# THE HINDU FAMILY IN ITS URBAN SETTING

# THE HINDU FAMILY IN ITS URBAN SETTING

• Aileen D. Ross •

*Department of Sociology
and Anthropology
McGill University*

UNIVERSITY OF TORONTO PRESS

*Copyright, Canada, 1961, by*
*University of Toronto Press*

*Reprinted 1962, 1967, in the*
*United States of America*

Reprinted in 2018
ISBN 978-1-4875-7321-8 (paper)

*To*
CARL A. DAWSON
*pioneer sociologist*
*of Canada*

# *Acknowledgments*

IN SPITE OF the fact that the authorship of a book is usually attributed to one person, sociological research is always a joint affair. Any project is a continuation of work that has gone before, and during its course many people wittingly and unwittingly contribute to it in one way or another. It is, therefore, only fitting that the author of this study, while bearing the full responsibility for the interpretations and conclusions, should pay tribute to at least some of the people who assisted at its different stages.

First of all, my thanks are due to the many people in India who helped to set up the research, or gave advice or encouragement during its progress, namely Vice-Chancellor V. L. D'Souza, Professor G. S. Ghurye, Professor C. N. Vakil, Dr. Irwati Karve, Mr. M. S. Gore, Mr. C. S. Paul and Mr. R. Benjamin.

An indispensable group were the research assistants who undertook the major task of interviewing. In this respect Nirmala Pawar, Nina Krishnamma, N. S. Shanta and K. K. Kuttappa did efficient work. In particular the interest and enthusiasm of Lalitha Krishnaswamy, C. S. Suryanarayana Rao and T. K. Karunakaran, and their insight into Hindu life, were of invaluable assistance. Dr. S. Gopalaswamy played a unique role in this study as chief counsellor. His wisdom eliminated many mistaken interpretations.

Encouragement and understanding are always valuable props to the researcher. For assistance of this sort I am deeply indebted to the many friends in India who took an interest in my study, especially Miss Muriel Robinson, Dr. and Mrs. VanDuzen Kennedy and Dr. and Mrs. Edward Harper. I am also very grateful to Dr. (Mrs.) R. Rajalakshmi for her careful criticism of the manuscript.

In Canada my thanks are due to Professor Oswald Hall and Professor Nathan Keyfitz for their helpful criticism of the study, to the Faculty of Graduate Studies and Research of McGill University for financial assistance for the research and typing the manuscript, to my colleagues in the Department of Sociology and Anthropology who gave practical and moral support, and to Mrs. Judy Friedl who so patiently assisted in the mundane task of correcting foot-notes and typing the manuscript. I would also like to thank the Canada Council who granted funds to assist the publication of the manuscript. This does not imply, however, that the Canada Council endorses or is responsible for the statements or views expressed.

This then is the study. It is to be hoped that the deep satisfaction which comes from getting to know people of another culture will be shared, at least to some extent, by those who read it.

# *Introduction*

THE POPULATION of India is made up of an infinite variety of castes, religions, and language groups, which have lived side by side, in an intricate division of labour, for thousands of years. Many customs, and much of the social structure, historically isolated from modern technological and industrial developments, have remained essentially the same. Such deeply laid patterns of behaviour do not respond easily to change. Some of the more superficial aspects may alter fairly readily—grandsons, for example, may ride tractors when their grandfathers used bullock carts—but underlying ideologies and deeply embedded patterns of relationships are more resistant.

This study analyses one of the Hindu structures—the family—which is considered by sociologists to be very resistant to change. Its purpose is to show the effect of industrial and technological change on the traditional middle- and upper-class urban Hindu family. In doing so, it will attempt to develop a sounder theoretical framework within which the many dimensions of family change can be studied.

Up to the present, apart from a few novels and sociological studies of urban life, it has been the traditional rural joint family which has occupied the attention of students and writers. However, it is the middle- and upper-class urban families which are facing the full impact of the rapidly changing conditions which have accompanied India's growing industrialization. It is in the city, too, that people are in closest contact with Western influences. The educated middle- and upper-class families, in particular, are exposed to the influences of the new techniques of mass communication, such as journals, magazines, radio, and movies. They are of particular importance in a study of change, for they themselves are its disseminators through their positions as journalists, writers, teachers, scientists, and businessmen. The urban middle and upper classes are thus in a strategic position, for their adjustment will set many of the patterns which other Hindus will follow.

India is also an instructive area in which to study social change because many of its urban families are still so close to their village backgrounds that the changes which are occurring in them are more drastic, and therefore easier to note, than are the changes in families living in countries which have gradually become industrialized over a period of several centuries, countries which have now reached a higher and, therefore, more complex degree of industrialization.

It may not be true, as some people claim, that a society is lost if its family system disintegrates. But it is true that some kind of family structure still plays such a vital role in all societies that changes in it will profoundly affect other institutions. Moreover, considering the intimate emotional nature of family relationships, it is likely that such changes will lead to a good deal of personal and familial disorganization; and, as the family sets the basic patterns for social conduct and adult roles, it is also likely that this disorganization will have repercussions throughout the whole society.

It is not the purpose of this study to try to prove, or disprove, the familiar thesis that the large joint family in India is giving way to the smaller nuclear type typical of middle-class, urban, Western societies. Its purpose is rather to study the strains and problems which arise when families do, in fact, change from one form to the other. One of the conclusions of the study, however, is that, if the industrialization and urbanization of India continue as rapidly as they have in the last thirty years, many more families will have to face the problems and strains that come in the wake of structural change.

The material for this study is arranged first to describe the traditional form of the joint family and then to show how industrialization and urbanization are forcing changes in its structure and relationships, and causing many families to break down into smaller units. This breakdown entails moving out of the main family household and establishing separate homes. An analysis is then made in more detail of the effect of this change in the areas of authority, sentiments, work, education, friendships and marriage.

This study is the outcome of one year of research in India. There are both advantages and disadvantages in studying people of other cultures, for, although an outsider can make many mistakes in interpreting the behaviour of another society, he has the advantage of viewing the new culture with a fresh perspective. This enables him to see the basic behaviour, and its interrelation with other aspects of the society, more clearly than a native could.

One of the possible biases of a Westerner in studying an Eastern country is that, as he lives in a dynamic culture, change to him is normal. So he may tend to exaggerate the changes, in contrast to an Easterner, who might stress the stabilities. It is possible, too, that an Indian student of his own culture might overemphasize its infinite detailed differences, whereas a Westerner would tend to see more of its universal similarities. Such biases will be gradually overcome when East and West not only meet more often, but also exchange enough students to add to our knowledge of each other's cultures.

# Contents

| | |
|---|---|
| ACKNOWLEDGMENTS | vii |
| INTRODUCTION | ix |
| I. THE JOINT FAMILY SYSTEM AND CHANGE | 3 |
|     The Traditional Joint Family System | 8 |
|     The Changing Hindu Society | 18 |
|     Theories of Family Change | 27 |
| II. THE ECOLOGICAL SUBSTRUCTURE | 33 |
|     Size of Household and Type of Family | 33 |
|     The Spatial Arrangement of Households | 38 |
|     The Interior Arrangements of the Household | 40 |
|     Reasons for Remaining in One Household | 41 |
|     Reasons for Separate Dwellings and Atypical Living Arrangements | 46 |
|     Summary | 49 |
| III. THE SUBSTRUCTURE OF RIGHTS AND DUTIES | 52 |
|     Division of Labour within the Household | 54 |
|     Responsibility to Family and Relatives | 67 |
|     Summary | 86 |
| IV. THE SUBSTRUCTURE OF POWER AND AUTHORITY | 91 |
|     The Authority of Different Relationships | 92 |
|     Punishment | 121 |
|     Obedience in Later Life | 128 |
|     Summary | 131 |

| | |
|---|---|
| V. THE SUBSTRUCTURE OF SENTIMENTS | 136 |
| The Affectionate Intensity of Different Relationships | 138 |
| The Closeness and Affection of the Family Circle | 175 |
| Summary | 177 |
| VI. WORK AND THE FAMILY | 180 |
| Some Effects of Industrialization | 181 |
| Occupational Problems | 190 |
| Summary | 205 |
| VII. EDUCATION AND THE FAMILY | 208 |
| Education in India | 208 |
| Education and Ambitions | 217 |
| Education versus Marriage | 227 |
| Summary | 231 |
| VIII. CHANGING FRIENDSHIP AND MARRIAGE PATTERNS | 235 |
| The Social Life of Men and Women | 236 |
| Changing Marriage Patterns | 245 |
| New Marriage Trends | 268 |
| Summary | 277 |
| IX. SUMMARY AND CONCLUSIONS | 280 |
| APPENDIXES | 299 |
| BIBLIOGRAPHY | 309 |
| INDEX OF AUTHORS | 315 |
| INDEX OF SUBJECTS | 317 |

# THE HINDU FAMILY IN ITS URBAN SETTING

• *Chapter One* •

# THE JOINT FAMILY SYSTEM AND CHANGE

THE JOINT FAMILY, the caste, the linguistic group and the village were the main units which formed the core of the traditional Hindu society.[1] These groups circled each individual Hindu, radiating out like rings around a thrown stone, from the central and most intimate family circle to the larger kin group, then to the caste, then to the territorial village circle and finally to the boundary of the language group. Each of these circles set limits to the individual's conduct, but on the other hand gave him certain securities and the psychological satisfaction of identification with groups which he felt to be his own.[2]

In early days the linguistic divisions marked off the total culture of each group, and separate ways of life evolved within them. Their literature, proverbs and folksongs tell of these distinctive features.[3] The village boundary marked off the individuals' effective living area and, the fact that so many urban Hindus still identify themselves with their "native place" indicates the deep feeling of belonging to a geographical locus which village life engendered.[4] This is also shown in the extent to which older people still desire to spend their final years in their native villages.

---

[1]Irawati Karve, *Kinship Organisation in India*, Deccan College Monograph Series, 11 (Poona, India: Deccan College Post-graduate and Research Institute, 1953), p. 1. "Three things are absolutely necessary for the understanding of any cultural phenomenon in India. These are the configuration of the linguistic regions, the institution of caste and the family organisation. Each of these three factors is intimately bound up with the other two, and the three together give meaning and supply basis to all other aspects of Indian culture."
[2]*Ibid.*, p. 114. Karve says that of these three the family and the caste have had most influence on the individual.
[3]*Ibid.*, p. 5.
[4]*Ibid.*, p. 14.

Some knowledge of the caste system is a necessary prelude to understanding family life in India. The numerous castes and sub-castes are "arranged in a vertical hierarchical manner" so that each caste member knows his position of superiority, or inferiority, in relation to all other caste members.[5] One reason for the evolution of the system seems to have been to provide an effective division of labour. In early times each caste was identified with a particular occupation, and even today many people can be occupationally placed if their caste or sub-caste nomenclature is known. This means that names in India not only place the bearer regionally, and denote his linguistic group, but also indicate his occupational background and his general social position.[6]

The Indian Census of 1901 was the last to tabulate the many different Indian castes. At that date it was estimated that there were 2,378 "main" castes and tribes. Some of these had several million members, others only a few.[7] The larger ones have gradually broken down over the years into many sub-castes, which are usually still endogamous groups. Blunt has emphasized the great difficulty of finding suitable mates when endogamous, exogamous and hyperagamous restrictions are strictly observed. In the largest castes these rules restrict marriage to a possible few thousand people, in smaller castes to a few hundred, and in the smallest castes there would be only about ten possible marriage partners at any one time.[8] If age restrictions are also taken into account, then the father's problem of finding a suitable mate for a daughter can be better understood.

Karve claims that each linguistic region has over fifty major castes. The Brahmin, Vaisya and other main castes will usually be found

---

[5]*Ibid.*, p. 7. "Thus the whole caste system is a very intricate structure which places social groups on innumerable and minute steps indicative of status and function."

[6]Caste names still have some bearing on a person's attempt to climb to higher prestige positions in India. In North America, the names of immigrants may mark them as belonging to a country which does not rate high in the North American hierarchy of ethnic acceptance, but the name will seldom denote occupation or general "class" position. Occupational identification with caste has probably never been complete in India, except in a few castes or sub-castes, and the new occupational openings which have arisen with the changing economic basis of life have enabled caste members to move into occupations different from those of their fathers. Thus the former fairly close relation of caste to occupation is now no longer true, but a caste name still denotes position in a hierarchy of prestige.

[7]*Census of India*, 1901, vol. I, Part I, p. 537. Kingsley Davis, *Human Society* (New York: Macmillan Co., 1949), p. 379. In 1931, the Brahmin caste had over fifteen million members. The main caste was split up into many sub-castes. In one province alone there were two hundred major castes of Brahmins, all endogamous. These different sub-castes were arranged in a hierarchy of prestige within the larger caste grouping.

[8]E. A. H. Blunt, *Social Service in India* (London: H. M. S. O., 1946), p. 49.

in each linguistic area, but they will differ in size and certain distinguishing characteristics. In other words, the boundaries of the main castes overrun linguistic lines, but sub-castes, which are more intimate groups, are usually only found within one language group. Srinivas claims that today they are the real basis of identification for a man.[9] Although most writers have described caste systems as stable and/or static, in reality many castes and sub-castes have gradually changed their positions in the hierarchy of prestige down through the centuries.[10] This has been accomplished largely through the ability of caste members to take over some of the characteristics of the higher castes and sub-castes. For example, the members of a sub-caste may become vegetarians, as this custom denotes high caste position; daughters with large dowries may attract husbands from higher castes; or caste members may achieve higher status by "passing," that is, by taking over the manners and customs of another caste so completely that they become identified with it.

Before the growth of central government in India the caste council, the panchayat, held the ultimate authority over each individual's life, and had power to apply sanctions which ranged from slight penalties for small misdemeanours to the exclusion of a caste member.[11] Its power was supported by the religious sanctions of the caste temples and gods. However, the establishment of central government agencies

[9]M. N. Srinivas, *Marriage and Family in Mysore* (Bombay: New Book Co., 1942), p. 22. Srinivas criticizes the statement in the Census of Mysore of 1901 that: "The rule of endogamy within the sub-caste, has of late years been relaxed to some extent by intermarriages, whose difference is purely conventional or territorial without any substantial basis in religious or social observances." Srinivas says that although there were some exceptions to marriage within sub-caste limits at that time, even now such marriages are exceedingly rare, and only happen in the most advanced sections of India. "The Non-Brahmin sub-castes are innocent of any attempt to violate their endogamous rules."

[10]Karve, *Kinship Organization*, pp. 6–7. Karve stresses the desire of castes to rise in the caste system very forcibly: "The endeavour of each sub-caste is to gain an ever higher position on the social ladder and of each sub-caste to gain a higher position within the caste." See also: Davis, *Human Society*, pp. 384–5.

[11]Kingsley Davis, *The Population of India and Pakistan* (Princeton, N.J.: Princeton University Press, 1951), p. 108, Davis quotes *General Report of the Census of India*, 1911 (Sessional Papers, Cmd. 7377, London: H.M.S.O., 1914). Davis points out the severe penalties which a caste can impose on members who transgress its customary behaviour. "Not only is he unable to marry beyond [the caste] limits; he may not even eat or drink with members of other groups, nor may he smoke from their huqqa. He often finds it difficult to get any one to cook his food; and if he dies, there will be no one to perform his obsequies, and his body may have to be removed by scavengers." Davis suggests that in some cases caste is a spur to migration, for it may induce an individual to move to a city where his identity can be hidden. This would be particularly true of people from lower castes.

under the British rule helped to eradicate caste barriers, for not only did the central and state governments gradually supersede the caste councils in authority, but they provided shelter for men who wanted to break away from the traditional customs by giving them jobs in the new government services.[12]

Consideration of these regional, linguistic and caste differences brings up the important question of the validity of making assumptions about "the" Hindu family. The answer seems to lie in the fact that, although details of life and custom vary markedly in different parts of India, the Hindu family everywhere has a basic structure which permits generalizations.[13] Moreover, students of families all over the world have shown that the factors which are of fundamental interest to the sociologist are similar in all large extended family systems, and tend to change in the same way when affected by similar technological and industrial forces. This thesis is given support by other aspects of Hindu life which are similar across India. Bachmann, in her intensive study of the folklore of India, for example, claims that from the tip of Cape Comorin to the Himalayas Indians have much the same moral code and outlook on life.[14] Others claim that the basic structure of the village portrays "a large element of uniformity over the whole of

[12]Karve, *Kinship Organisation*, p. 15. Karve says that these reformers probably made the government more forward in its outlook than most of the population.

[13]*Ibid.*, p. 117. Karve stresses the similarity of the families in northern India: "The organisation of family is essentially similar throughout Northern India and most of the castes conform to the same basic pattern, which has its roots in the Indo-Aryan patriarchal family. . . ."

David Mandelbaum, "The Family in India," in *The Family: Its Function and Destiny*, Ruth Anshen, ed. (New York: Harper and Brothers, 1949), p. 93. "India is so vast and her people seem so variegated that any generalized statement of the family in India must be subject to numerous exceptions in detail and amendments in local particular. Nevertheless, it is possible to depict Indian family organization in general terms that will have some applicability to a very large proportion of the Indian population."

[14]Hedwig Bachmann, *On the Soul of the Indian Woman: As Reflected in the Folklore of the Konkan* (Bastora, India Portuguesa: Tipografia Rangel, 1942), p. 145. See also p. 201. "The many different peoples of India possess a *fundamental common ethical trait* which, prescribed by the moral doctrines and laws of its ancient sages, was stamped upon even the humble classes of the people. Hence a peculiar popular unity is imparted to the whole folk, based on nothing but the heritage bequeathed by the moral teachers and philosophers."

M. N. Srinivas, *Marriage and Family in Mysore* (Bombay: New Book Co., 1942), p. 10. "Kannada society is fenced in by the Mahratta, Telugu, Tamil, Malayalam and Tulu cultures, and a complete understanding of Kannada culture would necessarily involve a study of the boundary-cultures. Culture-currents have flowed in and from Kannada culture to the outlying cultures, and a thorough understanding of the origin and nature of Kannada customs would imply a knowledge of these outlying cultures."

India."[15] It is also evident that the structure of the different castes and sub-castes must be similar throughout India. Otherwise, how could they fit into the general pattern of the village? Thus, if striking similarities can be found in the basic patterns of village and caste as well as in those of religion and philosophy, it seems evident that the joint family system will have a similar basic structure in all parts of India.

These similarities are partly due to the following: the customs people carried with them as they moved from one part of India to another gradually fused with those of the locale in which they settled;[16] all linguistic groups borrowed words from the classical language of Sanskrit, so that people whose languages were not originally related gradually developed common meanings and understandings;[17] as the state and provincial boundaries set up by the British were seldom co-terminous with linguistic divisions, state governments bound people of different languages together under similar rules, which developed many common ways of living.

Finally, and perhaps most important, the old epic stories of family life gradually spread to all parts of India from their original home in the north, became the models for all Hindu families, and were passed down by word of mouth by story-tellers and village dramas from generation to generation for thousands of years.[18] They are still repeated almost word-perfect by Indians in the north, southeast and west, no matter what their language or caste. Although these stories

[15]Karve, *Kinship Organisation*, pp. 9–10. "The structure of the caste-system encourages isolation and separateness but the necessity of economic co-operation, common social life in a village and the commonness of language are forces which encourage assimilation."

[16]*All-India Rural Credit Survey* (Bombay: Committee of Direction, Department of Research and Statistics, Reserve Bank of India, 1954) vol. II, p. 54. "In the social structure of the village (and social dynamics) may be discerned both a diversity from region to region and, running through the diversity, a large element of uniformity over the whole of India. . . . the largest single sociological aspect, which is the institution of caste, and the largest single economic factor, which is the penetration of the industrialized economy of the cities, have combined to produce broadly the same results throughout the country-side; and that the regional variations are largely related to variations in the nature of the class structure on the one hand and in the character of the agricultural economy on the other."

[17]*Ibid.*, p. 5. Karve claims that the languages of people living in Andhra and Karnatak, as well as such tribal peoples as the Oraons and Gonds have incorporated over 50 per cent of Sanskrit words into their kinship terminology. Also that the literature of the first two groups contains many Sanskrit words and many Sanskrit epics.

[18]Karve, *Kinship Organisation*, pp. 21, 195. The two main epics which tell of family life are the Mahabharata and the Ramayana.

do not always apply to present family life, there is no doubt that they still have great influence, and their heroes and heroines are important models for many aspects of family life.[19]

## The Traditional Joint Family System

In former days, life in India centred around the village. Even when towns arose, they retained their rural character, for they were simple in structure and inhabited by rural people. Families lived on their properties or on small holdings of land. When they increased in size, kin members broke away to form new units. It was a self-contained and self-sufficient life, and social contacts were usually confined to blood relations.

Literature shows that, as far back as records can be found, the joint family system has always existed in India. In fact, the early Sanskritic literature describes much the same type of family life as can be found in many parts of India today.[20] The Indian economy has until recently depended basically on agriculture which only needed a very rudimentary specialization of labour and little scientific knowledge. It was the type of environment which developed a stable way of life, with tradition and custom its dominant features. It is only in such an environment that the traditional joint family in its "ideal" form could exist. Somewhat similar family systems have existed in such agricultural societies as those of ancient China and Japan.

[19]*Ibid.*, p. 5. "Both these factors [i.e. inter-regional agencies which transmit this cultural material from one region to another and the common source from which all regions derived their culture] are at work and show us the inter-relation of various regions to one another and ultimately reveal the common fabric which we understand as Indian culture."

[20]Karve, *Kinship Organisation*, pp. 10, 21–33. The accounts of family life described in the Mahabharata and Ramayana show that even in 1,000 B.C. much the same type of family existed. These two epic poems are "the sources of all the later literature in Sanskrit consisting of works on grammar and linguistics, medicine and arts, drama and poetry, philosophy and logic." They also contain a great deal of mythical material and contradictions. The Ramayana tells of a struggle between Aryans and southerners which occurred around 1,400 B.C. The Mahabharata relates the story of a battle fought near Delhi in which a whole line of kings are supposed to have been destroyed bringing their era to a close. These stories depict the family system which existed at the time. For example, the description of a family feud shows how the kin relationship worked. "It is almost a complete record of usage and law, norms and actualities, sentiments and attitudes found in an ancient joint family." Karve says that these stories show how stable the joint family system has been down through the ages. "The Mahabharata family is found today all over India and a Mahabharata battle is being fought in most joint families. The ideas of status, duties and rights of members of the joint family are those inherited from and deeply rooted in the traditions of these epics."

An ideal picture of the traditional large joint Hindu family can be drawn up from the definitions given by various students, and by material taken from literature and case studies. It is, of course, easier to describe an extended family pattern which has been relatively stable for many centuries than to evolve a definition of it which will be adequate for research purposes. Karve's definition is one of the most precise. "A joint family is a group of people who generally live under one roof, who eat food cooked at one hearth, who hold property in common and who participate in common family worship and are related to each other as some particular type of kindred."[21] Agarwala includes the characteristic of authority.[22] Desai adds common income as well as property, and also stresses mutual rights and obligations.[23]

*Who generally live under one roof.* The traditional large joint family household was composed of a number of separate family units living under one roof, sometimes called the "Great House." Each family unit might have one or two rooms for its personal use, but the whole family shared a common room for worship, a common kitchen, and meals were eaten together in a common dining hall. When the large house became overcrowded, a son and his family, or two brothers with their families, might set up separate establishments, thus forming the nucleus of new joint families. These offshoots would generally locate as near the former household as possible, sometimes building their

[21] *Ibid.*, p. 10.

[22] B. R. Agarwala, "In a Mobile Commercial Community," in "Symposium: Caste and Joint Family," *Sociological Bulletin*, vol. IV, no. 2 (Sept., 1955), pp. 141–2. "[Members of the joint family] are under the authority of the elder in matters of family and religion, joint investment of capital, joint enjoyment of profits, and of incurring birth, marriage and death expenses from the joint-funds." Agarwala feels that it is not essential for members of a joint family to live in one place and eat in a common kitchen: "For management of business a brother may stay at Calcutta, the father may stay at Delhi, a cousin may stay at Madras and the grandfather at the native place, and manage the affairs allotted to them. . . . What constitutes the essence of the joint family is their common way of living or way of living common to their constituents."

[23] I. P. Desai, "The Joint Family in India—An Analysis," *Sociological Bulletin*, vol. V, no. 2 (Sept. 1956) pp. 147–8. In this article Desai has gone further than any other student in attempting to evolve different family types which exist in India today. He criticizes census definitions, which have correlated the type of family to the size of its household. Instead, "the type of family is not to be determined by the fact of co-residence, commensality or the size of the group. It is the relationship between the members of a household among themselves and with those of another household that determines the type of the family of that household." Unfortunately, Desai's analysis appeared after the data for this study had been collected, and the author had left India. Otherwise his analysis would have been more carefully followed. See also his article "An Analysis," in "Symposium: Caste and Joint Family," *Sociological Bulletin*, vol. IV, no. 2 (Sept., 1955) pp. 97–117.

houses within the family compound. Family members would often feel so attached to this locality that even after living away from it for many years they would return to visit the elder family members, or to keep vows made to the local gods which they still worshipped, or to live there in old age. This ancestral village would be referred to by them as "home."[24]

*Who eat food cooked at one hearth.* The wife of the head of the house, or the eldest woman, would supervise the work of the other women in a common kitchen. Men and women did not eat together. In fact, the typical pattern was for women to first serve the men of the household, and later to eat by themselves, but as conversation was carried on while the women were serving, meals played much the same socializing function in the joint family as they often do in the modern Western family.

*Who hold property in common.* The traditional joint family was both a producing and consumption unit, for not only was family property held in common, but there was also a common purse into which all members put their earnings, and from which money was taken for the expenses of earners and non-earners alike.

The ancient prescriptions of the *Mitakshara* still form the legal basis of the present-day Hindu joint family. They outline the rights and duties of family members and stipulate the way in which family property should be handled.[25] It is assumed that a family is a joint family unless it is proved not to be one.[26] Theoretically, property is divided equally among the sons on the death of the father. In fact, every male member is legally a co-owner of the family property when he is born.[27] And he in turn divides his share among his sons. How-

[24]Karve, *Kinship Organisation*, p. 10.

[25]Mandelbaum, "The Family in India," pp. 94–5. "The legal framework of the joint family was crystallized about the eleventh century, in the *Mitakshara*, a commentary on earlier sacred writings. For some nine centuries, the rights and duties of family members toward each other, the general structure of the Hindu family, and the processes of family partition have followed, without great deviation, the prescriptions of the *Mitakshara*. Just how great an antiquity may be ascribed to this classic form of the joint family is not now known. . . . In any event, the eleventh-century author of the *Mitakshara* only formulated practices that must then have been . . . in operation for centuries, and were to continue functioning for centuries thereafter." See also K. M. Kepadia, *Hindu Kinship* (Bombay, 1947), pp. 122–5.

[26]Desai, "An Analysis," pp. 110–11.

[27]Agarwala, "In a Mobile Commercial Community," p. 144. ". . . every male member as soon as he is born becomes a copartner." An informant told me that in some parts of India a male child has a right over the family property as soon as he is conceived.

ever, it is obvious that this "ideal" pattern has not been followed down through Hindu history; had it been, each male would now own only an infinitesimal bit of land.[28]

The senior male member of the traditional joint family usually manages the family's finances, ". . . such is the respect commonly paid to the parent that his decisions are seldom countermanded by the will of his sons. Legally, however, he acts only as a representative of the males of the family in the administration of the family property, and his responsibility is that of a trustee."[29] The *Mitakshara* allowed sons to ask for a division of property at any time, but in effect few sons seem to have taken advantage of this legal right, at least before the father died.[30]

The sons may all help to look after the lands and estates if they are extensive, otherwise one son, generally the eldest, may be manager while the other sons earn additional incomes in other occupations. Sometimes the eldest son who takes over the management of the property on his father's death will be assisted by his mother.

The property of the joint family was passed down in a strictly prescribed way from father to sons.[31] Daughters only occasionally shared in this inheritance, although they could inherit property owned by the mother. The inheritors received their share of the property in terms of their family responsibility—not for their own individual use.

*Who participate in common family worship.* Hinduism accepts many representatives of the "creator"; so each family has its own gods which help to bind that particular family but set it off to some extent from other families. Religion is in integral part of a Hindu's life. All important family events and festivals are deeply steeped in religious rituals and ceremonies and daily family worship has always been part of the family routine.

[28]Desai, "An Analysis," p. 110. ". . . if the law of partition was carried to its logical conclusion the time would come when nothing remained to be divided." That is, the joint family would die in the eyes of the law. In one of the cases studied the ancestral property had been given to the family by a tribal chief. Now, this property, consisting of two thousand acres of land and a village, is divided among twenty-five families.

[29]Mandelbaum, "The Family in India," p. 94.

[30]Desai, "An Analysis," p. 111.

[31]Davis, *Human Society*, p. 422. Davis quotes L. S. S. O'Malley, *India's Social Heritage* (Oxford: Clarendon Press, 1934), p. 123. "Every male child acquired at birth 'a vested interest in the ancestral property, becoming a co-owner with his father, brothers, and other male relatives.'" In its essence, this system implied the obligation of members to contribute to the support of the whole joint family, and the right to receive a share of the total product.

In these families religion and ceremonial rites are performed when all the members of the family gather together and the eldest performs the sacred rites. In a joint family the eldest, the "Karta," is the guardian, the man who has the controlling voice in the family, he performs all the family and religious rites. The marriages are arranged with the consent of the older members of the family, and the individual member cannot arrange a marriage by himself nor can he perform religious rites.[32]

The religious devotion of Hindus is indeed so great that one of the closest ties of the Hindu joint household lies in the fact that it is the "place of intimate worship and hallowed religious associations.[33] Often members of families which have become nuclear units and have moved to a city away from the ancestral home will return to worship the family gods of the larger kinship unit. Eventually, however, when they have lost close ties with their ancestral family, they establish their own family gods.

*Who are related to each other as some particular type of kindred.* The limits of those accepted in any kinship circle change with changes in the systems of lineage and authority. A good deal of the difficulty in studying family relationships in India lies in the fact that the present families have descended from two separate lines, the one patrilineal and the other matrilineal. The Dravidians, the indigenous population, had a matrilineal and matriarchal system. When the Aryans, whose family system was patrilineal and patriarchal, penetrated India from the north between 1,400 and 1,000 B.C., the Dravidians were gradually driven southward. However, as the two peoples often lived side by side for many generations, each tended to take over the customs of the other. The assimilation of the two groups was probably hastened by the shortage of women among the invading Aryans which resulted in a good deal of intermarriage. Hence the structure of southern families is now largely patrilineal and patriarchal.

In Karnatak, Andhra Desh, Tamilnad and among certain important castes of Malabar the predominant form of family organisation is the patrilineal and patrilocal joint family. . . . The males are born and live all their lives in the house of their paternal kin, while their wives are brought in from other families and the girls born in the family are given away as brides into other families.[34]

[32]Agarwala, "In a Mobile Commercial Community," p. 142.
[33]Urquhart, *Women of Bengal*, p. 25.
[34]Karve, *Kinship Organisation*, 181. Bachmann suggests that the various contradictions found in the code of Manu can be traced back to this mingling of the two ways of life of Aryans and Dravidians. "Although generally speaking moral laws of Hindus from North and South can be traced back to the same foundations —small exceptions are found which show the influence of each group." See Bachmann, *On the Soul of the Indian Woman*, p. 173.

In spite of this turnover in structure, interviews revealed some traces of the matrilineal system, such as the strong influence of, and affection towards, the maternal uncle, and cross-cousin marriages. This type of marriage has a profound effect on the husband-wife relationship, for when a girl marries a relative she will not go into a completely strange household to a husband and in-laws whom she has never seen. Several interviewees spoke of their daughters marrying their nephews, perhaps the youngest son of the eldest sister. In such a marriage the bride's aunt would also be her mother-in-law, and she would have established a close and perhaps affectionate relationship with her before marriage. After marriage her own family and in-laws will be much closer than in the patrilineal system.[35]

[In the matrilineal system] one's own extended family is also one's family by marriage and so the complete separation between one's family of birth and family by marriage, which is evident in the Northern terminology, is absent in the Dravidian kinship terms. . . . Marriage in the south is not arranged with a view to seek new alliances, or for widening a kin-group but each marriage strengthens already existing bonds and makes doubly near those people who were already very near kin. Because of this one difference the pattern for the development of the personality of a man and woman must be entirely different in the north and the south. No special norms need to be evolved for the behaviour of the married girl or no special precautions need be taken for ensuring her loyalty to the husband's house. Neither does marriage symbolise separation from the father's house for a girl.[36]

Karve goes on to say that because the young bride is not going into a strange house on marriage she can move freely in her father-in-law's house. "In folk literature . . . woman is certainly not the weak link in the chain of family solidarity that she is in the north." Furthermore, "The southern man may be more natural in his attitude to women. He is the cross-cousin and the playmate of his future wife, not her lord and master. Marriage or sexual life is a culmination of friendships started in childhood."[37] This type of marriage arrangement completely precludes any choice on the part of the parents or young people, for it is predetermined from the moment of their birth.

Many factors are now causing cross-cousin marriages to break down. One is that there is a growing feeling that there is something shameful about them, particularly if it is an uncle-niece marriage. In

[35]Karve, *Kinship Organisation*, pp. 228–9. Karve shows how the patrilineal and patriarchal system in effect leads to a wide circle of kin, whereas that of the matrilineal and matriarchal develops a "clustering of kin group in a narrow area."
[36]*Ibid.*, p. 219.
[37]*Ibid.*, p. 220. As husband and wife are predetermined mates it does not include the idea of romantic love; this is reserved for concubines.

fact, it has been proposed that they be abolished by law. Moreover, it is often difficult to find suitable mates within kinship groups. And finally the new ambitions of an industrial age make families more anxious to marry sons or daughters to outsiders who are in better economic positions than relatives.

The patrilineal-patrilocal system presents a quite different experience for the young bride. Instead of going into a household whose ways she may know intimately, she must accommodate to a completely new set of customs and people. Moreover, the woman is of relatively little importance in this system for it emphasizes the son and the son's son. In earlier days, when she married as a child, she was also apt to lose touch with her own kinship group except for occasional visits, and therefore had little protection from them.

Considering the distinct difference in the emphasis which each system placed on different family relationships it is likely that much family strain in the past, and present, is due to the inconsistencies of behaviour caused by the mixture of the two systems.

*Functions of the Joint Family*

The large joint family is family-centred, characterized by intimacy, mutuality of interest, strong primary group controls and mutual assistance in time of need. In it family tradition and pride are strong, and individual members are dominated by the opinions of the larger group. Such a family can only remain stable when a number of generations succeed each other in the same locality, occupation and social class. It is a system which "strongly limits social mobility and social change because it binds the individual to others on the basis of birth, forces him to contribute to the support of a large group independently of their ability, introduces nepotism into both business and politics, and assures control of the younger generation by the elders."[38] In India it is supported and upheld by the caste system which "introduces unusual rigidities into the social order." Caste adds another primary group, in addition to the joint family and the rural village, to the custom-bound control of the individual for it "is an effective brake on geographical mobility, ready contact with strangers, and the formation of large-scale business organizations."[39]

The joint family is a system which is eminently suited to a stable society in which life is relatively simple, and there has as yet been no need to develop separate institutions to care for the needs of the

[38]Davis, *Population of India and Pakistan*, p. 216.
[39]*Ibid.*, p. 216.

group. Thus, where separate political institutions have not appeared, the patriarch of the family is an important element in the authoritative and controlling system of the society. When there is no organized church, the family gods are the centre of religious faith.

Because of the nature of the society in which it exists, the joint family also carries out welfare functions. It includes so many members that there is always someone to help look after the indigent ones. Often older women, familiar with most of the crises of life, will give advice as well as practical aid to the needy. Because of the large number of members, the large joint family also serves as a recreational agency.

A joint family . . . is always an exciting group to live in. All the time something of interest is happening there. Now it is the marriage of a girl or a boy, now it is an initiation ceremony, the birth of a new baby, the puberty rites of a new bride, some particular family ritual, a fast, a feast, sometimes a death. The great extent of the family always ensures the coming and going of guests. The brothers of the brides come to invite them to their mothers' houses, the daughters of the house are being brought home for a family feast or wedding. There is always bustle and expectation, laughter and quarrels, discussions and plans. Life may be complicated, sometimes full of bitterness but rarely dull, at least from the point of view of the children.

The joint family is a miniature world, in some ways standing apart, in others inextricably bound up in a never-ending ceremonial of exchanges and gift-giving with all the other joint families with whom it has affinal connections.[40]

In the joint family, affection as well as dependence is diffused among so many relatives that the loss of even an important member, such as a parent, is less critical for the group or individual member than in the nuclear family system which is so small that every member plays a decisive role. In reality, the joint family is a revolving system which provides a full complement of young and adult people at all times to carry out its various functions.

Each family and kin position is a complex of detailed duties and rights, attitudes, sentiments and expectations, which must be carefully balanced if the whole unit is to function effectively. The stable character of the joint family means that its roles are precisely and clearly defined, but on the other hand, it also means that little initiative or independence is possible for its members.

In summary, the traditional family, along with caste membership and village life, provides the individual family member with a secure

---

[40]Karve, *Kinship Organisation*, p. 14.

environment. In it he can fulfil not only his survival but his religious and recreational needs as well. However, the very factors which make it such a satisfactory haven make it a frustrating unit for deviant members, or for those who are affected by changing conditions and desire to exert their own initiative and independence.

*Strain in the Joint Family*

"Distant fields look green," and the traditional large joint family is often eulogized by people who are alarmed about present family changes. Considering the simple, uncomplex milieu in which it is typically found, it would be expected to be an organization which worked as much like the proverbial well-oiled machine as possible.

> There are some cultures which seem to be built like finely adjusted clock movements. Every element interlocks with every other. . . . Value systems and actual behavior patterns are consistent, and even the cosmology and mythology explain and reinforce the status quo. Such cultures are most commonly found in societies which have lived for a long time under relatively stable conditions. As long as these conditions remain unchanged, the cultures function smoothly, taking care of every need of the society and of its normal members and providing answers to all problems.
> At the other end of the scale there are cultures which are so loosely organized and so full of both ideological and behavioral inconsistencies that one wonders how they are able to function at all.[41]

Linton goes on to say that the problem of the first type of culture is that when a new cultural element is introduced, it sets in train a series of dislocations, for the closer the integration of a culture, the more extensive is its disorganization likely to be. On the other hand, loosely integrated societies can absorb new elements more easily since they are not as resistant and inflexible.[42]

It is evident from many written descriptions of the traditional joint family system that, although it existed in a culture of the first type mentioned by Linton, it was continually faced with internal and external crises. Some of these were due to personality clashes. "In the joint family there is abundant scope for the clash of wills. In the individual family the couple live away from their parents, and thus

[41]Ralph Linton, "Cultural and Personality Factors Affecting Economic Growth," in *The Progress of Underdeveloped Areas*, Bert F. Hoselitz, ed. (Chicago: University of Chicago Press, 1952), p. 86.

[42]*Ibid.*, p. 87. Linton tells of a Swedish economist's surprise that the American culture could function so effectively with such a loose integration. Other students support Linton's idea that the very looseness of the American culture enables it to assimilate change more easily than societies with more rigid structures.

the tug-of-war between the daughter and the mother-in-law will be lessened, if not totally destroyed."[43]

This quotation refers to the traditional mother-in-law–daughter-in-law conflict, but many other strains can occur when a large number of people live together, particularly when the women of the household are largely confined to each other's company and have little opportunity to discharge their emotions on outsiders. Sometimes the very size of the joint family makes it difficult for members to live together peacefully. "When I was growing up in the joint family, the hatred between our family and my uncle and aunt prevented us ever playing with our cousins. Uncle was a drone, and father had to finally go to court to get our share of the money from the family property from him. My aunt too always dominated my mother, and they had lots of quarrels." (Case 142)

The women of the household often seem to have to bear the larger share of family strain. They may have cruel mothers-in-law, strife over their children with other mothers, a husband who is unfaithful or takes a second wife, or they may become widows or their children may die.

Children, too, can be just as unhappy in joint families as in smaller ones. Although the relationship between parents and children is typically close in the traditional joint family, interviews showed that conflict often occurred between them. A joint family may be very frustrating for an independent, individualistic child, particularly if he or she has been influenced by modern ideas. One such case showed that there had been continual serious conflict between mother and son. The son was one of four, and although the typical close tie may have existed between the mother and some of the other sons, the relationship was a very painful one for this particular son. This case shows the jealousy which may arise when children feel that sisters or brothers are preferred or get better treatment.

> I had serious fights at home when I was young, especially with my mother. I still fight with her, and it will always be that way. One reason for this is that she pampers my eldest brother and ignores me. Then we are both short-tempered. And she often complains to father about me, so that I feel she has no affection whatever for me. Once I was so angry that I nearly beat her. After that we didn't speak to each other for seven years. (Case 32)

The necessary conformity for living in a large unit may not be difficult for those who fit in, but it may be a great problem for the

[43]Srinivas, *Marriage and Family*, p. 193.

deviant member since the penalty for non-conformity is high. Karve sees a connection here between the Hindu religion and the traditional family form: "The philosophical urge towards asceticism and realisation of complete freedom may be a reaction against the thousand chains by which the joint family and the kindred hold the individual in terrible imprisonment."[44]

## The Changing Hindu Society

*Industrialization and Urbanization*

India had been invaded by many types of people before the advent of the British, but it was they who brought in the new technological age which upset the former relatively stable Indian society. This age introduced India to new technological knowledge which was instrumental in bringing in new types of economic and industrial organization, new modes of communication and a new type of urban life.[45] Railways gradually wound their way across the Indian continent and, along with the new roads, provided India with a communications system through which new ideas could travel even to remote villages.

The British also established new kinds of political organization, which slowly bound the scattered religious, caste and language groups into a semblance of unity, and a new system of education, transferred in its principles and almost all its details from the British Isles. Along with the new education went the dissemination of the English language, bringing together Indians who had formerly been separated by language barriers,[46] and introducing them to Western books, magazines, newspapers and finally radio.

---

[44]Karve, *Kinship Organisation*, p. 136.

[45]Although the majority of Indians lived in villages which were self-sufficient enough to be able to maintain their traditional way of life, there were also many large cities in India when the British arrived. In fact, "India was, comparatively speaking, a highly urbanized area, but after its own fashion, of course, when the first European travellers appeared on the scene." See Robert I. Crane, "Urbanism in India," *American Journal of Sociology*, vol. LX, no. 5 (March, 1955), p. 468; also T. C. Das Gupta, *Aspects of Bengali Society from Old Bengali Literature*, (Calcutta: University of Calcutta, 1935), pp. 123–36. Das Gupta here describes such early cities as Agra and Lahore in the sixteenth and seventeenth centuries. However, these early cities were primarily for administrative purposes, or served as handicraft or trading centres, and their way of life was not very different from that of the villages and small towns (Crane, "Urbanism in India," pp. 469–70).

[46]The new educational system and the introduction of a common national language were probably the main channels through which a feeling of national identity came to India. Linguistic lines began to blur with the increasing movement of Indians to jobs and homes outside the boundaries of their mother-tongue language. It is now not unusual to find that even illiterate Indians can speak three or four languages efficiently enough to handle the main problems of life.

The "new urbanism" was evident in the rapid growth of cities at the beginning of the twentieth century, a trend which was accelerated by migration from rural areas as the result of World War II.[47]

Because of its relatively late beginning, India has not as high a proportion of urban population as many other countries, but statistics show that in the last decade her rate of urbanization has been higher than that of many Western countries which started at an earlier period.[48] Nor does this increase seem likely to slow down in the near future. Kingsley Davis notes that there is no sign yet that the rate of urbanization will slacken for the world as a whole, "the human species is moving rapidly in the direction of an almost exclusively urban existence." Moreover, Davis estimates that, although the highest levels of urbanization are now found in the countries of northwestern Europe, and in the regions where descendants of these people have settled, their rate of increase is beginning to slow down, while the rate of urbanization of the underdeveloped countries is increasing. In India, "the fastest urbanization has occurred since 1941." Davis believes, too, that the industrial revolution began an era for all countries "from which there was no return." According to Davis, "urbanization represents a revolutionary change in the whole pattern of social life. Itself a product of basic economy and technological developments, it tends in turn, once it comes into being, to affect every aspect of existence." Therefore, the old patterns of life developed in simple, agriculturally based societies will never return.[49]

---

[47]Crane, "Urbanism in India," p. 470. See also Kingsley Davis, "The Origin and Growth of Urbanization in the World," *American Journal of Sociology*, vol. LX, no. 5 (March, 1955), p. 433, "It can truly be said that the hinterland of today's cities is the entire world." And, I P. Desai, "An Analysis," in: "Symposium: Caste and Joint Family," *Sociological Bulletin*, vol. IV, no. 2 (Sept., 1955), p. 115.

[48]Crane, "Urbanism in India," p. 463. Crane shows that whereas in 1921 only some 11 per cent of the Indian population was urban, it increased to 13 per cent in 1941 and to 17 per cent in 1951. This 17 per cent amounted to about sixty-one million people. "Between 1921 and 1941 the total urban population grew by 33.5 per cent, while in the most recent decade its rate of growth is even more rapid. . . . Furthermore, while the urban population was growing by one-third between 1921 and 1941, the general increase of the population was only 15 per cent. Thus there is a strong trend toward urbanism, of which the most recent decade has seen the greatest development."

[49]One reason for this is that the social structure of the city is distinctly different from that of the simple village. "The continuance of urbanization in the world does not mean the persistence of something that remains the same in detail. A city of a million inhabitants today is not the sort of place that a city of the same number was in 1900 or 1850. Moreover, with the emergence of giant cities of five to fifteen million, something new has been added. Such cities are creatures of the twentieth century. Their sheer quantitative difference means a qualitative change as well." This discussion comes from Davis, "Origin and Growth of Urbanization," pp. 429–37.

Davis sees that cities of Asia and Africa are not evolving in the same way as did Western cities in the eighteenth and nineteenth centuries. Since their growth has occurred mainly during the twentieth century, their development will be affected by contacts with fully industrialized Western cities. "Their ecological pattern, their technological base, their economic activity, all reflect the twentieth century, no matter how primitive or backward their hinterlands may be."[50] Indians moving into the cities from the rural areas of India now meet a much more modern urban way of life than did rural Westerners when the great rural-urban trek began in their countries: that is, when the proportion of urbanization in their countries was similar to that of India today. This means that Indians will be faced with a much more drastic and dramatic adjustment than their Western counter-parts.

Another difference noted by Sriñivas is of basic importance. "For industrialization does not merely refer to the use of large and complicated machinery, and urbanization does not only mean the great concentration of human beings in small areas; they both require certain types of socio-economic relationships and a *weltanschauung* which are in conflict with the social system, which obtained in pre-British India."[51] One of the most important qualitative differences which sociologists see in urban life as compared to rural is the difference in social contacts. People in large cities come from different economic, racial, ethnic, caste and social backgrounds, and thus the city person is surrounded by a much more heterogeneous population than in rural areas. Moreover, the contacts which a person has with others tend to be secondary, quite different from the primary relationships of village, caste and kinship. The city, too, with its extensive division of labour, is a place where there is a maximum of occupational choice, and this favours both vertical and horizontal mobility.[52] Thus the ideology of city life encourages new ambitions and aspirations.[53]

All these factors stimulate individuality, for each person is more spatially separated from the customary ways and primary controls of his kin group and caste, and the new city opportunities he en-

[50]Davis, "Origin and Growth of Urbanization," pp. 436–7.

[51]M. N. Srinivas, "The Industrialization and Urbanization of Rural Areas," *Sociological Bulletin*, vol. V, no. 2 (Sept., 1956), p. 79.

[52]Desai, "An Analysis," p. 112. "In order to avail of these opportunities people had to leave their native villages and go to the towns and cities. This gave rise to the phenomenon called migration and occupational and social mobility, which are believed to shatter the old social pattern."

[53]Davis, *Human Society*, p. 318. "By its very nature it [the city] throws people into close contact with strangers, facilitates the rapid diffusion of news and fashions, permits a high degree of individualization, stimulates invention, social mobility, secularization, etc."

counters "force the individual to make his own decisions and to plan his life as a career.[54] His behaviour becomes more controlled by secondary contacts, and the divergency of opinions on all subjects tends to make him more tolerant in his outlook on the conduct of other people.[55]

Many historical and sociological studies have shown the operation of the above influences in societies which have come within the orbit of the new technological, industrial and urban forces. It is thus to be expected that the changes in India will continue, and that the former simple village structure and the rural ideology which it supported, will gradually give way to the more impersonal, secular life of the city.

*Changes in the Traditional Joint Family*

A perusal of the studies which have been made in regard to changes in the traditional joint family in India reveals conflicting views. One of the main problems in this controversy is the lack of an adequate definition of the joint family itself, so that students are often arguing at cross purposes.[56] Evidence that city life does not necessarily cause the joint family system to disintegrate comes from several studies.[57]

---

[54]*Ibid.*, p. 334.
[55]*Ibid.*, p. 331. "[The control of the city] is impersonal and general, that of the country personal and particular."
[56]A. Aiyappan, "In Tamilnad," in "Symposium: Caste and Joint Family," *Sociological Bulletin*, vol. IV, no. 2 (Sept., 1955), p. 120. "When, for example in the Loka Sabha, a member says, 'joint families have broken down,' in nine cases out of ten, he is repeating a slogan. He will not be able to say whether in fact all the joint families in a particular area have partitioned; if not, what is the proportion of those who have partitioned and those that have not? Even after legal partition, we know there are other familial obligations which large numbers of people continue to maintain." See also Desai, "An Analysis," p. 99. "The opinions about the joint family to-day are largely the subjective reflections of the individuals based on extremely limited and partial observations and largely conditioned by the socio-economic strata to which they belong. . . . hardly any studies of contemporary joint family worth the name exist."
[57]Jean L. Comhaire, "Economic Change and the Extended Family," *Annual of the Anerican Academy of Political and Social Science*, vol. 305 (May, 1956), p. 45. "One of the consequences expected from the introduction of a money economy and from urbanization is the dissolution of the joint family. . . . But if the threat to the extended family—or even to any form of family—looks obvious, the degree to which other institutions, and more particularly the small patrocentric family of the Western type, are going to replace the old-style family offers ground for considerable doubt. In the Western world, everything combined to bring about the triumph of the nuclear family. Institutions inconsistent with the needs of an industrial society were slowly undermined, and the extended family broke up the more easily that Indo-European societies had a millenary tradition of simple kinship structures." Comhaire goes on to show that the African native middle-class family in Leopoldville, Belgian Congo, has not yet broken down into a nuclear type. It is not clear from his description whether these families have been exposed to the full forces of a technological age or not.

One of these is by Agarwala, who describes the Marwadi community which has been living for centuries in different large cities all over India. Agarwala claims that it is "an outstanding example of the obdurate continuance of the joint-family and caste-system in spite of industrialization, technocracy and Western education and in some respects, rather because of them."[58] Possibly a parallel could be found for this group in the large closely knit kinship groups among the upper classes of the old white southern plantation families in the United States.[59] If so, it would be another illustration of the tendency of kin groups to "close" either when they have gained a high level of prestige or when they are facing persecution or annihilation. Several informants said that the Sindhis who suffered at the time of Partition tend to cling together and live in large joint families even in cities. The royal families of Europe are a clear example of the closure of high-class kinship groups. This point is supported by Aiyappan who believes that higher castes and income groups living in cities tend to have a larger proportion of joint families than the lower castes, and also display a greater amount of family solidarity.[60] Thus tendencies to family closure or to separation must be considered in terms of the total position of the group concerned.

Other writers have shown that men who go into cities for work in the large factories tend to maintain their connections with their joint families in their native villages: they return for wives, or family festivals, or retire to their villages after making some money in the city.[61] A large number of these studies have been of families of lower income groups, who barely made a living on the low factory wages and did not share in the satisfactions of urban life. They typically lived miserable lives in crowded housing districts. It is well known that early conditions in boom industrial cities all over the world have been so deplorable for the labouring classes that there has been little

[58]B. R. Agarwala, "In a Mobile Commercial Community," pp. 138–45.
[59]Allison Davis, Burleigh B. Gardner and Mary R. Gardner, *Deep South* (Chicago: University of Chicago Press, 1941).
[60]Aiyappan, "In Tamilnad," p. 121.
[61]Karve, *Kinship Organisation*, p. 12. ". . . instead of founding independent families in the towns where they are employed they tend to keep their ties with the family at home. They send money to the impoverished farmers at home, send their wives home for child-birth and go themselves for an occasional holiday or in times of need. The urge to visit the family for certain festivities and at sowing and harvesting times is so great that there is seasonal migration of mill-labourers in all industrial towns. Even if a man earns good wages it is difficult for him to find a bride from a decent house if he has no family with some land in some village."

inducement for them to remain if they can eventually escape back to their villages. Some students believe that it is these early conditions which have caused many writers and poets to eulogize country life at the expense of the cities. However, it is fairly evident that very few middle- and upper-class people would now wish to return to a simple rural way of life in Western countries. And even factory workers show no signs of going back to rural life. It is thus conceivable that higher standards of living will eventually make city life in India more attractive for the labouring classes, and thus make them cut their ties with their native villages.

Desai suggests that in India it is necessary to distinguish between the attitudes of pre-1939 and post-1939 migrants, for the latter moved to the cities when relatives and caste members were already established there, and thus were not as open to urban influences as the first migrants. He also stresses the importance of knowing the age, income, occupational and social groups, and the former positions of the migrants in their villages before we can understand the full impact of urbanization on them.[62]

All these studies, and the many controversies over whether family structures are changing or not, point up the complexity of the processes of industrialization and urbanization, and show the necessity of analysing the many variables in the total situation in which each family is found, before definite trends can be established or predicted. The present sample of urban middle and upper middle-class Hindus was particularly chosen as they were thought to be more open to urban influences than other classes or rural people.

India like every other country has, through such phenomena as invasions, internal wars, famines, floods and epidemics, always experienced some sort of change. These crises, in altering the composition of the population, forcing people to move from one part of India to another, and introducing many new cultural patterns, must necessarily have affected the structure of the Hindu society. Desai points out that the fact that the Hindu joint family system has "always been changing" is evident from the history of changes in such matters as the rules of exogamy, the laws of succession and inheritance, and the composition of its households.[63]

[62]Desai, "An Analysis," pp. 115–16.
[63]Desai, "An Analysis," p. 97. See also: Alan R. Beals, "Interplay among Factors of Change in a Mysore Village," in *Village India*, McKim Marriott, ed. (Chicago: University of Chicago Press, 1955), pp. 78–101; and the descriptions of many other anthropologists of changes in village life when they are influenced by urbanization.

It is, therefore, to be assumed that the technological forces which have caused so many changes in family structure in other countries will also have affected the structure of the family in India; this, in spite of the fact that no clear trend can be observed, nor has a sudden drastic change of the family pattern in general occurred as it did in Soviet Russia at the time of the revolution. Thus, the question does not seem to be, "Has the family changed?" But rather, "What has been the rate of change? Is the family changing more rapidly now than before? If so, what is causing this more rapid change?"

Many more studies must be made of the family structures of the many diversified groups in India, and in fact of family systems all over the world, before we will be able to isolate the effect that all the separate factors which make up the complexes of "industrialization" and "urbanization" have on family structure. Some of these factors have already been isolated, and the following sections will discuss those which tend to break up, and those which tend to strengthen the joint family unity.

*Factors which Tend to Break Down the Joint Family System*

Even before the advent of the technological age many factors were instrumental in causing joint families to split up, or one member to leave and establish a separate family of his own. The growth of the family itself often made it too large a unit to be manageable in one household. Family feuds made brothers or sons anxious to live separately. The custom of dividing the family property among all the sons of the joint family gradually cut up the property into holdings which were too small to support large families and so literally forced young men off the land to find shelter in the growing towns and cities.

India's fight for independence was undoubtedly one of the major factors in shaking up the older customary patterns of behaviour. It forced both men and women to move out into a wider world and break many previous habits. In fact, it might not be too great an exaggeration to say that for Hindu women, in particular, this movement ushered them into the modern world.[64] Two important facets of this movement were first of all that Gandhi, the great spiritual leader, insisted on lowering caste barriers, and secondly that participation in the struggle gave great prestige to the participant; so both men

---

[64]Nayantara Sahgal, *Prison and Chocolate Cake* (London: Victor Gollancz, Ltd., 1954). This autobiography gives vivid insight into the change which took place in the lives of many men, women and children during the fight for independence.

and women were able to engage in types of behaviour which would not ordinarily have been countenanced.[65] Another factor which affected family life was that, as the last stages of the struggle for independence coincided with World War II, it was a time which demanded initiative, and in which there were opportunities for many Hindus to try out new occupations, and move around India more than before. Although much change has occurred in India since 1946, the pioneer stage of the break into the modern world is over, and in this sense the India of the present generation is possibly more stable than that of the last generation. This idea was supported by a number of interviewees who felt that they had been less affected by radical change than their parents.

Recently, the heavy expense of weddings and religious festivals, lavish hospitality, costly dowries, and increased pressure to spend money on the higher education of children, all have tended to make middle- and upper-class people, in particular, leave their joint families and seek the new opportunities in the cities to augment their incomes. Higher education is more easily obtained in cities, and one important outcome of the move to obtain it is that children develop ambitions which their parents do not share. They also tend to see life in a new perspective, and the relative freedom of the city makes them reluctant to return to the tutelage of their elders. Thus the influences of city life tend to separate children and parents in interests and outlook. If the children remain in the city, the problems of building up a business or professional career are so great that little time is left over to spend on thoughts of those at home.

It can be stated as a theorem, valid in a very high percentage of cases, that the greater the opportunities for individual economic profit provided by any socio-cultural situation, the weaker the ties of extended kinship will become. Modernization of the unmechanized cultures, with their unexampled opportunities for individuals with intelligence and initiative, cannot fail to weaken or even destroy joint family patterns. This in turn will entail a whole series of problems for the societies in question. They must develop new mechanisms to provide for the economic and psychological needs now taken care of by family organization.[66]

Higher education for girls may make them want more independence, including their own homes when they marry. The city, too, often engenders desires for a higher standard of living, with its attendant

[65]This is a common occurrence in times of war and struggle. Even though the controls may be reimposed when peace arrives, some breach in the mores has been accomplished, and the new freedom is to some extent established.
[66]Linton, "Cultural and Personality Factors Affecting Economic Growth," p. 84.

comforts, and new types of recreation and leisure. Urbanization, also, seems to emphasize individuality and privacy, which gives another incentive for being independent of the large family group.

Another important factor which affects joint family solidarity lies in changing laws relating to family life. Dr. M. A. Rauf considers that the Hindu joint family, particularly in the cities, has been greatly influenced by the introduction of English Common Law.[67] Agarwala claims that the Income Tax Law and the new Estate Duty will go even further in disrupting the joint family.[68]

These then are some of the forces working to break up the extended family system. There are others, however, which are still important in maintaining its unity. One of these is India's comparative geographical isolation from Europe. This has kept India somewhat removed from the most vigorous results of the industrial revolution. In the second place, the rural-urban trend has not been as extensive as in other countries. In his study of population movements in India and Pakistan, Davis says that although internal migration in India has been large in actual numbers, it has been small in proportion to the total population. This means that India has not been as disrupted by internal migration as many other countries have. Chief among the many factors responsible for this lack of migration have been the caste system ("suppression of social mobility tends to suppression of geographical mobility"); early marriages, which have bound young Hindus with family responsibilities at an age when they might want to wander; the lack of a period of restlessness among adolescents; the laws of inheritance, which have served to look after all family members and not worked to send them out to seek their fortunes as in the West; the diversity of language and culture, which has made it difficult for Hindus to move easily far from home; and the lack of education ("migration is the result of an idea of what lies beyond").[69]

The relatively rapid industrialization and urbanization which are now taking place in India are changing many of the above-mentioned

[67]Dr. Rauf illustrated his point by describing the "Gains of Learning Act" which provided that a man could keep his income from his professional or civil service earnings as his own separate property. This did not always have great practical effect, for the moral pressure of his family would still often compel the man to contribute to the common pool. But if the man wanted to be free from family liability he could always plead this Act. Another law which helped to dissolve joint families was the Income Tax Act, for in order to reduce this tax families would break up. Dr. Rauf also considers that recent legislature, such as the right of daughters to equal inheritance with sons, will probably also affect the solidarity of the joint family.

[68]Agarwala, "In a Mobile Commercial Community," pp. 144–5.
[69]Davis, *Population of India and Pakistan*, pp. 107, 108.

conditions. This would seem to suggest that, on balance, the factors which are tending to break up the joint family are now stronger than those which are helping to maintain its unity.

### Theories of Family Change

The research for this study was carried out in Bangalore, a city of 778,977 persons in South India.[70] Owing to its position, the city is somewhat isolated from the sharpest impact of industrialization and modern Western influences, which bear much more heavily on such large northern cities as Bombay and Calcutta. However, as it has many industries, formerly included a British cantonment, and has grown at a very rapid rate since 1941, the urban middle and upper classes must face many of the changes which are occurring in the larger Indian cities. A contrast to those interviewed in Bangalore was provided by including in the sample a number of young men who had moved from villages and towns in South India to Bombay to seek their fortunes. The main interviewing was done by a research team of six Hindus. In addition to the 157 interviews, general information was obtained and interview material tested by countless talks and interviews with people familiar with, or especially qualified to know about, changing family conditions in different parts of India. A full description of the sample and the method will be found in Appendix I.

One of the major theoretical problems of this study was to find a precise enough definition of the "family" to use as an analytical tool, for most anthropological and many sociological definitions did not include the more subtle aspects of family structure. Moreover, although sociologists have made a great many limited studies of particular aspects of family life, there are very few of these that give an all-round picture of the family as a changing system, related to changes taking place in other parts of a society.

E. W. Burgess and H. J. Locke have, perhaps, gone the farthest in attaining this goal by their construction of two Ideal Types, the Institutional Family and the Companionship Family. The first type is found in small isolated societies with a simple economy, where conditions have been stable enough to evolve a large extended family system. The second type is found in large complex modern cities on

---

[70]*Census of India*, 1951, vol. XIV, Mysore, Part II, p. 6. (Bangalore: Director of Printing, Stationery and Publications, Government Press).

For an understanding of the ecology and social organization of Bangalore see Noel P. Gist, "The Ecology of Bangalore, India: An East-West Comparison," *Social Forces*, vol. 35, no. 4 (May, 1957), pp. 356-65.

the American continent, where the processes of industrialization and urbanization have presumably exerted their greatest influence.[71]

The Burgess and Locke theory presupposes that the forces of industrialization and urbanization will affect the basic structure of families in the same way. This proposition can be at least tentatively held, for many studies of different societies have shown that the impingement of these forces on family systems produces similar basic results—although details may vary considerably. These abstract types are thus methodologically useful, for they permit a somewhat accurate estimation of the degree to which any family system has moved from one type to the other. As they represent extremes on a continuum, they can be used as standards, and indices can be worked out to measure relative amounts of change.

In applying this theory to the Hindu family, the traditional large joint family would be very near to Burgess's description of the Institutional Family, and the few small nuclear families, which can now be found in some of the larger Indian cities, would approximate the Companionship Family.

There is no suggestion in Burgess's theory of Ideal Types that change will occur rapidly unless the full quota of industrial and urban influences impinges on the family unit. Indeed, history shows that in some countries it has taken many centuries to change from the large extended family form to the small unit, and in others the period of transition often appears suspended in space, and families retain the characteristics of one type for generations.

Linton gives a concise description of the way economic changes affect family structure:

Economic change is always destructive to a joint family system. This can be seen even in Europe, where the early Roman and Germanic families were not unlike the oriental joint families. Such families broke down under the impact of developing mercantilism with its increase in individual opportunity, while their complete destruction came with the rise of modern mechanized civilization. Here in the United States we have reached the low point in a process of breakdown of kin structure which has reduced our functional kin group to the primary, biologically determined one of parents and children.[72]

[71]E. W. Burgess and H. J. Locke *The Family* (New York: American Book Co., 1953), pp. 26–7. "The family has been in historical times in transition from an institution with family behaviour controlled by the mores, public opinion, and law to a companionship with family behaviour arising from the mutual affection and consensus of its members. The companionship form of family is not to be conceived as having already been realized but as emerging."

[72]Linton, "Cultural and Personality Factors Affecting Economic Growth," pp. 83–4.

Other authors are more positive of the effects which they believe occur when the influences of highly industrialized societies impinge on relatively non-industrialized ones.

In case after case the initial patterns of family organization, of production units, and of authority and responsibility have broken down. In the sphere of family patterns tendencies in the direction of multilineal conjugal patterns, the "emancipation" of youth, "romantic love" as a basis for marriage, etc., have been noted again and again. Furthermore, it would seem that no known case has yet started such a trend and reversed it.[73]

Perhaps the most dramatic effect of these changes can be observed in peasant families from central Europe who migrate to the cities of the North American continent and are suddenly faced with the problems of a new way of life, without any supporting kin group.

The present study uses Burgess and Locke's Ideal Type theory as a working hypothesis, and classifies the families interviewed for this study into four types, in which the large joint family approximates Burgess's Institutional Family and the nuclear family approaches the Companionship Family. It attempts to see how the various substructures of the family system are affected as the family changes from an approximation of one Ideal Type to the other.

First of all, however, the "family" must be defined so that its component elements are understood. Students use the term "family" in many different ways. The common thread of meaning refers to a more or less closely integrated group of people who are related to one another through ties of kinship, blood or adoption. The variations in the use of the word are accounted for by the fact that each particular specialist defines the family in terms relative to his own particular purpose. Even anthropologists and sociologists, both interested in social structure, differ markedly in their definitions, a difference which makes it very difficult to relate data from anthropological studies of families living in pre-industrial societies to sociological data collected after these families move to the city. For example, both Karve and Mandelbaum define a joint family as one whose members are related by bonds of kinship, and generally lives in one household. Karve adds three kinds of necessary family behaviour to her definition: eating food cooked at one hearth, holding property in common and worshipping together.[74] These anthropological definitions only include the physical

[73]Marion J. Levy, Jr., "Some Sources of the Vulnerability of the Structures of Relatively Nonindustrialized Societies to Those of Highly Industrialized Societies," in *The Progress of Underdeveloped Areas*, p. 124.

[74]Karve, *Kinship Organisation in India*, p. 10. Mandelbaum, "The Family in

and biological aspects of family life and tell nothing of the sentiments, the systems of power, and the rights and duties which constitute the effective binding elements of the family unit. Nor do these definitions give an adequate framework for analysing shifts in family relationships in a rapidly changing society.[75] Another problem that has arisen from inadequate definition is that the multi-dimensional character of family life has not yet been fully analysed.[76]

Most sociological definitions include some of the psychological elements of family life as well as its physical and biological elements. Green's definition is clearest in this context: "By structure of the family is meant its formal patterning of rights, duties and living arrangements and its defined statuses of age, sex and kinship."[77] This definition can be seen to include the elements of three separate substructures, a biological substructure of age, sex and kinship; an ecological substructure of household groups; and a substructure of rights and duties. But it omits two which have been the subject of many family studies, although they have not been systematically worked out, namely, authority and sentiments. This study analyses the four last-mentioned substructures separately in order to clarify the way in which each

India," p. 93. See also Blunt, *Social Service in India*, p. 45. Blunt states that the chief criterion of a joint family is that they "Eat food cooked on one cooking place."

[75]Desai, "An Analysis," p. 117. Desai stresses this point when he says, "The residential joint family group is the three generations group. But the functionally effective group is much wider."

[76]Talcott Parsons, *Max Weber: The Theory of Social and Economic Organization* (New York: Oxford University Press, 1947), pp. 424–6. Max Weber recognized this same problem in his analysis of social class. He showed that this phenomenon cannot be fully understood unless its multi-dimensional character is taken into consideration. The three dimensions which he recognized were the economic order, the prestige or honorific order and the power structure. Each dimension constitutes a separate rank order, although the different orders are interrelated. According to his analysis a person or family of a certain class would have at least three relative class positions in a society at any given time. In a changing society these three dimensions may not correlate with each other.

Marion J. Levy, Jr., *The Family Revolution in Modern China* (Cambridge, Mass.: Harvard University Press, 1949), pp. 4–5. In his study of the family revolution in modern China, Levy was probably the first to systematically work out some of the family substructures. He contends that a kinship structure cannot survive unless it has certain generalized structural elements. The substructures he selected for analysis were: role differentiation, allocation of solidarity, economic allocation, political allocation and the allocation of integration and expression. He then analyzed the changes which have taken place in the traditional Chinese family since its encounter with modern technological forces in terms of the above categories. Levy's work was not known to the present writer until she had evolved a separate series of substructures, based more on interpersonal relationships between kin members than on the survival categories evolved by Levy.

[77]Arnold W. Green, *Sociology: An Analysis of Life in Modern Society* (New York: McGraw-Hill Book Co., 1952), p. 370.

one is affected by family change. The analysis is based on the theory that each family position is composed of a variety of elements, such as duties, rights and affection, and these elements form separate substructures through the related family positions. In the traditional Hindu family system, for example, the warmest, most enduring feelings are expected, first of all, between mother and son, and secondly between brother and sister. Whereas in the modern American family the most affectionate relationship is expected between husband and wife and secondly between mother and children.

It is necessary to analyse each substructure separately because they are not necessarily affected by the same factors of change. That is, changes in the affectional patterns of the family may not be accompanied by corresponding changes in the structure of obligations or in the hierarchy of power. The data collected for this study seemed to suggest that affection for relatives, for example, weakens much sooner than a feeling of obligation for them when the small family unit is separated from distant kin.

It is easier to describe changes in each substructure than to show how one substructure is related to the others at any one period of time. This study goes no further than the first abstraction of substructures, and does not attempt to give more than a superficial understanding of the complex problem of the interrelationship of the substructures that form the Hindu family system. The definition of a family which will be used is that a family is a group of people, usually related as some particular type of kindred, who may live in one household, and whose unity resides in a patterning of rights and duties, sentiments and authority. A distinction will be made between the family—typically a household unit—and relatives, who will be thought of as related kin living outside the household boundaries.

Individual or group behaviour cannot be fully understood unless it is related to the total situation in which it occurs. The second major task of a study of family change is to understand how the family relates to the other structures of the society,[78] for changes in one

[78]Levy, *Family Revolution*, pp. 7-8. "It should never be forgotten that these kinship substructures are inevitably in some cases and in some degree part of the more generalized substructures for the whole society. Take for example, the status of women relative to men. . . . The role differentiation of women relative to men in the kinship structure can never vary independently of that for women in the society at large. It is, however, methodologically permissible to abstract the kinship sector of the general status of women and hold it up for investigation. As a corollary of this, it follows that the analysis of the kinship sector of a general social substructure never completely describes the total substructure unless all the activities of that substructure are in terms of kinship, that is, conterminous with that section of the society which is the kinship structure."

structure will inevitably affect the others. Change in the economic structure, for example, is bound to affect the family, for new types of occupations may arise which may demand a totally different outlook on life, and drastic changes in behaviour. This can be seen in the behaviour expected of a village landlord as compared to his son in business in a large city. In the same way the educational system is intimately related to the family from which it draws its recruits, and is at least partly shaped by the economic and other social structures which it serves.

The analysis of family change in this study will begin with a discussion of the ecological substructure and the patterns of rights and duties, authority and sentiments. This will be followed by a description of the effect of some aspects of the educational and economic structures on the Hindu family, and of the way in which the development of new primary groups relationships, based on friendships rather than kinship, and changing marriage patterns, alter family relationships.

• *Chapter Two* •

# THE ECOLOGICAL SUBSTRUCTURE

A THOROUGH STUDY of family change must start with an analysis of the spatial arrangement of family members and their households. For as contacts tend to be more intimate and controls more effective when relatives live geographically close, so separation of the members and household units will tend to have the opposite effect. It is easier to maintain family solidarity if people are continuously in contact with each other. The old saying that "distance makes the heart grow fonder" is only true over a short period of time, for common meanings and understandings inevitably weaken as the members of a family go their separate ways. Contact through letters and visits may be maintained for some time, but it is highly likely that children of the second generation will not retain close ties and will gradually lose all contact with distant relatives.

### SIZE OF HOUSEHOLD AND TYPE OF FAMILY

The 1951 Census of India classifies all Indian families into three types, according to the number of household members.[1] In this classification, the large-sized family, presumably the traditional large joint family, has seven to nine members; the medium-sized family four to six and nuclear or small family has under four members.[2] Size, how-

[1] The size of a sample of rural and urban households in Mysore State will be found in Appendix II. Appendix III shows the composition of 1,000 households in Mysore State.
[2] I. P. Desai, "The Joint Family in India—An Analysis," *Sociological Bulletin*, vol. V, no. 2 (Sept., 1956), pp. 144–5. Desai claims that size alone is not a reliable or sufficient criterion by which the jointness of a family can be established. Of the Census, he says: "The classification seems to have been entirely arbitrary. The central defect of the Census approach is that the family is understood as a conglomoration of individuals whose classification can be derived solely on the basis of the number of persons composing it."

ever, does not give an adequate basis for understanding the subtleties of jointness, and so it was thought appropriate in this study to classify the sample of families in terms of: the number of generations living in one household; the presence or absence of married couples; and the number of dependent members. In this way, four distinct types of family households were found: the large joint family, the small joint family, the nuclear family and the nuclear family with dependents. This classification will be used throughout the study.

*Type A*

The large joint family is composed of three or more generations living together in the same house, cooking in the same kitchen, owning property in common and pooling their incomes for common spending. Several families of this type may live close together and claim a common ancestor. The father is usually the person who maintains family solidarity, for married sons do not always continue to live together after his death.[3]

All families change in size during their life cycle, but the composition of large joint families seems particularly susceptible to change, for not only are children continually being born, and older members dying, but the crises of life may bring back dependent members.[4] Widowed sisters or unemployed or sick relatives may also return to its shelter, or sons may move away and daughters leave when they marry. Thus joint families seldom have the "ideal" composition of members at any one point of time, but have rather a scattered arrangement of people. For example, at the time of the interview, one large joint family was composed of ego, her husband, her father-in-law, mother-in-law, mother-in-law's brother, his wife and two sons, as well as ego's brother-in-law and his family.

The composition of the household may be changed for a period of time through the Hindu custom of daughters returning home for their pregnancies. Their other children may accompany them.[5] Illness or emergencies may bring daughters back with their families until they

---

[3]I. P. Desai, "An Analysis" in: "Symposium: Caste and Joint Family," *Sociological Bulletin*, vol. IV, no. 2, (Sept., 1955) pp. 108–9.

[4]A number of the people interviewed for this study had never known their grandparents, for they had died before they were born.

[5]Irawati Karve, *Kinship Organisation in India*, Deccan College Monograph Series, 11, Poona: Deccan College Post-Graduate and Research Institute, 1953, p. 233. This custom is followed particularly in the case of the first confinement. It is thought to be humiliating for a woman to have no home to return to. She usually goes in her seventh month of pregnancy and returns when the child is three months old. Visits home are more numerous for the daughter during her

can again stand, economically, on their own feet. The large joint family may also include visiting relatives whose visits may last a year or more. Even the poor and needy of the locality may swell the ranks of the family for meals or lodging.

There were lots of people living in our house when I was growing up. As well as my paternal grandparents, father, mother, my six brothers and myself, relatives often stayed with us all through the year. Mother's brother and sister often visited us and my other grandmother stayed with us most of the time. Father's brother and his three sons and daughter only lived six miles away, so they too were frequent visitors. Then, as Father was one of the richest Zamindars in the province, everyone—rich and poor, employed or unemployed, old or young—came and lived with us for as long as they wanted to.

The house always looked like a marriage house, it was so full of people. There were so many around that we had no set times for meals, people ate at any hour at all. (Case 66)

## Type B

The small joint family is, by definition, composed of a household in which parents live with their married sons and other unmarried children, or two brothers live together with their wives and children. The most typical pattern in the sample studied was a family in which one son and his family lived with his parents in the ancestral home, or parents lived in the son's home, or two married brothers lived together.

This type of family may only be a temporary stage in the family cycle. It usually forms when a son breaks away from his original family on getting a job in another city and sets up his own household; one or more of his sons may then continue living with him after marriage. Many of the people interviewed had spent their early years of married life with the husband's parents.

## Type C

The nuclear family is composed of two generations, usually one or both parents with children. In most cases this type of family also tended to be one phase of the family cycle. However, thirty-three interviewees had always lived in nuclear families and a number of these had established their own separate homes on marriage. This type of family is found more often in large towns and cities than in villages.

---

first years of marriage. Her absences do not inconvenience her husband when he is living in a joint family, for he will be looked after by other women in the household. But a husband living in a nuclear family will have to look after himself during his wife's absence. If he was brought up in a joint family, he will not be able to do this, for the women of the household will always have waited on him.

## Type D

The nuclear family with dependents consists of parents, their children and one or more dependents. The latter may be grandfathers or grandmothers (if both are living with the family it would be classified as a joint family), uncles, nieces, etc.

It is difficult to define a "dependent" precisely, for a widowed sister living in her brother's home may be a dependent in the sense of not earning money, but she may do the work of a servant and so save the family that expense. Another problem is to make a distinction between a dependent and a visitor. For example, children who are boarded by uncles while at school, sisters returning to their homes for confinements or relatives staying for a year or more could be put into either of these classifications.

Finally, the following distinction was made: a brother who lived with ego and his wife and contributed to the family income would be a true member of that household and it would be classified as a joint family; a younger sister living with ego and his wife until her marriage would be called a dependent and this household would fall into classification D. The main distinction between these two cases then, lies in the fact that when a person has no authority or responsibility in family matters he is a dependent.

Lack of adequate information on the above subtleties made it impossible to classify all extra family members according to the above criterion; so doubtful cases were classified as Type D families.

The 157 interviewees were asked to describe the composition of their family households at two periods of time: first, when they were growing up and, secondly, at the time of the interview. They were then classified into the four family types.

### Type A

6 interviewees had remained in large joint families throughout ego's life.
3 had lived in large joint families when ego was growing up, but had changed to Type B families when ego was older.
7 had changed from large joint families to nuclear families.
3 had changed from large joint families to Type D.

### Type B

14 had remained in small joint families throughout ego's life.
22 had changed from small joint families to nuclear families.
8 had changed from small joint families to Type D.

### Type C

33 had remained in nuclear families throughout ego's life.
29 had changed from nuclear families to small joint families.

13 had changed from nuclear families to nuclear families with dependents.
2 had changed from a nuclear family form to a large joint family.

*Type D*

9 had remained in nuclear families with dependents throughout ego's life.
2 had changed from Type D to small joint families.
6 had changed from Type D to nuclear families.

The above figures show that nineteen of the interviewees grew up in large joint family households, forty-four in small joint families, seventy-seven in nuclear families and seventeen in nuclear families with dependents. Twenty-two of the sample were living alone when interviewed.

Describing family composition at two points of time in ego's life does not, however, give a full idea of the number of family forms that ego may actually live in during his lifetime. For example, ego may grow up in a large or small joint family and after marriage move away to another city and establish a separate household. This new nuclear unit will typically have dependent family members living with it for periods of time when ego's children are growing up.

Finally, when ego's son marries, he may remain in ego's house with his wife and children for a number of years before moving out and establishing a new home of his own. Thus ego's nuclear family changes once again to a smaller type of joint family and may eventually revert to the nuclear type if and when the married son leaves. The typical middle and upper middle-class urban Hindu thus moves through a series of family forms during his lifetime. Each type will alter his relations, to some extent, with his family and relatives. Similar kinds of change in family form have been noted by Dube in his study of a South Indian village, and by Kapadia in his study of Navsari, a town of 44,663 people:

A man leaves the parent family to start his nuclear family. In course of time his sons get married and they do not generally leave the family on marriage but stay there and, in course of time, as they become parents of children, extend its circumference. A family of three generations is thus once again formed. Theoretically it does not much differ from the traditional family. The difference lies only in the perspective of the individual who heads it. . . . He now heads the family which consists of his sons and grandsons, his daughters and daughters-in-law, who are dearer to him than his brothers and collaterals. . . .[6]

[6]S. C. Dube, *Indian Village* (1955), p. 133, quoted by Desai, "An Analysis," p. 104. See also K. M. Kapadia, "Rural Family Patterns: A Study in Urban-Rural Relations," *Sociological Bulletin*, vol. V, no. 2 (Sept., 1956), pp. 120-1.

In summing up the trend of family form in India today, it could be safely said that, if the sample of families interviewed for this study represents a change that is taking place in the composition of Hindu middle and upper middle-class urban families, then this trend is towards a break away from the traditional joint family form into nuclear family units.

### The Spatial Arrangement of Households

In the traditional large joint family, all sons theoretically remained under the paternal roof, keeping their wives and children with them. Daughters would leave for the joint households of their husbands on marriage. Relatives typically lived close by, perhaps in the same village. Few lived so far away that they could not return for special family ceremonies.

Should the family become too large to remain under one roof, one or more of the sons, or two brothers, would break away and set up a house of their own. However, they would typically remain nearby or even build in the same family compound, so that all family members had constant close contact with each other.

When Grandfather was alive his four sons and their families lived with him in a joint family. His two daughters were married but lived quite near. After Grandfather's death, the property was divided and all the sons and daughters were given land on the same street; so they all built separate houses quite close together. Therefore, although the family property was divided, they met every day and consulted each other whenever help was needed. (Case 48)

The custom of cross-cousin marriage, formerly typical of the matrilineal family system of the south, binds families even closer together, for the daughter might marry a cousin who lived close by and whose family had been so intimate with her own that she would know her new "in-laws" very well before she entered their home as a bride. As one interviewee reported: "When my Grandfather died, my parents bought a house next to my uncle's. I married one of his sons and after that our two families were very close and always went everywhere together." (Case 62)

A grandmother may often be instrumental in holding the family in close contact with each other even when they live under separate roofs.

I come from a big joint family which has lived for generations in Madras. My father had six sons and five daughters. The daughters were all married and went to stay in their husbands' homes. The six sons lived with their wives and children in Grandfather's house. When Grandfather died, the brothers gradually spread out into nearby houses, but they continued to eat in the "big house," for Grandmother thought that the unity of the family would remain as long as the kitchen and oven weren't broken in two. (Case 74)

More spatial separation of families occurs when sons move out and build their homes in other parts of the town or city. This will make it more difficult for family members to meet, particularly in large cities. However, although this distance can be used as an excuse to remain separate by those who wish to escape from close family controls, it still may not relieve them from the obligation of looking after any relative who wishes to visit them. "My husband and I, and our three children, live in a separate house, not too close to our in-laws, but this does not mean that we are a separate family, for my mother-in-law often lives with us for months at a time. Moreover, any time the elders want they can come and live with us, or they can tell a younger family member to go to visit us. So, even though we live in a separate house, our independence is not recognized." (Case 53)

A further separation occurs when family units move to different cities. Here again, however, close enough contact may be retained through visiting or emergencies to make the distant members still feel close to the core family. "Two of my brothers-in-law are married and live in Bombay and Hyderabad, but they are still considered as belonging to my husband's joint family and spend their holidays with us whenever they can. When my sisters-in-law are ill or when there is an emergency, they also come back to the joint family." (Case 54) This interview shows that many sons still feel that it is "natural" for them to return to their parents' home for vacations although a much more formal attitude exists in relation to visiting the wife's home.

Geographic separation only becomes completely effective in separating family members when a son moves far away to a large city and becomes so absorbed in the new life that he has little inclination to retain family ties and returns home as seldom as possible. He may eventually break away completely from his relatives.

The increasing occupational mobility of sons, the growth of cities which often necessitates separate family units living far apart in the same city, and the marked tendency for sons to divide the family property on the death of their father, all seem to point to a growing spatial separation of urban Hindu households, particularly in the middle and upper middle classes. This gradual separation will lessen inter-family influences over the day-to-day affairs of the different household groups, so that even though they may continue to consult each other on the major issues of life, families will grow more independent until, when the nuclear family system is well established, the control of the family "trunk" will be at a minimum.

### The Interior Arrangements of the Household

The large joint family usually still share a common living room, worshipping room and kitchen. Different arrangements may be made for the use of bedrooms, usually depending on the size and wealth of the family. Sometimes each separate family unit will have its own separate bedrooms, or all children of the household will sleep together in one room when small. "Our house was more or less like a hostel and our bedroom was like a dormitory." Or, all the boys might sleep in one room, the girls in another.

Most of the families included in the sample for this study shared a common kitchen and worshipping room, but each family had its own sleeping rooms. Sometimes there would be one living room for women, one for men. It was only in cases of family conflict that each family unit living under the same roof had a separate kitchen. Eating meals together, however, was not a common practice. In the more traditional large joint families the custom still prevails of men eating first, then children and finally women.[7]

When the family changes to the nuclear type and former eating customs are no longer appropriate, the pattern of eating tends to vary to suit the convenience of each family. The various members of some families may eat at different times during the day and then have their evening meal together. Sometimes a servant will serve, thus freeing the women of the family to eat with the others.

A major change which has come about with the shift from joint households to nuclear is that the two sexes are now no longer as completely separated. Whereas formerly the women often had a separate living room of their own and did not eat with the men, in the nuclear household all sexes and ages are brought into much closer contact.

[7] J. H. S. Bossard, *The Sociology of Child Development* (New York: Harper and Brothers, 1954), pp. 164–175. Bossard speaks of the unifying function of family meals. In the Hindu family mealtime may be a gay time for the children as they insist on stories being told. For the grown-ups there will be local gossip and politics to discuss. In former times, this was the main way in which the women of the house learned about outside world affairs.

## Reasons for Remaining in One Household

Not enough data were available to show the extent to which family members formerly remained in joint family households during their entire lifetime, but it has been shown that in recent years the complications involved in the movement of families to cities mean that many Hindus now live in a number of different types of family households in the course of their lives.

Information on the movement of brothers who were over eighteen years of age was given by 135 interviewees. Of the 207 brothers mentioned, 110 were living away from home, often in distant cities. The remaining 97 still lived with their families. Twenty-two interviewees either did not have brothers or had none over eighteen years of age.

As no studies could be found on the former mobility of sons, it is impossible to know whether their movement away from home is accelerating or not, but a consideration of the increasing pressures to do so leads to the conclusion that many more are now living away from their families than in former times. On the other hand, economic insecurity may force sons to remain under the parental roof even when they are married and desirous of setting up separate homes of their own. Desai suggests that families sometimes stay together because "there is nothing to be divided except the ancestral debt."[8]

Economic factors have probably been the main determinant of the increasing number of family separations, for the inability of the land to support the growing population has forced many sons to leave home to seek their livelihood in the growing cities. In early times the total income of the joint family generally came from land. All members worked on it, and their mutual gains were pooled in a common purse. However, as technological and industrial changes provided new occupational opportunities at a time when the gradual impoverishment of the land, and a growing population, made children anxious to find new ways of maintenance, many different ways of contributing to the joint family income developed. Although the rural-urban trend meant that the unity of the family as a producing unit was undermined, joint families still seem to have retained their unity as a consumption entity, for many of the families of this study still maintained a common purse to which the earning members, women as well as men, contributed. Even sons who leave the joint family for other cities customarily send money home, either regularly for the general family expenses or for

[8]Desai, "An Analysis," p. 109.

special occasions such as marriages. In this way most joint families now have rather complex financial arrangements.

In a money economy many tensions and strains may centre around the family income. One reason for this is that money is a clear measurement of a person's contribution to the family, and spending money is just as clear an indication of his claims to family support. No matter what the source of income is or what spending arrangements are evolved, the hypothesis could be at least tentatively held that any arrangement will maintain peaceful relationships within the joint family provided that all are agreed on this particular arrangement; some members do not feel that they are bearing more of the financial burden than others; and too many financial crises do not arise to upset the customary way of handling money, and make it impossible for some members to carry out their obligations. However, when desires for a higher standard of living develop, and when family income is derived in the form of salaries rather than from family property, joint family financial agreements become increasingly subject to strain. For instance, one brother may have a higher monetary income than the others, and after paying his share into the common purse, will have more money left over for his own family's personal expenses. This may cause invidious comparisons between co-wives and cousins, and strained relationships may ensue. Allied to this problem is that, although all members of a joint family theoretically receive the same amount from the family purse, brothers with lower salaries often felt that they were discriminated against, or looked down on for their relatively small contribution. Such conflicts may be accentuated in families which have been influenced by urban ambitions, and have acquired a high standard of aspirations.

One of the main safeguards to the solidarity of the traditional joint family was that the rules of inheritance gave all brothers an equal share in the family property, and that they could demand a division of the property at any time. Thus the amount of inheritance which each son was to receive was clearly defined, and also the appropriate way of transferring it from generation to generation. Any change in this age-old arrangement generally caused trouble. In one family, in which the father sold some of the family property without consulting his eldest son, the son was furious, for as he was responsible for his father's liabilities he felt he had the right to help determine its disposal. In another family a son beat his younger brother because he objected to a division of the property, and the two did not speak for two years. A father in still another caused a great deal of family trouble by leaving his share of the family property to his brothers instead of to his sons. And in another family the father and elder brother refused to speak to the younger brother for a long time because he insisted on getting his share of the family property to finance his education.

All in all it seems that, if family relations have been harmonious and there is enough income from property to support a large family, sons will usually go on living together as a joint family after the father dies. But if family life has been unhappy there is a tendency for brothers to separate, either on the death of the father, or because of rivalry, disagreements, jealousy between wives, dissatisfaction on how the property is managed, or a desire to live separately. If sons are young when the father dies, relatives may be able to benefit by putting pressure on them for a partition.

Another problem which is probably a recurrent one, in that most large families produce at least one "black sheep," is created by men who will not support their children, and sons who will not work. Several such irresponsible people were mentioned in interviews.

The changing economic basis of middle-class urban families, which necessitates a gradual broadening, and redefinition, of family responsibilities, usually is not understood by all members at the same time; so conflicts often occur until new arrangements for financing responsibilities arise.

In one family, friction arose when the widowed mother-in-law was not content with the amount of money her son contributed to the family's support: "Our joint family property is not divided yet although my husband and I live separately. As I have an independent income I use it for our family expenses. My husband gives me a fixed amount each month and gives the rest of his salary to his mother. She lives with my eldest brother-in-law, and they manage the joint family property. They both feel that my husband should give his share of the family property to one of his brothers who hasn't a very good job. They often tell us this in front of him, and give examples of other 'good' brothers who have done this for their brother." (Case 53)

In still another family the father could not understand that the large income which his son was getting in the city did not cover the increased expenses of city life and a higher social position.

A man I know who grew up in Bangalore got a good job in Bombay which gave him a large income. On a recent visit back to see his old father who is 94 years old, the father asked him to increase the amount of money he sent him. His father is living with the eldest brother, who is 55 years old and retired. He hasn't much money and has six children to bring up. My friend is 45 years old and has two daughters.

My friend knows that his father doesn't need any more money himself, but will give any extra money he sends him to his brother. The father has also asked him to send him 1,000 rupees next year on his ninety-fifth birthday, which is always a very special event.

This request has made my friend furious, for he has many expenses, such as the coming marriage of one of his daughters, and the education of the other. Living too is expensive in Bombay, and he must also consider saving for his retirement. He is also gradually buying the jewelry his daughters will need for their weddings. His father cannot understand his expenses, or why they are important. My friend still has affection for his father, and wants to obey him, but resents his brother's hidden hand in all this immensely. (Case 53)

Thus changing circumstances and changing expenses often put strain on family relationships. It is fairly easy for a son who moves to another city and loses his feeling of family identity to withdraw his financial support. But for the son who continues to feel responsible for his joint family when he moves away, and who at the same time is faced with the expenses of urban life, conflict is inevitable.

Formerly, the wealth of the joint family rested mainly on revenue from estates or land holdings, and was usually relatively stable, and did not change radically over the years; now it tends, in most cases, to rest more on monetary assets, which may change in quantity much more rapidly than revenue from land. This poses the problem, which so often causes family strains in Western countries, of the distribution among sons of an amount of money which varies, rather than the division of a certain amount of land. It may also entail the problems of favouritism, since one son may be more favoured by his parents, and so inherit a larger part of the money.

An even more drastic change has been recently introduced through the passing of the Hindu Inheritance Bill, which gives women a legal share in the family property. Students believe that this right of inheritance may seriously affect the solidarity of the joint family, in that it will upset the customary system of family obligations,[9] for it gives the daughter a share in the property, without necessarily involving her in family responsibilities. Whereas it has been customary for sons to contribute to the support of their family as soon as they are earning,

---

[9] B. R. Agarwala, "In a Mobile Community," in "Symposium: Caste and Joint Family," *Sociological Bulletin*, vol. IV, no. 2 (Sept., 1955), p. 145. An informant said that, as a good deal of money is spent on the daughter's marriage, which often includes a dowry, it is felt to be unfair for her to share in the family property.

which often involves them in great personal sacrifice, there are no such customary obligations for daughters.[10] They have not been earning long enough to be expected to contribute financially. Moreover, some Hindus feel that, even should a daughter wish to share her family's financial burdens, she may be prevented in this by her husband, who customarily controls her money.

Economic circumstances also determine the number of dependent members that any one family can support. Indigent relatives or villagers were not too much of a strain on the joint family living in a village, for life there was simple and "an extra handful of rice in the pot" might be all that was required. But urban life makes many more demands on the family purse, particularly when responsibilities are redefined so that the urbanite becomes involved in the more impersonal obligations of a complex society, and his family budget must stretch to include an ever increasing number of charitable demands. Moreover, educated middle-class families now feel that it is essential for their sons to have a university education; so sons are often economically dependent on their parents until their education is completed and they are able to get jobs which will support them in separate households. If the son finds a job in another city, his wife may remain in his father's house until he can support her, as it is considered humiliating for him to have her return to her own home.

The son's turn to support the family will come when his parents are older, for middle-class parents are seldom able to save sufficiently for their old age. An informant said that the general tendency seems to be for sons who have moved economically ahead of their parents to want to meet their family obligations to them by cash remittances, rather than to have them live under their roofs. On the other hand, if the son has not done well economically, he tends to continue to live with his parents. In this way, the socio-economic differential is important in determining residence and size of family.

Other considerations, however, must also be noted and of these perhaps the most important in determining family and household size is the deep feeling of responsibility for elder family members which has been inherited from the joint family tradition. This attitude was particularly evident on the part of the young men interviewees who felt that their parents had made great sacrifices to bring them up. One spoke of the "tribulations" his mother had undergone; another said

[10] One informant who had no permanent job, and, as he was a Brahmin, was not at all sure of getting one, said that he would feel like a criminal if he did not send home money from his part-time jobs.

that as his mother had suffered a great deal, it was now his duty to look after her. Even one young man who had broken away to live in Bombay still felt this responsibility keenly. "After I marry I want to live with my parents, for I don't want them to have to shoulder any responsibility in their old age. I will look after them and my wife will see that all their needs are cared for properly. The modern fashionable girl from a university might not be able to do this, so I will never marry a girl with a graduate education." (Case 141)

Several other young men also said they wanted to marry girls who would be able to look after their parents, and thought it perfectly natural that their wives should share their feelings of responsibility in this regard. A few wanted to live with their parents because of their affection for them.

Other young men wanted to stay with their parents because they still felt dependent on them. "I have always been under my parents' wing." One extreme case was that of a young man who felt incapable of carrying the responsibility of a family by himself.

I don't want to go away from my family even if they drive me out. One reason is that I never had to take any responsibility at all, except to be a nice good little boy! Sometimes I think of setting up a separate household, and imagine myself as the boss—but I shiver in my shoes when I think of the responsibilities. I keep wondering if I could manage them.

I think that this is due to my father's domination over me. The moment I am confronted with problems of raising a family I feel I am incapable of facing it. So I always want to live with my parents. (Case 157)

Perhaps the most telling attitude was the surprise of several interviewees when asked whether they would like to live separately, for it had never occurred to them to leave their joint families.

The greater happiness to be found in joint families and their power and prestige were other reasons given for maintaining them. Even the usually criticized mother-in-law was mentioned by two daughters-in-law as being an advantage in a household. Finally, the housing shortage found in rapidly growing cities was mentioned as a factor which makes families continue to live together.

### Reasons for Separate Dwellings and Atypical Living Arrangements

Death is one of the most usual circumstances to upset the typical family pattern. In the following case the death of an important male member changed the composition of the family and pattern of dwelling.

I stayed with my parents for a few months after my marriage and then went to my father-in-law's place to live. But after my own father died we went to live with my mother's joint family for there was no older male member there to take the responsibility. (Case 90)

In another case, the death of a brother-in-law changed the type of dwelling and family for ego and her husband.

My husband and I lived with his family for a few months after our marriage, and then set up our own house. Shortly after that, my brother-in-law died and as there was no one left to look after the family interests, we closed our house and went to live with his family. After nine years with them, his son was old enough to take over the leadership of the family; so we left and again set up our own separate house. (Case 94)

The search for suitable jobs is another prime cause of the separation of family households. Some Hindus feel that better-educated and more sensitive young men often use migration to other cities for jobs as a device to enable them to escape from their families with a minimum of conflict. For it is very difficult for a son to live in a separate household from his parents in the same Indian city without causing gossip about possible family quarrels. This movement away to distant cities, therefore, could be looked on as a mechanism by which pent-up family tension and potential conflict can be relieved without any stigma falling on the family. The importance of this outlet can be seen when one studies joint families living in villages in which disrupting conflict may damage family relationships because there is no way to relieve the tensions through a "natural" separation.[11]

Another important reason for families' separating is conflict between different family members arising out of jealousy or quarrels. This is such a recognized possibility that some members may prefer to separate before too many irrevocable conflicts cause family feuds. In one family the grandmother insisted that the property be divided and her five sons live separately after the grandfather died to prevent disrupting quarrels.

The pursuit of education too, is often the cause of family separations. Children may move to a relative's home in a city where the educational opportunities are greater, or go to boarding school; young

---

[11] Mrs. G. B. Desai, "Women in Modern Gujerati Life," Unpublished Master's Thesis, University of Bombay, Bombay, 1945. In her study, Desai found that 42.6 per cent of the married women and 38.9 per cent of the single women favoured joint families. Whereas 57.4 per cent of the married women and 61.1 per cent of the single women preferred separate families. Considering that some type of joint family is still the norm in India these figures may indicate a growing restlessness with it, at least on the part of the women.

men and women may live in the ever increasing number of college hostels (residences). Thus, the young people separated from their families at a time when they are still very impressionable, will meet many more varied influences than in the family circle. This separation may give them their first independence from family controls. Moreover, they will gradually acquire an outlook on life which may make family members seem uncongenial when they return. It is possible that some correlation could be found between the amount of education and the desire to live separately from parents. Three of my interviewees mentioned young men who had gone to England or the United States for higher education and had not wanted to live with their parents when they returned.

Education too may promote high ambitions for lucrative and interesting jobs, which can be achieved only by evading family responsibilities demanding time or financial assistance. It will almost certainly promote desires for more freedom from family controls, and develop more individuality, which may all affect family patterns of dwelling. This trend was seen in the attitude of a number of the young married and single women interviewees who were desirous of living in separate homes.[12]

When child marriage was customary, a girl was not old enough at the time of marriage to handle a home of her own. Moreover, as she was typically married before puberty, she was too young to have sex relations with her husband. So she remained for the period between formal marriage and puberty in her own home before going to her husband's. One advantage of child marriage was that the bride was young enough to learn how to fit into the new strange household. Part of her training for her future adult responsibility was thus undertaken by her mother-in-law. This system assured the continuation of traditional family behaviour. A number of the interviewees for this study had been married as children, and accepted the system as naturally as they accepted other family arrangements..

If some crisis, such as the death of the mother-in-law, made a newly married couple set up a house of their own, the bride would have to take on the responsibilities of a home at a very early age. "I was ten years old and my husband nineteen when we were married. When I

---

[12]Another reason why the movement of a son to his own house does not cause conflict in the city is that city families seldom have to consider the division of large amounts of property when families separate. Sensible arrangements can be made for small amounts of property. But in the villages property is much more important. It must be formally and legally divided, which makes the separation definite and public, As this type of division of property often leads to grave family feuds, the sons normally stay with the father until he dies. For they do not want to distress their parents by demanding separation and division of property.

was fourteen, I went to live with him. By that time the family property had been split up; so I started to run my own home the day I stepped into his house." (Case 82)

The legal change of age of marriage for women has probably done more to influence women's desires for homes of their own than any other factor. A bride is now a young woman rather than a child, with greater experience of life and a greater feeling of independence. This is particularly true of girls who have attended college and/or university or have had a job outside their homes before marriage. There is a growing tendency for these more sophisticated young women to want to marry men who either live far away from their families, or else can afford to set up separate households on marriage. This will enable them to escape the tutelage of mothers-in-law and thus give them the opportunity of running their homes as they wish and training their children without interference.

A quite new pattern for young girls was shown in the desire of a few of the more modern girls to leave home even before their marriages.

I don't want to live with my parents now, because it is boring to just stay at home with nothing to do. And when I marry I want a home of my own, because I want to have a place that I can call my own and do as I like in. For example, I have just graduated in Home Science at college, and I want to try out my own creations and ideas in my own house. I will never feel completely independent while I live with my parents. (Case 22)

This desire will probably increase if the trend to individuality, which usually accompanies urbanization, continues. However, it is still so unusual for a woman to live alone in India that fear of public opinion often keeps them with their families. A woman who had been a child widow and was now self-supporting put it this way: "I would prefer to have a house of my own, but it would be a waste of money, and it would be difficult for me to break away from my family because they give me a secure social position. If I should live alone in a house, people would be very shocked." (Case 23)

Other reasons given for wanting to live separately included a desire to be economically independent, to avoid tension because of inter-caste marriage and a conviction that it would be more convenient and enjoyable to do so.

### Summary

Tentative conclusions from case studies and literature suggest that the small joint family is now the most typical form of family life amongst the middle and upper middle urban classes in India. However, a growing number of people now spend at least part of their lives in single family units. Living in several types of family during a lifetime seems so widespread that it is possible to talk of a cycle of family types as being the normal sequence for city dwellers. This finding faces the researcher with the problems of discovering the relative importance of each family unit to the individual. Feelings of responsibility and identity do not disappear overnight, and a short sojourn in a nuclear family might do little to remove the deeper emotional ties laid down over a long period in a joint family. These considerations also warn the researcher that the type of family that ego lives in at the time of the interview may have had little influence on his behaviour and attitudes.

One change that seems to be fairly well established is that distant relatives are less important to the present generation than they were to their parents and grandparents. They tend to see them less often and have less affection and feelings of responsibility for them.

Many factors are contributing to family decisions to remain together or apart. Economic conditions and quarrels have always affected family size. New factors which are now important in encouraging smaller family households are: widespread opportunities for higher education, heightened ambitions, increased occupational mobility, desire for higher standards of living, more individuality and more independence. On the other hand, there are still many factors which are helping to maintain the older family forms. Traditional attitudes of affection and responsibility do not give way easily, and are still supported by much of the Hindu way of life, which has not yet changed enough to alter the former patterns. Moreover, economic insecurity is still so prevalent that many families must remain together that might otherwise desire to break up. Higher costs of living also make it essential for some families to stay together. Thus, the socio-economic differential is important in determining residence and family size.

This study supports others in suggesting that young modern women desire to have separate homes more than the men. In particular, the more sophisticated ones are now anxious to marry men who either live far away from their families or else can afford to set up separate households on marriage, for this will enable them to become independent from their mothers-in-law. Modern mothers sympathize with this attitude and try to find husbands of this sort for their daughters, but at the same time are usually anxious to keep their own sons and daughters-in-law with them in their own households. A few extreme cases were found in which the daughter wished to leave home before marriage to live independently from her family.

When a son moves to the city and sets up a single household, it is usually not large enough to provide accommodation for many relatives, particularly when changing attitudes to individuality and privacy make visitors less welcome than in the large joint family. The city dweller thus becomes more spatially separated from all relatives and, consequently, less under their influence and control than in the tightly spatially bound joint family. Distance does not necessarily mean that family influence is not at work, but, on the other hand, if families do not come into contact over long periods of time, feelings of family obligation and emotional attachment to family members will almost certainly weaken and the authority of the former patriarch break down. When this happens, there will be little left to maintain a feeling of, and desire for, identity within the larger kinship group.

• Chapter Three •

# THE SUBSTRUCTURE OF RIGHTS AND DUTIES

IN HIS STUDY of the interrelation of power and responsibility in the Chinese family, Levy defines power as "the ability to exercise authority and control over the actions of others," and responsibility as "the accountability to other individuals or groups of an individual or individuals for his or their own acts or the acts of others." He shows that each of these forces must be institutionalized if the society is to attain its ends smoothly and efficiently. If "naked and whimsical force" is to be avoided, the way in which power can be used, and the people who are permitted to use it, must be clearly defined and predictable.[1] Likewise, the people who are to take responsibility, and those to whom they are responsible, must be clear in the minds of all concerned.

It is possible that in tightly structured groups, such as the ancient Chinese or Hindu families, power and responsibility do in fact coincide to the extent that Levy suggests. However, when these close groupings begin to break down, the two forces may not necessarily change at the same time or the same rate. It seemed more valuable in this study, therefore, to treat responsibility and authority separately, so that changes in each could be more clearly observed.

All societies use the criteria of age and sex as a basis for allotting rights and duties to different family members. Men are typically assigned the harder work outside the house, and women, mainly because of their child-bearing function, take over the household duties. Elders are usually responsible for younger members until they are past the age at which they can carry out their duties, then the younger members take over. Responsibility of the family for relatives, who do not belong

[1] Marion J. Levy, Jr., *The Family Revolution in Modern China* (Cambridge, Mass.: Harvard University Press, 1949), pp. 28–9.

to the immediate small unit of parents and children, will vary extensively in different societies. Those which are relatively isolated, and have a simple economy and a traditional way of life, are apt to think of the family in terms of the large, extended kinship group, and family members may feel as much obligation to look after distant cousins as they do their own children. At the same time, they will expect to be looked after as a right by these cousins when they, in turn, are in need.

In traditional societies one would expect to find clear-cut expectations of the duties assigned to each age and sex status. One would also expect that, as children grow up in an environment where there is no doubt about the allotted tasks of each member, and as they live in close proximity to the people whose roles they in turn will take over, they will be well fitted for these positions; furthermore, one would expect them to accept the responsibilities entailed in these roles as "natural," and thus display a minimum of resentment or revolt.

It is when the family moves from village to city and finds different patterns of behaviour, more individual choice and more incentives to engage in new types of behaviour that strains in role expectations occur. Change in family size alone, from a large extended group to a small nuclear household, will affect family expectations. Fathers who formerly relied on a group of older women to look after the children may find that they must now take a major share in their upbringing; and mothers, who formerly relied on women relatives to assist them physically and psychologically with their work, may now find that they must solve problems which they would never have had to face in the relative security of the large joint family.

The radical changes which occur in the family division of labour with change to an industrial society do not take place without frustration and strain. And it is usually a long time before new definitions of the work entailed in each position are established. In fact, there may be active opposition to the changes, as there is towards middle-class wives working outside the home, or husbands helping with the housework in Western societies.

Another problem which arises during the period of transition lies in the change in the breadth of family responsibility. Once the small family unit has been separated from the larger family group, and particularly when the new unit is a middle-class family which has been influenced by urban ambitions, it is no longer able—in terms of its needs in the new situation—to look after close, let alone distant relatives. As well as having to support the new family unit without assistance from siblings or parents, the family becomes involved in civic, national and even international obligations.

### DIVISION OF LABOUR WITHIN THE HOUSEHOLD

*Men's and Women's Work*

In the joint family system, men are responsible for the financial support and general administration of the large joint family. Women manage the household work and raise and train the children. Brothers, sons, uncles and/or cousins assist the eldest male member in providing the family income, which is typically jointly owned and spent. Daughters, sisters, aunts, and/or cousins assist with the household work.

The male members of the families studied either supervised the family property—which included collecting rents, or looking after the farm and doing the heavy farm work—or earned an income in business, a profession or government service. If the family lived on a farm, they might assist in such outside chores as splitting wood, drawing water or peeling coconuts. The eldest male member usually supervised the most important family purchases, such as land or jewellery. Very occasionally he might do all the family shopping, including the day-to-day market purchases. If the family lived on a farm women often helped with the chores, such as milking cows, looking after the dairy, or helping in the fields. Srinivas gives a picture of their work. "The housewife has her hands full always. In the morning she sweeps the house-front with cow-dung, and draws *rangoli* designs on it, grinds the corn, cooks, brings water from the tank and looks after the children. She carries the midday food to her husband working in the fields, helps him in his work, and so on."[2]

Housewives were also in charge of the Pooja, or worshipping room which had to have every ritualistic detail carried out to perfection. Children or servants usually did the daily marketing, but women assisted in the more important purchases. In the more modern families women would sometimes buy important household items without consulting the men.

One thing that was quite clear in the family division of labour was that the kitchen work—such as planning the menu and cooking—was the exclusive duty and privilege of the women. Male members were

---

[2]M. N. Srinivas, *Marriage and Family in Mysore* (Bombay: New Book Co., 1942), p. 188.

rarely allowed to interfere, and indeed were not anxious to do so (unless they had domineering personalities), as household work was considered to be beneath their dignity. It was the mother's responsibility, too, to see that her husband and children were well fed.

In our joint family the women served the children first and then our men. We served them the best food, and when it was hot and fresh. We would never allow them to be half fed. We women were hardened and trained to restrict our own tastes, for we were considered to be the protectors of the men's and children's health.

Today it is different. Young wives often eat first. The men are to blame, for they come home at any time they like, often after the girls are tired of waiting and have eaten when they felt hungry. The result is that when the husband comes home the food is cold and his favourite dishes are finished. But my older friends still always wait to eat after their husbands come home. And even if they are very late they never complain. (Case 57)

The women's work was allotted in a traditional way. The wife of the head of the house theoretically had complete authority over the organization of the work of the other women. She would usually retain the supervision of the cooking, or actually continue to do it herself.[3] When a son took over after his father's death, his mother might retain the authority over the household, particularly if she was very close to her son, or the daughter-in-law was not old enough or could not stand up for herself.

Contrary to the prevalent idea that women cannot work together, the household work was often carried on with a maximum of affection and co-operation.

When I was growing up, the children in our joint family were mainly looked after by my grandmother and my aunts. Joint families give the family a lot of loving help. The mother never felt the whole responsibility for the child's welfare; there were always others to share it lovingly.

When I take my children back home now I always have a lot of free time, for my mother and sister-in-law help with their oil baths and dressing. My mother-in-law once said that she had never had to work very hard for she had had so many helpful relatives to assist her. She had ten children, but the only thing she had to do for them was to feed them. They were bathed, dressed and looked after by aunts, cousins and nieces. Life was good in those days, for it was a thrill to live in such a family. (Case 59)

Other case studies show the way in which the women worked out the different household tasks:

[3]The great care given to the cooking of food is due to the strict dietary laws still maintained by most Hindu families, to the taboos on eating food cooked by certain people and the ritual defilement of kitchens.

When I was growing up, we lived in a joint family on a farm. My mother cooked the meals, and the aunts looked after the milking, made the curds and butter, fed the cows and cleaned the cowshed. Grandmother looked after the babies and the feeding of all the children. The eldest aunt was responsible for the Pooja room. She arranged the flowers, washed the idols, and lighted and cleaned the lamps.

The children were responsible for washing the clothes and vessels in the river and bringing water to the house. We did not have any servants. (Case 84)

When relatives came to visit, they fitted in easily to the general division of labour. "When our uncles and aunts visited us they all helped with the housework. One would cut vegetables, one prepare a special pickle, and one would be busy preparing some new dish for supper. Another would be preparing jam." (Case 89)

Allotment of home duties differed according to the number of relatives and/or servants in the home. In large joint families the young wife might have to look after only the personal interests of her own husband and children. In any case, the greater the number of servants the more her job became one of supervision rather than actual work. "When I was growing up, my father had a very good position and a fat income. Labour was dead cheap; so we had lots of servants. We had two coolies, one to cook the dishes and the other to serve and prepare coffee. We had a gardener, a peon, three ayahs, an attendant, a clerk and a driver." (Case 86) These servants often became "like members of the family." However, as in all countries, their tasks were the hardest and most unpleasant. They would clean the house, sweep, wash utensils and clothes, grind flour and spices, and look after the more menial tasks for the children. If the family lived on a farm, they would do the harder farm chores. Twenty-five of the ninety-six families reporting had not had any servants in their homes when the interviewees were growing up; fifty-five families had had from one to three servants; and sixteen families had had four or more servants.

The wife's part of the division of labour grows more varied as she grows older. As a young bride entering her husband's joint family, she will begin by doing the more menial and unpleasant tasks, such as fetching water from the well, cleaning vessels and preparing vegetables. "I was married at twelve years of age and was sent to my in-laws' house after six months. My three sisters-in-law (brother-in-laws' wives) and I did the outside work. There was no tap in the house so we had to go to the tank one mile away for washing water. We had to milk the four cows and look after them. We were busy all day long. After my mother-in-law's death the eldest sister-in-law did the cooking." (Case 57) After she has learned the ways of the new household and has acquired a more important position in it by becoming a mother, she will gradually take over more important work; but it will not be until her mother-in-law either dies, or is very old, that she will take over the main supervisory tasks.

In a wealthy household the mother must also see to the comfort and entertainment of many relatives and guests. This may mean looking after literally hundreds of people for many days during a wedding ceremony. In wealthy city families it may mean learning to entertain men guests as well as women, a task for which she is seldom trained. In more modern families the mother may also be expected to help her husband in business. There seemed no doubt that her role has become even more complex, and that she has to be more flexible in carrying out the family work in modern families than in the more traditional type.

We did not have any clear-cut division of the work at home. We all felt it was our home, and we were responsible for all of it. Mother was an educated woman; so she helped Father with his business as well as keeping house. When Father was at home, or had a holiday, she used to help a lot with the children and cooking. When my brothers didn't have morning classes at school they helped Mother with the cooking or house cleaning.

The preparation of the evening meal was a joint affair. All of us helped Mother. Or Mother rested while we did the work. When Father felt tired, Mother and all of us helped him a lot. (Case 79)

Finally, in city families women must now supervise the education of their children, for good education is essential to their future employment.

## The Training of Children

It is the women of the household who are responsible for the care and training of the children. They must, too, see to their moral training, and act as inspiring models for their behaviour. A few of the interviewees said that they had had a completely carefree life while growing up, with no family duties or responsibility. But in the great majority of Hindu families children appear to begin their training for their later roles by helping at home at an early age, even though there may not be set jobs for each particular child.

Although grandparents theoretically play an important part in socializing grandchildren, the short age span of Hindus meant that relatively few interviewees had known their grandparents, who had died before they were born or when they were very young. In only a few families had grandmothers played an important part in the children's training, and even in these mothers had been expected to take the major responsibility.

Very few fathers of interviewees had had anything to do with the supervision and training of their children although they seemed to take a more active part in their studies and education. A number said that their fathers had helped them with their school work. But in the large majority of cases fathers seemed to be too occupied in providing the family income to have time for their children. Some interviewees spoke of their father devoting his "heart and soul" to his business, others said their fathers neglected them when young. Several said their fathers had had no leisure time to help them or play with them. In several families in which the father was seldom at home as he had an occupation which necessitated a great deal of travelling the mother had almost the sole responsibility for the children unless she lived in a joint family.

The great majority of case studies, then, showed that the mother was the chief agency through which Hindu children were socialized. In only a few families was this role transferred to servants, as is often the case in wealthy English families. This is illustrated in a family whose father was a ruler of a state. "We saw Mother very rarely, actually only when she sent for us. We saw Father about once a day. He played with us a little, and listened to our doings. But he was very busy with the affairs of state." (Case 11)

The role of husband may change radically when he becomes head of a nuclear family. His wife no longer has a group of women to help her with the housework and children, and if she is ill or unable to do it all, he will have to help. Moreover, it is more difficult to keep servants in the city than the village. One case showed the difficulty the husband had had of adjusting to this new role, for it not only meant that he must do work which he was not fitted for, but tasks which were considered to be "women's" work and thus had little prestige.

"My husband was a spoilt son and so didn't help with anything around our house at first. He liked to be waited on. But now he does help, but is embarrassed if his mother comes in and finds him helping. Even if he is only standing at the kitchen door talking to me as I cook, he will move away quickly and look 'lordly' if his mother comes in." (Case 53)

*Boys' and Girls' Work*

In most families there was a rather clear-cut division in the tasks allotted girls and those allotted boys. The boys nearly always did all the outside work, such as shopping, marketing and running errands. If the family lived on a farm, boys would usually help with the farm work. These duties would include grazing the cattle, collecting fodder, assisting in paddy fields, coconut groves or gardens, thatching roofs, getting water from the well, and collecting firewood. In the city families their contribution was more in the nature of running errands and doing the marketing. Or they might assist with light work in their fathers' or uncles' business, or earn part of the family income. Those earning invariably contributed all or most of their earnings to the family purse. Several boys had washed their own clothes, and helped to prepare vegetables or cook when growing up. Occasionally a boy had had to look after his younger siblings, but on the whole this task was usually allotted to girls.

The sample showed a rather wide range in the actual amount of work done by boys when growing up. The wealthier families did not need the assistance of children in the housework. Another important determinant of the allotment of work to children was the relative ambitions which parents had for their futures. In the less well-off families, some children seemed to have spent most of their time at work, with little leisure for study or play. On the other hand, a number said that they had done little or no work, and a number of others said that their only work was to study. This was truer of boys living in cities than villages and of younger interviewees than older. In fact, much pressure was often put on them to do well at school and pass examinations. It is possibly significant that none of the families in which education was particularly stressed was a large joint family.

The children of the families under study had also had varying training in assuming responsiblity. Several boys who said they had had little or no responsibility at home, when growing up, came from the better-off families and tended to speak of their youths as carefree. In other families, the father was so domineering that he never gave his children the opportunity of learning to look after themselves.

> When I was a child, I had no family responsibilities at all. I played and went to school. I had no independence because my father completely dominated me. I could not even wear the clothes I liked. Father decided what I should wear, what I should eat, what I should read and when I should sleep. He was very strict, and I always shivered in my shoes when he was angry. My brothers and sisters and I were always anxious to get away from the house, for we were all very strictly and even severely disciplined. (Case 154)

On the other hand, the inculcation of a sense of responsibility was particularly noted in the less well-off families, and in those living in villages and small towns. "We children never shirked work." "We were keen to contribute, and loyal to our parents and teachers." "We never refused to help." It would appear from these remarks that the difficulties of an overpopulated continent makes the "struggle for existence," as one interviewee put it, of crucial importance, and children must learn that life is serious at an early age. The following is a typical case of children brought up with a deep sense of responsibility to their family:

I have never tried to escape any duty at home. Neither have my brothers or sisters. We simply could not do it. Each child in the family used to be given responsibility according to his ability; so we got a gradual training for our future life. For example, my youngest sister is now able to manage the house by herself. She can cook and look after the younger brothers. And my brother who went to Singapore by himself was able to get a good job there and has even been able to buy a car. For all of us, marriage and family responsibilities will only be a natural sequence to our early life, and we will not be upset by them. (Case 138)

The eldest son usually had special training for his particularly heavy family obligations. A lot of this was done unconsciously through the day-to-day attitudes and examples of the parents. But there was also conscious training. A rather extreme case points this up.

As I was the eldest son, Father wanted me to become independent and self-reliant as early as possible. So he pushed me into responsible positions. I had to do a lot of the work around the home, and as Father often had to be away, I had to bear the additional burden of his absence. Father always reminded me of my responsibility as the eldest member of the family. I had to take over all the marketing, and he also watched my studies.
Sometimes I think he made me do things that I was not ready for. For instance, when I was nine years old, he used to send me with money to pay the grocer's bill. Boys of that age are not usually allowed to handle money in my community. But he wanted me to become more and more responsible. One night he sent me to buy a blade for his razor. I had to go all alone a long way, and my path passed the cemetery of which I was very much afraid. But I didn't have the courage to disobey my father; so I mustered my courage and went to the shop. It was nine o'clock and there were very few people about. When I reached the cemetery, I ran past it as fast as I could. Unfortunately, when I arrived home with the blade, it was broken; so in the dead of night Father made me go back for another one. (Case 141)

As Hindu girls grow up in the milieu in which they will carry out their adult roles, their training begins early. The Hindu woman has traditionally spent most of her life within the confines of the home, and Hindu girls are still mainly brought up within it. Young girls are not given as many tasks outside the home as boys, particularly around the age of puberty, when they fear they may be teased by mischievous men. Although they are attending school and college in ever increasing numbers, and more young women are taking outside jobs, it is still not a generally accepted idea that middle and upper middle-class women should have careers; the central goal of a girl's life is still marriage. Thus, her training centres around the skills and qualities which will make her an efficient housewife and mother, and will help her to fit in with a strange husband and his joint family.

A great deal of this training is passed on to daughters as unconsciously as it is in other cultures. But as parents are fully aware that they will themselves be judged by the way their daughter acts in her husband's home, they take great pains to inculcate her with the "right" kind of behaviour. The mother, as her chief trainer, feels that she is particularly on trial for her daughter's conduct. Even today daughters are often trained in submission to their future in-laws as well as in household tasks. They are expected to "implicitly obey the instructions of both father-in-law and mother-in-law without any suggestion or feeling of resentment.[4] The mother, aware that her daughter may go into a house of nagging older women, often tries to tell her daughter how to handle the situation. "Don't be sweet as sugar, or they will overwhelm you with work, nor as sour as a nim leaf, or they will spit you out."[5] Even fathers sometimes give their daughters last words of advice, particularly if there is a strong bond of affection between them.

That this advice is necessary is shown by the caricature of the daughter-in-law's position current in literature, and in such songs as the following: "Oh my mother! *For thy sake* I endure the words of my parents-in-law and take them as sweet—although they are full of bitter poison."[6]

[4]Levy, *Family Revolution in Modern China*, p. 184. Levy describes the same attitude in the Chinese classical family. "For the sake of the face of her parents' family, she needed to know certain techniques and patterns of behaviour," M. N. Srinivas, *Marriage and Family in Mysore*, p. 195. "It is the mother's duty to train her daughter up to be an absolutely docile daughter-in-law. The *summum bonum* of a girl's life is to please her parents-in-law and her husband. If she does not 'get on' with her mother-in-law, she will be a disgrace to her family, and casts a blot on the fair name of her mother. The Kannada mother dins into her daughters' ears certain ideals which make for harmony (at the expense of her sacrificing her will) in her later life. There is no denying that this early training is very effective in reducing the conflict to a minimum."

[5]Mrs. Sinclair Stevenson, *The Rites of the Twice Born* (London: Oxford University Press, 1920), p. 106.

[6]Hedwig Bachmann, *On the Soul of the Indian Woman: As Reflected in the Folklore of the Konkan* (Bastora, India Portuguesa: Tipografia Rangel, 1942), p. 122.

Assisting mothers in the household work is a daughter's main responsibility. These tasks are at first simple, such as cleaning, washing dishes, washing and dressing their own hair, giving oil baths and looking after younger siblings. Total responsibility for siblings may be taken over at an early age. "When I was grown up, about twelve years old, I helped Mother with the cooking and took over the complete charge of the other children except for their feeding." (Case 24) Girls who live on farms may help with the farm work, such as looking after cattle and getting drinking water from the well. All learn through experience to nurse. "My sisters had a rigorous training at home, and I am proud of their ability to prepare delicious dishes at very short notice. They used to have to carry food to the workers in the paddy fields, and help with dehusking the paddy and grinding the grain into flour. They were also taught to nurse, and they have enough stamina to sit up all night to look after a sick person." (Case 48) More complex tasks, such as cooking, are usually learned from thirteen years of age on. Cooking is considered such a high art in India that young girls will never be responsible for it in joint families as long as an older woman is there to do it. One informant said that the elder members of her family would not eat food cooked by young girls until they became mothers. This is probably why many interviewees said that they only learned to cook when they went to their husband's home after marriage. However, in nuclear families daughters as well as the father, often do the cooking when the mother must remain aloof from kitchen work during her menstrual periods.

The amount and type of work done by daughters change according to the number of adult females and servants in the home. Like the sons, a few said that they had had no work at all to do at home while growing up. These daughters usually came from wealthy families. "We never did any work at home for Mother didn't think it necessary as she was sure she would marry us to rich men who held good positions. I was actually married to a man who wasn't very well-off, but Mother sent a cook and ayah with me whom she paid herself." (Case 72) But the great majority interviewed had had tasks to do and learn even when there were servants in the house.

We had two cooks, one to travel with Father when he went on his tours, and one for the house. We had a driver, a peon, a gardener and a night watchman. We had a maid servant to sweep the house and wash the women's clothes.

In spite of all these servants Mother used to do a lot of the work as we had a lot of guests. With so many servants in the house I did not have much to do. I had my studies and music lessons. But on holidays, and when a servant was away, Mother used to ask me to do some of the work. So I was trained to do even the maid's work of sweeping, washing clothes and grinding grain. I was taught to cook when I was about thirteen years old. I was also taught how to buy food in bulk, and to make preserves.

Mother and I also did all the work in the Pooja room, as we don't allow outsiders to do it. We would sweep and wash the room, wash and polish the Pooja utensils, and decorate it with flowers. (Case 53)

Another case shows the variety of work a girl must learn. In this case ego lived with her aunt.

I was brought up in my aunt's house, and she had four or five servants. But still we all had a lot to do. We were trained in all the household work, and my cousins and I did such things as helping the cook, chopping vegetables and running errands.

As my aunt was often ill, we sometimes had to run the house completely. We looked after the guests, and there were a lot of them as Uncle was a very important person. We had to look after the babies of relatives that my aunt took a fancy to and brought home to bring up.

Thank God for Aunt's training—for I am now able to run my own home quite easily. (Case 68)

In former times a married girl lived far away from her own family's guidance and support. Thus one important aspect of her training was to prepare her to stand on her own in a household of strangers. She typically entered a house where there were a number of older, well-trained women. Her chief task in the beginning was to adjust to the customs and personalities of the new household. Child marriage had the advantage of introducing her to this difficult position when she was young enough to expect the control and guidance of older family members, and when she was flexible enough to adjust rather readily. In any case, the great majority of Hindu women must have adjusted well, and those interviewed for this study on the whole also fitted in remarkably well to the new households.

In the urban families of this sample, the daughters attending college were, like sons, expected to spend more time on their studies than on housework. Several single girls said that although they had never learned to cook at home, they were quite sure that they could cope with it when married. This is probably due to the fact that girls now marry at a later age, and presumably have had more opportunity to watch cooking at home and are also more intelligent and experienced. A number of young married women said that they had learned to cook from their mothers-in-law. Thus, even when girls marry at a later age, mothers-in-law still play an important role in training daughters-in-law.

The modernly educated city girl also has to learn "accomplishments" such as fancy needlework, playing a musical instrument or classical dancing. They must learn, too, how to entertain guests and mix with outsiders more than their rural counterparts.

One of the new trends which is beginning to change the conception of women's part of the division of labour is that some daughters are now expected to contribute to the family income. Girls often use their college education and other training to obtain paid positions. One interviewee was financing her younger brother's education, a traditional "brother" job. Several were wholly supporting themselves as well as contributing to the family.

*Transfer of Duties*

The work of supporting a family and caring for it is continuous; so means must be found of transferring it when the appropriate family members can no longer carry on their part of the division of labour. In large joint families there is typically always a full complement of competent people to do the work. This occurs in all family systems which are relatively self-sufficient, and have not many outside agencies to assist when parents are too old to do the work or children too young.[7] As the family cycle revolves children are trained to gradually replace adults. As older sons grow up, they take over some of the work. If they leave the home for jobs in another city, the younger sons gradually replace them. As daughters leave to be married they are replaced by daughters-in-law. Soon grandchildren will be able to help. In this way the family is always assured of workers even when death or illness removes older members. Death is thus not always a crisis for the family division of labour. Usually, too, a certain amount of illness can be tolerated, as it does not always mean that a working member drops out for long. "We didn't have many servants at home when I was growing up. But as there were a lot of aunts and older women one of them would take over when someone fell ill."(Case 62)

A fairly usual situation in modern India, necessitating shifts in working roles, is occasioned by the father who has a job which takes

[7]In highly industrialized countries where the majority of families are nuclear in structure, agencies such as the government assist at points in the family cycle at which families themselves cannot manage, for example, the establishment of old age pensions and unemployment insurance. For a very good description of the family cycle of work in the Rural French-Canadian family, see Horace Miner, *St. Denis: A French Canadian Parish* (Chicago: University of Chicago Press, 1939), chap. 4.

him away from home for long periods of time. In this case the mother will almost certainly have to take over some of his family responsibilities, such as disciplining the children or making important purchases. However, she will not have to shift her role to such an extent if she still lives with her husband's joint family, for the other male members will take over many of the father's responsibilities.

Unemployment is another fairly common phenomenon which causes shifts in roles in India. Several families interviewed had had to rearrange their division of labour because of the father's loss of a job. The usual adjustment was for the family to go to live with one of the relatives until the father was able to support his own family again.

In all these contingencies the joint family cushions the shock, but makes its members more vulnerable to a wider number of crises. For the claims of family members and relatives will be much more numerous.

Most of the crises mentioned above occur in the normal process of family growth. Two particular points of strain occur either when a person playing an important role unexpectedly drops out, and there is no one to replace him, or when a person is brought up to play one sort of role, and then finds when he takes it over that the expectations for it have changed, and he is not prepared for the new type of behaviour.

The unexpected death of an important family member may put great strain on other members, particularly if it occurs at a crucial time in the life cycle of the family, for instance if a father or mother dies when the children are young. Twelve of the families interviewed had had to face this crisis. In nine of these, the mother became the sole or principal financial support of the family. In one family, she took the children back to her own wealthy joint family, where she still had to carry out part of her husband's role. "The servants relieved her of the kitchen work, but she had to pay especial attention to our education because Father was no longer there to do it. She also had to go often to our native village to look after our property. Later on the family went to Madras and I, as eldest son, took over the responsibilities. I did the marketing and my other brothers helped Mother in the kitchen." (Case 144)

Two other mothers managed to support their children by taking over the administration of the family property. In one of these families, the income was so small that "Mother had such great difficulty in supporting the family that she never dressed or ate well herself." In the other, the mother had great difficulty in keeping up appearances on a smaller income. Three others managed the family's finances by themselves. In one family the mother took a job and supported her children until her daughter was able, too, to get employment. Very little help was given these families by relatives. Ontside of the case quoted above in which the mother returned to her own family, which was a wealthy one, "relatives" were only mentioned as assisting in one other family. In a third family an uncle helped by financing the education of a son and in two others uncles acted as advisers. Otherwise, the mother bore the main burden of the crisis.

Typically, the sons assist the mother in providing the family income when they grow up. The burden in this case is apt to be particularly severe for the eldest son. One had to give up his university education to support the family. Only after providing a college education for his three brothers and marrying a sister could he himself marry.

In several families a father's death meant lower income, and servants had to be given up. In one instance the children had been brought up in great comfort, and found it extremely difficult to shoulder the responsibilities after their father's death.

The death of a mother does not usually bring a financial crisis, but it may be very difficult for the father to find competent people to look after the children if the family has been a nuclear one. A grandmother would normally be the one to replace the mother; or an aunt might come to look after the household, or take the children to live with her. If a daughter were old enough, she might take over the household responsibilities, aided by her sisters-in-law as her brothers marry. In three nuclear families in this study the fathers took over the mother's role. They did all the housework, gradually aided by the children as they grew older. In one of these families the daughter was only a few years old when her mother died, and received all her household training from her father. In another, the father took over the cooking when the mother died, and taught his sons to do the housework. As with the twelve families in which the father had died, the nine in which the mother had died had received little practical assistance from relatives.

Cases of children brought up to play roles that are no longer adequate when they are adults tend to occur oftener as families move to the city. A number of interviewees mentioned the problem of a mother's unexpectedly having to run a household of her own without the support of other older women; or a fathers' suddenly finding himself completely responsible for the finances of his family, without the assistance of older male members. Another problem of this sort arises when women have to help support the family financially by taking jobs outside for which they have had no practical or "psychological" preparation.

### Responsibility to Family and Relatives

It is, of course, not a new thing for family members to separate and gradually lose their feeling of identity and obligation to former kin groups. The point of this analysis is that changing circumstances in India are causing families to separate at an accelerated rate, and forcing many family members to adjust to new conceptions of rights and responsibilities almost overnight. It is highly probable that few nuclear families in India ever completely cut off all feeling of identity with, or responsibility to, their ancestral families, even if this feeling only takes the form of guilt when they avoid family obligations.

Actual acts of responsibility are better indications of sacrifice than people's expressions of their feelings of obligation. Feelings often do not materialize into action when the crucial moment arrives. Thus interviewees were asked to cite instances of help given, or received, from the kin group, as well as to tell how they felt about their family responsibilities. However the family feeling of identification is so close and the idea of individual property so foreign to the Hindu philosophy of obligation that it is quite probable that many instances of assistance, which would be considered extreme cases of self-denial by Western observers, were simply overlooked by informants.

Another problem in trying to estimate a possible trend in family assistance lay in the difficulty of interviewees remembering acts of assistance by their parents to relatives. For they would not always be aware of them when young, and not interested in noting them unless they impinged on their own interests.

One way of judging the extent to which a person still feels a sense of family obligation, even if he does not carry it out, is by studying the feelings of guilt which arise when responsibilities are evaded. Another is to observe the way in which the indivdual talks of his obligations. Of those studied, a number spoke of the privilege of helping others, and seemed proud and happy to be able to assist. On the other hand, others stressed their "duty" to help others, even when they did not wish to do so.

## Attitudes to Responsibility

The duty to help those in need is stressed in Hindu religious teachings.[8] It is thus intertwined with a Hindu's whole philosophy of life, and strongly affects attitudes to personal responsibility. In this philosophy the individual is not accountable to all humanity, as he tends to be in highly impersonal industrialized societies, but to his local groups, his relatives, his caste and finally indigent village members.[9] These responsibilities are thought of in terms of his debt to society.

The individual is but a vehicle of the social process. . . . A man is born with three debts—one to the gods, one to the sages and one to his ancestors. He pays them by (a) worship and ritual, (b) learning and teaching and (c) founding a family and raising children. If a man dies without paying these debts, he must be born again and final release will come only when the terrible creditors are fully satisfied. In the family he pays this debt with every act of his. He obeys the elders, learns his job, marries, gets children, gives gifts and receives gifts, attends ceremonials and rituals because his family had incurred the responsibility of doing these actions long before he was born. A terrible bondage indeed, but it is the common bondage of all human beings who inherit the culture of their ancestors.[10]

Thus, the individual is seen only to be important as he relates himself to his group and advances its interests. Karve's description does not mention the duty which Brahmins, in particular, had to villagers who could not look after themselves. The religious duty of

---

[8] "He who keeps his wealth for himself, without allowing his relatives and others to share it, goes to hell. He who is strong to work and does not support his family, the Brahmins and the unfortunate, is *dead* though he be alive." (Krishna: Bhagvat-Purana, X, 45, 7.)

[9] Margaret Urquhart, *Women of Bengal* (Mysore: Wesleyan Mission Press, 2nd ed., 1926), p. 28. "Devotion to family and obedience to caste rules must be reckoned as the principle controlling ideas in Bengali life. Duty to society in general comes a long way after these two loyalties and a real sense of social responsibility is still rare in the orthodox Hindu . . . such a sense has scarcely dawned on the great mass of women." See also Dhurjati Prasad Mukerji, *Modern Indian Culture: A Sociological Study* (2nd ed., Bombay: Hind Kitabs Ltd., 1948), p. 35.

Dr. Milton Singer at a seminar at the University of Chicago, 1955 said that the strong allegiance of family members to their family and to their native village often continues long after the individual member has gone to the city. Although these wanderers may not get back to their village more than once or twice a year, or in time of crisis, both the individual and his family continue to think in terms of their former obligations to each other. The people of the village regard their relatives as their outposts in the city.

[10] Irawati Karve, *Kinship Organisation in India*, Deccan College Monograph Series, 11 (Poona: Deccan College Post-Graduate and Research Institute, 1953), p. 136.

giving daily alms not only was a means of providing for these people but also gave the giver rewards in the next world, and enabled him to gain prestige in the eyes of his community. Shame would be felt by anyone who allowed a kinsman to go hungry or without a home.[11] Moreover, the assistance was not always in one direction, for poor relatives or friends could often be of great assistance in the farm or household work. This is shown in a family in which the father was so rich that he was practically a chieftain in his village. "As Father was very rich, he helped many people in the village. If any branch of the family was in trouble, they came to our house. The unemployed ones helped with the farm, or a widowed sister might assist with the household work or cows. That is why our family didn't feel their burden very much." (Case 6)

It is this deeply ingrained sense of responsibility to family members which, on the one hand, gives the individual the great feeling of security in the joint family. On the other it often burdens certain members, notably older male members or those with more money, with very heavy responsibilities.

The essential nature of family responsibility is that it is the *acceptance of responsibility without a sense of obligation*.[12] One informant said:

If one brother is affluent and the other is poor, then money is given as a gift, not as a loan, to the poorer one. If he should get on well, and feels like returning his brother's aid, he does this indirectly. Perhaps he may give his brother a gift, or he may board or educate some of his children, or give him a portion of the family property which was assigned to him.

The main point is that this assistance is *not* a business transaction, for the money given by the better-off brother in the first instance is not meant to be returned in kind. So the material transactions are not thought of as a "quid pro quo" arrangement. It is more the idea of a moral or social transaction.

Another informant put it this way:

When one brother does something for another, there is no sense of "obligation" about it. It is done so naturally that the brother doesn't in any sense feel put upon. Nor does he attempt to return the assistance in

[11] The village is a small enough unit to make gossip an effective control. It is also small enough for the poverty or illness of relatives to be seen by all, thus the effective care for those in need in small isolated communities. However, informants claimed that help was often given grudgingly and relatives later on were often treated as appendages rather than as members of the family. On the other hand, parasites were often a common phenomenon in large joint families.

[12] I am indebted to Professor M. S. Gore for analysis and descriptive material on this point.

kind, or in any other way. He will, of course, do the same or more for his brother should the occasion arise. My brother's daughter is living with us to attend school. I pay all her expenses. Of course, if I could not afford it it would be different. I sometimes have to cut down on things for my own family to do it, but I wouldn't think of asking my brother to pay his daughter's expenses. This obligation to educate one's relatives' children is taken as completely natural. No reciprocal services are expected. But my brother would be expected to do the same if my child needed it.

In the Hindu system of family obligations, the sons are expected to look after their parents in old age and illness. If there are no sons, then it is the duty of daughters. After daughters, obligations in order fall on brothers, uncles, aunts and finally any other relatives. Typically, too, these duties were not thought of as burdens, but as privileges. In fact, it was a matter of pride to be the son, or daughter, whom the parents chose to live with in old age.

The help given kin members took many forms. Relatives were not only taken in to live, or fed, looked after when ill or old, and given financial assistance, but also they were given much advice and sympathy. In recent years educating nieces or nephews, or getting them jobs or government posts, is an important part of the family obligations of middle- and upper-class families.

In a changing society the different feelings of responsibility of individual family members could be charted on a continuum. At one end would be found the individuals who feel that their responsibilities extend to immediate family, relatives and neighbours. Members of traditional joint families would hold this view. At the other end would be found the individuals who have broken away from joint family ties, thrown off all feelings of obligation to their kin group, and do not expect any reciprocation from them. However, they will feel responsible to their own small family unit, friends, the community, the nation and even the world at large. To lose a feeling of responsibility for kin members does not, therefore, necessarily mean a loss of all moral sense of obligation. In between these two hypothetical extremes will be found a variety of attitudes, depending on the upbringing and circumstances of each family member.

On the whole, then, one would expect that as the joint family breaks down into smaller family units, as families move spatially away from each other, and as the complexities of urban life develop outside agencies responsible for the general welfare of the community, individual feelings of responsibility for relatives and even family members would tend to lessen. This tendency was shown in interview material. It was often accompanied by feelings of greater self-reliance and at the same time of resistance or resentment at having to take help from family members. A few wanted to cut themselves off completely from all responsibility to relatives. One of these was a daughter whose parents had been rejected by their relatives when they married without their consent. "My motto is that self-help is the best help. I don't believe in looking after relatives and I don't expect to be looked after by them. I have seen both my father and mother get on in the world without the help of relatives, and I'm sure anybody can do the same if they have courage and a will to succeed in life." (Case 80) The parents had both spent much of their time in political and social action, had gone to prison during the fight for independence, and the daughter had been trained to a wide circle of responsibilities.

In several other families, sons had moved far enough away from their native villages to be rather out of touch with their relatives back home. They were ambitious young men, fascinated by the game of "getting ahead," and realized that all their efforts had to be concentrated on themselves if they were to achieve success in the highly competitive large cities.

There is a tendency now for children to become more and more independent of their original family. My father was very much attached to all his relatives, and helped many of them. My grandparents were also very helpful even to distant kinsmen. But my generation is not very interested in helping relatives. We are becoming more and more self-centred and want to look after our own affairs only. I don't even see much of my two sisters who are now living here in Bombay.

I feel that we shouldn't waste our energy and time in helping or bothering about relatives. For everyone should be independent and self-sufficient. The joint family tends to kill people's initiative, and make them a burden to other family members. I can definitely say that the loyalties of my brothers and sisters towards our relatives are becoming weaker day by day as they become more and more engrossed in their own lives. (Case 144)

One or two of these young men felt more responsibility to the society as a whole than to their own blood relatives. "I have a very strange philosophy of life, for I feel that there is no need to discriminate between relatives and non-relatives in the matter of extending help. Instead, help should be given according to the need of the person. My parents and other older relatives were very clannish, but I feel that that sort of attachment to relatives is unnecessary and undesirable." (Case 145)

Thus, the claims of modern urban life, and the wider perspective which it presents, has caused a number of young people to change their attitudes to their responsibilities.

Other changes in attitude to relatives seemed to have occurred because of a bitter experience in the past when the interviewee's family was in need. One young girl, who could not forgive her aunt for the way she had treated her mother when in trouble, said she would now help outsiders, but never her relatives. Another young girl said that even if she were a millionaire she would not help her relatives, but would rather give the money to a public institution. Past experience is thus a strong conditioner of philanthropic attitudes. This point was emphasized by a refugee family at the time of Partition, which would have been destitute without the help of relatives. "What would have happened to us? How pathetic it would have been if they had driven us away at that time!"

Although giving alms is part of the religious duty of Hindus, to be the recipient of public charity is considered to be a calamity.

Generally people will first go for help to their inner, close circle of relatives, and when they refuse go to the outer circle of relatives. Next they go to close friends, then to next close friends. Then comes acquaintances and then at last when all the above mentioned refuse, they go to the general public to beg. So it is our duty to help them when they first come to us so that they will not be forced to finally arrive at the stage of seeking public sympathy. (Case 87)

This feeling was also observed in some of the interviewees' attitudes to government assistance. One of the main reasons for this was that it meant that the recipients' need was made public; whereas assistance to relatives need not be publicized and thus would not shame the recipient. On the other hand, some felt that help from relatives can be a bitter experience, and even although it is supposed to be given as one's "right," recipients may feel inferior and shamed to receive it.

My father was a sort of vagabond; so we children spent most of our younger days with our grandparents. Sometimes we would be sent to our paternal grandparents, where they looked on us as strangers. After a few months, when they got tired of us they would send us back to our maternal grandparents. Sometimes we would be sent to an aunt's house for a few months and then again sent back to grandparents.

Except for my maternal grandmother and aunt I hate all other relatives. I will never help any of them when they are in need. And even when I am old, I would rather die in a hospital or old people's home than stay with a relative. (Case 67)

A number of cases, too, showed that some family members felt it was a blow to their self-respect to have to live with a close relative. One of these was a father who occasionally visited his daughter, but would not live with her. "Once when my father was visiting us he must have been without money, for he had to pawn his watch to get money for his train fare home. We only knew this later when he sent the pawn-broker's ticket back to my husband and asked him to get his watch. It was only then that we realized how deep his feeling of self-respect was." (Case 70) This attitude was also implied in several other interviews, which showed that many family members are too proud of their independence to receive help from relatives.

Father was working at Kolar, and we lived with him at the time. All of a sudden his pay was reduced and he was told to move to another place. This came just at that time when he was expecting a promotion; so it was an emotional blow as well as a financial one. We had practically no money; he became ill. Mother was pregnant at the time. Those were hard days for us. We children didn't have proper clothing or food, and finally we too became ill, mainly owing to malnutrition. In spite of all our miseries Father wasn't willing to ask help from his relatives, especially from his maternal uncles.

Mother very willingly sold all her jewels and ornaments, and Father sold all he had; so we were able to tide over the situation ourselves. (Case 141)

At first all feelings of allegiance to family, and dependence on it, may be hard to break. Sons who move away from home can usually manage their own affairs as long as things go smoothly. But in all major crises, such as illness, death, or choosing a wife, they may have to turn back to their families. Having such a "secure haven" to return to in time of need is important for the inner security of the individual when he first breaks away.

One example of family strain, occasionally noted in case material, occurred when the husband and wife did not agree on the amount of assistance to be given, or the person to whom it should be given. It is possible that, as the lines of traditional obligation become dimmer, and the wife remains more closely attached to her own family than in the days when she married as a child, and as she becomes more independent, this is an area where strain will increase. This has happened on the North American continent where small families are expected to maintain loyalty to both family lines, and where there are no clearly defined lines of responsibility to either the paternal or the maternal side.

The above analysis has shown that many attitudes to personal obligation now exist in India. People who have separated themselves from the bonds of kin find that they are not relieved of responsibility for others. It is typical of a highly industrialized society that financial charitable obligations tend to increase. This is due to the fact that impersonal city life develops many situations in which individuals cannot look after themselves, and having no help from relatives, must turn to governmental or charitable agencies.

The following interview shows very clearly the transitional stage at which many Hindus have arrived in the ever widening circle of obligations: that is, a point at which while they are conscious of their new insecurity they still feel the emotional pull of former responsibilities.

Charity begins at home. These hard days it's very difficult to look after oneself and family. We may manage to save a little for ourselves and our children, but if we use this for others, then we will have to suffer in times of need. I have seen too many people who belong to big families spend all the money they save to help their relatives, who are either poor or in some difficulties. Then, when the benefactor's family is in need no one will help them. So I feel each one of us should save something for a rainy day and as far as possible try to avoid troubling others during our time of need.

Only in extreme cases should we go and trouble others. In the days when we lived in big joint families it was quite different. If one brother helped the other, he was sure of help when he needed it. Now an intermediate stage has come about in India where a man belongs to his family for certain things, and is not considered a member for other things. For instance, take the case of an elder brother belonging to a joint family who goes out of his native place and gets a prosperous job in the city. He will be pestered for money for every marriage, and every boy's higher education. But suppose he dies, or is in financial difficulties, the joint family will say: "He doesn't belong to us. He has gone out with his wife and children and was earning a lot. He must have saved a lot. Why can't the wife go to her father's house?"

This is the general attitude, I have seen it many times, even among my own relatives. But if near relatives are in need, and we are prosperous, we will have to help them whether we like it or not. (Case 55)

Desai suggests that the extent to which the joint family is still assuming its responsibilities could possibly be observed by its number of dependent members.[13] These members may stay with a family until their financial crises are over, or, as in the case of a widowed sister or a grandparent, may remain with the family all their lives. It has already been noted that these dependents may be welcome because of their contribution to the farm or household work. Most close family members have been typically taken in, in the past, without question or resentment, and usually did not feel any shame in becoming dependents. It is probable that in most Hindu families close family members who are in distress would still be taken in as willingly as before, but there are indications that distant relatives are no longer as welcome as they were when families lived in villages.

[13] I. P. Desai, "An Analysis," "Symposium: Caste and Joint Family," *Sociological Bulletin*, vol. IV, no. 2 (Sept. 1955), p. 107.

Parents, brothers and sisters were usually specifically mentioned by interviewees as family members who would be assisted when in need. Next in line came uncles and aunts, cousins were occasionally mentioned. After these "close" relatives would be helped, then distant ones. Often a father, because of the close brother-sister tie, would have a special affection and particular feeling of duty towards his widowed sister and her children.

However, the help the interviewees were willing to give these people was often qualified. Some would help only close and blood relatives willingly; others would be helped as a duty. A few mentioned their in-laws as worthy of help. But one wife did not like her husband foregoing his personal conveniences to assist his brother and his wife. Another qualification which was repeatedly stressed was that only "deserving" relatives, or those who had been sympathetic or understanding, should be helped. This implies a moral connotation to giving. It is possible that one of the implications here is that the "deserving" relative is one who has maintained or aided the family in the past, or has assisted in raising the family's general level of prestige. Another attitude which gave a moral interpretation to assistance was that giving must be carefully done for it could have a demoralizing effect on the recipient. Relatives should only be helped if beset by a calamity—and while the crisis lasted—not as a permanent proposition.

> I have seen that helping people continually with money makes them lazy and lose their initiative. We have a rich relative in our family who took pity on another branch of the family who were in poverty. He gave them a monthly allowance. This has been going on for twenty years, and the family is still not self-sufficient. Two of the grandsons have started earning, but the mother still goes to my relative each month with another story of need. I feel that too much help makes people more evil than good, so I would suggest that help only be given in extreme cases, and then for only a short time. (Case 77)

The attitude expressed in this interview may have always existed in India or it may be a trend in thinking which develops as societies become industrialized, for it is very prevalent in current North American thinking in regard to charity.

The criteria which were most often stated as determining assistance were old age, illness and unemployment. A few would not include the unemployed on their list for they felt that there were so many unemployed, and so much economic insecurity, that no one could possibly stand the burden of unemployed relatives. "If we start keeping a relative who is unemployed we will get dozens and scores of them at our house within a week. Unemployment has become such a common problem that it is quite impossible for any single person to remedy it." (Case 76)

These qualifications which interviewees made to assisting others may have always existed. However, they show that the actual responsibilities which many Hindus are now willing to assume do not fit in with the ideal picture of unreserved help to all kinsmen, which was typical of the large extended family. Moreover, when these attitudes are seen in relation to other family changes, it is possible to maintain the hypothesis that many outside contingencies now force Hindus who are reluctant to give up cherished family responsibilities to at least modify their feelings about them, and possibly their acts.

*Acts of Responsibility*

To what extent are attitudes of willingness to help transferred into action when the need arises? Tables I and II can only be considered as a minimum indication of the actual assistance undertaken by interviewees and their families. Many interviewees would forget past acts, many would not know of them, and many would have the conception of family obligation so deeply ingrained that they would not recognize acts of assistance on the part of their family members and relatives. Tables I and II are, therefore, given only as an indication of the type of assistance commonly offered and to show the family members who are more often the givers and those who are usually the recipients.

TABLE I

TYPES OF ASSISTANCE GIVEN BY FAMILY MEMBERS

| Type of help | Number of cases* |
|---|---|
| Help | 48 |
| Board | 37 |
| Financial | 31 |
| Education | 24 |
| Marriage | 16 |
| Illness | 10 |
| Jobs | 6 |
| TOTAL | 172 |

*Of the interviewees, eighteen said that their families had never assisted other family members or relatives.

The term "help" was not defined by the interviewees. It can be taken to infer that some sort of assistance was given. Financial assistance for education or boarding nieces and nephews while they are completing their education is a very usual recent type of assistance amongst middle and upper middle-class Hindu families. This is such a normal type of assistance that Desai says: "To ask a relative for help for education is not considered anything out of the way and it is just taken as a matter of course that such help is given. The person who helps may not think of getting anything in return. But the person who receives such help considers it his duty to help some other relative. This is the approved and approbated norm of behaviour."[14]

Assistance with marriages includes help in providing dowries, or in financing the actual wedding ceremonies. This is also such an accepted part of the family pattern of responsibility that many instances which occurred may not have been mentioned by interviewees. With relatively low incomes and few nurses, illness often involves the women of the family in nursing and can take up a great deal of the time and effort of older women. Not many interviewees spoke of assisting relatives to get jobs, but as nepotism has been characteristic of societies with joint family systems, one would presume that many more instances had occurred than are noted here.

One type of help which is not listed in Table I was the amount of advice and sympathy given relatives. However, "consoling" relatives was often mentioned, and, given a large kinship group, it is possible that this often takes up a good deal of the time of certain family members. "Father had six sisters and all of them came to him for advice."

TABLE II
GIVERS AND RECIPIENTS OF ASSISTANCE

|  | Grandparents | Parents | Brothers | Sisters | Uncles | Aunts | Relatives | Husband | Total |
|---|---|---|---|---|---|---|---|---|---|
| Assistance given by | 10 | 64 | 36 | 19 | 14 | 10 | 12 | 7 | 172 |
| Recipients* | 3 | 26 | 46 | 22 | 4 | 8 | 58 | – | 167 |

*Additional categories of recipients were widows, in-laws, and neighbours.

The figures in Table II suggest that the parents are the main people who bear the responsibility for assistance given family members and relatives. In analysing the amount of assistance given by different types of families there appeared to be no appreciable difference in the help extended by the large joint families of this study as compared with the other types. However, the number of families involved was too small for the analysis to be definitive.

In some families the burden of financing all crises seemed to be the lot of one particular member. In one of these the father was the only

[14]*Ibid*, p. 116.

elder male member with a prosperous job. As well as supporting his own family, he educated his brothers, got them jobs, and married his sisters. Then he kept two of his brothers who were poor with him, educated their sons, and married their daughters. Another case shows how one member may never be free of the responsibilities of family members and relatives and of what sacrifice this family went through to help relatives.

> My husband started earning when he was twenty-two years old. His father had just died and from that age on he has done everything for his family. He married one of his sisters and educated his two brothers. He also supplemented the income of another brother who wasn't very well off.
> Then our eldest daughter was old enough to be married. Her marriage and dowry cost us 10,000 rupees. After that we thought that all our financial responsibilities were over and we could indulge in some luxuries. But just then another calamity hit the family. My sister-in-law's husband lost his job. Most of his savings had gone to marry two of his daughters. They have five sons and three more daughters to support; so my husband is giving them a large part of his income.
> We now have another daughter of marriageable age and I don't know how my husband is going to manage her marriage. Two of our sons too will have to go to college in the next few years so we will have to prepare for more expenses. (Case 58)

A rather large number of interviewees implied that although they had occasionally received help, or moral support, from relatives when in trouble, they could never be sure whether they would respond to their needs or not. Relatives who were classified as "poor" seemed even less sure of their reception when in trouble. They were sometimes spoken of as "burdens," and seemed to be regarded in a different light from relatives who were ordinarily self-supporting, but were unable to look after themselves in times of crisis. It was not clear whether this uncertainty has always existed or if it is an indication of a trend to less support of relatives.

Although a few husbands were said to treat their wives' relatives like their own, a problem sometimes arose when they were in trouble. As most of the families studied were patrilineal in lineage, and as the wife is now maintaining closer ties with her own family till a later age, it is quite likely that this type of strain will be more common in the future.[15]

---

[15]*Ibid.*, p. 117. Desai says that, if the couple develops close relationships with the wife's family, they in effect leave one family and join another. An informant has said that, even in joint families, women would sometimes help their own families in subtle ways, such as passing on scarcely used saris and dhotis or giving them grain or groceries.

As my husband and I have no children to leave our money to we help all our relatives and the people around us. Soon after my marriage I got TB and was very ill. It was the self-sacrifice of my own relatives that saved me; so now I help them in their troubles. My in-laws constantly criticize me for spending my husband's money on them, but I never pay any attention to their complaints, for they never helped me when I was ill. They would have been quite happy to have me die and marry my husband to another girl.

When my sister became a widow without any money, she had two daughters, and I took them all into my house and looked after them until the girls were married. At another time one of my brothers wasn't earning very much; so I kept him and his wife and three girls until they were able to stand on their own feet.

The only ones I don't like to have living in my house are my in-laws, for I am sure that they will make trouble instead of helping me. (Case 86)

In several other families daughters who had married well assisted their families. Two of these had taken their brothers and sisters to live with them.

The type of assistance given varies with the age and sex of the giver. Men are usually the only ones who can help financially, for they control the family income and are the ones appealed to when money is needed. Women typically give their labour, either taking people into the house and caring for them when ill, or actually helping with the physical work entailed in a marriage or other important family ceremonies.

One important aspect of family obligation is the way sons take over financial responsibilities as soon as they are earning. They are expected not only to contribute to the family purse when living at home, but to continue to send money to the family when they move away for a job, even though earning very little themselves. One young man who was supporting himself on a scholarship sent part of it home regularly. Others who were struggling to finance their own education also continued to send money home. They are usually fully aware of the father's great financial burden, and as they still feel an integral part of the family it is their burden as well.

The time at which sons begin to make money usually coincides roughly with two of the major family expenses, the marriage of daughters and the education of the younger sons. The eldest son being the first to earn will have to contribute more than the others, especially if he is much older than his brothers. When he becomes head of the family his main responsibilities will be similar to the father's—supporting the family, educating his younger brothers, and marrying his sisters.

Eighteen of the interviewees said that they had never known their families to assist relatives. This might mean that help was not needed.

But if it was, and none was given, then it can be seen that some family members can escape their responsibilities. In fact, several cases showed that, when young men feel that they should no longer bear family responsibilities, they cannot be forced to do so. One young man, who had achieved an important career in a large city, had never felt close to his sister, and when her daughter was being married, refused to give his share of the marriage gifts. His father then sent him a bill for thirty of the saris given as presents. The son paid the bill, but he now avoids the family when he goes back to the home city on business.

If the above eighteen families are added to the number of interviewees who said that their generation did not help relatives, or feel as close to them as members of their fathers' generation had, a trend away from kinship responsibility is evident. Some interviewees even said that members of their generation did not help their brothers and sisters to the same extent that their parents had helped their siblings. It is also significant that most of the conflicts mentioned by interviewees with relatives were due to failure to carry out expected or anticipated obligations.

In speaking of those who gave help, interviewees almost invariably mentioned one member of the family only: that is, "father" was nearly always mentioned instead of "father and mother," "uncle" rather than "uncle and aunt" and "brother" instead of "brother and his wife." This suggests that male roles are the ones which are meant to bear the major responsibilities, or it may indicate the dominance of these roles, or that the men of the family have complete control over charitable contributions. However, as the interviews revealed that a good deal of family consultation occurs, and as the women of the house must bear much of the extra burden of work when relatives are helped, there must be a considerable concurrence on the part of all responsible family members if assistance is given which will demand some sacrifice from all members. In fact, relatives often are said to appeal to the pity of the wife, to try to win her affection and intercession on their behalf before appealing to the husband for help.

Family members assume new financial duties and the responsibilities entailed in them when the family's division of labour changes with changing circumstances. For example, when the husband becomes the sole family earner, he may become involved in personal relationships with friends, that may necessitate his assuming financial and other responsibilities towards them rather than to relatives.

Another phenomenon which is becoming more evident is the increasing role which educated women are playing in helping to finance the family. If a widow or married woman continues to work in a paying job outside the home, her money usually goes mainly to help support her immediate family, but if a single woman works, she may be called on to help even distant relatives. One woman, a doctor, showed the change in her feelings of responsibility when she decided to marry. "As I am the eldest child, and up to now had a good job which gave me a decent salary, many of my relatives expected me to help them. I have done my best to do so. Now I am going to marry; so I will have to consider my husband and own family first. But I will do my best to go on helping my relatives if I can." (Case 29) When another woman started to work she became the sole support of her mother, sister, and uncle.

My grandfather was very wealthy, and so he looked after my mother, sister and myself after my father died. My maternal relatives, too, helped us in many ways. They gave us jewels we used for our family expenses. Now that I am earning, our family is no longer a burden to our relatives. My paternal uncle has come to live with us, and as he will not work, I have to support him, too. Our maternal relatives are very sympathetic about my working, they feel sorry that I am forced to support the family instead of staying at home and getting married. (Case 85)

*Reciprocation*

An exact estimate of mutual assistance is extremely difficult to achieve. For the essential nature of responsibility is such that the amount of reciprocation can never be clearly measured. This is particularly true of family relationships, as ordinarily the older members have the duty of looking after the younger ones, and younger members seldom reciprocate fully in kind, but rather carry out their duties in turn in relation to their own children.

Nevertheless, some sort of reckoning is consciously and unconsciously done of even the subtler aspects of family help, and the recipient is expected to pay in his turn when other members are in need. But reciprocation is not necessarily to the *same* family member, for one's debts may be paid to another relative. Nor need it be of the same type. In one family an uncle financed his nephew's education, and that nephew's mother gave a cousin a loan for his marriage. But it must eventually be paid back in terms of the family's expectations of the member's ability to repay, even if it is only the duty of a small child to pay back by being "good." Thus, a system of insurance is set up against the crises and vagaries of life, so that even if a family member gives all he has to a relative in trouble, he is fairly sure that he will be assisted in turn when his need arises. Several interviewees made remarks of this sort: "If we help our relatives when they are in need, they will help us when we need something."

Mutual obligations and duties may not be verbally voiced, or even explicitly acknowledged by any one person, but underneath lies a shrewd estimation of what each family member has given, and of what they have received. The subtlety of these mutual expectations are lost to all but intimate family members. Should a member refuse to carry out his obligations, he is open to the severe condemnation of the group, for he is threatening the family system of security which is essential to its survival. Several interviewees mentioned the criticism and shame they would suffer if they did not help relatives; some said relatives had called them "misers" and "small hearted." Several also mentioned the quick change that could come in relation to the amount of help needed: "Our relatives were very sweet to us when they needed help, but once we had given it they cut off all contact with us, and didn't even write to us."

Several interviewees reported cases in which family debts had not been repaid. In one case a wealthy family had helped relatives generously, but when they lost their money found that these same relatives would not assist them. In another, the husband was the eldest of eight brothers, and sent home money regularly to help with their education. "Now that he has lost his job, his brothers, who are now in good positions, won't help him. Even my father-in-law and mother-in-law are no longer willing to have us live with them."

Failure to carry out obligations are not always allowed to go by without a good deal of protest. One man's failure to fulfil his expected obligations was so flagrant that he was ostracized (Case 106). "When my uncle was ill my brother-in-law would not look after him. When he died my brother-in-law went away for fear that he would have to bear the cost of the funeral. He didn't even attend the death ceremony; so I have dealt with him mercilessly. I have sent him out of our joint family, and won't allow him to come back again." In another case a father had helped the families of his two brothers when he was alive, but when he died one of these brothers, who lived only a short distance away, never visited the family. The second brother went to see them, but avoided asking them about their financial position as he was afraid he might have to do something about it. An outside friend and an aunt helped the family until the eldest son could get a job to support them. This family has refused to see the uncles since that occasion.

On the other hand, recipients may be so grateful for help that they sacrifice themselves when their turn comes. In one family an uncle had financed ego's brothers through school and college. When he wanted ego to marry his daughter, ego could not refuse although he had no wish to do so. "The suggestion of my uncle left me no option."

Family members will not always agree about the amount of help they should give, especially if family generosity falls heavily on one particular member. In one family, in which the parents and sisters were very hospitable to relatives and friends, and boarded a number of nieces and nephews, the son was very irritated and would have preferred the money to be saved for his education. On the other hand, help is often given "most willingly" and a good many instances of self-sacrifice were mentioned, such as taking relatives in to live when in trouble even though the family income was so small that they were deprived of many things.

*Ritual Participation*

One of the main functions of family rituals and ceremonials is to emphasize and renew the feeling of kin solidarity, for they are outward symbols of this unity. Kinship contacts probably last longer in these areas than in any other, for they are the main way of publicly demonstrating family identity. Formal kinship gatherings were considered so important in former days that a fine would sometimes be imposed on members who did not attend.[16]

One reason for concern about family ceremonies is that a marriage, a birth or a death may affect the family continuity, and thus is a potential crisis for all family members. Weddings have always been very important occasions in India, for in the past they were one of the few times at which relatives could meet and enjoy themselves. As in other countries, they have always been overt marks of a family's social position. This is still seen in the anxiety of even distant relatives to help with the preparations, so that the family of the bride will not be shamed in the sight of the new in-laws. Every detail of the rituals must be scrupulously followed if criticism is to be avoided. This shared responsibility, and the co-operation in the actual work, were a strong binding factor for family members. The decline in this participation

[16]Bryce Ryan, "The Sinhalese Family System," *Eastern Anthropologist*, vol. 6, pp. 143–63. Ryan noted this in Ceylon: "At household ceremonies one expects greater loyalty from kinsmen than neighbours—more accurately their absence is more sharply noted. The failure of . . . a kinsman-neighbour to be absent (from a funeral or in times of grave illness) may be reason for enduring coolness between the households."

as weddings have become less elaborate, and relatives less inclined to attend family ceremonials, may be an important factor in assisting to break up the unity of the large kin group.

The most important Hindu ceremonies are those attending birth, the naming of a child, the thread ceremony of the twice-born, marriage and death. The less important ceremonies occur at feasts and festivals such as Divali.[17] Today only close family members attend the more important ceremonials of city families, and the other festivals are normally celebrated by each family unit in their own homes. The men of the family usually represent the family at funeral ceremonies. Close blood relatives or older women may also attend, but children are not supposed to be present.

If the wedding is one of a close relative all the family will attend, but if it is a distant relative one person will represent the family. The father is the main ritual representative of the family, especially if it is his side of the family that is involved. After a girl's marriage, she will be more responsible for the ceremonies of her husband's family than for those of her own.

Assistance to relatives on these occasions takes the form of both financial help and actual household work Usually the members of a joint family will jointly bear the expense of religious or marriage ceremonies, but sometimes more distant relatives will help with the dowry money or the actual financing of the wedding. Presents to the young couple may take the form of financial help. The actual assistance required with the wedding arrangements, such as cooking, serving, looking after guests, etc., is usually very great because of the elaborate nature and length of the ceremonies. Even in the city close family members may house as many as fifty guests for several days.

The women of the family usually undertake the cooking and serving for a small number of guests. Men assist if there are a large number. Aunts, and other older women such as sisters-in-law, do most of the work, but sometimes all relatives will help. Occasionally one woman, possibly a widowed sister, bears the greatest burden of the work. One interviewee said that his widowed mother was taken to all the family ceremonies to serve this function. Sometimes relatives will evade the work. In one family the mother's relatives were so wealthy that they considered themselves to be honoured guests, and expected to be waited on rather than to assist.

Most of the interviewees said that family celebrations were not now as elaborate as in the past, or as strictly attended. One reason

[17]Srinivas, *Marriage and Family in Mysore*, see chaps. 7, 8, 11, 12, 13, and 14 for an account of different Hindu ceremonies.

for this lay in the comparative anonymity of the city. In the village no one could escape the censuring eye of neighbours, let alone that of relatives; thus attendance and assistance at family ceremonies of even distant relatives were unavoidable. This pressure lessens in towns and small cities. But it is probable that cities must be very large before relatives living in the same city can escape their ceremonial obligations. Cost and time often now prevent distant relatives from attending. Other reasons which now prevent people from attending as many ceremonies as before are seen in the following interview:

In the past, weddings and other celebrations were shared with relatives. The whole family went and stayed at the wedding house for weeks. In these days of food and housing shortages, it isn't convenient to be either the host or the guest. In those days, too, the parents weren't very particular about their children's education, and didn't mind their losing school to go to the weddings; so whenever we went to any celebration we took the whole family. Nowadays it is quite different. Children have strict schooling and music, dancing, and painting classes as well; so now it has become the habit to have one member represent the family at weddings and ceremonies. (Case 82)

Most of the single young men who had moved from the South of India to Bombay were no longer interested in attending family ceremonies, or found the obstacles to attendance too great. Only one or two said that they still enjoyed them and went to them as enthusiastically as their parents had before them. One young man had not even returned home for his sister's funeral: "Why waste all that money?" Another said that his present close attachment to his friends had made his meetings with relatives so formal that he disliked attending family ceremonies. Another ambitious young man did not now want to associate himself with his relatives for he felt that he had gained a higher position of prestige. Several said that they were now more and more engrossed in their own interests and thus were not interested in family celebrations. A few of these young men still felt the compulsion to return, even though they had little inclination to do so, for they were afraid of the "fuss" if they did not, or that they would disappoint a parent or close relative. The majority, too, still felt some responsibility for the important ceremonies of their own immediate families, even though they did not want to continue to go to those of relatives. It is quite possible that the cost of ceremonials is now so high that it is difficult for the host to offer the same hospitality as in former times. Finally, other types of entertainment and recreation now compete with family celebrations. Several young men said they were bored with them.

The variety of responses to family responsibility noted in this chapter shows that neither the joint nor the nuclear family is now a completely secure haven for family members, especially if they are only distantly related to the core members. When the different cases of this study were analysed in terms of family type, it was clearly seen that members of the younger generation, in particular those who have moved to cities, tend to narrow their circle of family obligation. This trend is in keeping with changing patterns of rights and duties observed in other countries which are becoming urbanized and industrialized. Feelings of guilt may continue long after members refuse to help, but even when these are very disturbing, the new claims of the urban surrounding will often outweigh them.

However, it should be remembered that the son who moves to the city, and confines his duty to his own small family unit, does not escape wider responsibility. For the pressures of city life make him vulnerable to the needs of friends and even strangers. And the gradual development of civic and national agencies to look after indigent people may involve him in just as heavy financial contributions as did his former family responsibilities.

### Summary

An analysis of the division of labour in the large joint family shows that it was clearly allotted according to age and sex. Except in farm families, women did not work outside the home, and men typically had little to do with household tasks. The amount of actual work, as compared to administration, done by the chief women of the household varied according to the wealth of the family and the number of servants employed. But usually the women in middle-class homes had a busy life, for there were many guests to entertain, and family festivals and ceremonies always entailed a lot of work. Children's part in the division of labour also depended on wealth and servants. In poorer families they often shared so extensively in the housework that they had little time for play; in better-off families they sometimes had to learn the practical aspects of household work even when there were servants.

A boy's work pertained more to the outside jobs than those within the house. Through them he learnt to deal with the outside world as well as take responsibility for family matters. A girl's work was specifically designed to train her for her married life in a strange household. Through it she learnt to be flexible and self-sacrificing, so that she could fit in easily to a subordinate role in the new home. Her care of younger siblings fitted her to look after her own children when married.

The mother was the main trainer of children, assisted by the other women of the household and grandparents. When a mother today finds herself alone to do this task in the small household, she will find that outside agencies, such as nursery schools, paediatricians and many other experts, have gradually taken over much of the child's training.

One of the main differences between the division of labour of the large joint family as compared to the nuclear family lies in its distinct duties, and that it provided many workers, especially at times of weddings and family festivals.

The close association of family members and relatives under one roof also gave children the opportunity of becoming familiar with their future roles so that they could take them over efficiently. On the other hand, the nuclear family is by definition a small unit in which children and parents have such different work and interests that parents cannot be used as models for future roles. This often makes it difficult for young people when the time arrives for them to begin their careers.

The division of labour on the basis of sex tends to break down in cities, for women often have to help earn the family income, and men, in turn, have to help or substitute for their wives, as there are no other adult women in the home. Boys, like their fathers, may have to share in the housework. Girls tend to move outside the home and obtain more education; so their share of the work becomes more like that of their brothers. The result is that there is no longer as clear a difference in the training for sex roles as before.

Strain can occur when an adult must take over a new work role for which he has not been prepared as a child, particularly if the prestige of this new assignment is not equal to that of the former role. The new division of labour in the nuclear urban family is, therefore, probably harder for the men of the family to adjust to than it is for the women: as women's tasks in all societies have less prestige than those of men, women taking over "male" business or professional roles are moving to a higher level of job prestige, whereas men are moving to lower levels of work. Strain can also occur when a crisis, such as death, removes an important family member, and his part of the work must be taken over by others.

One important change in a mother's role that comes about in nuclear families with the new division of labour is that she becomes the pivot around which the family revolves. In families which approximate the companionship type, mothers are the chief organizers of the complicated schedules of family members. Meals, work, education, sports, religious activities, holidays, health and countless social and associational claims must all be co-ordinated skilfully if the family is to function at all smoothly. This is a mammoth task in a busy urban family, and the mother needs to be a particularly adaptable person to carry it out successfully. If this analysis is correct, then perhaps one of the major changes in family structure, as it moves from an approximation of the institutional ideal type to a nuclear form, is this change in the positions of father and mother, for the patriarch of the large extended family played much the same pivotal role as the mother now does in nuclear families.

The forces of industrialization and urbanization bring a gradual change in the expectations of responsibility. On the one hand, they shrink to the immediate family of parents and children, but, on the other, they widen to the community, and may even become national or international in scope; so that finally a stage is reached at which even close relatives in need are considered "public" problems rather than personal ones. Attitudes correspondingly change as outside agencies—such as governments—take over, so that public assistance gradually ceases to be a stigma, and people accept it without shame or guilt, as "naturally" as they formerly accepted the help of close relatives. This change will, of course, not come evenly or easily, particularly if individuals are brought up to the traditional deep sense of family responsibility which is firmly implanted in the Hindu joint family by religious sanction. One of my informants and her husband were so thoroughly inculcated with feelings of family responsibility that after they had taken legal action against their family for their share of money from the family firm, they were so overcome with remorse that the husband went back and worked in the firm for nothing to expiate their feelings of guilt.

Many of the interviewees were brought up in joint families where the traditional norms of responsibility seem to have been adhered to almost perfectly. However, practical necessity cuts down strict compliance with family obligations when the family moves to town, and the higher cost of living makes it impossible to treat relatives as liberally as before. Smaller city houses prevent an influx of too many extra people although one city-dwelling couple may serve as a sort of family hotel for nephews and nieces who are sent to them for free board and education. The data showed that these sibling obligations seem to be still carried out without question, as naturally as grandfather boarded distant relatives in the villages, but distant relatives are *not* welcomed or treated as hospitably as in grandfather's day. Thus the circle of personal responsibility is beginning to narrow.

Once the traditional attitudes of responsibility have cracked and families live so far apart that acts of responsibility cannot be checked by other kin, the lines of expected obligation become vague, and even close relatives cannot be counted on in times of trouble. Thus the clearly delineated patterns of responsibility in the joint family become confused as the family changes to a small nuclear unit. Even in the nuclear family the feelings of obligation do not necessarily coincide with the household unit—for several young men claimed that, whereas in the village it was considered an insult for family members to have to go to outsiders for help rather than relatives, in the city they personally went to their friends for help rather than to brothers.

Not enough detailed data were available to show the specific pattern of rights and duties entailed in each family relationship, such as mother and child, as clearly as in the areas of authority and affection. In general the elder male members and those with more money are expected to bear the greater share of responsibility. This tends to put a good deal of strain on the ambitious son who moves to the city and gets a lucrative job, for claims on him by relatives will tend to increase just when he is beginning to achieve higher ambitions, and perhaps needs more money to carry them out. Illness was a common problem for the families of this sample. But the responsibility of family members for each other was still so well institutionalized in regard to it that it was never mentioned as a cause of tension or conflict. One outstanding theme in the case studies was the underlying feeling of financial insecurity, and the idea that economic crises would arise in the future. Moreover, as it is very difficult for middle-class urban families to save, they are very uncertain about their financial futures. This is beginning to promote the idea that one should "save for a rainy day" and that "charity begins at home." In other words, urban life tends to break down the mutual assistance of the larger family unit.

Types of assistance given also change with the times. Education is now considered an insurance for the family's future; so relatives may help a young man to get a degree because of its potential effect on the family finances. There are also indications that many families prefer to help relatives with money rather than to have them live with them when they are in trouble, for fear of conflicts and misunderstandings. The type of person responsible for giving assistance also changes. Women are now having to take an increasing share in providing the family income and even in assisting more distant relatives financially.

One significant aspect in the study of changing obligations is to find the point at which the "privilege" of helping becomes a "burden." This point probably arises when self-interest becomes more important than the welfare of the group, in other words, when familism gives way to individualism. It must, therefore, be related to a loss in the feeling of family identity.

In conclusion, the extent to which a family member will feel himself responsible for other family members depends on his feelings of loyalty to and identity with the family unit. In a changing society a seeming disregard of responsibility for relatives on the part of those who live in cities cannot be "morally" measured against those who still live in the native village surrounded by kin and caste members. The situation is quite different, and necessitates a different system of rights and duties.

Finally, it is highly probable that obligations will be more willingly and "unconsciously" carried out if affection and love exist between the people concerned. This affective dimension of family relations will be discussed in chapter v.

• *Chapter Four* •

# THE SUBSTRUCTURE OF POWER AND AUTHORITY

EVEN IN SUCH a small intimate group as a family, responsibilities and rights must be distributed in order that the group may function smoothly and efficiently, and a hierarchy of authority be established to direct and co-ordinate the activity. Weber never specifically mentions the family in his discussion of authority, but his analysis of the "traditional" authority of corporate groups is applicable to the family unit. The family's authority is "traditional" in the sense that, as its rules are traditionally received, they are much more difficult to change than those of "rational-legal authority." Moreover:

> The order underlying a system of traditional authority always defines a system of statuses of persons who can legitimately exercise authority. Such a status is different from an "office." It does not involve specifically defined powers with the presumption that everything not legitimized in terms of the order is outside its scope. It is rather defined in terms of three things. There are, first, the concrete traditional prescriptions of the traditional order, which are held to be binding on the person in authority as well as the others. There is, secondly, the authority of other persons above the particular status in a hierarchy, or in different spheres . . . and finally . . . there is a sphere of arbitrary free "grace" open to the incumbent.[1]

Traditional family authority is usually accepted by children as easily and naturally as other types of family training. It does not always need naked power to enforce it, but uses persuasion to entice the individual to follow the dictates of those in control. This kind of power can be called "indirect authority" for the recipient is not always aware of its existence. A child may become so used to obeying the

[1] Talcott Parsons and A. M. Henderson, *Max Weber: The Theory of Social and Economic Organization* (New York: Oxford University Press, 1947), pp. 60–1.

family mores that he may even experience feelings of deep guilt if he transgresses them long after he has been separated from his family, or even after his parents are dead.[2]

On the other hand, "direct" authority is usually felt to be compulsive and is, therefore, often distasteful to the recipient and may call out resentment and resistance. This type of authority is usually employed by an insecure person, such as a father who, in changing times, is not sure of what his relationship to his children should be. However, in all groups which exist for any length of time, authority will become an integral part of each status.

Every person fills a variety of authority positions during his lifetime. He may even have to occupy several different positions at the same time. For instance, as well as filling the position of father, he may also be son to the grandfather of the house, brother to a sister, uncle to a nephew or niece, and husband to his wife. His authority will vary in all these positions. It is only when the complexity of an individual's adjustment to others in his different roles is understood that the amazing flexibility of the human animal, and the delicacy of the balance of each social system is fully appreciated. These positions become even more difficult to fill when family relationships are changing. A more detailed description of the structure of authority of the joint family will emphasize the areas of strain in this substructure when the family grows smaller.

### The Authority of Different Relationships

#### Head of the Household

The eldest male, whether grandfather or father, was the acknowledged head of the family.[3] He may never have had the power of life and death over family members as was common in ancient Roman families, but his authority was theoretically complete.[4] Moreover, the hierarchy of authority of the joint family has always been supported

---

[2]David Riesman, *The Lonely Crowd* (New Haven: Yale University Press, 1950), pp. 11–16. In this study Riesman gives a very good analysis of "tradition-directed" "other-directed" persons.

[3]E. Kathleen Gough, "The Social Structure of a Tanjore Village," in McKim Marriott, *Village India* (Chicago: University of Chicago Press, 1955), p. 44. "Within each patrilineal extended family all submit to the oldest man."

[4]E. W. Burgess and H. J. Locke, *The Family* (New York: American Book Co., 1945), p. 20; also Olga Lang, *Chinese Family and Society*, published under the auspices of the International Secretariat, Institute of Pacific Relations, and the Institute of Social Research (New Haven: Yale University Press, 1946), p. 54, for a description of the patriarchal family in China.

by caste and religion, and was formerly absolute and predictable. Particularly in isolated villages it is still upheld by attitudes of respect and fear, and acts of deference.

One of the clearest descriptions of the hierarchy of authority of the traditional Hindu family is given by Beales in his study of the six main families of a village near Mysore. Each family had more than thirty members:

... each formed an economic unit, and each was under the leadership of a single headman. The functions of family leadership were, to some extent, shared by the brothers of the family head. The family head was in charge of finances. He sat on the village panchayat, or council, and represented the family in dealings with consanguineal and affinal relatives living outside the village. Of the brothers of the family head, one was usually in charge of dry-land agriculture; another managed the garden lands, the cattle, or the family industry. Such a division of labour persisted in large families even in 1953, although the largest families of 1953 could count only twelve to fifteen members.

Allied with each of the six large families in 1900 were a number of small households composed of distant relatives and dependents, such as widows and impoverished brothers in law, as well as servants and debtors of other castes. In this manner, the six large families included many other families within their respective spheres of influence.[5]

The grandfather was theoretically the head of the family until his death. This gave him power over his wife and children, his younger brothers, and his sisters until they were married. Even those who moved away to distant cities, or overseas, were theoretically still members of the family and therefore under his control although he could not supervise their day-to-day affairs. On his death, the authority passed to the next eldest male.[6]

Interviews showed that the grandfather's authority in fact varied in the different families studied. At times it was strong and his role was much like that of a dictator; at other times it was weak and the family relationships were more equalitarian. But on the whole, case studies tended to show at least one dominant grandparent in most large joint families. They did not show, however, that grandparents were as influential in the life of the joint family as had been expected, for the

[5]Alan R. Beals, "Interplay among Factors of Change in a Mysore Village," in *Village India*, McKim Marriott, ed. (Chicago: University of Chicago Press, 1955), p. 87.
[6]David Mandelbaum, "The Family in India," in *The Family: Its Function and Destiny*, Ruth N. Anshen, ed. (New York: Harper and Brothers, 1949), p. 94. The traditional authority has passed down without too much change and with only slight deviations for some nine centuries and was prescribed in the *Mitakshara* which outlines the rights and duties of all family members.

short life span in India means that one or both of the grandparents usually die at a comparatively early age.

Only a few of the grandfathers mentioned in interviews had had personal characteristics which had prevented them from carrying out their traditional roles. In one family the grandfather had been so reckless with money that the control of the family finances had been handed over to his son before his death. Apart from these few exceptions it was clear that control over important family decisions is still maintained by the older generation in large joint families.

The following interview indicates the rather typical way in which authority is handled in a family of several generations. It shows that the authority of the head, or grandfather, is in effect only over the major matters which affect the whole family life, whereas the grandmother holds authority in her own domain and can control the minute details of household life. Not all grandparents, however, exerted influence over their son's family. Nor were they necessarily stern in their discipline; a grandfather was quite often pictured as a loving, gentle person.

All the important decisions at home were made by Grandfather and Father. Grandmother was the authority in the domestic side, but she and Mother had no voice in outside matters. Mother did not even have the right to purchase her own saris. Grandmother was responsible for the children's training and behaviour. She taught us eating manners and caste duties. Grandmother, and sometimes Father punished us, not Mother. Grandfather never punished us. When he got angry, he used one or two abusive words, but nothing beyond. (Case 84)

On the other hand, the position of head of the family entails so much potential power that a harsh incumbent can disrupt family relationships. In one family, both grandfather and father had been extremely severe.

My father was terribly afraid of his father. And when Grandfather died and Father became head of the family he in turn made us all afraid of him. He made my uncles obey him implicitly. He beat Mother when she didn't carry out his orders. He harassed and punished all of us children. But Father felt guilty after he had punished us, and had terrible nightmares about Grandfather coming back and threatening him with a stick, because Mother was Grandfather's favourite daughter-in-law. (Case 47)

This extreme kind of discipline sometimes had unexpected results and it is quite likely that many sons rebelled against it. The following case study is an illustration of an unsuccessful rebel.

My great-grandfather was a dictator and believed in the strictest discipline. He used to give Grandfather and his brothers, five rupees for pocket money a month and they had to write accounts of every pie they spent. Grandfather had an independent spirit and resented this discipline; so he went off with friends and spent a lot of time with them. He used his school money and got into bad company and evil ways. When Great-Grandfather heard he stopped his allowance. Grandfather was desperate; so he started borrowing. Then he got in with a famous actress who promised him 500 rupees if he would drive in a chariot with her in a big procession—as he was the son of a famous man. Grandfather wanted to hurt his father for the way he had treated him so he went with her. Great-Grandfather was furious, his anger knew no bounds. He beat Grandfather mercilessly, and sent him and his wife to live in another town. Finally he disinherited him and left all his properties to his grandson—my father. Grandfather then had to live under the authority of his son, who had all rights over him. (Case 72)

The changing attitudes to such strict authority was shown in several interviews in which the grandfather who "wanted everybody under his thumb" was called a very old-fashioned man.

In the traditional joint family women were theoretically allotted a subordinate position to men. Even today they do not have controlling positions before the law, or in many economic or social matters. However, a closer analysis of joint family life shows that, in fact, women did have important positions in their own sphere. The wife of the eldest male member, usually the grandmother had a clear position of authority as head of the domestic side of the household. Important household matters were theoretically controlled by the grandfather, but day-to-day routine matters were completely under her control. She administered the household, supervised or did the cooking, organized the work of the women of the household, and saw that the children were properly cared for. In the close confinement of the house, from which women rarely escaped, her main task must also have been that of mediator although this element of her role is never mentioned. If she had exceptional qualities, she could even wield great influence over the male head "behind the scene." If the grandfather died before her, as he often did, she might inherit his mantle of authority over all family affairs since her influence over her sons was usually so strong that she could dominate the family. The many facets of her duties and power are shown in the following description of a Hindu widow.

The widowed mother does nothing, but she manages everything. She has absolute rule over the family members. She sees that the daughters-in-law behave, that the house-father [the oldest son] receives the respect due to him from other family members, that servants of the household are well behaved and orderly, that the community thinks well of the house, that the family priest is respected and honoured, that enough money is contributed for feeding the Brahmans, that gods are venerated properly, and that there is some substantial saving in the house every month.[7]

In spite of her theoretical control different arrangements of authority between the grandmother and her sons were revealed in case studies. In one case, a grandmother had authority over all general family matters, while her two sons controlled their own immediate family affairs. In most families a son would continue to consult his mother on all important matters. The following case study shows how extensive a grandmother's influence can be in her son's household.

When I was growing up, Father was the chief authority in the home in all official and financial matters. He was a district commissioner and practically ruled the district like a king, and yet he would always go to his mother, who was nearly illiterate, for her final decision in any important family matter. Grandmother was the authority too in all household matters, and Father left everything to her. In such matters as settling weddings Father and Mother did the preliminary choosing, then Father would ask Grandmother for her final approval. I still remember how my brother's marriage was arranged. After all the preliminary arrangements had been gone through, the girl's parents came to visit us. Grandmother was cutting vegetables in the kitchen; so Father went to her and said: "The girl's father has come to enquire about our final decision. The girl is good looking, and the boy has given his consent. The family seems to be decent and of a good class. What is your opinion?" Then Grandmother said: "As the girl is liked by the boy, and comes from a good family the wedding can be set." If Grandmother had said that she didn't like the match, then Father would never have gone ahead with the wedding. (Case 88)

A situation which is becoming increasingly typical is that in which a son moves away from his paternal home with his wife and children, and later takes his mother to live with him when her husband dies. This new pattern usualy causes strain, for technically speaking the grandmother is now living in someone else's home, and therefore the strict traditional definition of her position of authority does not apply. For instance, the wife of the house now seems to feel that instead of dealing with a revered "grandmother" she is rather coping with a "mother-in-law." It is a situation in which the lines of authority are less well-defined, and it is likely that a daughter-in-law feels more frustration and aggression towards a mother-in-law who attempts to exert her authority in her son's home than she would if she were still living in her mother-in-law's home where her dominance would be expected.

[7]Burgess and Locke, *The Family*, p. 19.

This situation is aggravated if the daughter-in-law was not the grandmother's choice, or if she had not been trained to the family ways, as in the days of child marriage. There would be especial tension if the daughter-in-law had more education than the mother-in-law, or was from another region or caste. For, the rigidity of caste and regional customs increases the areas of possible conflict for the women of the household when they come from different milieus. Peaceful cooperation between the two would further depend on whether the grandmother was from the maternal or paternal side, and whether the wife had been married as a child or an adult.

Case studies showed more grandmothers living with the families interviewed than grandfathers. This would be due to the earlier age of girls on marriage and the longer female life span. It seemed too that grandmothers were more often mentioned as strong authoritarians than were grandfathers. This may be because her two roles of grandmother and mother-in-law are played concurrently. It is useful to remember here that a "beloved" grandmother to the children and a "revered" mother to a son may be a "nagging" mother-in-law to the wife. If a grandmother had a strong personality, the grandfather would allow her much say in family matters. On the other hand, the grandmothers mentioned in case studies sometimes had personalities quite different from that expected of their position. One was referred to as a "very quiet, timid person." Such unexpected characteristics might mean that the grandmother would be unable to fill her role in the expected way, and thus might cause just as much conflict and tension as a person who had a particularly overbearing personality. If a grandmother carried out her role in an authoritarian way and was also a grumbler, the family often found her hard to endure. "Grandmother was always finding fault. She nagged a lot. She was the chief authority over the family until her death, which was a relief to us all." (Case 51)

The close mother-son tie in the joint family meant that the person who could handle the grandmother best was her son. If he had a domineering personality, she would be no trouble in the household.

The grandmother tended to exert most authority and influence over her daughters and daughters-in-law, even though the grandfather was theoretically head of all members of the household. Her control even extended to daughters-in-law living in separate households, for the social separation of men and women means that women are still somewhat confined to spending most of their leisure time with other relatives, even when they live in nuclear family units.

The position of the grandmother in the large joint family has been shown to be one of considerable importance. In it she had much power —explicit in her control of the other women, implicit through her influence over her husband, and through her close affectional relationship with her son. When the traditional joint family changes to a nuclear type, the power of the grandmother dwindles until she may only have symbolic or ritual influence and authority over her children and grandchildren.

*Father*

Many of the laws of Manu deal with the sovereignty of the head of the family, and prescribe his conduct towards subordinate members, always recommending forebearance and patience.[8] His position of authority is not out of line with his duties, for he is responsible for the well-being of all under his roof, particularly the women. Among other things he must preserve their chastity in order to secure pure-blood progeny.[9] The great authority of his position in the joint family meant that a man of strong personality could exert his personal preferences over the whole household. In former days little could happen without his consent, and he made all decisions even down to such matters as when babies should be ceremonially named.

A father of a family only has this position of complete authority if he is the head of a joint family. A man who was merely the father of a family unit within the joint family, and not the senior male member, did not appear to have much power. Very little is, in fact, recorded of his actual authority, but a few hints of it appeared in interviews. They showed that his power was fairly well confined to the day-to-day affairs of his own wife and children. In other words, his own small family unit was merely part of the large whole.

However, his actual relationship with his father was determined largely by their different personalities, for in several families the grandparents were merely the formal authorities, and the sons took much of the initiative in family matters. Most heads of houses were wise enough to consult their sons on important family matters when they were adults. This meant that even younger sons might have a good deal of power.

In nuclear family units a father's power is extensive over his children when they are growing up, and may extend over into their ado-

---

[8]Hedwig Bachmann, *On the Soul of the Indian Woman: As Reflected in the Folklore of the Konkan* (Bastoria, India Portuguesa: Typografia Rangel, 1942), p. 82.

[9]*Ibid.*, p. 104.

lescence. But consultations with sons and daughters normally begin early, and the children are fairly independent as adolescents. As adults they are, theoretically, completely independent of their father's control, particularly when they are married, but in the nuclear Hindu families studied many sons and daughters continued to consult their fathers when adults, and most still regarded them with piety and respect.

The change in authority from father to son over the practical aspects of family life in the joint family was so institutionalized that it seldom caused strain or conflict between them. The eldest son's initiation into his responsible position would begin early, and even though the father would retain the reins of power in his own hands, the son would be gradually assuming control through consultation. The strict discipline of the father over him as a child would thus gradually change until the son became the real authority in the household. "When Grandfather was old, Father still held him in great esteem, and Grandfather always looked to him for advice on important decisions such as weddings or buying property. Grandfather was always told of Father's decisions, but as he hero-worshipped his son, Father's ideas always seemed best to him." (Case 61)

When the family structure changes from the joint pattern to the nuclear type, the problem of adjustment to new patterns of authority are probably greatest for father and son, husband and wife, and mother-in-law and daughter-in-law. All these relationships become more equalitarian, and before the adjustments are institutionalized there may be attempts on the part of the older generation to carry over the old patterns of domination. Levy believes that the two most crucial areas in family change will be found in the attempt of the son to emancipate himself from the dominance of his parents, and in women to change from their subordinate positions.[10] One case study shows the conflict which occurred between father and son before the son freed himself from his father's close supervision by leaving home.

> It is no exaggeration to say that Father completely dominated us when we were children. He even dominated Mother. We never used to discuss things with him at home, and he never reasoned with us. When I was young, I just accepted his attitude, but later I felt great tension over some of the restrictions he wanted to impose, such as my going out at night, or going with certain friends.

[10]Marion J. Levy, Jr., *The Family Revolution in Modern China* (London: Oxford University Press, 1949) p. 175.

My father and I did not agree, either, on my career. I wanted to go in for a professional course, but he wanted me to remain at home and teach; so I decided to leave home, and went to Bombay. I got a job there and cut off all contact with my home. Father was very annoyed at this. He sent one of my cousins to fetch me, and this man finally persuaded me to return. At home I tried to get a seat in a medical college, but when I failed to I had nothing to do. I led a very idle and rather loose life. Father began to grumble, and tried to persuade me again to go into teaching, which I hated. Mother was very worried because she thought that the situation would develop into a real fight between us; so she persuaded him to give me some money and I returned again to Bombay.

I have not gone home since then; so I have almost completely extricated myself from the clutches of Father's rigorous discipline. Now I do things according to the dictates of my conscience. (Case 138)

Not all young men, however, are able to emancipate themselves from their father's authority. In fact his control over his sons is still such an integral part of Hindu thinking that even at college young men will threaten or tease each other by saying "suppose your father knew what you had done!"

Case studies showed that fathers sometimes beat their sons up to sixteen or seventeen years of age. After that age there is no physical way of dealing with indiscipline, and a father who has not gained the confidence and respect of his children is at a loss. His only resort is to "nagging," which often turns his children still more against him.

In several cases fear seemed to be the dominant feeling towards the father, and when this was so it was such an effective deterrent that little or no punishment was necessary. "Father never had to cane us as we were all afraid of him. We never dared disobey him." On the other hand, the father's affection for his children often served to control their behaviour as effectively as fear.

On the whole the relationship between father and children is seldom completely free and easy, for as the main family disciplinarian the father tends to maintain distance from his children. Several interviews with older men indicated that they were often bewildered about how they should treat their sons.[11] "Fathers insist on their children studying, but how can they make them when they are adolescents? They tell them to, but the boy will be reading a novel under his books. The father can beat or thrash him when he is young, but this is harder when he grows older. It is finally impossible when he gets to be nineteen or twenty years of age; so the father gets desperate."

[11] An informant who had spent several years in the United States thought that fathers were surer of their authority in that country, and therefore did not have to assert themselves by physically punishing their children as much as did Indian fathers. In other words, the relationships of the nuclear family are more firmly established on the North American continent.

The father's main problem in a changing society is to gradually relinquish his position of dominant authority as his children grow older. This is most difficult for a father who has only ruled by virtue of his position, and has not gained the co-operation and real respect of his children. It is still more difficult when the traditional respect to older people weakens, and fathers no longer have the esteem of their children. Conflict between them will be most likely to occur if the father tries to maintain his power while the son insists on his freedom.

One father's dilemma in trying to handle his son and daughter after they had gained some independence is shown in the following interview:

> I have serious disagreements with my daughter and son. My daughter is in her last year at college. She is a wild girl with the modern ideas of the day. She sings well, is good at sports, and always wants to be in the limelight. I don't like this; I don't like my daughter singing in a public auditorium or dashing about like a tomboy. We don't seem to be able to settle our differences of opinion. I don't want to oppose her too firmly in case she does something foolish, like running away. I do my best to keep up to the times and change my attitudes about the new things that have taken place, but I feel they are for the worse. I can't reconcile myself to them, although lately I have been quieter about my feelings.
>
> My quarrels with my son are about his spending more time on college activities, such as sports and cadet corps, than on his studies. He hasn't actually failed any of his examinations, but merely passing them won't get him anywhere. He smokes, sees many movies, never is home early, and seldom studies hard. (Case 46)

## Mother

A woman's authority in the joint family household was determined by the length of time she had spent in it, and the position of her husband in relation to his brothers. She entered her husband's home in a completely subordinate role, particularly if she married as a child. Her position improved when she became the mother of children and when she gave birth to a son she was given some "esteem in the family, a greater degree of independence, and the right to have her voice heard in the women's quarters."[12] If she was the wife of the eldest brother, she would eventually be expected to assume complete authority in the domestic sphere.[13] Occasionally if her husband's mother was dead, she might have to assume authority immediately. In one case a young bride had to run her husband's household from the moment she

---

[12] Mandelbaum, "Family in India," p. 103.
[13] *Ibid.*, p. 101. "The mother of the eldest male in the family is in the position of authority. After her death the wife of the eldest male succeeds to her position; if she should become a widow before her sons are mature men, then the wife of the next eldest brother becomes head of the household."

entered it, for she was the oldest woman, even though a child bride. Later, as grandmother, should her husband die, although theoretically subordinate to her eldest son, she might have to take over the complete authority of the whole joint family.

The traditional attitude is that Hindu women get influence through their relationships with men; their positions as "mothers of sons" gives them their authority in the household. Moreover, their traditionally close relationships with their sons meant that they could dominate them through affection and love. It might even mean that a son would be so overpowered by his mother that he would not develop leadership qualities, and would, therefore, be dependent on her when he became head of the family. Many older Hindu men still lean heavily on their mother's decisions. Bachmann says that she has often heard a man, when taking an important step, say: " 'It was the wish of my mother.' ... In all circumstances, even when a mother urges a resisting son to go to battle, there is no way for him but obedience."[14]

In the cases studied, the position of the mother varied from that of being the chief authority of the family to that of being completely subjected to her husband. But in the majority of families, and particularly in those of the more traditional type, the mother had a position between these extremes. Her traditional role of dominance in the domestic aspects of family life has not been as publicized in literature and lore as the father's position as head of the family. But her position as consultant meant in reality that in most families she shared the responsibility of making the major family decisions with the father. These responsibilities increase in importance to the extent that her family unit is separated from the paternal or maternal stem. The mother is well qualified to act as adviser to the head of the house, for as she is the pivot around which the family revolves she is in a strategic position in relation to the whole gamut of household intrigue. Through her relationships with the women of the household and larger kin group she knows all the intimate details of the lives of family members and is thus in a position to advise her husband and later her son, and so control their decisions. Interviews also showed that she often influenced her husband's decisions by acting in the role of mediator between him and the children. She is closer to her children than he is and often they are afraid to go to him directly for what they want. In one family in which the father was hot-tempered, "Mother often intervened for us and shielded us from his wrath." In this way, "mothers," may have great power although the traditional picture of

[14]Bachmann, *On the Soul of the Indian Woman*, p. 25.

the Hindu woman shows her in a state of submission to husbands and elders. Several interviewees told of mothers who had played exceptionally authoritative roles even when their husbands were alive. "Mother was so authoritative and domineering that no relative tried to interfere with us, it would have been simply impossible." (Case 48)

In nineteen of the families interviewed, mothers were said to have complete authority in the family. These were mainly families in which the father was dead, and the mother had taken over control of affairs. But in one or two, the mother seemed to be the one who dominated the husband and could even stand up to her mother-in-law.

Mother was the complete authority in our home when I was young. She made the important decisions. She consulted Father, but she had the final say, and she always overlooked and ignored Father's opinions. Now, Mother is still the authority. She has a strong hold over everyone in the house. Father is insignificant. I don't want to obey her because I want to be completely independent. But this is impossible for Mother is too domineering and I am very much afraid of her. Grandmother is still alive, but she and my uncles have absolutely no authority over my parents. (Case 26)

At the other extreme were the families in which the wife had a mild personality and did little to influence family decisions. "Father dominated Mother. At first she used to make suggestions, but Father thought he was better informed and had had experience—in the end Mother just kept quiet." (Case 125)

If the families of this sample are indicative of Hindu families in general, there is no doubt that the father is still the most influential person in the Hindu home from the point of view of authority. In ten of the homes of the 168 interviewees who spoke of discipline the grandfather had been the chief authority, in ninety-three the father and in nineteen the mother. Besides this, grandfathers had had some authority in ten families, fathers in seventeen and mothers in thirty-nine. In fifteen families uncles were said to have had some authority, and aunts in nine. In only a few cases in which a father's personality interfered with his assuming his traditional role was he said to have no authority over the family.

A father's authority continues to be important when the children have grown up, for in ten of the families of married interviewees, the father was still the chief authority, and the mother in three. This implies that parents continue to exert influence over their married children, particularly when the young couple still live in the joint family. However, as some children marry they gradually pull away from the influence of parents, for nineteen interviewees said that the husbands were now the chief authority, and sixteen that the wife had more authority than either of the parents-in-law. Older brothers were also said to have had some authority in thirteen families.

Other relatives were seldom mentioned as having any authority or influence over immediate families except when some crisis had caused the withdrawal of one of the main supporting family members, such as the father or mother.

Very little has been written of the mother-daughter relationship, for when the daughter was married as a child she usually lived so far away that the occasional visit was their only contact after the daughter left for her husband's home. Now that daughters tend to marry at a much later age, the relationship between mother and daughter is changing. This change is not yet well enough established to permit full description, but some light was thrown on it in interviews. It would appear that even daughters who seemed to have broken away from many of the family controls still wanted help and advice from their mothers. In fact, this reliance will probably increase, for daughters who set up single families on marriage cannot count on guidance from their mothers-in-law or other older women, and so are more likely to turn to their own mothers for help.

One interviewee whose family had gone through the rigours of partition, and in which the father had died at an early age, had developed such a close relationship with her mother that they were more like sisters than mother and daughter. In another family, a very domineering mother supported her married daughter when she left her husband. These cases emphasize the point that even daughters who have achieved the mature state of married women may still depend very much on their mother's support. This adult dependence on mothers is understandable in the light of the strict training still given most daughters even in nuclear families. "Our girls are not allowed to go out alone after dark. Even in daytime they are expected to have some company when they stir out of the home. In any case parents must know where they go, when they expect to be back, what they intend to do, and whom they are likely to meet." (Case 47) However, the modern daughter tends to resent her mother's dominance, for she has learnt to become more independent, particularly if she has gone to college.

> Now that I am going to the university Mother ought to treat me more like an adult and not expect me to obey her in everything. But she still treats me as though I didn't know anything, and wants me to live a sheltered existence; so I often rebel against her and do things which I know she will

not like, such as reading "realistic" books, dressing in the very latest style, wearing heavy make-up, or going out with friends to pictures or restaurants without telling her of it. I don't feel guilty about this, because it's her fault for being over strict with me. (Case 12)

This desire for more independence will probably cause a greater amount of friction between mother and daughter, particularly when daughters are influenced by their growing outside contacts at college or work. On the other hand, the fact that they remain longer at home before marriage, may tend to develop a more companionate relationship between the two. If this latter trend develops, it may compensate a mother for her loss of control over her daughters when they marry. However, the strain in her relationship with her son may become more intense, particularly in the period of transition from one family type to another, for she not only loses her power to sway his decisions when he moves to a household of his own on marriage, but also has to accept a less important position in his affection.

*Husband and Wife*

In customary thought and before the law, the wife was on a level with servants, slaves and other members of the lower social classes in the traditional Hindu family.[15] The attitude of Hindu women to this subordinate position has not often been understood by Western observers, for they have seldom seen it in the context of the total family setting. Bachmann interprets the satisfactions which the Hindu woman did, in fact, derive from her seemingly "lowly" position:

To us "I am the servant of your feet" is humiliating, but later Hinduism so deeply impressed the ideal of a wife's complete devotion and self-denying service to her lord and master, whether he be human or God, as the only means of attaining bliss . . . that there is no humiliation in the expression to them. . . . With religious enthusiasm the wife took up her "Dharma"—not the Dharma of Brahmins which had to be fulfilled through knowledge, sacrificial worship and contemplation—but the Dharma of the slave who demanded complete devotion, obedience and service to her lord and master. . . . So the bride, in blissful joy, allowed bangles to be put on her wrists even though they were the symbols of slavery."[16]

Bachmann also illustrates this feeling when she writes about Gandhi's wife: "Whoever knows her is bound to believe that the self-surrender of the widow which led to the custom of self-immolation on the funeral pyre, must in certain cases have been quite voluntary."[17]

[15]*Ibid.*, p. 60.
[16]*Ibid.*, pp. 57, 148, 150.
[17]*Ibid.*, p. 156.

Thus, the term "obedience" as related to the husband and wife does not mean the same thing in India as it does in Western countries, for it does not imply external compulsion, but rather is seen as "the natural wifely desire and duty to please him, to serve him."[18] It is in this sense that the subordinate position of the Hindu wife cannot necessarily be said to be restricting, for, as it is accepted as "natural," she has a sense of freedom in her relationship to her husband which Western wives would not have.

The power of the husband over the wife was shown in several cases which cited husbands who had slapped or beaten their wives. The fact that the interviewees were not particularly disturbed by these instances implies that it is not an unusual practice for husbands to punish their wives in this way.

It has already been noted that a wife's authority in the household depended on her husband's position. If she was the wife of the oldest son, she might have power in household matters above an older sister-in-law. Any power she had over her husband depended on her personality, and on her ability to influence him to her views. It is quite possible that this influence was often considerable, and in some circumstances so great that she literally became the "power behind the throne." Such cases are found in literature and also in families interviewed for this study. In one family the mother of the interviewee had been so beautiful that the father worshipped her and became her complete slave. In a number of other families the wife dominated through her personality.

> Father has never dominated anyone. He was very tolerant. But Mother tried to dominate everyone. It was in her blood to rule. When Father married her he made the blunder of going to stay with her in her ancestral home; so Mother felt that she was providing his shelter. This caused a lot of quarrels between them.
>
> When I was growing up, I used to hear my parents constantly quarrelling and abusing each other. Mother always thought she had a higher social position than Father, and she used to abuse his ancestors. These quarrels reached a height when Father's business failed and he retired and depended on his properties for support. Sometimes the quarrels reached such extremes that Father would leave the house, and live separately for a long time. (Case 48)

However, not every woman attains a controlling position in the household, and even in old age some may still have "junior" status. Urquhart

---

[18]Margaret Cormack, *The Hindu Woman*, Teachers College Studies in Education, (New York: Bureau of Publications, Teachers College, Columbia University, 1953), p. 133.

speaks of the docility of gray-headed "juniors" in a large household, who never lost a certain childishness of demeanour.[19]

The frequently made statement that the power of women was supreme in the domestic sphere, in so far as it is true, applies chiefly to women who were wives of the head of the household. In a large household a number of the wives would never obtain any power at all except over their children, and their husbands—if they were susceptible to their wives' persuasions.

Another factor which determined the authority between husband and wife was their respective ages. The wife was generally a number of years younger than her husband, probably had less education and certainly had less experience in the ways of the world because of her close confinement to the house. Thus the husband's greater experience and age put him more in the relationship of an adult to her than in that of an equal. This would be particularly true when widowers married second wives, who were often very young girls, a forty-year-old man sometimes marrying a girl of twelve.

However, it should be noted that, even in the joint family system there is usually a gradual change in the relations of power between husband and wife with time. According to an informant, "The husband is at first completely in control of his wife. But as they live together, and especially after children are born, they develop binding interests; so their relationship will gradually work out to a more even basis, where they share responsibilities and authority."

When industrialization affects the structure of the joint family and it breaks down into a single family unit, the relationship between husband and wife undergoes a major change. The wife gains a position of more importance because she is older when married, typically has more education, and there are no longer elder relatives in positions of authority over her. Moreover, if the wife grows up in a nuclear family she will be more accustomed to equalitarian relations between husbands and wives, and will tend to expect them in her own marriage.

On the whole, however, the traditional outlook on the husband-wife relationship is still so strong in India that it may be long before the more equalitarian ideal becomes part of the "natural" expectations of marriage. In a recent study, Desai found that although some Hindu women objected strongly to the complete obedience expected of them by their husbands, the large majority accepted the older concept of their subordinate position.[20]

[19]Margaret Urquhart, *Women of Bengal* (Mysore: Wesleyan Mission Press, 2nd ed., 1926) p. 43.
[20]Mrs. G. B. Desai, "Women in Modern Gujerati Life," Unpublished Master's Thesis, University of Bombay, Bombay, 1945, pp. 162–6.

Material from interviews supported Desai's study in that the majority of wives still accept their subordinate position to their husbands as natural, and look up to his superior knowledge and judgment. But the data also showed that many wives are consciously and unconsciously now wielding more authority. One interviewee illustrated the wife's position today by saying that in former days husbands would be seen striding along the street with their wives following behind carrying the bags and children, but nowadays the man carries both and his wife walks beside him. However, the new conception of their relationship is not yet clear, and the more modern husbands and wives often do not know exactly how the role of authority between them should be carried out. An older woman said:

When we were married, our husbands took so much responsibility on their own shoulders that we women did not have very much to worry about. Nowadays men are not so courageous. For instance, my son-in-law asks my daughter for her advice. But if anything goes wrong, he blames her for making the decisions, and this means a lot of quarrelling between them. (Case 57)

## Brother–Brother

In the traditional joint family the authority of brothers followed their age sequence, with the eldest brother holding a particularly powerful position, for not only did he have the highest position of prestige next to the father, but also, as he passed through the usual experiences of life before his younger siblings, he was in a position to lead and guide them. Another factor which bolstered the eldest brother's position of authority was that new privileges accompanied the ability to handle new situations, and as the eldest son normally attained these privileges before the others, his position always entailed more prestige than theirs.

A great deal of responsibility fell on the eldest son's shoulders when he replaced his father, for he took on economic responsibility for family members as well as moral and ceremonial leadership. His economic obligations included marrying his sisters, in the higher castes, and seeing that his brothers were educated and well settled in life. Nowadays he is often also expected to see that his sisters get higher education. A consideration of these heavy responsibilities shows why his position had to be one of considerable power, even before his father died. Normally this power increased with age until he was supposedly in control of younger brothers, even when they were adults. The continuation of such control was shown by one young man who had lived by himself in Bombay for a number of years yet still obeyed his distant elder brother.

The death of a father could bring about a crucial situation if brothers did not get on. Jealousy could also be the cause of conflicts between them, particularly if aggravated by wives who feared they were not getting as much attention or family goods as other wives. When the joint family breaks up, and brothers move into their own separate homes, day-to-day frictions are avoided. But they may not be separated from each other's authority, or responsibility for each other's families. And these responsibilities may become irksome as interests and ways of life tend to differ. All these factors show why the brother-brother relationship was one of potential conflict. The eldest brother's gradual increase in authority means that his relationship with his father changes as well as that with his siblings. Ordinarily their relative positions of power slowly equalize, and the son may finally wield authority over his father in all areas of family life except ceremonial rituals, for the father remains the symbolic head of the house even when he has relinquished all other prestige and power positions.

The eldest brother may have difficulty in taking over his position of leadership when he is not sure of his power, or in families in which a younger brother has a more forceful personality. If he is not sure of his authority, he may develop bullying techniques. Several elder brothers were reported to have beaten their younger brothers for small misdemeanours, and several interviewees said they had been completely cowed at home by their elder brothers. On the whole, however the elder brother enforces his will by building up attitudes of respect and fear in those who should obey him. This can best be done by keeping himself somewhat apart from his younger siblings.

The strict discipline which elder brothers were often able to maintain over younger ones in the joint family gives way to a relationship of more equality in nuclear families. In the transitional stage, elder brothers may consult their younger brothers more frequently, and, particularly when younger brothers move away from the ancestral roof, may find that they have little if any actual power over them. However, as in other changing family relationships, the notion of respect and obedience to elders will still carry over for some time, and younger brothers will probably not transgress their elder brother's wishes without some sense of guilt. On the other hand, the elder brother will be conscious of a loss of prestige or of failure if they so do.

## Brother-Sister

In the traditional Hindu family, the brother-sister relationship was an extremely close one. Their companionship began in early childhood, particularly if they were close in age. If the brother was older, he assumed the expected pattern of male dominance. If the sister was older, the relationship was more equal, as the respect due her age tended to balance the respect due his sex. However, in most instances the sister's authority over younger brothers depended as much on her personal ability to dominate them as on their relative ages.

Strain could arise in their relationship if the sister became jealous of the privileged position of the eldest son. But tension of this sort was not a threat to the family stability, for the sister normally left the house at an early age. Her power ended with her marriage unless she married a wealthy or powerful man who might influence her former family's affairs.

A girl's training for her subordinate position to men began early, and at the same time her brothers would be being trained for their more authoritarian roles.

> Mothers and grandmothers conscientiously watch over young girls and train them into complete submission and see that they also learn to worship males. In games, sisters must defer to brothers and be self-sacrificing. Even as little girls they see their brothers served first at meals. They see the mark of respect that the mother shows to brothers, which they do not get. They are therefore brought up in an environment where nothing special or great is either promised to them or expected of them."[21]

After a girl married and moved away to her husband's home, her brother's authority over her was theoretically at an end, for she then came under the authority of the men of her husband's house. However, a brother might be called in to protect his sister from her husband and in-laws, and to the extent that he looked after her, to that extent he would reassume his authority over her. If she was widowed and went to live in his household, she would assume the same subordinate relationship to her brother that all the women of the household had to him. If, on the other hand, she had money of her own, or had married a wealthy man, she might retain a very honoured place in her brother's family, and be able to exert more authority in his household than was generally expected of a widow. One interviewee said: "My aunt inherited 10,000 rupees when her husband died. She invested the money and brought property; so she always had an honoured place in our household. She had a lot of authority in the

[21] Bachmann, *On the Soul of the Indian Woman*, vol. 2, p. 1.

family too, and ordered us all about and scolded us. When she died, her four brothers performed her obsequies in a very grand style." (Case 57)

Brothers and sisters are on a much more equal basis of authority in nuclear families, particularly when the sister is the elder. In fact, unless the father dies at an early age and the eldest son becomes head of the house, no obedience is expected of sisters to brothers. However, in the transitional stage from one family form to another, sisters will normally still consult their brothers on important decisions, for the latter's wider experience in the outside world will make their guidance desirable.

*Sister–Sister*

The authority of sister over sister also followed an age sequence in the joint family, and the eldest sister's power over younger sisters was clearly defined and seldom questioned. She had an important position in the family in regard to the supervision of her younger siblings, and this gave her prestige as chief assistant to the mother. This task, along with a little housework, was her chief responsibility, but the change in age of marriage has given her heavier duties, and with these has come the possibility of assuming greater power in the household.

The death of a mother was a contingency which gave an elder daughter a much more important position, for then she might have to take over the organization of the household work.

In nuclear families sisters tend to maintain contact with each other and other family members to a much greater extent than in the traditional joint family. However, as the relationships within the nuclear family tend to be more equalitarian, older sisters are not as likely to maintain positions of authority over younger ones.

*Uncles*

If an uncle is older than the father, he may eventually become head of the joint family. In that case his role would be similar to that of the grandfather when holding the same position. But if the uncle is the father's younger brother his role is more that of consultant and adviser. An uncle's authority over his brother's or sister's family increased if the father died, for he then theoretically took over the father's responsibilities. In the families studied, this seemed to be particularly true of maternal uncles who on the whole seemed to have more influence and closer ties with the families than paternal uncles. However, this may have been due to influences carried over from the former matrilineal family system of South India.

The few families who mentioned that uncles and aunts had had much say in their family affairs were those in which: the uncle was head of the joint family; one or more of the parents had died and the children had been adopted by an uncle and aunt; children had been sent to live with an uncle and aunt in the city for their education; or childless uncles and aunts had grown so fond of nieces and/or nephews that they had taken almost complete control over them. In the last case the actual authority of the uncle and aunt over the children would depend on whether they were living in joint or separate family units. Sometimes they would be able to check a parent's authority over their own children when living in joint families. "When Grandfather died, Father became the chief authority of the family. But when I was punished, my uncle or aunt would object and speak highly of me to Father. On the other hand, if my cousins were punished, my father would remonstrate with my uncle, and tell him that his children were the best children in the world." (Case 173)

Unmarried uncles living with a family would sometimes have some power over nephews and nieces. One interviewee mentioned an uncle who was not only living with the family but also working in the father's business. This appeared to give him a lot of influence in family affairs. Another interviewee said that he hated his uncles and aunts because they spanked him when he was young, even against his father's wishes.

In spite of some of the above instances in which uncles played prominent roles in the control of nieces and nephews, their main role seemed to be that of family adviser. Maternal uncles were more likely to play this role for mothers, paternal uncles for fathers. However, if the father died, the mother would consult paternal uncles as well. Several interviews also showed that in important family matters, such as weddings uncles had to be consulted, and their consent obtained before the important event could take place.

In nuclear families uncles theoretically have no authority unless appealed to by family members. Moreover, the gradual separation of household units, and the decline in expectation of mutual responsibility, are usually accompanied by a weakening of control over relatives living outside the household unit.

## *Aunts*

The authority of an aunt over nieces and nephews is not nearly as extensive in the joint family as that of the uncle, and theoretically would only last while they were children. As little is said of this relationship in Hindu literature, all that can be done is to describe it in the light of the data collected for this study.

The aunts mentioned in interviews were often widowed sisters who had returned to the family on the death of their husbands, with or without their children. Such an aunt might have a good deal of influence in the family if her bond with her brother was close, or if she had wealth of her own. Otherwise she might play a very subordinate role. Very little was said in interviews of the relation of the aunt to the mother, except when the mother was a young bride. It is probable that, as the mother was the chief authority over the domestic side of the household, the aunt, even if older, had to conform to her wishes. It is also possible that, as the dependent member of the family, she was relegated the hardest and least attractive household tasks. On the other hand, if she had been the eldest sister of the husband, or very close to him, she might be able to dominate the wife.

Nuclear families are not expected to look after widowed aunts, and they theoretically have no influence over nieces or nephews. However, the closer contact of sisters in such families may mean that they will continue to have some indirect influence through the mother. But their formal authority would certainly not be recognized. Thus both the direct and the indirect authority of aunts, as well as that of uncles, lessens when family units become spatially separated.

*Father-in-Law–Daughter-in-Law*

The authority entailed in the father-in-law–daughter-in-law relationship is not as clear in literature and legend as that of the position of the mother-in-law in relation to her daughter-in-law. Moreover, the only time the relationship was mentioned by interviewees was when a mother-in-law had died and a father-in-law was living with his son, and his family; or when the couple were living in a father-in-law's house, and he was domineering.

Still less is known of the husband–father-in-law relationship. A few remarks in interviews indicated that it was a very formal one, except when the wife's father came to live in the young couple's home. Ordinarily a father-in-law would be expected to live with his sons when his wife died, or in his old age.

His relationship with his daughter-in-law as a young bride in the joint family was supposed to be a very formal one. The mother-in-law was her custodian and the young bride would not see much of him because of the customary distance maintained between males and females. However, just as the head of the house can be considerate and gentle to his own children, the father-in-law can play the same role with his daughters-in-law.

In our house Father-in-law was the authority, but he was very sweet in some ways. He knew the dishes liked by each one of us. He used to say: "This vegetable is a favourite of daughter-in-law number one and so we will have something that the second daughter-in-law likes tomorrow"; so not one of us felt left out or uncared for. He bore his authority so well that we never felt that it was authority.

When he bought saris for us and clothes for our children he used to bring the same colour and pattern for all of us. Even for the children he used to buy one single bale of cloth from which everyone cut his requirements. Not one evening did he forget to bring us flowers for pooja for our hair and pan-supari. He looked after all our comforts very well. He never punished us, but preached sermons instead to make us obey, which in a way were punishment enough! There was no unpleasantness in the family. Father-in-law saw to it that every member was satisfied and happy. (Case 57)

In nuclear family systems the father-in-law will not have any authority over his daughter-in-law, and control over his son-in-law only if the latter becomes dependent on him.

*Mother-in-Law–Daughter-in-Law*

It is perhaps the potential drama entailed in the mother-in-law–daughter-in-law relationship that has caused it to be one of the most publicized of all family relationships. Traditionally, a mother-in-law was able to wield more "naked" power over her daughter-in-law than could be exerted in any other family relationship except that between parents and children. However, although children are in completely subordinate positions to their parents, they are trained into family discipline gradually, whereas a daughter-in-law comes into her new home suddenly, and has no one but her husband to protect her. Moreover, a mother-in-law's position of authority over the women of the household enables her to abuse her power over her daughter-in-law more than is possible in any other family relationship.

In the traditional joint family a daughter-in-law entered her husband's home to a position of very low prestige, because of her age and the fact that she was a stranger. Her lowly position only changed when she became the mother of sons, but even then her control extended only to trifling matters, and sometimes even the care of her children was taken out of her hands by the older women.

However, a young bride would be at least partially aware of her future position and so would be somewhat prepared for her new role. First of all, the model daughter-in-law was pictured in folklore and religious writings, and was well known to all young girls. One of the model wives was a heroine called Sakhu, who lived in the eighteenth century, and is still worshipped because of her heroic toleration and silent suffering in her husband's home. She was, moreover, a good-looking, modest and docile girl.[22] Moreover, down through the centuries Hindu girls have been carefully trained for the daughter-in-law role. Urquhart quotes from the *Gava Halud*, a book which was written for young wives to advise them on their conduct as brides: "No matter what is being said about you, you must behave like a Siddhapurusha [Holy Man]. You must not give any sign of being hurt or annoyed. You should not even smile at the remarks. You must keep your eyes fixed on the ground."[23]

In the second place, the young bride had seen the treatment of daughters-in-law about her, and had also had many warnings from her parents. If they were loving parents they would probably advise her carefully about her conduct in her new home, for they knew the problems she would face.

Her exact position within the new household was strictly defined. If she was the wife of the eldest son, she had an important place, second only to the mother-in-law, and would eventually replace her as head of the household. The mother-in-law's direct and complete authority over the young bride was due to the necessity of integrating the new wife into the female side of the family.[24] The new wife's obedience to her parents-in-law came first, and her husband was not expected to interfere in their treatment of her. The only members of his family who were expected to treat her with respect were her husband's younger brothers, but she could not count on their support. She had no one to whom she could appeal to if the discipline was too severe.

If she was attractive enough to elicit her husband's support, her position might become even more difficult. If he sided with her, the delicate balance of family relationships was upset, and tensions created which might react back on her. Her supervision was not given over to her husband for this might have developed a warm, personal relation between them, which again might have caused strain to the joint family system.

[22]*Ibid.*, p. 122.
[23]Urquhart, *Women of Bengal*, p. 42.
[24]Levy, *Family Revolution in Modern China*, pp. 106–8. From the point of view of the family: "The daughter entered an unfamiliar family, and from the point of view of her new family, she posed the problem of the integration of a stranger into a tightly knit disciplined group."

Karve says that Hindu folk literature singles out certain relationships as being those of natural enemies. One of these is the mother-in-law–daughter-in-law relationship which seems to have been almost universally harsh, or at least strict in extended family systems.[25] Mandelbaum thinks that there is a tendency to institutionalize the strictness of the mother-in-law in the Hindu family so that they are *expected* to be harsh.[26] He quotes a poem to show the ambivalence of the mother-in-law's attitude to the new bride:

> Joy at the prospect of her coming
> But from you your son she's stealing
> Gape your dismayed mouth at the heavens.[27]

For although it is essential for her to have grandchildren, the daughter-in-law challenges her authority as well as her close affectionate relationship with her son. Srinivas believes that the mother-in-law is strict because her house is her kingdom and she does not want her daughter-in-law to rival her power.[28] The actual transfer of authority from one to the other must eventually take place, and it is institutionalized and expected. But it is not easy for the mother-in-law to reconcile the growing independence of her daughter-in-law. Her watchfulness over her daughter-in-law is at first so constant that many songs talk of the "ever-wakeful" mother-in-law who would interfere even if the bride goes to her own husband at night.[29]

Another reason for their conflict is that, as wives often outlive husbands, the mother-in-law is apt to be longer with the young couple. Moreover, as they live in the same house they cannot avoid each other, and the two women may spend most of their time together in cramped quarters. As their leisure time is also spent largely in each other's company they have fewer outside interests on which to release frustrations and aggressions.

In one case both mother-in-law and daughter-in-law had no escape from each other.

> I have a lot of problems with my mother-in-law. While my father-in-law was alive she was busy, so did not have too much time to criticize me, but now she has a lot of time on her hands.

[25]Irawati Karve, *Kinship Organisation in India*, Deccan College Monograph Series, 11 (Poona: Deccan College Post-Graduate and Research Institute, 1953), pp. 129–30.
[26]Mandelbaum, "Family in India," p. 101.
[27]*Ibid.*, p. 101.
[28]M. N. Srinivas, *Marriage and Family in Mysore* (Bombay: New Book Co., 1942), pp. 191–8.
[29]Karve, *Kinship Organisation*, p. 130.

She has very few near relatives and as my husband is her only son, she hasn't any other place to go, but stays with us all the time. The same is true for me. My parents are dead and I have cut off all connections with my only brother; so I have no place to go for a visit or a change. Day in and day out all through the year we have to be together. We have a lot of fights about my children for among other things she teaches them to disobey me. (Case 71)

Srinivas says that conflict between the two women may last until one dies or gives up: "But in some cases the struggle goes on, ending only with either separation of the pair from the joint family, or death of one of the fighters. Sometimes the mother-in-law might succeed in having the daughter-in-law driven out of the family."[30]

However, even living in separate houses does not always protect the daughter-in-law, for mothers-in-law can still exert a great deal of control over their sons from a distance or pay them long visits. "My mother-in-law comes to visit us for two or three months every year. Then the trouble begins." In another family, the daughter-in-law had to visit her mother-in-law two or three times a week, the son every day.

So many current proverbs stress the cruel mother-in-law that she must have been a fairly common phenomenon. Interviewees claimed that she could be utterly merciless, and the daughter-in-law could only escape her tyranny through suicide. Interviews showed that, out of thirty cases mentioning the relationship, thirteen had entailed a great deal of conflict, eight a good deal, and nine had been amicable. In several of these the conflict was specifically related to the question of authority between the two women, particularly in families in which the mother-in-law never relinquished her authority while alive. The worst conflict between mother-in-law and daughter-in-law for the leadership of the household probably occurs when the father-in-law dies, and the daughter-in-law theoretically becomes the wife of the head of the house.

A daughter-in-law may have a very difficult position in the joint family if her husband is absent from home for long periods of time, and so cannot protect her from the cruelty of the mother-in-law. "Grandfather lost his wife and immediately remarried a young woman. She became ruler of the family and Father suffered untold miseries from her. When he was married, his wife was also cruelly treated by the step-mother. Father was a doctor, and enlisted and sailed away when Mother was pregnant. He didn't come back for seven years, and

[30]Srinivas, *Marriage and Family*, p. 198.

Mother had to stay with her in-laws all that time. She was very badly treated by all of them and was unhappy the whole time." (Case 55)

In one or two cases the mother-in-law–daughter-in-law position of dominance was reversed, and the courage or aggression of the daughter-in-law enabled her to dictate to her mother-in-law. In one instance, a young bride of thirteen years of age "had the courage to speak up to her father-in-law and mother-in-law." This woman showed great aggression all her life, and completely dominated her own daughters. In one extreme case the daughter-in-law treated her mother-in-law so badly that they finally severed all connections.

> The break over the mother-in-law's power is a point at which the old and the new come into serious conflict. Once the problem is posed in a family, the young couple can either submit or revolt. If they revolt, they break the old family entirely, for its interlocking solidarities permit little compromise. If the son refuses to enforce his mother's wishes, she can ask his father to order him to do so; if the son defies his father, the old family structure is finished. Thus the break of the mother-in-law's power almost inevitably involves other crucial aspects of family structure.[31]

The dominance of the mother-in-law would be expected to decline as family structures change from large joint families to nuclear units, first of all, because they will be spatially separated and each will be in charge of her own household. Conflict might arise, however, when the father-in-law dies and the mother-in-law must live with her son and daughter-in-law. In the second place, the later age of marriage means that the daughter-in-law has her first contact with her mother-in-law as an adult, and so the relationship between them is more equal from the start. It will be even more equal if the daughters-in-law have more education. On the other hand, interviews showed that unequal education often caused friction between the two. Moreover, the factors which now enable a daughter-in-law to be more independent are precisely those which make her a stronger rival to the mother-son bond. "From the beginning of my marriage I couldn't get on with my husband and mother-in-law, for they had very narrow ideas. They couldn't understand modern ways. Their idea was that women should stay at home and cook and have children. Finally I separated from my husband and went back to live with my mother." (Case 74)

This relationship, then, is one which does not change easily. For although friction between the two may be lessened by separation, older women tend to try to maintain some supervision of their

---

[31] Levy, *Family Revolution in Modern China*, p. 316.

children's lives even after marriage; so that, even though the daughter-in-law escapes her mother-in-law's tutelage in some matters, in others, such as the care of her children, she may still find her interference. Finally, it should be noted that the picture of the mother-in-law as a disrupting factor in family life is still prevalent in Western countries, where nuclear families have been established for a much longer period than in the East.

*Other Relationships*

Just enough information was obtained on the authority entailed in the following relationships to make a few comments about them.

*Brother-in-law to wife.* Formality usually existed between the wife and her husband's eldest brother in the joint family, but her relationship with her younger brothers-in-law was normally friendly. Should her husband die, her brother-in-law theoretically took over the position of authority over her. In the transitional stage of family change, brothers-in-law usually become the wives' chief advisers rather than their controllers. "After my husband's death I was the authority in the family, but I left the important decisions, such as the marriage of my daughters, the education of my son, and buying property to my brother-in-law. Now that my son and I have moved away to another city I consult my son on important decisions. However, if they are very important I still write to my brother-in-law. He will be the head of the family while he is alive." (Case 57)

*Brother-in-law of husband (wife's brother).* Occasionally, in both joint and nuclear families, a husband will go to his brother-in-law for advice or assistance, but on the other hand he may be too proud to take help from him. In one family a husband was not as well educated, nor as financially well off, as his brothers-in-law, and would not accept anything from them.

Considering that in the joint family the husband's brother-in-law normally had a close brother-sister relationship with the wife, it may be that jealousies sometimes existed between him and the husband. If this is so, it cannot have been very disruptive, for little is written of this relationship in Hindu literature, and it was very seldom mentioned by interviewees. Jealousy might particularly occur in families where there is still a "psychological" trace of the matrilineal line, and in which the sister relies on her brother as chief adviser and protector.

*Sister-in-law.* A new bride coming into a joint family household, particularly in the days of child marriage, was in a subordinate position to her sisters-in-law unless they were a great deal younger, for the sisters-in-law would be in established positions in the household when she arrived as a stranger.

Conflict between them has not been as widely publicized as that between mother-in-law and daughter-in-law, but writers show that it often occurred in the joint family. "The girl has no harmonious relations with her husband's sisters. . . . Her sisters-in-law take sides with their mother and wage a ruthless war against her. The only persons to support her are her husband and her father-in-law. . . . The males support her, and the women are against her. But the men will be absent from home most of the day. And the women will always be there ever ready to get at her. Hence many daughters-in-law have jumped into tanks to end their lives."[32]

Srinivas goes on to tell of how the sisters tend to get the best of everything in the home, while the new wife may be insulted. They often combine against her and report any of her misdemeanors to the mother-in-law. Even after many years there may be trouble when the sister returns to visit her family.

In several of the cases studied sisters-in-law were the chief cause of trouble for their brothers' wives.

> My sisters-in-law were the chief mischief-makers in my home. They overheard our conversations, opened our letters, and sometimes even destroyed them. They carried tales to my mother-in-law. Whenever she was away from home, she put one of them in charge; so we were never free.
>
> They never considered it worth while discussing things with us because we weren't thought of as human beings. I might be standing right in front of my mother-in-law and yet be ignored. But the daughters of the house had a very important place in the family council. We were always treated like outsiders. We had to ask about our work, but the daughters of the house did theirs the way they wanted to. We even had to ask our mother-in-law's permission about how much of the provisions we should measure out for the cooking. (Case 81)

The relationship was saved from too much strain by the fact that the sisters-in-law normally left home at a fairly early age for their husbands' homes.

The husband had very little contact with his wife's sisters, and consequently they were almost strangers. If the vicissitudes of family life brought them together, their relationship would follow the usual pattern of the subordinate position of women to men.

The gradual emancipation of the brother's wife comes as she replaces her mother-in-law in the hierarchy of household authority, and as her sisters-in-law are married and leave for their husbands' homes.

---

[32]Srinivas, *Marriage and Family*, p. 194.

A quicker way of accomplishing her independence from them is to persuade her husband to live in a separate house.

*Husband to his in-laws:* Normally this relationship was very distant in the joint family, for, although the wife might return home for visits and for her pregnancies, she would not always be accompanied by her husband. If a family crisis arose in which the wife was forced to return to her own home with her husband and children, strain might occur in working out the authority arrangements between the husband and his father-in-law. The balance of power in this case would probably be determined by the personalities concerned, and the relative social and financial position of the husband and his male in-laws.

In nuclear families the influence of all the above relationships will depend on the intimacy of the different separate family units. However, little control over in-laws will be expected, and normally the families will depend more on close-by friends for advice.

*Summary*

The structure of authority, as the family moves from the joint to the nuclear form, weakens, and, as the small family units beome separated from the large extended family group, comes to reside in each separate family unit. Moreover, the relationships within the small nuclear unit become much more equalitarian in character. These trends are in keeping with the general need for children to be brought up to be more independent in a world in which they may have to move far away from the original family stem, for, when separated from the control and advice of the extended family group, they will have to handle their problems and responsibilities by themselves.

### PUNISHMENT

The authority to wield power, and the methods by which it can be implemented, become institutionalized in all stable societies. According to Levy, the function of this institutionalization of power in the classical Chinese family was to prevent confusion over the distribution of power and responsibility among the different family members, and to ensure the acceptance of methods of enforcing them. "Succession to position of authority and responsibility was also clearly institutionalized, and thereby the disruption of the structure by the death of old members or the introduction of new ones was virtually eliminated."[33]

[33]Levy, *Family Revolution in Modern China*, p. 245.

The institutionalization of power includes legitimate sanctions that can be applied to transgressors. The histories of many family systems show many varieties of accepted kinds of disciplinary measures which parents can take to children. If these are clear to the child, he may not feel that they are excessively strict. But if the child feels that he is being unjustly disciplined, or that the punishment is too severe, then resentment is likely to arise.

The answers of interviewees to questions about the amount of discipline they had had when growing up is shown on Table III. No interpretation of the term "discipline" was given them, for it was thought that it was more important to get their own feelings towards family controls than the researcher's interpretation of it.

TABLE III
STRICTNESS OF FAMILY DISCIPLINE WHEN INTERVIEWEES WERE GROWING UP

| Interviewees | Strictness of family discipline | | | |
|---|---|---|---|---|
| | Very strict | Fairly strict | No discipline | Total |
| Married | 10 | 26 | 13 | 49 |
| Single | 16 | 36 | 15 | 67 |
| TOTAL | 26 | 62 | 28 | 116 |
| Men | 24 | 24 | 21 | 69 |
| Women | 2 | 38 | 7 | 47 |
| TOTAL | 26 | 62 | 28 | 116 |

TABLE IV
PUNISHMENT OF CHILDREN WHEN GROWING UP*

| | Punished by | | | | Types of punishment† | | |
|---|---|---|---|---|---|---|---|
| | Father | | Mother | | | | |
| Interviewees | Complete | Some | Complete | Some | Spanking‡ | Scolding | Reasoning |
| Married | 18 | 18 | 16 | 13 | 38 | 53 | 34 |
| Single | 13 | 14 | 17 | 13 | 67 | 50 | 20 |
| TOTAL | 31 | 32 | 33 | 26 | 105 | 103 | 54 |
| Men | 22 | 23 | 5 | 19 | 67 | 48 | 26 |
| Women | 9 | 9 | 28 | 7 | 38 | 55 | 28 |
| TOTAL | 31 | 32 | 33 | 26 | 105 | 103 | 54 |

*The figures were broken down in both Table III and Table IV into marital status to see whether difference in age affected the family discipline, in other words, to see if the strictness of discipline is changing.
†Several respondents mentioned more than one type of punishment.
‡This term also included mention of slapping, caning, beating and thrashing.

Table III shows that roughly a quarter of those answering felt that the discipline in their homes had been very strict. About half thought it had been fairly strict, and the remaining quarter felt that it had been so light that they had hardly noticed it.

When the answers are broken down for sex, many more men than women thought that their home discipline had been very strict. But about the same number of men (about one-third) considered it to have been fairly strict, and the remaining third thought it had been very mild. A large percentage of the women who answered this question thought their home discipline had been fairly strict. Only a few said that there had been little or no discipline in their homes.

The fathers and mothers of both married and single interviewees seem to have handled the punishment of children about equally. Table IV shows that nearly the same number (31 fathers to 33 mothers) had taken complete control of punishing children, and about the same number (32 fathers to 26 mothers) had done some of the punishing.

Difference for sex, however, shows that whereas fathers were the main punishers of sons, mothers tended to punish daughters. In only a few families had the mother been the chief punisher of sons, and these were nearly all widowed mothers who were the main authority in the home. In about twenty of the cases cited, fathers and mothers had shared the task of punishing the children.

When the type of punishment given children in the homes represented by the sample is considered, it can be seen that of the 262 incidents of punishment mentioned, 105, or about 40 per cent, were spankings. Nearly twice as many single people as married, and nearly twice as many men as women had been spanked.[34] Only 54, or about 20 per cent, grew up in homes where parents reasoned with them and the punishment of the remaining 103, or 40 per cent, consisted of scoldings.

Other types of punishment mentioned by female respondents were:

---

[34]Cormack, *The Hindu Woman*, pp. 44–6. Cormack claims that punishment is used much more liberally in India than rewards. "In the East there is much less conscious guiding of the child than in the West. There is a lot of punishment; there are a lot of spankings." Spanking means slapping the child on the face, head or shoulders, not on the buttocks, which is considered to have a "sexual connotation" by the Hindus. This punishment continues for both boys and girls up to the age of twelve. Cormack's remarks do not agree with my interviews in saying that it is the mother who does the spanking, and that the father rarely touches them. On the contrary, my material showed that the father does a large share of the punishment of boys. Nor does physical punishment stop as early as twelve years. It may for the girls, but a number of boys mentioned being physically punished by their fathers until well on in their teens.

being deprived of food, being compared invidiously with cousins, being nagged or lectured, and being shown displeasure. Men interviewees had also been deprived of food, nagged, and shown displeasure. Additional punishments had been the use of ridicule, sarcasm, curses, swearing, threats, confinement to room, and promotion of fear. A few extreme cases of punishments were mentioned: "I was severely punished at home. Once my legs were strapped and I was suspended to a peg head downwards and caned." (Case 98) On the other hand, some parents tried persuasion as a way of training their children to family norms. Probably more parents used this technique than were reported, as respondents might not have recognized it as a means of coercion. A number, too, said that they had been persuaded to be good through affection, guidance, by advice, and expressions of regret. The following case illustrates a family in which persuasion was used rather than physical means of coercion.

Both Mother and Father were very affectionate towards us and they shared the duties of bringing us up together. Our house was a model one. If we did anything wrong Father and Mother would first preach about our morals, and how we should be thankful to God for bringing the whole family together and how affectionate and happy we were. Generally this was enough to stop us. If we still misbehaved, we were asked to go to bed early or stay in our rooms the whole day. Sometimes we were left behind at home while all the others went out. I never remember any other kind of punishment given to any of us. (Case 79)

Many interviewees considered "nagging" the worst punishment, for beating, although painful, was over in a few minutes whereas nagging continued and made the recipient eventually lose confidence in himself.

The punishment usually varied according to the seriousness of the misbehaviour and the relative anger of the parent. Children were punished for disobedience, mischief and not doing their work properly. In addition, boys were punished for spending too much time with friends and going to too many pictures. Punishment also tended to change with the age of the child, typically beginning with severe physical measures, then passing through a stage of scolding and finally ending with reasoning and remonstrating.

Fathers and mothers usually used different types of punishment: "Mother scolded, father beat me." Usually too, in families in which the discipline was not too strict, there was often one member whose discipline was strict or harsh. If this observation is correct, it might lead to the hypothesis that one strict person is usually necessary to maintain a family system, and, on the other hand, this person permits other members to be more lenient in their discipline. One interviewee said: "We were never punished. Father and Mother never even scolded us. But we were afraid of Grandmother. Her way of punishing was generally scolding. No doubt she had a great deal of affection for us, but we were all afraid of her. We would be eating our meals, shouting and discussing when Mother would say, "Grandmother is coming," and suddenly the noise would die down, and everyone would eat silently or talk very quietly." (Case 88)

No information was obtained in this study on the treatment of babies. Cormack says that her Hindu informants felt that the idea of punishing babies was so repugnant that they would hardly discuss it. When they did, they claimed that babies were only punished occasionally when the mother was in a bad temper, and that the punishment consisted of slaps. On the whole Hindu babies are so loved that they are normally kindly treated.[35]

Although much of the above analysis of discipline and punishment might be interpreted by Western standards of child training as excessively strict, the Hindu children seemed to show relatively little resentment of it. For family authority was so clear and definite, particularly in large joint families, and was such a normal part of the child's training, that they seldom questioned it. Moreover, although it was similar in many ways to the type of family discipline found in Western countries during the Victorian era, it seemed to have a different character, for the relationship of the mother and often the father to their children was usually relaxed, and the discipline seldom seemed to have the effect of promoting life-long distance or conflict between parents and children.

Informants said that parents who punished their children harshly usually regretted it, and tried to make up by showing affection for the child afterwards, or giving him small gifts. And the child would soon forget. Moreover, as "right" and "wrong" are clearly presented in the Hindu family, children usually know when they have done wrong and therefore feel that the punishment is deserved.

> Whatever punishment we received we took in the most natural way and without any resentment. We knew that it was for our own good. We never felt that the authority and discipline were too rigid, for they were always governed by affection and enlightenment. My parents never tried to reason with us when we were children. But later on, when we grew up, Father started consulting us on important matters. At present, although I am

[35]*Ibid.*, p. 15.

completely free of parental control, I still feel very strongly that it is good for me to be guided by my father, who is experienced and mature in his views. I don't do anything now that I know my parents would disapprove of. (Case 143)

However, occasionally, a child who felt that he had been punished unfairly, or that his parents had been unreasonably strict or harsh, would feel resentment. In several families life-long separation and antagonism developed between parent and child. The resentment of boys was usually against their fathers. This was heightened when their relationship with their fathers was not close and there was no bond of affection between them.

My father thrashed me until I was eleven years old. After that a crueller type of punishment was given me—that of admonishing me and speaking badly of me. I resented my father's punishment when I was a child, but couldn't do anything about it. But now I sometimes oppose him boldly—at other times still feel helpless.

My father always insisted that I should get home early, and as a boy this meant by 6:30 o'clock. If I was late, there would be a scene. Father would call me names and say that I was a vagabond and good for nothing. He used to compare me with my cousins, and show that I was useless.

I knew that he did all this for my own good, but he overdid it. Having always called me names and told me time and again that I was no good, he has made me feel helpless when I have problems. When I meet people I feel shy, and when I am with my teachers, or have examinations, I feel that I am stupid. I am always scared when I have to write exams, and even scareder when the results come out. I feel very inferior in spite of my degrees and the fact that I come from a good family.

It is Father's strict, even brutal, control that has killed my initiative and made me unsure of myself. I never can look him in the face when we talk, and avoid him as much as possible. (Case 157)

Interviews showed that a good many of the children in the families interviewed had been good, obedient, even docile children, and punishment had not been necessary. Several said they had never thought of going against their parents' wishes.

Most children learn at least some ways of avoiding punishment. Perhaps the most typical of these is by hiding behaviour which they think will anger their parents. Many of the interviewees used this method effectively. Secrecy was particularly successful for students who lived in hostels while attending college or who had moved away from home to live in large cities. An informant said:

I have often seen students hide their smokes and drinks, and even change romantic novels and detective stories for serious books when their fathers are coming to visit them at college. College men don't tell their fathers anything about what they are doing. They *won't* discuss their problems with them because, first of all, it would hurt their fathers to know, secondly, they want to avoid their displeasure, and thirdly, they know their parents simply won't understand them.

Students who change into European clothes at college often return to their native dress when they go home because they feel they would meet a lot of opposition from friends and relatives; so when the boy goes home for a visit, he conforms to the old ways of the family. I once went home with one of my students to his village. The boy was thoroughly westernized at college, but when he got back home, he sat on the floor for his meals, said early morning prayers, etc.

Husbands too often used secrecy to avoid quarrels with their wives, for they knew that their more conservative wives would not understand or countenance their failure to follow caste rules in the impersonal business world. In one case both father and son knew that the other broke caste rules at business, but neither acknowledged it to the other, nor spoke of it at home.

Sometimes children avoid punishment by keeping quiet when lectured by their mothers or fathers and then doing as they want, or by running away from home. Usually their absence is of short duration, and they are brought back by parents or return when tired or afraid, but in adult life this type of behaviour has more drastic consequences and sometimes results in final separation.

My life was full of quarrels and fights when I was growing up, mainly because of the fights Father had with the other members of his joint family. His mother and sister finally made it impossible for him to continue living in his native place because of their jealousy and intervention. The climax came when grandmother accused him of selling the ancestral property to buy new land in his wife's name. This insinuation enraged Father. He couldn't stand it any longer. He beat his brother and my mother and said that as he wanted peace, he was going away for good; so he said good-bye and left us, and went to Delhi, where he has lived ever since. He sends back money to Mother for our expenses, but he has only come back once since then. (Case 67)

This means of escape was so frequently resorted to that parents and wives were often forced to give in when sons or husbands threatened to leave home for fear that the man in question would never come back. In one case a wife who was very badly treated by her in-laws did not dare tell her husband for fear of his leaving and not returning. The suicide of several young people could be listed as the ultimate escape.

Several mothers who called themselves "modern" said that they stressed reasoning with their children rather than punishment. This typifies the method of instilling controls more commonly found in nuclear families of highly industrialized societies than in traditional societies, and is due to the need to fit children to adjust to complex and varying patterns of behaviour rather than to conform to clearly established roles.

## OBEDIENCE IN LATER LIFE

In the traditional Hindu family, children were expected to obey their parents, especially their fathers, without question. This implicit obedience gradually declined as children became more able to look after themselves and in turn took over positions of authority. More education than parents and jobs which make them economically independent are two important new factors which now permit sons and daughters to become more independent of parents' controls. Sons and daughters, too, may go away from home to school or live in hostels while at college, which are new mechanisms which enable them to gain earlier independence from parents.

Some insight into the extent to which early training in obedience carries over into adult life was obtained from the interviewees. It was evident that as adults they were more willing to have their parents control moral matters than the practical details of their day-to-day lives. The practical matters included: for women, choice of friends, dress, careers, spending money, children's education, and ordering meals; for men, clothes, food, smoking, spending money and cutting their hair (taboo in some castes). Of the seventy-one who mentioned the moral aspect, only seven wanted to be completely independent of their parents. Whereas twenty of the sixty-one mentioning practical details said that they did not want interference from parents in this area. When these figures were broken down for sex, approximately the same number of men and women felt that they still wanted to be under their parents influence in both moral and practical matters. However, less than half as many men as women felt that they should consult them in all matters.

About twice as many single men as married ones, and a few more single women than married women felt that they should obey their parents in moral affairs. The men showed almost the same proportion in practical matters, but the single women showed slightly more independence than married women in not wanting parents to influence the day-to-day details of their lives.

These attitudes could be roughly classified into three categories:

(*a*) *Completely dependent.* In this category, the interviewees still felt completely dependent upon their parents, and wanted to obey them even though they might be married, and perhaps living in separate households. Fifteen men and two women fell into this category. One was influenced by his complete acceptance of the family hierarchy of authority: "I cannot be independent. My father has a right to interfere and to influence my course of action and pattern of life. . . . My brother to whom I am much attached has also the right to advise me. I can't marry anyone I like without the prior sanction and approval of my father, brother and uncle. I can't take up any job without consulting my parents. I feel I am bound to take their suggestions and advice." (Case 117) Another was motivated by his deep feelings of affection: "I don't want to hurt the feelings of my parents, brothers or sisters in any way. I never keep secrets from my parents. I don't want to be free of their authority and influence. I have done nothing to displease them and feel I will never go against their wishes. I am an obedient and faithful boy, and my parents are proud of me." (Case 101)

In another case, a dominant mother had retained control over her children.

Mother never punished us for she said it made children timid and curbed their spirits. Even if neighbours complained against us, Mother always took our side. When a person is fortunate enough to get a mother like mine, I think I should obey her all my life. I should bow to her superior knowledge and judgment. We all obey her implicitly. My two younger sisters are married and live with their husbands, but they often write her for advice and act accordingly. I do feel guilty if I do anything that Mother forbids, and naturally it goes wrong and I have to go to her again for advice. (Case 72)

(*b*) *Partially dependent.* In this category, the interviewees were partially independent of their parents' control. The great majority of men and women fell into this category. They came from families in which comradeship existed between parents and children. Children were not afraid to tell when they had done wrong, and relied on parents as a "great source of help and strength in time of need." They stressed the experience and wisdom of parents as important in guiding them. Several of the interviewees were single young men who had left their families and yet still wanted their advice and help. One of these said: "In spite of being educated and independent, I feel I should obey my father. All of us feel this, not because we are financially dependent on him, but because father is enlightened and broadminded and has our welfare in view. The influence of our elders should always be with us. It will act as a check on our excesses. Their influence should be in the form of mild advice and directions. I don't wish to be cut off from them under any circumstances." (Case 98)

These cases showed that many young men and women who have at least partially gained their independence from their parents have not enough self-confidence to feel that they *can* direct their own lives without help from people they can trust.

On the other hand, several interviewees felt that when a difference of opinion arose between them and their parents they would be able to persuade their parents to change to their point of view. This meant a reversal of roles in that the children had to some extent taken over the guidance of their parents. These interviewees thought that parents should be consulted on important matters, but not implicitly obeyed. Women interviewees tended to qualify their remarks by such statements as that children should obey their parents only until able to make their own decisions, or in times of trouble.

(c) *Completely independent.* The men and women in this category felt that they were completely independent of their parents. One man and fourteen women gave this answer. A few of them wanted to break away from their parents' authority completely, expressing this in such phrases as: "Parents shouldn't poke their noses into their children's affairs," "Parents shouldn't dictate or interfere," "I feel I should be independent of my elders' authority and influence; I don't like to be treated as a kid and ordered about."

Sometimes early independence made the interviewees reluctant to now follow the advice of elders. "All these years I have made all my decisions by myself. I don't feel like asking anyone now and don't feel like obeying them either! I have never felt guilty, because my parents and husband never insist on too much obedience. I don't bother about my relatives." (Case 87)

Although these figures are small in number they suggest that the traditional idea of woman as the more dependent family member may be changing. However, it is possible that the sample of respondents was biased in that it contained a larger proportion of women who have become independent than men. It may be too that women who are somewhat more sheltered from the problems of family independence than men, may pay lip service to it without being as fully aware of its consequences—at least in the financial area—as men.

Further indication of the way in which childhood training is carried over was sought in the relative feelings of guilt interviewees had on going against their parents' wishes or orders.

Among the fifty-seven men and fifty women making this point, opinions were almost equally divided: thirty men and twenty-four women said they would not or had not felt guilt. Single men and women were more apt to feel guilty than married ones. These young people, being still at home, and not having had much opportunity of working out problems on their own, were still close enough to their parents to feel guilty if they transgressed their wishes. It is quite probable that their guilt is reinforced by fear, for they are still subject to various types of parental punishment, such as remonstrations and scoldings.

A slightly smaller number of women felt guilty than men. However, more women were restrained from going against their parent's wishes by this feeling than men. A few of the latter said that, even though they felt guilt, it did not restrain them from doing what they wanted. Several men and women qualified their feelings of guilt by saying that the pain they felt when they had misbehaved was due to hurting their parents, rather than guilt over transgressing some important value. This attitude seems to indicate that a large component of the guilt feeling does not necessarily arise from a violation of the moral norms of the society but rather from a feeling of guilt for personal hurt.

There are some indications that the boys who were more adjusted to life in the small or large joint family were more docile and less likely to have done anything to incur a feeling of guilt than those who were more independent of family life.

This analysis suggests that the training given Hindu children is still effective enough to ensure that as adults they will follow lines of discipline instilled in childhood. Guilt is still a deterrent to action and guilt feelings probably will increase as more young men and women, brought up to obey and trust their elders, find they must change from the customary way of doing things as adults.

## Summary

Although the structure of authority is well integrated with other aspects of family life and with the general structure of the society as a whole, it can be separated out as a distinct entity for purposes of analysis. In the traditional large joint family the power allotted each member was clearly institutionalized, and the means of transferring authority was so well defined that it was not upset by the birth of new members, or the death of older ones.

At only a few points, such as the possible rivalry of mother and son for power on the death of the father, was there a possibility of major disruption. Moreover, the hierarchy of authority was supported by well-instilled attitudes of respect to those in top positions, and distance between these members and those they controlled was a means of retaining these attitudes.

In this hierarchy the older generations were in authority over the younger, with the eldest male member the dominant figure. Studies of many societies have shown that, when the large extended family breaks down, the authority of the patriarch gradually diminishes, and each individual family unit eventually becomes an independent self-governing entity. This change in turn promotes changes in the hierarchy of authority within each family group. The father's authority tends to equalize with that of his wife, and his children, while still supposed to respect and love him, are no longer expected to obey him when they grow up.

In the extended family, male authority always preceded that of the female, except when age intervened: for example, an elder sister could sometimes control a younger brother until he became an adult. But in general the authority of a woman depended on the position of her husband in the household. In a patrilineal family system, her own family line is subordinate to her husband's, but in a matrilineal society her own family gains in importance. As some traces of the matrilineal system are still found in South Indian families, a maternal uncle often still has some authority over his sister's family.

A son has little need to take initiative in exerting power in a large extended family, for he always has an elder male member, uncle or father-in-law if not a father, to whom he may refer. He is therefore not usually trained to take responsibility by being given it, as is typical in highly industrialized countries. And yet, sons appeared able to step into positions of complete authority in times of crisis. As very little light was thrown on this area in the present study, it is one of utmost importance for further study.

The means of disciplining children differ from society to society. As long as they are institutionalized, and part of the normal expectations, they are not resented unless used cruelly or unreasonably; so, although the interviewees reported more physical punishment of children in India than is usual in most Western countries, very few showed resentment. Many of the subtler means of coercion, such as ridicule, persuading through affection, and playing on feelings of guilt, were not apparently thought of as means of coercion by interviewees, and therefore not mentioned by them; so an important area of family control was not investigated.

It is only when conditions change, and parents find themselves helpless to handle disobedient children that tensions, frictions and conflicts ensue, and parents must reconsider their methods of promoting obedience. In the period of transition parents are unsure of their authority, and both they and their children feel resentment towards each other.

The extent to which training in obedience is carried over into adult life can be seen both in the extent to which adult men and women are still willing to follow their elders' wishes, and in the degree to which they feel guilty if they transgress them; that is, to the extent to which these patterns are internalized, and become part of the person's conscience.

A number of families studied showed that the family's authority often remains as strong when the children have grown up as when they were young. But on the whole the interviewees experienced a gradual change-over from looking upon their parents as arbiters of all the details of life, to at least desiring to decide the practical aspects of their lives themselves. Not as many wanted to part from their parents moral precepts. A slightly smaller number of women felt guilty when transgressing their parents' wishes than men, but those women who did feel guilty were more restrained by it. Several maintained that they never felt guilty if they themselves were convinced that there was nothing wrong in what they were doing. But the majority still had some, if not complete faith in the wisdom of their parents.

Interview material showed that the family is still the chief enforcer of discipline. Closer contact of the mother with the daughter often makes her more concerned with her obedience, but many fathers punished daughters as well as sons.

Fathers and fathers-in-law lose their power over married children when they move to separate homes, especially if these are located far away, for they no longer have financial control over them. Nor is the son likely to be following the same occupation as his father; so the father no longer can guide and advise him in his work. Uncles and aunts also lose authority in the small nuclear family system. Only in times of crisis, or if the bonds of affection are very close, are they still influential.

One important question that arose during the study, and has not been answered, referred to the checks to personal power, for even when authority is strictly institutionalized, it is possible that the personality of a person, who takes over a position of authority will be such that he will be able to dominate people in positions who are theoretically superordinate to his own. Several reports of dominant mothers showed that people can in fact get away with a good deal of deviation from the expected norm.

The degree to which a person with a strong personality can extend his power into a series of roles is another aspect of this problem. A domineering wife, for example, will probably find it easier to be a domineering mother-in-law or grandmother as well. But, on the other hand, interview material showed that a woman can play an excessively dominant role as mother-in-law, and yet does not display this aggressiveness in her roles of wife or mother. It may be that in such cases the personalities of husband and son check any encouragement of this dominance in her relationship with them. More would be learnt on this point if the successive and concurrent statuses taken over by, say, a woman, were followed into her roles of mother, mother-in-law, sister, aunt, etc. A full understanding of interaction in role situations cannot be achieved until more is known of the way in which personality factors influence role performance.

When the extended family breaks down into single units, the father's authority tends to equalize with that of his wife, and children become more independent of parental control, particularly when other agencies such as schools and youth organizations develop and impinge on the former total authority of parent over child. Changes of such a profound nature cannot occur without strains and tensions among family members. Case studies showed conflict in many areas where the power structure is changing or confused. Children will first try to gain their independence by gradually achieving freedom in relatively unimportant areas, such as clothing or smoking. Other areas where the battle is typically carried on are in spending money, caste or religious deviations, education, careers and—perhaps the last stand of parental control—marriage. In his study of the problems of Chinese youth in a period of transition, Ai-Li says that their two main problems were, first of all, their conflict with parental authority and, secondly, the problem of finding new patterns and cues which would help them readjust to the new conditions.[36]

Boys and young men are more likely to come into contact with new situations than the more secluded girls and young women. They are also able to get away from the supervision of parents; so they can often practise new types of behaviour in secret. But, as girls are typically still more confined to the home, it is difficult for them to

[36] S. Chin Ai-Li, "Some Problems of Chinese Youth in Transition," *American Journal of Sociology*, vol. LIV (July, 1948), pp. 1–4.

hide their transgressions. Young men, too, are apt to move away from the family for education, to live in college hostels or to take jobs in other cities.

Parsons and others have shown that one of the great differences in societies in which nuclear families are the norm, rather than the extended type, is that the power structure of the family in the former covers only a small part of the individual's life, for in such societies such substructures as the religious and economic lie almost entirely outside the family system and its jurisdiction. The individual family member is, therefore, not as restricted by his family when he lives in a highly industrialized society, for other organized systems become more influential in his life. The changing Indian economy, for example, has enabled both men and women to achieve independence through their ability to become economically independent of the family. This ability to challenge the authority of their elders has enabled them to obtain freedom in other areas such as religion, caste attachments, marriage, and residence.

On the whole there is not yet evidence, among urban middle-class families, that even when they live as separate units, the control of the elders completely disappears. However, there is evidence that the older generation no longer dominates the younger to the same degree, or in the same way. Nor do they maintain their dominance throughout their entire lives, as was customary in large joint families. There is a growing tendency too for the younger family members to be treated as individuals rather than as family members. The distance the single family unit lives from the joint family, the length of time which they have been separated, and the relative age of those separated are some of the factors on which the continued authority of the main family depends.

The three major points of strain in the substructure of authority which occur with a changing society are found in the relationships of father and son, husband and wife and in the mother, son and daughter-in-law triangle. But the problem of a more equalitarian distribution of power will cause some strain in all the constellation of family relations, throughout the transitional period, until a new equilibrium and some stability are achieved.

• *Chapter Five* •

# THE SUBSTRUCTURE OF SENTIMENTS

AFFECTION AND LOVE are two of a society's strongest binding elements. Their opposites, dislike and hatred, can be extremely disrupting, particularly in such close intimate groups as families. Since the family is an informal structure, whose stability rests on sentimental attachments rather than rational planning, it is peculiarly dependent on maintaining cohesive rather than disruptive relationships between members. The very intimacy of its contacts means that the love or hatred of family members for each other can be very intense. It is thus imperative that the sentimental aspects of the various family relationships be institutionalized in such a fashion that conflicts and jealousies are kept at a minimum. This is why, while certain affectional relationships are permitted in long-established family systems, others are avoided. When they must be avoided, attitudes of respect and fear often replace feelings of affection and these help to maintain a distance between the two people concerned that eliminates the disrupting relationship of love: for example, in the traditonal Hindu joint family the father-in-law is expected to avoid his daughter-in-law.

Hindu epics and literature give a good deal of information on the relative affective feelings involved in a few of the major joint family relationships, and many hints of others. Those of mother and child, husband and wife, and brother and sister are clear. Some of the less important relationships are harder to define, but enough is known to enable the student to rank the relationships in an order of preferential attachments, which has been fairly well maintained in its original form down through the ages. Many studies of the affective elements of nuclear families in modern industrialized societies show a completely different rank order of affection and love. Green has described some reasons for the realignment of relationships in these families.

The structure of the modern American family represents in some respects a continuation of the earlier extended conjugal family and in other respects is partial dissolution. The outstanding unique characteristic of the modern family is its well-nigh complete isolation of the conjugal unit from previous generations, from following generations and from extended lines of kin. Husband, wife and children, if any, make up the typical household. Ours is a restricted conjugal family form and for that very reason its emotional ties are uniquely close. In most societies, the individual spreads his identification and loyalty thin over a large household and an extended line of kinsmen. In our society, the individual contracts his identification and loyalty within a small household; each other family member becomes of critical importance to him. In combination with other factors, this raises severe problems of adjustment.[1]

The above excerpt shows the profound shift that gradually occurs in the affective feelings of family members as family structure changes and helps to explain some of the important reasons for the intense family conflict which often occurs during the shift from one family form to another: for example, the mother-son relationship is the closest in the traditional joint Hindu family, but it becomes much less intense in the nuclear family and its supreme position is replaced by a strong husband-wife tie. Green's quotation also helps to explain why such deep feelings cannot change suddenly and clearly and why confusion and strain arise during the transitional period.

Table V represents the rank order compiled from direct and indirect statements of the interviewees of their feelings for various family members. It should be noted that as the interviewees were not actually

TABLE V
EMOTIONAL ATTITUDES OF FAMILY MEMBERS FOR EACH OTHER

| Relationships | Affection and love | Dislike and hatred |
|---|---|---|
| Mother-son | 115 | 5 |
| Brother-sister | 90 | 1 |
| Brother-brother | 75 | 1 |
| Father-son | 74 | 16 |
| Grandparents-grandchildren | 48 | 4 |
| Mother-daughter | 42 | — |
| Mother-children | 29 | — |
| Father-daughter | 27 | 1 |
| Father-children | 24 | 5 |
| Husband-wife | 16 | 10 |
| Sister-sister | 5 | — |

[1]Arnold W. Green, *Sociology: An Analysis of Life in Modern Society* (New York: McGraw-Hill Book Co., Inc., 1952), p. 370.

asked to plot their order of family preferences, this ranking is suggestive rather than definitive.

The data show that the mother-son relationship is still much more often stressed as being one of love and affection than any other and that the brother-sister tie is extremely close. The fact that the feelings of husband and wife were so seldom mentioned, and when they were, were spoken of as entailing dislike and hatred as well as affection, tends to suggest that the rechanneling of emotions which has occurred in the Western World with the change to a predominantly nuclear type of family structure has not yet progressed very far among Hindu families.

An analysis of the intensity of the various elements of each relationship shows that the expected strength of the affective element often differs from that of obligation or authority. For example, the Hindu sister is expected to have a very close and loving tie with her brother, but she is not expected to undertake any serious obligations on his behalf nor is she expected to have any authority over him; so a rank order showing the relative strength of each element would analyse her relationships to her brother as being very high in affection but very low in obligation or authority: that is, a total picture of her relationship to her brother would show variations in the intensity of its different components.

### The Affectionate Intensity of Different Relationships

*Grandparents*

In traditional family systems, grandparents have very important positions and are usually regarded with veneration and respect, for, having lived long and through many family crises, they have gradually assimilated the wisdom of the group.

As grandparents grow older and are relieved of the more arduous family duties, they will have more time for their grandchildren and deep bonds of affection often develop between them. However, the comparatively short Hindu life span meant that many of those interviewed either had never known their grandparents or had only known one at all well.

Although some grandchildren expressed feelings of affection for grandparents, respect and fear were more often mentioned. Fear was particularly felt towards a grandfather if he was head of the family, although not more so than fear of a father or uncle in the same position. This implied that when the grandfather was head he held himself more aloof from younger family members and his relationship with them was different than when he relinquished leadership to his son. The grandmother, too, when she was head of the domestic household, was sometimes looked on as a figure of authority, rather than as an object of affection. If the relationships of grandparents and grandchildren were warm and affectionate, it meant a great deal to all concerned and the death of a grandparent would mean the loss of an important emotional bond. The extent to which a grandfather could play this role is shown in the following interview. "We all used to adore our grandfather. He deserved it. He was a very kind-hearted and noble man. He could instil high ambitions and ideals in the hearts of his grandsons. He was a symbol of love and sympathy. He never punished us." (Case 141)

The affection and love between grandparents and grandchildren were more marked in the joint families interviewed than in the small modern city families. This was partly due to the custom of older people returning to their native villages when old, and so being separated from the city family. Separation means that the contact of grandparents and grandchildren becomes less frequent; so warm intimate bonds between them do not develop as readily. However, these are usually replaced by stronger bonds between father and children and between children and friends. Another effect of diminishing contacts is to decrease the transmission of traditional ways of behaving. This tends to make the family less stable; but, on the other hand, it permits grandchildren to learn more up-to-date behaviour and attitudes than would have been taught them by their grandparents and so makes them better fitted for modern life.

*Parents-Children*

The intense desire of Hindus for children stems partly from the necessity of having a son to perform the funeral rites of his elders and partly from the fact that the son is the safe-guard of his parents when they are no longer able to look after themselves; but, more important, children are desired because they are loved.[2] They are, too, so much

[2]Gardner Murphy, *In the Minds of Men* (New York: Basic Books, Inc., 1953), p. 32. "Children are not individuals only—individuals to be prized, magnified, pushed forward, warned, threatened, rebuked, idealized, fancied in grandiose terms of future achievement. Children are the stuff of one's being. It is warmth and closeness to them that makes life important, meaningful, and continuous. The continuity of Indian life, without which one's own momentary existence is meaningless, is conceived naturally in terms of fruitfulness, in terms of the health, welfare, reproductive capacity, long life of all the individuals who issue from one's own body."

a part of the normal pattern of family expectations that a childless couple is pitied or looked down on.

The mother in the joint family was closer to the children and had a stronger affectionate bond with them than the father. Bachmann says that, as there are no proverbs that help us to understand a Hindu man's character clearly, it is difficult to determine the traditional attitude of the Hindu father to his children.[3] In fact, more material was found in literature and interviews on the attitude of Hindu children to their father than on his attitude to them. A few comments, however, showed that the father often had great affection for his children in the traditional joint family.[4] Interviews told of a few modern urban families in which this affection existed, but, on the whole, the relationship appeared to be one in which there was mutual co-operation for the family ends without too strong feelings of affection.

A few interviewees gave instances in which their relationship with their father had been extremely close, particularly in childhood. The father had spent a good deal of time with his children, reading to them, and taking them for walks. He took an interest in their education and spent much time discussing matters with them.

At the opposite extreme were a few families in which the father was an object of great fear to his children. "When we knew that Father was coming home we all trembled and locked ourselves in a room until we knew the frame of mind he was in. Our childhood was very unhappy because of him. None of us liked him. He had the tendency to quarrel with everyone. He bullied Mother and quarrelled with my uncles." (Case 67)

In a number of families, too, the father tended to stay so aloof from his children that they had no feeling of knowing him as a person. This type of father was often very authoritarian in character and would insist on their working hard all the time either at their schooling or at household tasks.

The greater distance between father and children than between mother and children is partly due to the household division of labour, for the father works outside the house, and is separated from his

---

[3]Hedwig Bachmann, *On the Soul of the Indian Woman: As Reflected in the Folklore of the Konkan* (Bastoria, India Portuguesa: Typografia Rangel, 1942), p. 82.

[4]*Ibid.*, p. 151. "When the husband gazes at the children of his wife as though he were looking at his own image in a mirror, he experiences the same joy as does the pure man who has been given his place in heaven."

children for most of the day. Several interviewees said that they had had little contact with their fathers while growing up.

Father was busy all day long with the affairs of our estate. When he came home at night he was tired, and had to entertain his guests; so we did not have any intimate contact with him. Father never worried about us; sometimes he even forgot the classes we were in at school. He never really worried about the family at all; he left everything to Mother. He wanted perfect comfort for himself. (Case 66)

The mother's warm relationship with her children was partly due to the fact that consideration and respect in her new home depended on her ability to produce the family descendants. Indeed, children were such an important aspect of her married life that even an expectant mother was made much of. She was given special respect and gifts, and was surrounded by every possible means to make her happy. Special ceremonies marked the different stages of her pregnancy.[5] Conversely the barren woman was so looked down on that childlessness is still a matter of dread for most Hindu women, and countless prayers are offered in hopes of a child, preferably a son.[6]

The mother was expected, too, to have utmost devotion for her children throughout her life.

It is the glorious devotion of the mother which invests her with that halo of sanctity before which the Hindu at all times bows in reverence. She gives life, gladly sacrifices everything—she was compared with the true deity already before the arrival of the Aryans on Indian soil. But it isn't in the conception of her creativity and preserving power as "mother of the

[5] Johann Jakob Meyer, *Sexual Life in Ancient India* (London: George Routledge and Sons Ltd., 1930), p. 199. The following quotations from Meyer show the attitude to a mother as distinct from a woman: "Above ten fathers or even the whole earth in worth stands the mother; there is no guru like the mother." On p. 204, Meyer again shows this attitude by quoting a scene from the Mahabharata in which a youth speaks of his feeling for his mother: "If one has a mother, one is sheltered, but unsheltered if one has her not. He does not grieve, age does not weigh on him, even though fortune betray him, who comes back home to his house and can say "Mother!" . . . He is old, he is unhappy, the world is an empty desert for him, if he is parted from his mother. There is no shadow like the mother, there is no refuge like the mother . . . there is no beloved like the mother."

E. M. Forster, *The Hill of Devi* (London: Edward Arnold and Company, 1953), p. 41. Forster shows that this attitude still prevails in recounting the story of a young maharajh: "To his mother . . . he was devoted. Years after her death he still mourned her, and one day he lamented to us, while tying a turban, that he no longer took pleasure in tying it, now that the beloved voice which could praise his skill had gone."

[6] Bachmann, *On the Soul of the Indian Woman*, p. 56. Bachmann quotes Kanarese proverbs to show this: "The field full of weeds is inferior, the barren woman is inferior." "It is evening where the barren woman goes." See also, M. N. Srinivas, *Marriage and Family in Mysore* (Bombay: New Book Co., 1942), pp. 175–6 where he tells of different rites to cure barrenness.

world" through which she has attained her greatest heights, but because of her immeasurable kindness, self-sacrifice, conciliating gentleness and her merciful forgiving heart that she was elevated to that pedestal on which she still rests today.[7]

Classical Hindu literature and proverbs also portray this close relationship. In Vedic literature the mother was compared to the light: "The mother died; then one feels the need of her as at the fall of night one feels the need of a light."[8] Children in turn are expected to have a "deep, earnest veneration" for their mother, whereas their relationship with their father was expected to be one of respect.

In the traditional joint family, the parents' relative affection for older or younger sons and daughters may have been so institutionalized that there was a clear order of preference, but interview material did not give a clear picture of this. Eleven parents had preferred their eldest son, and five their eldest daughter. A few expressed preference for their youngest son, and one father said that his youngest daughter was his favourite. In view of the importance of sons to Hindu families it was not unexpected to find that an only son was preferred to daughters.

On the whole, the in-between children were shown the least interest by parents. This interview material is supported by a Hindu legend portraying the order of affection of parents for their sons. "A father, mother and three sons met a demon who wanted to eat one of the sons. The eldest son offered himself, but his father objected. Then the youngest son said he would go to the demon, but the mother refused to let him go. Finally, the middle son said he would be the demon's victim, and no one objected."

In consideration of this indecisive attitude of parents to the order of their affection for their children, it was to be expected that a certain amount of sibling jealousy should be shown by interviewees. Usually this was felt between siblings of the same sex.

Our eldest brother was the favourite of the family. Everyone liked him, but as he was head of the family and belonged to another sex it didn't hurt much.

But I felt very badly when my eldest sister was preferred to me. Grandmother started it. She made a lot of my sister. To this day I feel sore about

---

[7]Bachmann, *On the Soul of the Indian Woman*, p. 38. See also, Meyer, *Sexual Life*, p. 210.

[8]Bachmann, *On the Soul of the Indian Woman*, p. 38. Bachmann is quoting a Hindu proverb which implies that when the mother is absent there is fear, uncertainty and insecurity. p. 35. "The holy reverence which, in the Hindu household, is regarded as due to the mother, is noticeable again and again in the daily life, for, to the Hindu, it denotes true religion."

it! My parents followed grandmother's example and mother consulted my sister on all important matters. We took out our jealousy by making fun of her. We would say, "Here comes the queen!" We used to feel very hot inside when she came out triumphantly from family conferences. (Case 52)

On the other hand, no system can endure if there is excessive jealousy between family members. More families said that there had been no jealousy amongst siblings than that there had. Some of the reasons given for this absence were that, when there were many children in the family, the parents simply had no time for favouritism and poor families had to put all their energies into fighting poverty and seemed to have no time for disruptive emotions of this sort.

*Father-Son*

There are many reasons for the preference of Hindu parents for a son rather than a daughter. In olden days a male offspring was desired because he could help protect the family from its enemies. He would also be an economic asset, for not only would he bring in income through his work and his wife's dowry, but he might eventually become the family's main economic support. From the day of his birth, therefore, a son was a potential source of family income, whereas the birth of a daughter meant economic deprivation.[9] She was also a possible source of disgrace to her family and caste should she remain unmarried.[10]

Another reason for joy on the birth of a son was that only a male descendant could shorten the period of penance of his father and grandfather after death, for he was the intermediary between them and the gods, and the only person who could perform the *sraddha* ceremony essential to salvation after death among the higher castes.[11] For these reasons the birth of a son was welcomed with pomp and

[9] Mrs. G. B. Desai, "Women in Modern Gujerati Life," Unpublished Master's Thesis, University of Bombay, Bombay, 1945, p. 16.

[10] Bachmann, *On the Soul of the Indian Woman*, pp. 116–17, 129. The undesirability of having daughters is shown in many sayings and proverbs: "The son is like the coconut palm, the daughter is like the monkey" (Dalgado, l.c., Proverb 1618). This proverb contrasts the queen of the trees with the stupid, useless monkey. Certain passages in the sacred Vedas even refer to them as being a calamity. Sometimes they are thought of as being the result of bad behaviour on the part of their parents: "He who is guilty of sin easily begets daughters" (Mainwaring: Proverb 1505). The economic burden of daughters to a man is implied in this proverb: "The head of him who has daughters is always bowed" (Dalgado: Proverb 1624). One story which illustrates the unhappiness of wives who do not give birth to sons is that in which the wives of a king were neglected: "We are just as unhappy as the slaves of a slave" (Bader, C., Proverb 106).

[11] Srinivas, *Marriage and Family*, p. 173. Informants said that occasionally a daughter, if an only child, was allowed to perform the funeral ceremonies.

splendour. After begetting a few sons, however, a daughter was desired as most of the Hindu festivals, such as Dasara, are centred around girls. A house without daughters was considered drab and inauspicious.

Informants said that in large joint households the comradeship between fathers and sons was sometimes strong, and they were closer in patrilineal families than matrilineal homes. But, as the father was always the law-maker and the one to impose restriction, the main attitudes of the son to him were of respect, awe and fear, rather than love. "Respect is the affect best suited to such purposes. It permits a high intensity in the relationship and forges a strong positive bond between the individuals concerned but it does not commit them to any primacy of concern for any individual's personal interests, as would be the case with a bond based on 'love.' "[12]

As the father was supposed neither to respect or fear his son, nor necessarily to have very strong affection for him, the son's feelings for him were much stronger than the father's feeling for his son. This was shown in interview material, in which the son more often expressed feelings of affection for his father than vice versa.

One or two interviewees said that there was a very close bond of affection between father and son and one or two said that they preferred their fathers to their mothers. At the other extreme were several expressions of deep resentment, hate and fear towards fathers. The majority of the interviews indicated a fairly affectionate relationship when the son was young, combined with a certain amount of fear and respect, and then a gradual drawing apart of the two at the age when the son had become a "young man" and yet had not quite gained his independence. Little companionship was mentioned between father and son as adults. One informant said: "There is no closeness between father and son. They never seem to get to know each other. The father is always a little like a stranger to the son and the mother acts as intermediary between them. The father learns what goes on in the family from her, for the family never gets together and 'chit-chats' over things as you do in the West."

On the other hand, the greatest incidence of dislike and hatred in family relationships was mentioned as occurring between fathers and sons. Since no institutionalized antipathy is expected in the relationship, this may be an indication of the strain attendant on the change to the more equalitarian relationship expected between the

[12]Marion J. Levy, Jr., *The Family Revolution in Modern China* (Cambridge, Mass.: Harvard University Press, 1949), p. 173.

two in nuclear families. It is a contrast to the father-daughter relationship where not one instance of hatred or dislike was mentioned.

One interesting suggestion that came out in interviews was that a close father-son tie caused less trouble for the son's wife than a strong mother-son relationship. Another was that sons who had a warmer, closer relationship with their father than with their mothers were more independent and had wider interests.

*Father-Daughter*

The Western World tends to follow the Freudian idea that presupposes a close relationship between sons and mothers on the one hand and fathers and daughters on the other. This view is probably responsible for the inclination to make the same interpretation of Hindu family relations, and postulate that because of the close mother-son relation the Hindu father will conversely have the warmest feelings of affection for his daughter rather than his son.

Interview material did not bear out this hypothesis, for whereas one hundred and fifteen cases of affection and love were mentioned between mothers and sons, and the mother-daughter score was forty-two, the father-son rating was seventy-four and the father-daughter score only twenty-seven. Although these ratings are suggestive rather than definitive they tend to show that Western interpretations cannot be imposed indiscriminately on other societies.

Some students believe that a strong relationship between father and daughter was not crucial in the traditional joint family system, for the daughter was only a temporary family member, particularly if she was married as a child. Her position in the household was one of complete subordination to her father, but his jurisdiction was over when she married and left for her husband's home. Consequently, the father's responsibility for his daughter was not as great as for his son. His duties to her consisted of supporting her until marriage, and providing an adequate dowry and a suitable husband.[13] As the daughter spent most of her time with the women of the household she might, in fact, have very little contact with her father while still at home. All in all, then, the father-daughter bond was so slight and of so little importance to the functioning of the family as a whole that it was seldom stressed in Hindu religion or mythology. But just because it was the least

[13]Bachmann, *On the Soul of the Indian Woman*, p. 178. Bachmann quotes the sacred laws: "If the father does not give his daughter in marriage before her maturity he becomes guilty of a great crime which increases with every month." The amount of effort entailed in finding a bridegroom is shown in the following proverb: "To get a daughter married it is necessary to wear out twelve pairs of sandals" (Dalgado: l.c. Proverb 195).

strategic relationship as far as the family continuity was concerned a strong bond between them was in no way disrupting.

In the large joint family the father did not need the companionship of his daughters. Informants told of families in which daughters never even talked with their fathers, but sent word to them through their mothers when they wanted anything. But when the family group grows smaller, the relationship seems to grow closer, for all family members are then more dependent on each other for companionship and affection. Moreover, as girls are married at a later age and have more education than their mothers, they tend to be better companions for their fathers. Interviews showed that some fathers enjoyed discussing matters with their educated daughters and were proud of their achievements.

On the whole, the affectional nature of the father-daughter relationship appears to strengthen as family structure changes from joint to nuclear.

*Mother-Son*

Male interviewees had had more than twice as many conflicts with their fathers as with their mothers. However, in spite of the close mother-son tie, fifteen men spoke of conflict with their mothers when they were young, and a few when adults.

One of the main reasons for the close mother-son relationships in the large joint family lies in the fact that the bearing of a son improved a woman's position in her husband's family more than any other single factor.[14] Urquhart says that love of her son was a ruling passion of a Bengal woman. It surpassed her devotion to her husband which, although raised to the level of a religious cult, had not the spontaneous quality of sheer devotion seen in the mother-son relationship.[15]

[14]Bachmann, *On the Soul of the Indian Woman*, p. 151: This is shown in the songs of a Hindu mother:
"Oh my little son, God's image of good omen.
Through thee my house becomes complete.
O my little son, gift of God,
Thou are Amrita (release) to me."

[15]Margaret Urquhart, *Women of Bengal* (Mysore: Wesleyan Mission Press, 2nd ed., 1926), p. 83. See David Mandelbaum, "The Family in India," in *The Family: Its Function and Destiny*, Ruth N. Anshen, ed. (New York: Harper and Brothers, 1949), p. 104. "For a young wife, her son in quite a literal sense is her social redeemer. Upon him she ordinarily lavishes a devotion of an intensity proportionate to his importance for her emotional ease and social security. . . . Even when a woman has several sons, she cherishes and protects and indulges them all to a degree not usually known in the Western world." An informant quoted the following proverb: "More exacting than the neck-husband [one who ties the wedding string or tali around her neck] is the belly-husband [the eldest son, i.e., the husband who has emerged from one's own self]."

Interviews showed clearly that this pattern of intense devotion between mother and son still exists in urbanized Hindu families. In fact, it was the relationship which was most often mentioned as being close and affectionate. Sons often maintained veneration for their mothers even as older men. "Father had great reverence for his Mother. As soon as he got his salary, he would heap the money at Grandmother's feet and then prostrate himself before her. Tears would glisten in her eyes when he did this. She would proudly say: 'My son rules a district but he is still very humble before me.'" (Case 61)

Another reason for the intense emotional bond between mother and son is due to the fact that, as she was not his main disciplinarian, there was not the same barrier between them as between father and son. Their relationship probably served the same function of releasing emotions as did the father's affection for his daughter. Another function it served was to give the mother a warm affectionate bond in her husband's home which she entered as a stranger.

Levy's analysis of the mother-son tie in the classical Chinese family may help to throw light on its relation to the mother-in-law–daughter-in-law and husband–wife relationships in the Hindu family. He believes that, although sexual relationships between mother and son were completely taboo, the extreme cruelty which the mother sometimes showed her daughter-in-law suggests at least a psychological incestuous attachment to the son. On the other hand, the reason their closeness did not cause strain to the husband-wife relationship was that, although the mother might act as a buffer between husband and son, she was not likely to stand up for him against her husband or incite him to defy his father. The father, too, was not apt to be jealous of their love because his own relationship with his wife did not depend primarily on affection.

Still another reason for the strength of the mother-son tie lay in the fact that they were not separated by his marriage. In fact, the English saying that, "A son is a son till he gets him a wife, a daughter a daughter all her life," is almost reversed in the joint family system. A daughter was married at such an early age that she became more like another woman's child, whereas sons remained at home and had a continuously close relationship with their mothers all their lives. She was their first responsibility; their duty to her transcended their duties to their wife and all elders, including fathers.[16] This great attachment, and the son's sense of duty as compared to his wife, is shown in the following saying from Bengal: "Shall I prefer my wife to my mother?

[16]N. A. Sarma, *Women and Society* (Baroda: Padmaja Publications, 1947), p. 75.

Oh, wicked thought! A man may forsake his wife without sin; but for a man to forsake his mother is the greatest of all sins."[17]

A mother's love accounts for her desire to monopolize her son's affections, particularly after her husband dies, for her subordinate position as a widow will make her lean even more heavily on him. It also accounts for the strain between the modern wife and her mother-in-law in regard to their relative position to the husband. As on informant put it: "It is terrible for the son, for he may be 'bound to his mother's apron strings.' She may always be telling him that he must look up to her, and take care of her; so he feels guilty if he ever goes against her wishes, and won't take his wife's side against her."

A number of the sons interviewed were so devoted to their mothers that they never wanted to part from them. "I love my mother more than myself." "Mother is the embodiment of love and affection." "Tears well up in my eyes when I think of my mother. Nothing interested me for six months after her death." Others spoke of her being their companion and guide. For several their mother was their main confidant. They told her all their troubles, and she acted as an intermediary between them and their fathers. One spoke of the high pedestal on which he had placed his mother; another said he found it almost impossible to disobey her or displease her. Several mentioned their deep gratitude for all their mother had done for them.

A number of other sons were much more moderate in their attitude to their mothers and one spoke of his violent dislike of her. This son was a very wilful boy, but as he had strong affection for his father, sister and brothers, it was not a case of revolt from the entire family. "I have never loved my mother as a son usually does. Sometimes I even feel contempt for her. And I have even treated her very unkindly and cruelly several times. I always feel sorry afterwards, even though I still feel that she deserved it." (Case 32)

If the data from interviews are correct in showing that the two closest relationships in the joint family are those of mother and son and of brother and sister, this means that a man's strongest emotional ties came in the period when he was growing up, for although the mother and son remained close together throughout life, the sister typically left while young, and although her relationship could remain

---

[17] Urquhart, *Women of Bengal*, p. 82, (quoting Rev. Lal Behari, *Bengal Village Life*.) See also: Bachmann, *On the Soul of the Indian Woman*, p. 25. "The duty of reverence to the mother goes so far that a son may in no circumstances desert his mother, even if the latter, through improper conduct, is ostracized and excluded for all social life."

warm and affectionate, other interests for both of them would intervene. It remains to be seen whether the changing relationship between husband and wife will compete successfully with the brother and sister relationship which may now be strengthened owing to the later age of marriage of women. And to what extent the tendency for sons to move into separate homes of their own, as soon as they are self-supporting, will affect the closeness of the relationship between mother and son.

The over-all impression from informants and interviews was that the husband-wife bond is becoming stronger. It seems true that the son is still on the whole more attached to his mother, but he will now protect his wife a little more from her demands. In any case, many variables will now affect the mother-son relationship, such as the growing importance of peer group relationships and new emotional outlets.

The close mother-daughter tie in nuclear families may somewhat compensate the mother for the transfer of much of the son's affection from her to his wife. The mother will also have less emotional dependence on her son when her affectional relationship with her husband intensifies.

However, no matter how the relationship changes, it is bound to cause much tension and strain, particularly for the mother. That some mothers are already aware of the growing competition of daughters-in-law for their sons is shown in the following interview with an informant:

The mother is in perpetual fear that some day her son may leave her. This makes her stick to him like a leech and try to make him more dependent on her by doing all possible loving services for him and even choosing his wife. All the time she wants to reassure herself that he still belongs to her.

In spite of all her attempts to keep him and of choosing his wife herself, she is finding that the mother-son bond is loosening little by little and the girl is gaining ground. This has developed a new situation, and the mother is preparing herself anew for retaliation, and so the conflict deepens. This is the main reason why mothers don't mind their daughters choosing their husbands but are critical of their sons if they do.

The mother-son relationship is still stronger in cases in which the father is dead. For the mother has nothing else to interest her, or keep her busy; so she dotes on her son. I have heard mothers of that type proudly say that their sons are completely dependent on them for everything. "Although he has a job he is just like a baby. I cannot leave him for a single minute. He wants me every second for everything, even to help him dress." The son who can manage everything himself and does not require anyone's help or advice is called a "rough man" or even a vagabond. Even if a man feels a little independent, he feels guilty to feel it. He feels contented, but not happy, in being dependent, and uncomfortable in independence.

## Mother-Daughter

The mother-daughter relationship, in the traditional joint family, is not as clearly defined in Hindu writings and literature as the relationship between mother and son. As the daughter was only a temporary family member, particularly in the days of child marriage, her role was always that of a child or very young girl. This meant that little strain was likely to occur in her relationship with other members of the family. She was, however, an economic liability. For one of the father's strictest duties was to see that she was married and in most communities this meant supplying an attractive enough dowry to procure a suitable groom.

The daughter theoretically owed complete obedience to her father as head of the family. But, as most of her activities were centred in the home, her mother was her chief supervisor and disciplinarian. Her mother also had the responsibility of training her for her future married role, a duty which she did not undertake lightly. For the mother's prestige as well as that of the whole family depended on the way the daughter reacted to the work and discipline of her new home. However, she was not the mother's most important responsibility, for her duty lay first of all to her parents-in-law, then to her husband, then to her sons, and finally to her daughters.

On the other hand, the mother's close intimate contact with her daughters, their mutual household interests, and the fact that she did not owe them much may have allowed a warm informal relationship to develop between them. And the bond of affection usually remained between them after the daughter had left for her husband's home.[18] Indeed, the mother's sorrow when her daughter leaves for her husband's home is expressed in many folk tales.

In earlier times the daughter often married into a family from a distant village, and afterwards had few contacts with her family. Even if married daughters lived close by, or returned to their parental home for long visits or for the birth of their children, the mother was not

---

[18]Srinivas, *Marriage and Family*, p. 185. Srinivas stresses the tender sentiments which are found between mother and daughter. The daugther living in her husband's home is always thinking of her, and contrasting her present difficult position with her happiness in her parental home. "The memory of the million kindnesses of her mother surge up within her, making her nostalgic for home. . . . Home is home only as long as mother is alive. But once mother is dead, the knot is severed. Mother would have fought for her daughter's rights and privileges (some of them exist only to the mother!) as a tigress for her cubs." See also Urquhart, *Women of Bengal*, p. 84. Urquhart believes that the mother is often so eager to maintain her first place in her daughter's affections that she encourages her to complain about her in-laws and criticize them.

expected to have much influence over them after marriage. The daughter's return home was often a time of great physical and emotional relaxation, for she escaped from the strict discipline of her mother-in-law, and as she was older her relationship with her mother was much closer and more companionable than before her marriage.

It is not only the early separation from her daughter that saddens a mother at her marriage and helps to make her less anxious to have daughters than sons, but the fact that she will no longer be able to protect her when she leaves her home. "[In her new home] the girl's life bristles with dangers. Her husband may ill-treat her. Her mother in-law may torture her. Living as she does in her husband's joint family, she might be subjected to insults by her husband's brothers and their wives. They might look down on her if she is dark, and be suspicious of her if she is fair. Worse, she might be barren. Any scandal about her is a slur on all her relatives."[19] The daughter is, therefore, often looked after with special care, and everyone in the household, except perhaps a new daughter-in-law, will have a warm spot in his heart for her. When visiting her own home after marriage, she will be given special attention, particularly if her husband's position is higher than her father's. But even if she is poor, her mother will treat her with sympathy.

The mother-daughter relationship has probably changed more markedly than any other family relationship since child marriage has been abandoned. The daughter no longer leaves home when a child, but remains close to her mother until a young woman, and in this longer interval they develop common interests and comradeship. This is bound to strengthen the relationship between them.

This changing attitude of mother and daughter can be seen in the following interview:

Now that I'm a graduate and working as a tutor, Mother treats me more like a friend. She confides her domestic problems about running the house and managing the servants to me. She also takes me with her to all the women's functions she attends. Mother introduces me to her friends and feels proud of the fact that I did excellently in my B.A. examination. She insists that I wear her jewellery for these special occasions and also wants me to wear her lovely saris.

Mother and I talk quite freely with each other on all subjects. But with

[19]Srinivas, *Marriage and Family*, p. 173. Srinivas quotes a poem in the *Garatiya Hadu*, a collection of folk songs, in which the mother, when sending her daughter away covers her tear-stained face with the end of her sari, and says she does not want any more daughters. Another poem advises women: "Don't give birth to a daughter, for, if you do, you will have to give her away to someone, weep at her departure, and angrily curse Shiva for causing you this pain."

Father I don't feel as free. Perhaps it's because I only see him occasionally on holidays. He seems to me to be rather aloof.

I know I'll miss Mother dreadfully when I get married, because she is such a jolly sort of person. She always welcomes all my friends and is very considerate of all our feelings. (Case 7)

Several important points come out in this interview with a modern young woman. As well as showing the closer attachment of daughters and mothers with later age of marriage, it also describes the difference in relationship between fathers and mothers and their children. The father is respected, but he seldom has a close relationship with his children. The mother is the one who is relied on for affection and for psychological support. It also suggests that the changing relation between her and her daughters may be rivalling that of her relationship to her son.

In summing up the parent-child relationship, it could be said that marked changes take place when the small family unit breaks away from the large extended group. For one thing, children must be trained for more independence, for they may have to move away from the protection of the family. This puts them on a more equal plane with their parents, and this, in turn, makes them more companionable.

The mother-son relationship probably retains much of its affection in the nuclear family, but the new emphasis on love between husband and wife means that the mother will no longer have first place in the son's affections. On the other hand, her compensation will come in a more loving and companionate relationship with her own husband, and probably a much closer affectionate and friendly tie with her daughter.

The transitional period, in which the new relationships are not yet clearly defined, will probably cause much strain and conflict, for the deep family love of the intimate family circle can very easily turn to bitter jealousy and hatred. The children will have less respect and fear for their father, but on the other hand, may have more affection for him. It is difficult for him to remain as aloof in the small family group as he did in the large joint family and the loss of his close group of brothers will throw him back on his small family group for both companionship and affection.

*Husband-Wife*

The emotional tie between husband and wife is probably the most difficult of all Hindu family relationships for North Americans to understand. For the latters' stress on romantic love as an essential pre-condition to marriage, and as an important binding element of the marriage relationship, makes it hard for them to conceive of a satisfactory relationship without it.[20] There is no doubt that although the bonds which bind the Hindu couple are different from those of North America the relationship is often an extremely close one.

It has already been pointed out that many contradictions appear in proverbs and sacred Hindu writings concerning family relationships. These are due to the points of view of the writers, who consciously or unconsciously stress the elements of the relationship which seem to them to be true. When it is also taken into consideration that India presents the writer with many different regional, caste and language variations of behaviour, and even with different family systems, the surprising thing is that the husband-wife relationship has remained relatively the same, down through the ages, in most parts of India. This is due to the continuation of the same family structure and to the supporting models of family behaviour described in the early sacred writings, and passed down from generation to generation, largely by word of mouth, and also to the absence of other models of husband-wife behaviour to confuse the traditional ones.

Thus the norms of husband and wife behaviour presented in such writings as the *Mahabharata* and the *Ramayana* have had great influence in shaping the behaviour of husbands and wives in India even though the actual attitudes and behaviour of the two have often been far from the general expectations.

It is important to first show the way in which this relationship fits into the total family structure before describing it in detail. In the large joint family, the husband-wife relationship was not as structurally crucial as some of the others, for the wife came into her husband's home as a stranger, and could be fairly easily replaced if she did not adjust to her new family, or if she displeased them or failed to produce heirs. Her main familial functions were to produce the children who would in turn carry on the family line, and train them for their adult roles. Thus, her personal qualities in relation to her husband's personality were not as important as her ability to fit into his family in which she at first played a very subordinate part. It was only when her husband became head of the family, her mother-in-law died, and she became supervisor of the household that she took over a crucial family position. Her early function in the family, then, was mainly a servicing one, and the husband-wife relationship structurally quite

[20]Implicit in this attitude to romantic love is the notion that marriage without it is "immoral."

different from that of the North American family, in which it is the pivot around which the family revolves.

From childhood on, religious teachings prepared Hindu girls for their subordinate position in their husband's family. They were brought up to regard their future husbands as "lord and master."[21] Although modern Hindu girls do not now accept these religious interpretations as completely as their mothers and grandmothers did, and so do not dedicate themselves completely to their husbands, they are still expected to venerate them. This attitude is in some measure due to the fact that the husband is the only means through which the wife can gain respectable status in this world, and that she is also dependent on him for her salvation in the next.

On the whole the degree of emotional feeling expected between the two in the joint family was low, particularly in the early years of marriage. But as the wife's attitude was expected to contain at least an element of adoration, she probably got more emotional satisfaction from it than he did. However, there were probably many deviations from this norm and husbands and wives sometimes fell as romantically in love as their Western counterparts do today. If they did, it could be another binding factor between them, but its very intensity might cause friction in regard to other family relationships: for example, it would challenge the strong emotional mother-son tie. Thus, in view of the total family structure, romantic love could be a disruptive element and was not a necessary aspect of the marriage relationship.

On the whole, then, the relationship between husband and wife seems to have been more in the nature of the love which sociologists define as companionship, as opposed to the romantic type.[22] And yet, husbands and wives had relatively little in common in the large joint family besides the interests of their children. Urquhart describes this relationship: "To many a little wife her husband is almost a stranger, and she regards him with awe if not with actual dread. Comradeship does not thrive readily in an atmosphere so laden with inhibitions, and does not, as a rule, occupy much of a woman's time. Attention to

---

[21]Bachmann, *On the Soul of the Indian Woman*, p. 180 "Her object of worship and devotion was a mortal God. To him she dedicated all her thoughts, works and devotion in the most perfect yielding up of self." Mandelbaum, *"Family in India,"* pp. 102–3. Mandelbaum quotes an Indian woman who says that the husband sometimes comes to take the place of her father to his wife. And as her father was due respect and obedience from his daughter, "she was apt to find this substitute-father more comforting, or at least more approachable, than her own parents had been."

[22]E. W. Burgess and J. H. Locke, *The Family* (New York: American Book Co., 1945), pp. 366–82. See also other textbooks on the family.

his creature comforts is her first duty, but for companionship he goes to the men's quarters, she to the women's."[23]

The large joint family supplied the husband and wife with contemporaries in age and sex with whom they could get "companionship" satisfactions. This may have been one reason for their relatively good adjustment, for they were not wholly dependent on each other for deep affection or companionship. The wife had her closest emotional ties with her children, the husband with his mother, and each had a large group of their own sex in the same household with whom they could share their interests.

Their relationship changed as they grew into more responsible positions in the household. The wife might become her husband's main adviser and consultant. This would give them binding interests, and the solidarity of their relationship would undoubtedly increase as older family members gradually died off to whom they owed prior allegiance. The husband's emotional dependence on his wife would probably grow stronger when his mother died and he was separated from his sisters.

That the romantic component is not an entirely unexpected item in the relationship, is shown in a number of love poems speaking of married, premarital, and extramarital love, as well as love between young boys and girls.[24] But no matter how little romantic love or companionship was entailed the bond between the two was strong. This can be seen in the emphasis placed on the "oneness" of the two in early and later Hindu writings. "Whatever may be the qualities of a man to whom a woman binds herself by legal marriage, the woman herself acquires these qualities—in the same way as the river by its union with the ocean."[25] This sense of oneness implied that the chief duty of a husband and wife to each other was a "mutual faithfulness" until death "[the wife has] complete absorption of her soul in that of her husband, who becomes the lord of her soul and life of her life. She becomes so very much one heart with him that her spirit—her thinking and her doing—becomes completely rooted and absorbed in that of her husband."[26] The oneness is symbolized in the marriage ceremony, when their garments are tied together. It implies that they are one in

[23] Urquhart, *Women of Bengal*, p. 80.
[24] Srinivas, *Marriage and Family*, p. 188.
[25] Bachmann, *On the Soul of the Indian Woman*, p. 125. Bachmann quotes the writings of Manu (10, 67, 9 and 2). Also the following proverb: "They have their heart in each other's heart and their soul in each other's soul" (Dalgado: l.c. Proverb 61).
[26] *Ibid.*, p. 125.

religious rites, fasts, sacrifices and domestic co-operation. This view has been more recently expressed in the writings of Gandhi: "It is just as impossible for me to describe my feelings towards the Hindu religion as my feelings towards my wife. She moves me more than any other woman. . . . I feel that between us there is an indissoluble bond."[27] It was also expressed by interviewees. "My father was affecton personified but with strictness. My mother was kindness personified with love. They gave us moral support and taught us to cultivate inner strength, righteousness and truthfulness. They were so close to one another that we failed to see them as two personalities. They were just like one single authority with two sides of beautiful character." (Case 92)

There is no doubt that the husband-wife relationship was not always as amicable in traditional joint families as some of the epics would lead us to believe. And many wives have doubtless remained with their husbands in the past because there was literally nowhere else for them to go. They could not support themselves, as they were not trained to work outside the home; so their only refuge was their own family, which might not always be eager to have them back. Sometimes the wife would have a difficult relationship with her husband from the beginning of her married life.

At puberty I went to my husband's house. Then he had the usual tantrums of a young husband, for in those days a young man would be considered cheap if he was fond of his wife; so families usually expected trouble after the marriage, and also expected the troubles to cool down after a child was born.

My husband followed this pattern. He used to go away for months at a time, and we all worried about him. Then he would come back for a few days, then pretend to get angry at one of my little mistakes and go away again. This went on for two years. (Case 84)

Sometimes a very bitter relationship can develop between husband and wife owing to different backgrounds. In the following case the girl had married a man who had a much lower socio-economic position.

My husband and I used to have terrible quarrels. He was very angry when my mother sent my grandmother and two servants to look after me when I went to live at his house. After our baby was born, the responsibility of looking after it, and its illness were too much for me; so my mother took it back with her. My husband was enraged. He was jealous of the luxury and comfort of my mother's home. He wanted me to work night and day

[27]Mahatma Gandhi, *Young India*, p. 286.

like a beggar. Finally, the fights between us became too many; so I went back to live with my mother. After a while he wrote to me asking me to come back or he would marry again. My mother wrote back to him and said I would never go back to a man who didn't know how to behave to a wife who was well born and well brought up. (Case 72)

No family structure could have lasted down through the centuries unless the relationship between husband and wife was established in a way which would give satisfaction to both. The binding elements in their relationship were: the acceptance of marriage as a "natural" and inevitable part of life; common interests and goals developed in working together for their family and children; a strong sexual relationaship, which has always been a very important part of Hindu married life; a clear-cut division of labour between them, each having an essential role to play in the household; and the expected subordinate position of the wife which eliminated much conflict and tension. The husbands and wives interviewed found it very difficult to describe the relationship, partly because it seemed so "natural" to them that they had never tried to analyse it. Several laughed when asked whether it was companionable or not. Summing up their answers: sixteen respondents considered that the relationship between husband and wife was "very close"; one said it was "indifferent"; six that it was one of "dislike"; and four gave examples of "hatred" between husband and wife. On the whole it could be described as a relationship in which affection or love is not necessary, for other factors are present which make it a durable enough tie to carry out the function for which it was intended.

Perhaps it can be best summed up in the words of an informant:

They understand each other, for they have lived together for many years and so know each other thoroughly. Each even knows what the other thinks; so they often do not have to discuss matters with each other.

A man's relations with his wife are so natural that he can't describe them. It is a casual relationship with no fuss or emotion about it. There is no companionship between them.

The following more detailed accounts of the role of husband and wife will throw further light on this relationship.

*The Wife's Role*

There are many more allusions in sacred and secular Hindu writings to the role of the wife than that of the husband. This means that her expected behaviour was clearer and more definite in the minds of people and may imply more control over her conduct than that of the husband.[28] The two most important models for wifely conduct are Sita and Savitri. Sita, the wife of Rama, embodies the ideals of utter unselfishness and complete self-sacrifice. She never returns an insult and has all the characteristics which are idealized in womanhood. "Sita is wholly the Indian ideal of a woman: tender and mild, soft and dreamy as moonlight, self-forgetting, filled with love, devotion, sincerity, faithfulness, and yet, where it is a case of defending womanly virtue, nobility of soul and purity of body, a strong heroine, great above all in long-suffering, but great, too, in her unyielding, daring pride."[29] Savitri is another example of feminine perfection. She represents greatness of soul and limitless wifely love.[30]

Bachmann suggests that the custom of Sati only becomes understandable in the light of the complete self-surrender of the wife to the husband which is embodied in these models.[31] They represent, too, her complete submission to her husband and her sexual faithfulness to him.

This dedicated devotion was shown to be still prevalent in the attitude of some of the older interviewees:

[28]Srinivas, *Marriage and Family*, p. 195. Srinivas quotes M. S. Puttanna in describing the "perfect" wife: "She never got angry at anything said by her parents-in-law and by her husband. She never answered them smilingly. (A smile may indicate lack of respect!) She never laughed while talking to anyone. She avoided all talk with men. When she had to speak to a man, she turned her face away from him. She believed that her husband was her God. She did her work well and spent her leisure in listening to the sacred myths. She avoided bad people. She never talked much with the servant-maids. She never complained that she did not possess a grand sari, or a costly bodice. She never dressed gaudily . . ." An informant quoted the following passage to show the different roles a wife was expected to play:

> "In counselling like a minister,
> In companionship like a friend,
> In caring like a mother,
> In giving pleasure like a mistress."

[29]Meyer, *Sexual Life*, p. 427. Even as late as 1906 Swami Abhedananda wrote of Sita's influence: "Sita . . . noblest, purest and most perfect ideal of woman that India has produced—is now the exalted spiritual ideal of every Hindu woman, old or young. . . . She was the most wonderful character that the world has ever seen. To show her faithfulness to her lord she sacrifices everything; she was, indeed, like the personification of loyalty and purity."

[30]Bachmann, *On the Soul of the Indian Woman*, p. 154. See also Meyer, *Sexual Life*, p. 427. "A wonderful fineness of feeling and strength of soul is shown by the pearl of all Indian women, Savitri."

[31]*Ibid.*, p. 54. Sati is the custom of widows dying on their husbands' funeral pyres.

When I was growing up we believed in religion and that our husband was a lord who we must love and worship. Our lives were completely dedicated to his service and we were amply satisfied when we were paid back with affection and love. We were so devoted to our husband that there was no place in our heart for anyone else. Whatever we did we did for him. Our jewellery, our decorations, our dresses and our beauty were all dedicated to him for his pleasure.

When my husband died all was dark. I felt that I had lost everything. I was quite prepared to shed all my decorations, jewellery and beauty for his sake. If I had no lord to enjoy my beauty, why should I be beautiful? I gladly requested my relatives to shave off my hair, and only wore white saris.

I live now through prayer, and eagerly look forward to the day when I will attain eternal bliss at the feet of my god. (Case 82)

However, although young Hindu girls are still brought up on models portraying selflessness, self-denial and sacrifice, the desire for mutual affection and love is beginning to appear in their conception of their relationship with their husbands. Some interviewees said that whereas in the West love is supposed to precede marriage, in India it is meant to follow marriage. A few suggested that their attitude to their future husband contained the idea of romantic love. This may be partly due to the romantic type of love which is often portrayed in Indian as well as Western movies and to a wider acquaintance with Western literature.

As it is still rare for husbands and wives to share their social life, the companionship element in the relationship was not mentioned by many interviewees. In fact, one of the problems which the family faces when it moves to the city is for the husband and wife to develop common outside interests to replace the comradeship of the large joint family. One informant said:

In the city there is rarely any companionship between husbands and wives; so they have nothing to chat about at home. The husband may take his wife shopping, but seldom to the movies. They have probably never shared a social life in the past, and now haven't the common interests to develop one. They are not together in the evenings. The husband may have many friends, but he will never introduce them to his wife, and won't take her to parties with them; so she won't share many of his views, and he won't want her to.

Any companionship between them is, therefore, largely confined to the planning which must be made by them as joint partners in marriage. In this relation it is important to note that although the father is theoretically the head of the family, in reality he often consults his wife on important matters. "Father discussed all important matters with Mother for he had great confidence in her. Once when he had had some bad financial difficulties Mother was very cheerful through the whole affair. She could instil a sense of confidence in Father and make him very optimistic about the future." (Case 141) This interview hints at one of the underlying bonds of the marriage, that is, that the husband receives psychological support from his wife. Probably too this pattern of consultation of husband and wife will increase as the women marry at a later age, and when they have received enough education to be a more intelligent adviser. In the large joint family wives were never consulted by their husbands until they grew old enough to take on important family positions. The change which has come about in their position in three generations is shown in the following excerpt from an interview:

My father and mother did not have anything to discuss and they never even talked with each other before the other members of the family. In those days there was nothing to discuss, for the elders decided everything for them. But my husband and I discussed all important things together, and consulted my mother and brothers, or sometimes my sisters when we wanted their advice. Nowadays my daughter decides everything herself. She doesn't even write to tell me that she is going to do certain things. Her children seem to be quite independent and I do not think they will want her advice when they are married. (Case 84)

*The Husband's Role*

As the attitude of the husband to his wife is not as clearly depicted in Hindu literature as her relationship to him, one might be tempted to expect them to be complementary in intensity.[32] But this does not seem to give an accurate picture of the real situation, for although the husband's importance to his wife is often emphasized, her importance to him is only occasionally stressed: for example, when Manu spoke of the man as incomplete without a wife and son.[33] But it is doubtless that devout Hindus took their duty to their wives seriously in the joint family, for they believed they came to them from the gods. A husband's obligations to his wife included his duty to be an ethical and moral

[32]*Ibid.*, p. 82. Bachmann says that no proverbs exist that tell of a Hindu man's character, or his relationship with women. She says that this is because women's feeling about them would obviously have to come from women, and they have never written the books and seldom composed the proverbs.
[33]*Ibid.*, p. 200. On p. 81 Bachmann quotes Mitter: "In the writings and in the law book, as well as in life itself, woman is intended to be one half of the body of her husband, sharing with him the fruits of pure and impure deeds; he whose wife has not died, leaves half of himself to survive."

example and to protect, cherish and care for her. Even when first married he was supposed to look after her interests and support her views unless contrary to those of the elders. However, as his parents were his first consideration, his feelings for his wife were not expected to be strong while they were alive. She became more important to him as a mother and as they took over the more crucial family positions. The relationship could have deep emotional intensity, either of love or of hatred because of their sexual intimacy, but romantic love between them was considered dangerous, for it might so engross him that he would neglect other family duties. They were never expected to show any affection for each other openly, nor was it the custom for other members of the family to show overt expressions of affection in public. The only family members who were expected to be demonstrative were grandparents, who were permitted to caress their grandchildren.[34]

The husband-wife relation changes radically when the family system alters from joint to nuclear. Whereas in the first type of family it does not become of great importance until they take over the leadership of the joint family, usually in later life, in the latter it is of crucial importance from the beginning. It is the pivotal relationship on which all the others depend. Moreover, as it is no longer necessary for the husband to marry a wife who will fit in with the many and varied relationships of the joint family, he is more at liberty to select one who fits in with his own personality. In fact, because of its importance to the whole family structure, it is imperative in the nuclear family that their personalities be mutually satisfying. It is important too for them to have strong feelings of affection and love for each other, for these will be the main cementing elements of the whole family unit. This is one reason for the strong emphasis on romantic love as a basis for marriage in modern industrial societies. The retention of the element of love between the two is facilitated by the fact that, in the

[34]As young men and women do not go out together socially there is no opportunity for them to hold hands or put their arms around each other in public, as is the North American custom. Young girls and women, too, seldom seem to touch each other in public. Boys and young men, and occasionally older men will often be seen walking hand in hand, or with their arms around each other. This has been attributed to homosexuality by Western observers, as it is not a custom in the West. But this is very debatable, for many informants said that to the best of their knowledge there was very little homosexual activity in most parts of India. The very close companionship between Indian men seems to indicate that what seems to be overt sexual behaviour is merely a cultural pattern, and can be compared to the way in which young girls in Western society often walk hand in hand, or with their arms around each other, with no homosexual connotation.

nuclear system, their relationship becomes more equalitarian in character and much more companionable. More freedom of choice in marriage is thus an accompaniment to the change in form of the family.

The attitude of the husband in the transitional stage from one form to another was described by an informant in this way:

> The husband now treats his wife with due respect and tries to understand her wishes. He tries to make her as happy as possible. He attempts to put into practice all the things he dreamed of as an adolescent. He also wants her to be a friend. However, he does not want his wife to be independent, and he certainly does not want her to be the type of woman who spends most of her time amusing herself and going to restaurants and with other men.

*Brother-Brother*

In family systems which are patriarchal and patrilineal, all male relationships are of crucial importance for the continuance of the family. Karve writes that "the ideal state in a family was good-brotherliness. . . . The most dreaded quarrel was the quarrel between 'brothers.' But that was also the most frequent quarrel."[35] In Levy's estimation, the relationship of brother to brother ranked next in importance to that of father to son. For a strong fraternal bond was essential to keep a family together for even two or three generations, especially as their competitive positions in the family could develop hatred and jealousy between them. A strong fraternal attachment also made it easier for them to maintain a solid front against the outside world, and helped to retain at least ceremonial solidarity if brothers separated on the division of the family property.

In the traditional joint family the relationships between brothers were close, for they were brought up in the boys' group and would often spend their whole lives in the same household. Living in villages, they had common problems and interests to bind them together and a strong system of mutual help. The relationship was particularly close in patrilineal families where women did not have much voice. Interviewees spoke of many minor quarrels over clothes and playthings when brothers were young. Severe quarrels sometimes occurred when the family property was divided, or when their wives and children had to live under one roof.

The greatest strain in the brother-brother relationship was likely to arise when the father died and the eldest brother became head of the

---

[35]Irawati Karve, *Kinship Organisation in India*, Deccan College Monograph Series, 11 (Poona: Deccan College Post-Graduate and Research Institute, 1953), p. 72.

family, for his authority then extended over all his brothers and their families and often meant that he had the power to determine their share of the family purse and control many details of their lives. Moreover, the difference in age between the eldest brother and his younger brothers was not as great as between father and son, nor did he have the status of an adult in relation to his brothers—which was one of the greatest supports to the father's authority.

A good deal of warmth and affection between brothers was reported in interviews. In fact, in the list showing feeling of closeness, the brother-brother relationship ranked third, next to the brother-sister relationship and before than of father-son. One brother said "I share everything I have with my three younger brothers. I take them to parties and introduce them to all my friends. We discuss all things freely together and are good friends." (Case 153) However, brothers in nuclear families were less close than brothers in joint families. "Nowadays brothers often do not feel at all close. They don't dislike or hate each other, they're just indifferent. They are like strangers except when they are in trouble, then they help each other willingly—but after it are not any closer. In only a few families brothers remain good friends, discussing their problems together, going out together and expressing their affection for each other."

On the whole, it seems that sentiments of responsibility and duty are more binding than feelings of affection. In spite of the fact that the intensity of the brother-brother relationships tends to diminish in nuclear families, interviews suggested that feelings of responsibility remained. It may be true, therefore, that a sense of duty will maintain a feeling of family solidarity even when no affection or love is felt.

*Brother-Sister*

Many stories and poems in Hindu literature tell of the strength of the brother-sister tie. In Table V it rates as the closest family relationship after that of mother and son. The depth of the feeling between the two can be estimated from three interviews, in which it was reported that brothers died with their sisters' names on their lips.

The affection between them begins in early childhood when they play freely together, particularly if close in age. "Brothers and sisters share everything, even to joys and sorrows." "Brothers and sisters do not need to explain things to each other because they understand each other."[36] In this relationship, however, there is no physical contact.

[36]Margaret Cormack, *The Hindu Woman*, Teachers College Studies in Education (New York: Bureau of Publications, Teachers College, Columbia University, 1953), pp. 20–1.

They do not touch each other, sleep in the same bed or undress in front of each other except when very young.

In olden days the close relationship lasted even when they were separated on marriage, for the brothers were the ones who carried presents or messages to their married sisters, and accompanied them back and forth between houses. "The brother-sister relationship is *very* close —almost psychic. We sense each other's loneliness, even when in different countries. At a girl's marriage this parting is especially keen. ... It is a much closer relationship than I have seen in America. ... The sister does everything for a brother a wife would, except have physical contact."[37]

In spite of the above interview with a modern Hindu girl, the opinion of the interviewees of this study varied as to the strength of this tie, today, in adulthood. A number of men interviewed, for example, said they did not feel as close to sisters as they did when they were children. Several spoke of severe conflicts with them. One man who had gone to Bombay to study did not even remember the names of his sister's children, although she too lived in that city. Another man seldom visited his married sister, who lived nearby, for he felt they had very little in common.

One woman interviewee complained that it was the brothers who turned away from their sisters when they married. If this is true, it would explain some of the jealousy which is commonly found amongst sisters-in-law when they first meet their brother's bride. On the other hand, eight interviewees claimed that their relationship was just as close as adults as when they were children. Three cases of exceptionally close feelings between brothers and sisters are given below.

> My uncle loved my mother, his sister, better than his own life. He used to bring her his salary and let her handle the household expenses because he believed so much in her ability. When uncle died in his prime, mother seemed more like his widow than his wife did. (Case 62)
>
> Father loved his sister so much that he said: "Give all your jewels and properties to your son and daughter-in-law and come and live with me in comfort till you die." My brothers are treating me in the same way now, they said: "Do not feel badly, but come to us and we will see that you are comfortable." (Case 65)
>
> When they were young my father and aunt [his sister] were very fond of each other. Aunt was very sickly and once stayed in bed for six years with tuberculosis. All those years Father would not leave her, even for a day. He gave up his B.A. and stayed with her to entertain and look after her. He was completely responsible for her feeding every quarter of an hour by spoon. Even to this day Aunt says that she would not be alive if it had not been

[37]*Ibid.*, p. 100.

for his nursing. They are still very close. I have never seen such basic unity of ideas between two living people. Father cared for his sister most, then his mother, and only after them for his wife and children. (Case 68)

In view of the close mother-son tie in the Hindu family it is interesting to note that there was no hint in the interviews that this close relationship caused jealousy between mothers and daughters, although several young men said they loved their sisters more than their mothers.

An informant summed up the brother-sister relationship in the following way:

In many families the brothers feel closer to their sisters than to their brothers. Sisters, too, often like brothers better than their sisters, at least until they are married. In the long run the sisters have a closer bond than the brothers.

Brothers, without exception, always do their best to see that their sisters are well married. They don't even resent having to give a lot of money for their dowries. They feel so strongly towards them, too, that they can't stand seeing them insulted by anyone in any way. They want them to have everything they want and are much more willing to help them than their brothers.

It is this strong attachment to sisters that often results in jealousy between them and the brothers' wives, for the sisters complain that their brothers' love for them declines after marriage.

Not a great deal of information was obtained about the intensity of this relationship in nuclear Hindu families. It is almost certain, however, that the bond will be less close, particularly in adulthood. For one thing, sisters are more independent, both economically and socially, in small family units. They have broader interests, and if the "dating" pattern is taken over in India, their affections will be more diffused over friends of the opposite sex. Brothers may even come to resent having to help support their sisters or pay their marriage dowries. Romantic love between husband and wife—one of the accompaniments of the nuclear family system—will also tend to concentrate their affections on their spouses rather than their siblings. On the whole, therefore, this is another relationship which will drastically change the alignment of expected family affections, and in the era of transition this change will probably cause a good deal of tension and jealousy between sisters and sisters-in-law.

*Sister-Sister*

The sister-sister tie is another relationship which has not been very fully described in Hindu literature. In earlier times sisters would not be together for long before their marriages, and after marriage might only meet occasionally at family ceremonies or when they returned home for a visit. However, interviewees said that it was usually a very warm relationship for they had many common interests when they were growing up and these were retained even when they were separated after marriage.

Jealousy could develop between them if the parents favoured one daughter, or gave a larger dowry for one to gain a better husband. But as older daughters had to be married before younger ones, there was no fear that a more attractive younger sister might be married off and an older plainer sister left unmarried.

The eldest sister's position was not very different from that of her other sisters unless a family crisis, such as the death of the mother, made her take on extra family duties. She was due some respect from her younger sisters, but as her responsibilities were not as heavy as those of the eldest brother, she did not have to maintain as much distance from them.

As interviewees gave very little information on this subject it is one of the family relationships which needs a great deal more study. As girls now spend a longer time at home before marriage, it is probable that the bond of affection between sisters will deepen. Changes in this relationship are perhaps the least likely to cause disruption and strain to the rest of the family structure.

*Uncle*

The uncle's relation to his nieces and nephews could be of great influence if they lived in the same joint family, particularly if the uncle was head of the household. The relation was supposed to entail affection and care on his part, respect and obedience on theirs. The greatest danger of strain in the relationship lay in the possibility of rivalry between cousins if a father paid too much attention to his nephews.

The uncle's obligation to his nephews is still often carried out in the economic and educational realm when he has left the joint family, and lives in another city. For he often boards and pays for the education of a nephew, or helps him get a job, as naturally and willingly as he would his own son.

The uncle-niece relationship only became important if her father died and the uncle assumed responsibility for her. Otherwise they did not see much of each other, even when living in the same household. The relationship would, therefore, be a rather distant one unless contingencies arose which permitted some affection to develop between them.

Case material showed that uncles and aunts, childless, or with children of their own, often adopted nephews or nieces or took them to live with them for long periods of time. In such cases they gave them as much affection as they would their own children, and the relationship between them would resemble that of parents and children.

In the nuclear family system there will be, theoretically, relatively little contact between uncles, aunts, nephews and nieces. Uncles will not be responsible for their nieces' or nephews' misfortunes, and the only tie will be ceremonial, in the sense that the uncles will be recognized as a member of the larger family kinship group, but will only be indirectly concerned with them and their families. Affection between them will depend on the closeness of their contacts, and the actual way in which their personalities agree. Very little was gleaned from interviews on how this relationship is actually working out in nuclear Hindu families today.

*Aunts*

In the large joint family the children were often in close daily contact with aunts who were the wives of their father's brothers. But as his sisters left the house on marriage, they did not usually know them very well. All aunts living in large joint families often looked after all the children in the house indiscriminately. But sometimes rivalry would creep in, and strain would be caused by fear that one set of children would be especially favoured. Or strain might arise when an uncle became head of the family and his wife head of the household. For this might create a completely different relationship between the aunt and her nieces and nephews.

The relation between aunt and niece was usually of shorter duration than that between aunt and nephew, and was confined to the niece's childhood, particularly in the days of child marriage. This would tend to make it a warm relationship, for children were loved in Hindu homes.

Data from interviews show that when an aunt became a member of a nuclear family she often continued to exert a good deal of influence over nieces and nephews, and might even take over the mother role. "We loved our aunt more than our father and mother when we were growing up. Mother had twelve deliveries; so most of the time she was either pregnant or convalescing. She always stayed in her room and didn't worry about anything. Our aunt did everything for us." (Case 65) In another family, the maternal aunt replaced the mother after her death so successfully that the daughter regards her as a mother.

The aunt on the whole, then, seems to have a very affectionate relationship with her nieces and nephews. As an elder they owed her obedience and some respect, but her close contact with them as children, particularly if she lived with them as a widow, engendered a good deal of mutual affection. Her relationship, therefore, depended on the extent to which she became identified with the family.

*Cousins*

A number of interviewees said they had played with cousins who lived in the same household when they were growing up. Otherwise they were seldom mentioned. Invidious comparisons, however, were sometimes said to have been made of their different children by parents, which led to strain and tension in the joint family. In one case, the mother-in-law used every possible opportunity to openly praise cousins to the detriment of the children of the daughter-in-law whom she hated. In another, the grandmother caused intense jealousy by favouring one of the cousins.

Otherwise the relationship was not mentioned enough to obtain a concrete idea of its influence on the families interviewed. It is probable that it tends to lessen when cousins are not brought up in the same household. If they are, it tends to be modified version of the sibling relationship.

*Father-in-law*

The expected emotional tie between the father-in-law and his daughter-in-law in the traditional joint family is somewhat obscure. The father-in-law was the person to whom the daughter-in-law was primarily responsible, and she owed him complete obedience. His duty to her was more concerned with her protection than her personal happiness or well-being. In the early days the relationship was one of avoidance. The father-in-law ordinarily spent little time with the women of the house, and his daughter-in-law was one of the last people with whom he was likely to come into contact. As she did not challenge his position in any way, he had no cause to fear her or to be jealous of her. He would respect her when she became a mother, and might eventually become fond of her.

From the point of view of family structure, development of intense affection or love between them might have seriously upset other family relationships: for example, it would have raised problems of sexual rivalry between father and son, and between mother-in-law and daughter-in-law.[38]

In nuclear families the affection between the two depends on the extent to which they are in contact with each other, and the adjustment of their personalities. Since they will live in separate households, they will not have the opportunity to develop strong affectional ties, but on the other hand, as the relationship will be freed from any element of authority or responsibility two possible barriers to the development of affection will be removed. This was another relationship on which too few data were obtained to see it clearly in its new form.

*Mother-in-law–Daughter-in-law*

The mother-in-law–daughter-in-law relationship is usually depicted as one of tension and conflict, and is used as a basis for many jokes and much ridicule.[39] In the days of child marriage, the daughter-in-law came into her husband's home in the subordinate role of "child." Her mother-in-law, particularly when in charge of the domestic work, was in a position of complete authority over her. In fact, one of her main duties was to train the strange newcomer into the ways of the household so that she could in turn take over its administration. In other words, she must see that the daughter-in-law became identified with her new family in such a way that its continuity would be maintained in all its traditional details. It was a relationship in which the daughter-in-law owed her complete obedience and respect, but the mother-in-law's only obligation was to keep her in good enough health to bear children for her son.

Thus the relationship was much more crucial for the daughter-in-law for it was not too difficult to find another wife for the son if the need arose.[40] As she was expendable, the daughter-in-law was of much less importance in the family structure than the son, for the loss of an only son was disastrous.

[38]Levy, *Family Revolution in Modern China*, p. 185. "It would have threatened the accepted political solutions of the kinship structure and the entire position of the mother-in-law on which the household organization depended. Few attachments could have proved more disturbing."

[39]Srinivas, *Marriage and Family*, p. 197. "Folk-lore is fully conscious that the entry of the girl into her mother-in-law's house is the beginning of the trial of her life." "Many poems express the agony of the daughter-in-law. 'I had a sinner for my husband and an ogress for my mother-in-law. I ate the food of sorrow and insult at the ogress's house.'" (Srinivas quotes B. Rangaswamy.)

[40]*Ibid.*, pp. 191–7. Srinivas says that many references in Hindu literature show the mother urging her son to get rid of his wife. However, as "society insists on a minimum cruelty," the mother-in-law cannot afford to get too bad a reputation for cruelty lest she find it difficult to get a girl to be her son's second wife.

As her survival depended on her ability to please her mother-in-law, her first major task was to adjust to her demands. This was made more difficult by the nature of the domestic set-up. As the women of the household were seldom apart, the daughter-in-law was under the constant supervision of her mother-in-law, and practically never out of her sight and command.[41] The classic and current Indian literature pictures the relationship as one in which the daughter-in-law often feared and hated her mother-in-law and the latter in turn was extremely jealous of her as a rival for her son's affections.

The jealousy inherent in the situation comes out clearly in the following excerpt from a case study.

My grandmother lost her husband (my grandfather) when my father was three months old and she was only seventeen; so she brought him up with the help of her brother. As she had not enjoyed the happiness of married life for long, all her suppressed feelings and unhappiness in being a widow came out on my mother when father married. All through her married life Mother had conflict and trouble with Grandmother, and once they lived in the same house for years without talking to each other. Grandmother had to wear the traditional dull sari of the widow and keep her head shaved. When mother dressed in her best saris, Grandmother used to cry for hours, she was so jealous. (Case 88)

On the other hand, the feelings of hostility between the two have probably been overemphasized, for if the conflict had been as constant and severe as suggested, the traditional joint family could not have borne the strain. Srinivas suggests that the stereotype of the mother-in-law was so prevalent that it often made them harsher than their inclinations would ordinarily have been.[42] Moreover, when the young

---

[41] Olga Lang, *Chinese Family and Society* (New Haven: Yale University Press, 1946), pp. 47–8. Lang shows the similar position of the daughter-in-law in the classical Chinese family. "The person with whom the new daughter-in-law was in close contact was her mother-in-law. And here the real drama of her life began. "The harsh treatment of the daughter-in-law by the mother-in-law is one of the most striking features of Chinese family life. The cruel mother-in-law plays in Chinese fiction and folklore the role that the wicked stepmother plays in European fairy tales. . . . In old China [the conflict between them] was particularly bitter because of the authoritarian character of the Chinese family and of the fact that so many young couples stayed in the husband's parents' home. . . . The husband, out of filial piety, had to side with his mother who often took advantage of her position. Perhaps she avenged her own unhappy life and bad treatment when she was a daughter-in-law herself."

[42] Srinivas, *Marriage and Family*, p. 196. "Generations of mother-in-law tyranny have crystallised into an approved social institution. Mothers-in-law who are very tender by nature are accused of lenience. Respect and awe towards the mother-in-law are the approved emotions, and weak mothers-in-law are forced to be harsh on principle."

bride came to her husband's home as a child, it is quite probable that the mother-in-law would often treat her as kindly as she would any child, and the daughter-in-law would be ready to treat her with the respect due all adults. Many epics taught that the wife must look to the comfort of her mother-in-law and father-in-law even before that of her husband. If the strain became unbearable the daughter-in-law could, and did, commit suicide or run away.[43]

This analysis of the traditional relationship helps to explain the extreme conflict that is likely to ensue between mothers-in-law and daughters-in-law when the family structure changes, for the closer husband-wife relationship necessitated by a smaller family structure directly attacks the former affectionate mother-son relationship. The old pattern of mother-in-law dominance will not change easily and as sons may continue to be trained to the expected pattern at the same time as they are being influenced to new conceptions of their relations to their wives, more conflict is almost bound to arise until the new relationships are established.

Two of the main factors which have increased the potential tension between mother-in-law and daughter-in-law is that, first of all, the daughter-in-law is now no longer a child when she is married but a young woman who has more self-confidence, knowledge and experience and is thus much harder to bend to her will. In the second place, daughters-in-law now usually have more education than their mothers-in-law. They have learned new theories of child care, housekeeping and personal behaviour. They know more about the outside world. All this challenges the mother-in-law's previous supreme position as adult adviser and source of knowledge, and tends to enhance the friction between them, particularly if they live in the same household.

An increasing number of young couples are now beginning to want to live in separate households when they marry. It is possible that young wives would often have preferred to live separately down through the ages. Today they are sometimes abetted by their mothers who are beginning to try to choose husbands for them who live far away from their parents.

This growing desire of young women to live separately tends to put the son in a difficult position, torn on the one hand between his desire for a calmer household and on the other by his feeling of duty

---

[43]*Ibid.*, p. 197. "A year ago a girl committed suicide at Mysore by jumping into a well because her mother-in-law always accused her of bearing only daughters." Interviewees told of several cases of suicide of young wives.

and affection for his mother. The growing strength of the husband-wife relationship in smaller family units definitely tends to weaken the affectionate tie between mother and son. It also enables the daughter-in-law to revolt more successfully from her mother-in-law's control, for her husband will be more likely to side with her than before.

The way in which some daughters-in-law spoke of their mothers-in-law shows the complete reversal of their position in the nuclear family as compared to the traditional joint family. The daughter-in-law now often speaks of her mother-in-law as "living with us" or "my mother-in-law helps *me* look after the house." This change in wording highlights a crucial change in the relationship.

The daughter-in-law now retains closer ties with her own family because of her later age of marriage. They tend to become her advisers and thus her mother-in-law loses her position as trainer and consultant, and even must share her grandchildren with her daughter-in-law's family.

In the Western family system it is the son-in-law–mother-in-law conflict which is emphasized in cartoons and jokes. This is an important indication of the profound change in relationships which occurs with changing family structure, for the nuclear family is typically a bilateral system in which the in-laws of both husband and wife have equal importance. But as the wife has already forged a very close relationship with her mother in her own home, it is often the wife's mother rather than the husband's who goes to live with her married daughter when her husband dies. At any rate, the husband is brought into much closer contact with his in-laws than he is in the traditional joint family. The current saying that the bride is "going home to mother" emphasizes this close relationship. She is never said to be "going home to father."

*Other Relationships*

*Husband–in-laws.* The husband's relation to his in-laws was very distant in early days, for his wife came to his home and contact with them only occurred on the occasional visit or family festival. Changing conditions are now often making the wife's in-laws as important as those of her husband. This means that, in spite of the son-in-law–mother-in-law tension which tends to develop in nuclear families, a man may develop closer affectionate relationships with his in-laws.

In the joint family the husband was supposed to respect his parents-in-law and his wife's older siblings. And they were supposed to give him special hospitality when he visited them. Yet no mother cared to take hospitality from her daughter's husband or stay under his roof.

*Sister to brother's wife (sister-in-law).* Relatively little has been said in Indian literature of the relationship between the husband's wife and his sisters. It can be assumed that because of its short duration the relationship was not of much significance to family structure, for the husband's sister would be marrying out of the home about the time the sons were bringing in their wives.

Having lived in the family all her life, the sister had a much more stable position in it than her brother's new wife. She would also probably be more favoured by her mother for she could reinforce her attitude to the new daughter-in-law.[44] This put the sister in a more powerful position than the wife although, theoretically, the position of the wife was more important.

The close brother-sister tie meant that many sisters were jealous of their new sisters-in-law, but since as daughters they did not have important positions in the household, the most they could do was to make the new wife's lot miserable, or help their mothers to do so. If they did this they could make it the second most difficult relationship, after that of the mother-in-law, for the new wife. But they must always bully her with caution, for their brother's wife might eventually get into a position in which she could get her own back.[45]

On the other hand, if they were about the same age, friendship might develop between them that could grow into love. Thus the personalities of the two would be more likely to determine the actual relationship than family expectations.

At any rate, as so little is known of this relationship in the traditional family it can be safely said that it was neither structurally important nor the course of much serious conflict.

*Brother's wife–brother's wife.* This relationship was likely to cause tension when brothers lived in the same household. Its strategic nature lay in the extent to which it could affect the relationship between the brothers. Ideally, the relationship between sisters-in-law was expected to be based on mutual respect, co-operation and affection. Although

---

[44]*Ibid.*, pp. 185–6. When the mother dies, the daughter-in-law is mistress of the parental home "and she pounces on every opportunity of insulting her husband's sister. She goads her husband to insult his sister. . . . The girl may have a very affectionate brother. But the brother is helpless before the real ruler of the house, his wife." "The sister cries out that she will live under crushing poverty at her husband's home in preference to a comfortable life at her brother's. For, the brother's wife has a tongue that insults."

[45]Levy, *Family Revolution in Modern China*, p. 199.

seldom mentioned in classical literature, it was in fact so important that the continuity of the family largely depended on it, especially after the father died, and the brothers had to reorganize their relationships of authority.

If their wives got on well, a good deal of affection probably developed between them; for they were not only in daily intimate contact with each other, perhaps for their whole adult lives, and their social life was largely confined to their small circle, but they might also share a disagreeable and even cruel mother-in-law. This gave them a mutual bond and an in-group in which they could get at least verbal release from her. This bond of sympathy would be enhanced if the daughters of the house were also against them.

On the other hand rivalry over their children, desire to be the favoured daughter-in-law or to get a larger share of the common purse, carrying tales to their husbands, or siding with the mother-in-law against each other tended to strain the relationship.

The first daughter-in-law had an advantage over the others, for by the time they entered the family she was already somewhat assimilated to the family way of life. The mother-in-law could always enhance the position of one by favouring her against another. The relationship between sisters-in-law might become very critical after the death of the parents-in-law, because the wife of the eldest brother then became the head of the household. As she could never exert as much authority over her sisters-in-law as the mother-in-law, she might have difficulty in keeping them in order.

In nuclear family units, there is much less opportunity for rivalry and strain to develop between brothers' wives, for they will not live together, or be dependent on each other. This may tend to make the relationship warmer and more affectionate, but on the other hand, the fact that they do not live in the same household will eliminate the intimate contacts on which deep love and affection often flourish.

*Brother-in-law to wife.* Mutual respect was expected between brothers-in-law and their brothers' wives. If this relationship was maintained, all went well; if jealousy caused by love or sexual attraction developed between them, it could cause much family disruption. This was particularly true of the junior levirate relationship between the older brother's wife and a younger brother. Several cases quoted in interviews showed that such a relationship still occasionally occurs, particularly in large joint families. It is thought to be partly due to their close association within the same household without other outlets for their affective feelings. However, it only actually upsets the family structure in so far as it affects the relationship of the brothers, and to the extent to which it causes jealousy on the part of a wife whose husband had been attracted to her sister-in-law. The extreme dislike of a brother and sister-in-law can also be disruptive, for it can cause rivalry between brothers and their wives for family advantage.

The brother-in-law–sister-in-law relationship tends to become less important when the joint family breaks down into small separate family units. Moreover, in modern cities both have many more outside interests and the opportunity of making a greater number of friendships outside the family circle.

### The Closeness and Affection of the Family Circle

As well as analysing the emotional intensity of each relationship, it is important to get an indication of the feeling of family affection as a whole. The majority of those interviewed looked back on their childhoods as happy, even though the discipline may have been strict. "Our family was very close." "Life was good and it was a thrill to live in such a family." "All elders were very cordial and amiable and lived happily for a long time."

One would expect that in large joint families, or in families that lived in close proximity to other kin members, the affection of children for nearby relatives would increase in intensity as they grew up. Murphy and others have pointed out the "rich emotional interpenetration of all the relationships" within the joint family.[46] Separation and the break-up of the large joint unit into smaller families is usually the main factor in loosening these affectionate ties. Contact with relatives may be kept up for some time through correspondence, festivals, family ceremonials and holidays. In fact, one's far-away relatives may remain closer in some ways than before, for the members are separated from the day-to-day frictions which often affect affectionate feelings. But, on the whole, these emotions need to be constantly refuelled by actual contacts or they gradually die.

Sentimental attachment to relatives is also lessened by outside interests and friends. The young men who had moved a long way from

---

[46]Murphy, *In the Minds of Men*, p. 31. "The term "family" has many meanings in India which it does not have for us. . . . In many parts of India, for example, the child may be nearly as close to its aunts as to its mother. In the same way, older sisters and all females of the group may be thought of by the small child as essentially similar or even identical in function. . . . In general, . . . the joint family is an emotional nexus of profoundly unifying value. One finds one's being in the family constellation."

home to Bombay were almost unanimous in saying that the home bonds were becoming steadily looser, especially after they had been six or seven years away from home and if they had interesting jobs. Friends were becoming increasingly important to these men. Often their only home contacts were with their fathers and mothers.

In the sample under study, about one-fifth of the respondents said that they still retained as strong feelings of affection and closeness to relatives as their parents. One-third more still felt some closeness to either maternal or paternal relatives, or to some particular family member, but on the whole, their feelings were not as strong as those of their parents.

I used to love and respect all my relatives and I know they reciprocated this feeling. However, as I grew up and left my native place to earn my living in Bombay, my attitude to all my relatives changed considerably. At present I don't see them very often and when I do, I feel that our relationship is rather formal. I don't feel the same need now for their company and I don't think that any of them are anxious to see a lot of me. (Case 143)

Some of these interviews also showed that, although affection was still held, the bond of common interests was weakening: "I visit my relatives about every three years and don't want to see them more often. I don't feel as close to them now as when I was living at home. Of course, I still love and respect them, but that is all—we have little in common. They no longer have any direct influence over me." (Case 50)

The remaining respondents rarely, or never, saw their relatives and were not interested in keeping in touch with them. Some had had severe conflicts with them and a few claimed that they hated their relatives and had no desire to see them again. One girl disliked her relatives so intensely that she wanted to move to North India to be completely free of them. Others were anxious to escape from close kinship control.

Time is another factor which makes it difficult for relatives to maintain contact in the modern world. "As far as I am concerned, I am very busy with my own affairs and I hardly ever find time to see my relatives. My contacts with them, and even with my parents and brothers, are becoming less and less frequent. My elder brother, too, doesn't see as much of them as before." (Case 137)

Finally, education may estrange families. The family of one interviewee was highly educated and gradually became separated from less educated relatives. A feeling of duty and responsibility to relatives was sometimes said to be the only factor that made interviewees continue their contact with them.

When these feelings of closeness to relatives are summed up, a decided trend can be seen in that most of the young interviewees claimed that their parents had been much closer to relatives than they themselves now were, even though the bonds between them had been very close as children. There had also been much more inter-family visiting when the interviewees were young. On the whole, relatives seem to have much less influence on the younger generation than they had on parents, although ego sometimes remained close to one branch of the family or to one particular relative—such as a mother, grandmother or uncle. On the other hand, interviews showed that "friends" are becoming increasingly important and influential in the lives of the younger generation.

There is, then, a gradual movement away from kinship and neighbourhood ties and local interests towards looser family ties, increasing outside friendships and broader interests with change in family form. At the same time, the bonds of the nuclear family tighten and stronger affections develop between husband and wife on the one hand and parents and children on the other.

## Summary

The stability of the joint family could not be allowed to disintegrate because of the personal feelings of family members, for it was the main stable unit of the society in which it existed. The relationships of the various members had, therefore, to be carefully maintained and were built up through attitudes of respect, fear, obedience and avoidance as well as love. The modern American family, on the other hand, is largely held together by the emotional bond between husband and wife.

If this analysis of the binding element of the nuclear family unit of modern industrialized societies is correct, then perhaps the greatest strain lies in reorienting the emotional intensities when family structures change.

The intensity of feeling within any one family system varies in emphasis from one relationship to another. When these are studied, a rank order can be discovered in terms of preferential feelings: for example, the warmest, most enduring tie in the Hindu joint family is found in the mother-son relationship. Next in strength of feeling is the brother-sister relationship. On the other hand, the husband-wife tie is the deepest emotional bond in the Western industrialized urban family. This comparison indicates the profound shift in emotional relationships which takes place with changing family structures. For the modernly educated Hindu girl who has been brought up in a single family unit which has begun to respond to changed conceptions of family relationships will find that, should she marry a man from a more orthodox background, she will have to compete for the affections of her husband against the two strongest traditional emotional ties—that of mother-son and brother-sister. On the other hand, the modernly educated young man who has been much influenced by Western depictions of romantic love will find his position difficult in relation to mother and sister when he himself marries.

Affective feelings are not always positive. Lines of antipathy become structured in family systems as well as affection. The strongest expected antipathy in the joint family system is between mother-in-law and daughter-in-law. This antipathy is likely to lighten as daughters-in-law live in separate households. They will also escape from the jealousy of sisters-in-law.

In the joint family a man has his closest and warmest relationships during his childhood when he lives in the same household with his mother and sisters. In adult life his sisters are married and have moved away, and even when close ties are maintained between them, their prior loyalty and eventually their identities become merged with their husbands' family and their sons. His mother may live in the same household with him all her life, but as the life span in India is short, this relationship may not last long.

As far as women are concerned, as children they have the warm relationship of brothers at home, and after an arid period when they first go to their husbands' home, develop the strongest bond of their lifetime with their sons. This analysis emphasizes the dependency of women on sons, for not only were they essential to their positions of prestige and authority but they were also necessary to their psychological adjustment.

In societies in which the nuclear family is the typical form, the pattern of affection for both men and women will be more similar, for they will both have strong bonds of affection with their parents and also with each other as man and wife. The time of least affection in their lives will be as older people when their own children have grown up, married and taken on closer affectional bonds with their own family. This will be particularly acute if one grandparent is left alone.

In the ancient joint family the Hindu wife was supposed to have greater affective feeling for her husband than he for her. This emotional intensity helped her to temper the change from her own family to that of her husband's. As the husband remained in the same household in which he had already built up strong attachments to his mother and sisters, his need for an emotional attachment to his wife was not as great. When the husband-wife relationship forms the core of the family group and he has not the same emotional relationship with his mother and sisters, then a strong husband-wife tie is important for both. In the North American family, which has adapted more fully to a highly industrialized way of life than any other family system, the husband-wife relationship is now the pivotal one and deep emotional attitudes have centred around it which act as a unifying cement for the whole family.

Other emotional intensities which will change with family form will be the strong mother-son tie, for the mother's affections will strengthen towards her husband and daughter and the son's to his wife and children. The brother-sister tie, too, will probably not remain as strong in the nuclear family, for the sister will not be as dependent on him nor have the responsibility of looking after him to the extent she did in the joint family. Sisters will tend, on the other hand, to grow closer, for they will be longer together before marriage and after marriage their greater freedom of movement will give them many more opportunities to be together.

Fathers will develop closer ties with their children as well as with their wives, but grandparents and grandchildren will possibly still maintain the same affectionate tie in nuclear as in joint families, for the longer life span of older people in highly industrialized societies will counterbalance the tendency in nuclear families for them to live apart.

The affection between uncles, aunts, nieces and nephews and cousins will depend on the spatial arrangement of households, their relative social status and common interests and their personalities. Close friends may completely replace these ties in importance.

The above analysis shows some of the potential areas of emotional strain when changes in family structure necessitate changes in the sentimental intensity of different relationships. Tensions and conflict will ensue until the affective feelings appropriate for the new structure become an accepted part of family expectations and the emotions of children are channelled along the new lines.

• *Chapter Six* •

# WORK AND THE FAMILY

PARSONS HAS POINTED out that, although all the structures of a society are interrelated, and so reciprocally influence each other, the family and the occupational system are particularly closely interwoven. He illustrates this point by describing the delicate balance that exists between the family system and the rapidly changing industrial economy of North America, and then discusses the main feature of the occupational system.

The most essential feature of our occupational system is the primacy of functional achievement as an ideal pattern which is highly institutionalized. This fact has a variety of implications.

In the first place, it implies that roles are organized about standards of competence of effectiveness in performing a definite function. That means that criteria of effective performance in a role and of selection to perform it . . . must be attached to impersonally and objectively defined abilities and competence through training. This contrasts sharply with the . . . role and status in a kinship group. Second, it means that the expectations of the role, together with its obligations and prerogatives, must be linked to the specific technical content of the function to facilitate its effective performance; . . . Third, procedures must be continually subjected to rational criticism, and a continual process of rationally founded improvement must be entered into. This is fundamentally incompatible with any traditionalized system of norms of behaviour—the rightness of behaviour is judged by its objective efficiency not by its conformity with models of the past.

Parsons also notes that when an occupational system forces many workers to move from locality to locality for work it is essential that their families should be able to move with them. Thus, the family form most suited to a mobile society is "an isolated conjugal family which [is] not bound to a particular residential location by the occupational, property, or status interests of other members."[1] The extent to which this family form has been achieved in India is still debatable,

[1]Talcott Parsons, "The Social Structure of the Family," in *The Family: Its Function and Destiny*, Ruth Anshen, ed. (New York: Harper and Bros., 1949), pp. 189, 190.

but it is clear that many Indians are now living in isolated conjugal families and that many more young couples are desiring to do so, for the new industrial economy allows ambitious young men to forge careers independently of their relatives.

A number of variables will affect the decision of a man who is able to choose his career in a mobile society. One will be the relative prestige of an occupation in relation to his family's expectations. Another will be the money income. Financial reward for work is possibly of less importance in a closed occupational caste system, but may be of paramount importance in determining choice in an open class society, where money is often the key to the fulfilment of an individual's physical and psychological goals. Thirdly, an individual must relate the probable income of the occupation to his dependency burden. If he is a member of a large joint family, he may eventually be the chief financial support of many family members. Finally, consideration must be given to the relative expense of living in city or village, for, the city dweller's expenses for housing, food, clothing, amusement and education are greater. He also typically spends more on medical care and hospitals. Thus, if there is choice in occupation it will be related to the person's total standard of aspirations.

## Some Effects of Industrialization

### Caste to Social Class

The history of the Western World demonstrates the way in which fixed social barriers appropriate for a stable type of economy, such as those of the feudal system, have given way to a more flexible type of ranking in the industrial age. Differences of history and geography have caused the changes to come about at different rates in different countries, but everywhere the trend has been the same, for a fast moving industrial economy cannot develop within a society whose hardened social barriers force every son to follow his father's occupation.

Ghurye and others have described the way in which the contemporary European class structure arose out of an estate system which had many of the same characteristics as the Indian caste system.[2] Ghurye expects that a somewhat similar social class system

[2] G. S. Ghurye, *Caste and Class in India* (Bombay: Popular Book Depot, 1952), p. 150. "The history of the industrialization of many countries shows that one of the fundamental changes in social structure which takes place with the coming of the modern industrial age is that the rigidly structured stratas of the feudal age gradually gives way to an open class society." The new era had few traditional barriers to contend with on the North American continent. This lack of traditionalism, combined with the freedom to exploit the rich resources of a new continent, were important factors in establishing an open class system.

will eventually supersede the caste system in India should industrialization continue.

It is important to note that, in fact, the caste system has never been a completely static system in India, for many external and internal factors have caused new castes and sub-castes to arise from time to time, and changed the prestige ranking of the caste hierarchy. However, all these changes usually came gradually enough to be almost imperceptible, and the Hindu society was always able to absorb them in such a way that the caste system itself was never seriously disrupted.

Although many caste customs have not yet changed radically in India, the tradition that sons should follow caste occupations has weakened enough among the urban middle and upper classes that little opposition occurs when young men choose new occupational lines, providing that those they choose have prestige equal to or higher than the traditional caste occupations. The wide variety of occupations of the fathers and sons in the sample under study bore out the above contention that occupational homogeneity of castes is no longer a fact.

The new occupational opportunities introduced by industrialization acted as incentives to lure the educated unemployed youth to the city, and also gave him visions of the possibility of getting a better or more highly paid job.[3] The first new fields to open up were in government service and the professions. The following quotation shows how an expanding industrial society stirs ambitions.

Under British rule government service gave prestige, security, and status, and later, when Indians were allowed to enter the Indian Civil Service, this service called the "heaven-born service"—heaven being some pale shadow of Whitehall—became the Elysium of the English-educated classes. The professional classes, especially lawyers, some of whom earned large incomes in the new law courts, also had prestige and high status and attracted young men.[4]

Ambitious parents do not exist only in open class societies, for even within a caste system parents may want their children to rise within the occupational structure of their own particular caste. However, it seems evident that more ambitions are stirred and released in societies which have more width of occupational choice and more opportunities

---

[3]*Ibid.*, p. 228. Dhurjati Prasad Mukerji, *Modern Indian Culture: A Sociological Study*. Second edition (Bombay: Hind Kitabs Ltd., 1948), p. 113. One hundred years of English education has enlarged the proportion of highly educated Hindus and increased the social mobility of the middle class.

[4]Jawaharlal Nehru, *The Discovery of India* (London: Meridian Books Ltd., 1951), p. 311.

to climb than in those where the occupational choices which lead to power and prestige are limited.

In his analysis of the social background of Indian nationalism, Desai refers to the common interests and ways of life which came to India when the industrial revolution developed new occupational classes. "These classes were unknown to past Indian society, since they were primarily the offspring of the new capitalist economic structure which developed in India as a result of the British conquest and the impact on her of the British and world economy. The Indian people were reshuffled into new social groupings, new classes as a result of the basic capitalist economic transformation of Indian society."[5] Desai shows that with the development of industry and the parallel growth of new educational institutions, the four following urban classes gradually arose: first, the modern working class, engaged in industry, transportation, mining and other similar enterprises; second, the modern class of industrial, commercial and financial capitalists; third, the class of petty traders and shopkeepers; and fourth the professional classes.[6] Desai stresses that the gradual development of industrial enterprises in all parts of India created in their wake similar occupational groups which found that they had many similar economic interests. Thus, the outlook of occupational groupings changed from a local to a national one.[7]

This brief description shows the profound change in social structure which results from a change in the basic economic pattern of a country, and how ambitions are stirred by new opportunities. It implies that once a higher standard of living is within grasp many families formerly

---

[5] A. R. Desai, *The Social Background of Indian Nationalism*, p. 157. "The emergence of new social classes in India was the direct consequence of the establishment of a new social economy, a new type of a state system and a state administrative machinery, and the spread of new education during the British rule."

[6] *Ibid.*, p. 163. Desai also shows that the British regime caused new openings in the civil service and that it needed more and more lawyers to carry out and interpret the many new laws made by the administration. Teachers and professors were also needed for the new educational institutions, and journalists and writers to "quench the thirst of the new literate masses."

[7] *Ibid.*, p. 198. "It was not so in pre-British India, when no single national economy or state existed. In pre-British India, the village artisan, for example, had no common economic ties or interests with artisans in other villages since he was a part of village autarchy. Similarly, the two handicraftsman had no common economic ties or interests with the handicraftsmen of other towns. India was, in fact, then divided into a conglomeration of almost unconnected local economies and a congerie of states. Hence, there were neither common political nor economic interests of all the artisans, handicraftsmen or agriculturists."

content with a moderate standard gradually succumb to the compelling vision of more comfort, security, and even luxury.

*The Changing Prestige of Occupations*

As the economic emphasis of a society changes from agriculture to industry, and people become urbanized in outlook, the values attached to particular occupations tend to change. The complexity of the industrial occupational structure and its constant incorporation of new occupations makes the actual prestige ranking of different occupations difficult to assess at any one time. Many students are attempting to do this for the occupational structures of different societies.[8]

In India the deeply rooted traditional attitudes to certain occupations have not radically changed as yet: for example, manual labour is still regarded as only fit for the lowest caste workers.[9] Moreover, the changes in attitude that have occurred have probably affected only a small percentage of urbanized people. However, as these are the people who control the media of mass communication, it is important to study their views for they will disseminate the new value system to the rest of the society.

One thing that seems likely is that, as many of the new industrial occupations will be ones which have already achieved high prestige in the Western World, they will appear desirable openings when they become incorporated in the Indian economy. Many of these new occupations will be highly skilled and require long periods of study for their achievement. These requirements have enabled people with the necessary abilities to command high salaries in the Western World. All these factors mean that a society which is late in entering the industrial era is likely to be presented with a somewhat "ready-made" ranking of new occupations. These occupations may stir the ambition of the younger generation, particularly if they are introduced to them in environments, such as the university, where they are regarded with

[8]Joseph A. Kahl, *The American Class Structure* (New York: Rinehart and Company, Inc., 1957), pp. 69–82.
[9]In spite of the acceptance and even encouragement of middle- and upper-class sons and daughters working in occupations demanding manual labour while at college on the North American continent, the idea of their taking on such occupations as careers would probably be as heavily frowned on in the Western World as it is in India by families of comparable social position. Another factor which reinforces the idea that the sons of middle- and upper-class Hindu families should not do manual labour is that unemployment in India is so extensive that the young Indian has much less chance of finding part-time jobs of this nature than his counterpart in North America.

prestige. Or, they may "pick up" the attitudes to these occupations from Western movies, magazines and novels. At the same time, the incorporation of new occupations into the Indian economy will tend to change the prestige rating of the older ones.

## A Rising Standard of Aspiration

A great deal of anxiety centres around the work world in India and, if the rising standard of living does not keep up with the rising standard of aspirations, then anxieties will probably increase. Out of eighty respondents, fifty-five said they desired a higher standard of living. Of these, the young married interviewees were almost unanimous in wanting one. The majority of single interviewees and about 50 per cent of the older married interviewees also expressed this desire. This difference in desire of the different interviewees may be an indication that the young married men are facing the difficulty of financing their families for the first time, and the older married men have either arrived at an adequate income, or else adjusted to the one they have.

The desire for a higher standard of living was also brought out when discussing the ambitions of interviewees, and is probably the main reason so many of them were not happy in their jobs. A college degree does not give much bargaining power in a country in which the supply of college graduates is greater than the demand for their services. One informant said that university graduates often have to take jobs as clerks, which is a white collar job far beneath the expectations of their families. He thought these young men among the most dissatisfied in India, for as they were always looking for better jobs they did not develop loyalty to the firms they worked in. If they were able to add a law degree or some other higher degree to their qualifications they had better bargaining power. But even a young man with a good job, was constantly afraid of being victimized or dismissed because of the great competition for jobs and promotion. "Insecurity is always there."

Added to the economic insecurity is the feeling of loss of prestige in not living up to parents' expectations. Several interviewees were unhappy on this account. One young man whose father had wanted him to attain great power and influence had only attained the position of lecturer at a college, which was not considered important.

The anxieties of parents for the future economic and social position of their children are reflected in the urgency with which they often goad their sons at school and try to direct them into certain occupations. One son told this story:

When we were young, Father would remind us every day that he was toiling hard just to give us the education which would make us prosperous. He was very anxious that we should all graduate brilliantly, get good jobs, and raise the family income; so he tried to make us study hard and come out first in our classes.

He forced me to take mathematics because he thought that we should all become engineers and earn a lot of money. I flatly refused. My second brother made his dream come true, but my third brother hadn't any aptitude for engineering; so in spite of a lot of private tutoring, he has failed his examinations for three years. (Case 97)

Other causes for frustration or dissatisfaction in the economic sphere lay in the fact that the ambitions of several interviewees had been thwarted because of lack of money to continue their studies. One had hoped to be a lawyer, but had failed his examinations and by then had a wife and children to support; so he had to give up his "heart's desire." Several were dissatisfied with the pay they received. A number of Brahmins had either failed to get seats in college for further study, or on obtaining degrees found doors to good jobs closed to them. A few felt that they were too old to change their occupations although dissatisfied with the type of work they were doing.

Since the occupational careers of middle-class sons are no longer clear-cut, they may have to go through a long period of trial and error before they actually settle down into one job. Differing ambitions of father and son and the difficulty of getting the desired kind of education may add to this problem.

My chief desire is to be a very rich man. I want to see that my parents have a luxurious life with the money I send them. When I was a child, my ambition was to read as much as possible and become a scholar; so I read a great deal and still do. Now I want to be a journalist, but I also want a much higher type of living than my parents and other relatives. I would go anywhere in the world to get a lucrative job.

When I was at college, my ambition was to be an engineer. I did well in the examination and got a first class standing, but I was refused admission to the university. I continued to study with mathematics as my optional subject, finally I got my B.A. and won four medals.

Then my father wanted me to become an auditor. But when I had an interview I was told that I must have a diploma in statistics as well. When I came to Bombay to take the course, I found it was a full-time job, and I could not possibly finance it; so I was forced to take a job, and finally became an upper division clerk in the railways.

I am not at all satisfied with the job, but what can I do? (Case 96)

Another case also shows the disagreement between father and son as to the son's future.

My father was very much interested in my education. He wanted me to take a college degree and then study law. He also wanted me to become a politician. He dreamt of my getting an important position. He had a lot of influence in politics, and knew the way to get ahead, for he himself was a politician. But somehow I wasn't interested. I didn't feel I had the ability to become a politician or lawyer. I was always afraid to speak on a platform, or even in a classroom. I couldn't imagine myself being either a lawyer or a politician.

I went to college just because it was a good way to spend the time and at the same time it pleased my father. But I was very relieved when I finished my B.A. and I never went on after that. I never liked learning and in fact even at college I didn't learn anything. I always wanted to be a big business magnate—a Tata or Birla. Finally Father gave in and helped to finance me in business. Now I am a business man, and although it has its drawbacks, I prefer it to any job with a steady income.

I would go anywhere, even away from the family, to do good business. (Case 45)

Still another factor which complicates the search for satisfying urban jobs is that young men who are moving out into new occupations will not get the assistance they formerly relied on from kin and caste members; for although nepotism probably always exists to some extent in all societies, it becomes less effective when the impersonal business world takes over control of placements from the intimate kinship group; so special privileges for sons cannot be relied on in the city. Even sons who intend to follow the traditional caste occupation will be faced with greater competition, for traditional caste occupations are now more open to competition in the open market, and they will have to compete against people from many castes for positions of which they were formerly assured.

To summarize these points, financial circumstances, caste discrimination, indecision about career channels and difficulty of getting adequate education appear to be the major factors in frustrating the job expectations of this group and their desire for a higher standard of living.

## The Self-Made Man

The children of any one family are not necessarily all inculcated with the same ambitions even in an era of rising aspirations: for example, girls in village families were not always fired with the same desires as were their brothers to get ahead by going to the city. Sometimes brothers shared the interviewee's ambitions, sometimes not. In one case the parents managed to give their sons enough education to enable them to make a modest start in the hotel business in Bombay. Their energies and drive helped them to make a success of the business, and they in turn were able to assist their younger brothers and other relatives when they moved to Bombay for studies or jobs. In this family the girls did not share their brothers' ambitions.

At first, parents will probably be the chief media through which new ambitions are instilled in sons. But, as industrialization develops, new techniques of mass communication, such as movies and radios, will inculcate sons with ambitions which parents do not necessarily share. There thus arises the phenomenon of the "self-made" man, whose ambitions are far ahead of those of his parents. All the sons of this study who had moved to Bombay for study or work fell into this category.

It is quite probable that many young men who move to large cities such as Bombay fail to find satisfactory jobs or lives there. The number who return home is impossible to estimate. On the other hand, many do manage to adjust to the new economic and social life and find satisfactory niches in the city. Of the seven young men of this study who had gone to Bombay of their own volition, only one was contemplating returning to his native village. not because he had failed to adjust to Bombay, but because he had always wanted to be an important man in his own community, and had gone to Bombay with the explicit purpose of training himself for an important position in his village. The other six had moved to Bombay with little or no encouragement or financial help. In fact, their families and relatives had sometimes discouraged the venture.

> I am not at all content with the life my father lives. He is not ambitious. He didn't take much interest in my education. Had I not topped the list in matriculation he would not have allowed me to go to college. I would have had the same fate as my sister who is now wasting her talents in an office working as a clerk. Fortunately, I got free tuition, and free board while I was at college, and secured a first class in my B.A. degree. Father was anxiously waiting for me to finish so that I could get a job, but the first class saved me, for through it I got a scholarship; so Father could not object to my going on for an M.A. in Bombay. I also got a prize from the Rotary Club for coming head, and besides that I financed my M.A. by giving private tutoring; so I did not have to trouble my father for money, but on the contrary I was able to send him money.
>
> Immediately after getting my M.A. I registered for my Ph.D. and simultaneously joined law classes. I also took a full-time job as lecturer. (Case 148)

These young men had often faced great hardship in financing their university education. Most of them had made additional money by tutoring, or had taken part-time jobs along with their studies. Several attempted to take two or three degrees concurrently to shorten the period of time in which they would have no financial support. A few were sending money back home as their part of the family responsibility. A number of them appeared to be the only ambitious members of the family—others had brothers and sisters who shared their ambitions even though parents and other relatives did not.

Interviews seemed to suggest that if ambitious sons did not get help from family or relatives that they had to rely on their own ability to get ahead, for not one interviewee mentioned a "friend" or outsider who had assisted him. A few said that they had had encouragement from teachers or professors, but this was verbal rather than financial.

Another group of young men who could be called self-made had moved from relatively poor village families to Bangalore and had managed by means of scholarships and tutoring, or jobs, to obtain degrees which enabled them to get higher positions than their fathers. These young men received little or no encouragement from parents or relatives. Only one contemplated returning to live in his village. His reason was that he had always wanted to be a landlord, and was taking law to enable him to practise at home.

Money appeared to be the sole incentive of some of these self-made men. An informant in talking of them said: "Those young men will go to the moon for good pay. The type of job isn't important, they just want lots of money to spend."

It is possible that the young men who moved to Bombay from South India will eventually break away from their families completely. Spatial separation is not the only factor which is involved in this, for the young men who had brothers or relatives living in Bombay had no close association with them. They quickly became engrossed in city life and their outlook and ways of life changed so rapidly that they felt they no longer had interests in common with their families. A similar change in outlook often occurs when young men leave India for foreign travel or study.

This analysis could be summed up by saying that some of the changes which have come about with the gradual industrialization of India have so loosened the former rigidity of the caste system that young men and women now have many more occupational opportunities. These new opportunities in turn have tended to stir ambitions, so that even when not encouraged at home, young men have launched out themselves with the hope of achieving a higher standard of living than that of their parents. This attempt often necessitates their moving away from home, and they soon become so engrossed in the new way of life that they find they have little in common with their family circle.

It is to be expected that this movement up the occupational ladder, away from former family occupations and interests, will increase if industrialization continues to gradually turn the former caste system of India into a more flexible open class system.

OCCUPATIONAL PROBLEMS

*The Educated Unemployed*

Chapter VII shows that the Indian system of education has turned out too many people for the number of jobs for which higher education is needed.[10] This oversupply of university-trained workers has meant chronic unemployment amongst the educated classes since the middle of the last century. The intense competition for jobs which it has engendered has meant that, on the whole, education has been seen as a means not of achieving a "good" job, but a job which will allow the bearer to be financially secure in his future life. "Education means a degree—and a degree means a job." The intense pressure on children to study and on young people to go on to college for degrees cannot be fully understood unless this factor of unemployment is taken into consideration.[11]

[10]A. R. Desai, *Social Background of Indian Nationalism* (Bombay: Oxford University Press, 1948), p. 183. The growth of modern education in India was not paralleled by a proportional economic development of the country. As a result of this disparity, unemployment among the educated class had already assumed serious proportions by the end of the nineteenth century. Political discontent born of the economic suffering due to unemployment among the educated middle class was an important factor in the growth of militant nationalism at the time of the fight for Independence.

[11]Countries which experienced the depression of the early 1930's can appreciate the great strain, anxiety and frustration that unemployment causes amongst the educated classes. Figures for unemployment in Mysore State in 1951 show the extent of unemployment in a fairly prosperous state. "The educated unemployed who constituted nearly four-fifths of the 1941 total (of unemployed), now form 75.1 per cent with 4,560 persons, including 231 women. Though the bulk of the job-hunters—68.8 per cent to be exact—are unmarried, as many as 1,838 or 28.8 per cent appear to have ventured into matrimony. . . . Of this number 618 have already seen thirty-five summers and more. . . ." *Census of India*, 1951, vol. XIV, Mysore, Part I, Report, (Bangalore: Director of Printing, Stationery and Publications at the Government Press, 1954), p. 147. The above figures were for Mysore State. A breakdown for men with Matriculation or graduate education for Bangalore Corporation were: 523 men with matriculation, 68 with their college intermediate, 135 graduates, 1 postgraduate, and 166 others with degrees in medicine, engineering, agriculture, commerce, law, etc. (*Ibid.*, Part II, Table B.IX, pp. 186–7.)

In this country a person that belongs to the middle class can't expect to educate their children just for knowledge. One has to choose the course that has got the best prospects for a good job. Of course, I would like to take my B.A. just for the sake of knowledge, and to broaden myself by travelling in foreign countries. But I can't do it, because I don't have either the finances or the facilities. (Case 78)

The detrimental effect of unemployment on young graduates is seen in the following interview:

A man may have to wait a long time for a job after graduating. This is very bad for him, he simply rots away. He loses confidence in himself and gradually has no security. Anticipation of being unemployed is so universal that just after graduation a boy ages ten years. His family at home push him into applying for jobs. But as he is constantly refused, he gets terribly depressed and loses all confidence in himself. Unemployed graduates are always pale and worried. (Case 42)

Unemployment, in fact, causes such despair that observers spoke of "waves of suicide" among educated unemployed boys.[12]

A Hindu psychologist who had observed many patients in mental hospitals said that it was his impression that the majority of Indians went to him because of economic problems, relatively few because of sexual problems.[13] To illustrate this, he quoted the case history of a man who married a well-educated woman who came from a family in which the brothers were highly educated, and economically well off. Mr. X. only received a salary of 150 rupees a month, and on that had to support his wife and eight daughters. When the time came for them to marry, he could not possibly pay the dowries for suitable husbands, namely, 5,000 rupees for each daughter. His own family could not assist him. His wife's could, but as Mr. X. had always felt inferior to them because of his lack of education he would not accept their help. These financial worries upset him to such an extent that he finally had to enter a mental hospital.

The pressure then is circular in its effect. The harder it is to get "decent" jobs, that is, jobs commensurate with expectations of the

[12] A recent Indian movie had this theme, which suggests strongly that the despair of the unemployed is a universal phenomenon in India. Many recent Indian novels also deal with the problems of the educated unemployed and stress as well the dissatisfaction which many young Indians feel with the jobs they eventually get. In 1954, an Association for the Educated Unemployed was formed in South India, which also is an indication of the wide incidence of this problem. For a very good description of the feelngs of these young men, see R. Prawer Jhabvala, "The Interview," *New Yorker*, (July 27, 1957), pp. 25–9.

[13] "Sex" only becomes a problem when sex mores are changing and disrupting former firmly established ways of handling this strong emotion. Sex mores in India do not seem to have changed to such an extent that many people need help in adjusting to the new patterns.

individual and his relatives, the more families attempt to see that their sons get university degrees. This increases the competition at universities and the competition for higher types of jobs. As a university degree is still an important symbol of ability, and as more men obtain them, pressure is put on parents to see that their children get degrees so that they will be able to compete too.

Another thing that enhances the problem is that although the number of universities has increased since Independence, and more are planned, there are still not enough to supply the number of seats which are sought. This means that pressure on sons to get degrees must begin far down in the school system, for unless a boy's family has some sort of influence which will assist him to get into a university, he must have very high marks to compete successfully for a seat.

Although, as it has been noted above, unemployment in the educated classes is not a new phenomenon in India, it is conceivable that present conditions now cause it to be felt more heavily by a greater number of Hindus. One reason for this is that as caste barriers to occupations have given way, more young Hindus are now imbued with industrial ambitions than before. Another reason might be that incentives to gain a higher standard of living have now spread more widely through such media as movies and advertising. Still another is that one's own caste members may have risen to more important positions in society in recent years. And finally, the energies of many unemployed educated men which for many years were centred on the fight for Independence are now released on their own personal problems. Moreover, fathers are no longer capable of assisting their sons to find suitable positions, for the impersonal mechanism of selection through examinations and efficiency has largely replaced the former more personal process of selection through caste and kinship background.

The educational system is not alone responsible for the number of educated unemployed in India. Other factors which have affected it are: the continuing belief in the indignity of manual labour; the fact that modern education often makes boys unfit for village life; and the fact that, since the plight of the educated is similar all over India, well-qualified men are not always able to move to other states or provinces for jobs.

The despair of an educated unemployed man is deepened by the change from the comparative freedom of the university to the responsibility of finding a job. As one informant said:

As soon as graduation is over it is very difficult. The rich boys are disillusioned because they can only get poor types of jobs. The fun and unity of college days are over. Some can't get jobs at all, and tend to go to pieces. Many commit suicide, it is almost a fashion. I know of two graduate students who have taken jobs as servants at 25 rupees a month, and one M.A. who is running a bus in Calcutta.

In reality, therefore, Hindu youths today are brought up in conditions resembling those of the great depression of the 1930's in the Western World. And unemployment in India has lasted over so many years that the greatest and most constant fear of growing boys is that they may not be able to find jobs when they arrive at the age to take up their life work. The situation has resulted in many graduate students having to take a type of employment that rates much lower than the expectations of families and relatives, particularly when much money has been spent on their education. This failure to achieve personal and family goals exposes many Hindu young men to frustration, and a consequent feeling of inferiority. Young women who are not yet expected to bear much responsibility for the family finances are spared this anxiety and frustration.

*Brahmin versus non-Brahmin*

One factor which has confused the occupational picture in the last few decades has been the growing antagonism to members of the Brahmin caste by members of other castes. This antipathy has upset the safe monopoly that Brahmins formerly had of government and teaching positions, and is an important aspect of the problem of the educated unemployed. Up to recent times the Brahmin caste has always held the highest position of prestige in the Hindu caste hierarchy.[14] They have been able to maintain their dominant position largely because their greater amount of education enabled them to take over the majority of civil service posts, which included most of the teaching positions. Their position was so favourable during the British régime that all other castes were lumped together and called "non-Brahmin" and were looked on as "backward" castes. When

---

[14]Ghurye, *Caste and Class*, pp. 6, 7, 44–114, 161: In the traditional order of ranking of the four main castes the Brahmins, who were allotted the religious and teaching duties for the Hindu society, were placed at the top. Next in rank came the military caste, the Kshatriyas, then the Vaisya caste, which was comprised of people carrying out business and agricultural occupations. The Sudras caste, beneath the Vaisyas in prestige, undertook the lower occupational duties. Finally, the so-called "untouchables," re-named by Gandhi the "Harijans," were the outcastes who did all the most disagreeable jobs such as scavenging.

changing conditions brought about a desire for more equality, the Indian government gradually gave the non-Brahmin castes some preference in education. "Backward Scholarships" were instituted to promote their education and certain government positions reserved for them. This policy opened up new opportunities for them and they were able to compete successfully for some of the higher occupational positions.

In this way many non-Brahmins were able to obtain important positions and so gradually enlarged their scope of influence by having quotas for civil service posts and for medical and engineering colleges established in their favour. This change did not come about without strong feelings of antagonism and rivalry between the two groups.[15]

The antipathy is now so intense that many young Brahmins in South India despair of finding jobs suitable to their former status, and thus tend to move to North India where anti-Brahmin feeling is not as acute. The Brahmins remaining in the South who cannot compete successfully for the limited occupational openings often become completely discouraged about their futures, for they cannot get the type of jobs which their parents, relatives and caste expect them, as Brahmins, to attain. Their profound feeling of discouragement was often expressed by interviewees not only of their own positions, but in terms of the future of the whole Brahmin caste.[16]

I am twenty-five years old, and in our state a Brahmin who is over twenty-five won't be able to get a job. So far I haven't been able to get a government position. Now the only course that is open to me is to complete my degree in education and teach in a private school. But I don't like teaching, for the salary is very poor and there is no scope for promotion or prosperity. I was unemployed for nearly two years after I got my B.Sc.; so all my ambitions to do well in life are thwarted. I am helpless to do anything about it. (Case 109)

The effects of the difficult position of Brahmins will be seen in some of the following discussions on the problems of work.

---

[15]Gardner Murphy, *In the Minds of Men* (New York: Basic Books, Inc. Publishers, 1953), pp. 104–6. Ghurye, *Caste and Class*, p. 227. "The Brahmin Non-Brahmin clash of interests has taken on a sullen aspect venting itself on occasion into violent out-breaks."

[16]Murphy, *In the Minds of Men*, p. 106. Although the picture seems extremely discouraging to those affected by it, Murphy warns: "It must . . . be remembered that though the Brahmins are on a quota system, still a higher proportion of Brahmins enter into desirable positions than is the case with members of other castes. We are dealing with a gradual relative displacement of Brahmins, not with a sudden equalization of all castes."

## Occupational Models

One of the main problems of parents is to inculcate their children with the desire to continue a way of life which they deem suitable. This inculcation is usually largely unconsciously done through the day-to-day contact of children and parents. One way models for the children's behaviour have been presented down through the ages is through stories of the family's past achievements, or of the group's heroes. A grandmother, a mother or a professional story-teller are often the main media by which these models are presented to the children. One interviewee whose mother had been very ambitious about his education told of how she had often told him stories of men who had had eminent academic careers. Books, movies and children's associations will be used in more highly urbanized countries to present models for the children's future behaviour. In stable societies, models will remain appropriate over a long period of time, for parents themselves will have modelled their behaviour on them and can thus easily pass them on to their children. This will mean that children will acquire the correct behaviour for the society they are to live in as adults. But in a rapidly changing society the group's traditional models are not up to date. And if children are taught their future roles in terms of these old-fashioned models, the behaviour patterns which they will expect to carry out as adults will no longer fit in with the times. This is especially true of children brought up in rural areas who later move to the city. Another problem that is closely connected with the above one is that rural parents often make great sacrifices to educate their sons, believing that a university degree is the open doorway to a position of prestige. And yet at the same time they are so ignorant of city life that they cannot guide their sons' careers, but only hopefully launch them off into an unknown world.

I'm not at all satisfied with the life and standard of living of my parents and relatives. This has caused great conflict within me, for I believe that I have the ability to get ahead. But I lacked proper guidance from my parents, and this was partly responsible for my recklessness when I first went to college. I felt that my energies weren't properly channelled there.

My parents were anxious to see that I got some sort of education, and Father spent a lot of money educating me up to my B.A. But they weren't in a position to assess my abilities, and to help me choose a career. Mother was very particular that I should get a college education. At home she felt competent to teach me and she used to personally supervise my homework. She used also to tell me stories of people who had risen to eminence because of distinguished careers. But after I went to college she felt she was no longer competent to guide me and I was left to myself to study. At first I wanted to be an engineer, but unfortunately I couldn't get admission to Maths in the intermediate college; so with great unwillingness I took physics and biology. I was so uninterested in them that I failed the intermediate exams a number of times before passing them. When I finally got through, there was no one to guide me about further studies. Then I decided to go on with physics and biology with the idea of taking up medicine. But I failed to get a seat in the medical course; so at last I got a job as a clerk. However, that job didn't satisfy me and I was still burning with a desire for some higher professional training. I decided that I wanted to be a chartered accountant, but the course cost about one thousand rupees, and Father wasn't willing to finance it.

At last I bade good-bye to my home and came to Bombay. Here I began taking an M.A. and an L.L.B. at the same time. I find law very stimulating, and at present my ambition is to become a practising lawyer and if possible to go abroad for further study in law. (Case 35)

One of the main problems in a changing society, therefore, is to keep the models on which children shape their adult behaviour up to date. As the most effective model is one that is close at hand, younger brothers often emulate older ones. Being of the same generation probably makes them more appropriate models in a changing society than fathers who often cannot, or do not, change with the times and so are unable to guide their children's future behaviour.

*Old Age*

Not much information was secured in this study on the reaction of family members to the father on his retirement. In the Western World, the position of older family members has recently often been extremely difficult, for besides becoming financial burdens to their children they may also have to make the psychological adjustment to relinquishing positions of authority and prestige.

When the middle-class urban father retires in India, he often has very little financial security. He may have a small pension or some income from property, but all too often he has used his savings and even gone into debt to pay for his children's education and his daughters' dowries.

A centrally important question in this context is the relationship of financial competence to prestige. Does a man necessarily lose his position of prestige and authority when he can no longer supply the family income? Students of Western middle-class men tend to see a man's ability to provide the family income as a crucial aspect of his position. Even when his children are able to support themselves, he is still expected to be able to provide adequately for his wife and himself. A working wife may imply that a man is not capable of earning a sufficient income and this will reflect back on the prestige of his position.

When the family changes to the nuclear form and the ambitions of a mobile society prompt both fathers and sons to attain higher standards of living, the father may have to bear additional economic responsibilities, for he may have to support his son until he has obtained one or more university degrees. In addition, he may have to support his son's wife and children as well—should the son marry before he is economically independent.[17] This must be done without the assistance of brothers, which the joint family system assured.

These economic burdens mean that many fathers are not only forced to work very hard but also may have to take on additional part-time jobs to eke out their incomes. One interviewee, a 50-year-old man said:

When I started work I became a clerk. Not that I wanted to, but because there wasn't any other job. I got 25 rupees a month. At that time this was enough if the couple had a house and a few acres of land. I had that job for ten years, and then, owing to the influence of a relative, got a job in the railways. I passed a number of departmental examinations there; so I got promotions without difficulty. But as there were always plenty of relatives to be looked after, and children's education and medical bills to be paid, I took a part-time job as well. This meant that I had to work from eight o'clock in the morning to nine at night. I have continued working that way ever since, and still haven't been able to save anything. I had to sell all my property to get money for my daughter's dowry. The only money I will have on retirement will be my pension.

It has been very difficult to give my children a good education. I wanted one of my sons to take up engineering at college, but lack of money forced me to send him into another course instead which doesn't lead anywhere. If I can borrow the money, I will put him through engineering. (Case 46)

The father of a nuclear family, therefore, in comparison to a father of a joint family, has a continual financial burden that never ends, and when he is ready to retire he is no longer sure that he will be looked after adequately by his children. This changing economic picture has been recognized in many highly industrialized countries and old age pensions have been instituted to help fill the economic gap.

*Women's Careers*

The actual number of women holding remunerative jobs is low in

[17]This pattern of parents supporting their sons and their families until they have finished their university training is becoming more and more common on the North American continent. Usually the wives of sons will work to help finance them until the son has finished his university education. As her salary will seldom be enough to support them entirely, parents frequently assist.

Mysore State compared with the rest of India.[18] The Census of Mysore states that the main reason for this is that the pressure for a higher standard of living has not yet been felt in that state to the extent it has in provinces containing more and larger cities. In large cities many of the middle- and upper-class families will have to live in small, expensive apartments. This will give the women more leisure time for jobs outside the home and will also put more pressure on them to add to the family income. Indeed, the main reason that so many married Hindu middle-class women work without reproach is because everyone understands the economic problems of the middle class, and that a wife's income is often essential to the family's standard of living. As one woman professor said: "Life is so hard now that families need the extra money a woman can make. I have been teaching for about fourteen years, and want to give up my job. But my husband says we couldn't possibly run our household the way we do without the extra money I bring in."

It has also become more customary for young single middle-class women to work before marriage. In the larger cities many now enter such glamorous fields as drama, classical dancing or work in the movies or radio.[19] To an increasing extent, young girls are also taking up professional careers in teaching, medicine or law.[20] In this study, twenty-nine sisters of interviewees were reported as working mainly as teachers, lecturers and research assistants. A few were also nurses although this profession has a low reputation except among Christians and Anglo-Indians.

Business too is beginning to open up to women. But the problem of unemployed men as well as the discrimination against their sex makes it difficult for many to find jobs in this field. A woman professor said:

[18]*Census of India*, 1951, vol. XIV, Mysore, Part I Report (Bangalore: Director of Printing, Stationery and Publications at the Government Press, 1954), p. 131. Not as many women are earners in Mysore State as in the other provinces of India. In Madhya Pradesh, 100 women out of every 1,000 earn their own living, and 377 out of every 1,000 women help to support the family. That is, roughly one-half are earners whereas in Mysore State the figure is roughly one-tenth. The *Census* concludes that the desire for a higher standard of living has not yet influenced women to become earners in Mysore.

[19]Kamala Markandaya, *Some Inner Fury* (New York: John Day Co., 1956); Prawer R. Jhabvala, *To Whom She Will* (London: George Allen and Unwin, Ltd., 1955), also published under the title of *Amrita*. These two recent novels, and others, deal with the stories of girls who have taken up these types of careers.

[20]The last years of the fight for Independence took a great many Indian women away from their former secluded lives, and gave precedence for their taking part in activities which would be of benefit to the country. This has assisted their entrance into such fields as medicine, although nursing is still considered a very questionable occupation for higher class girls.

It is very difficult for girls to get jobs after they graduate. About two hundred girls are taking post-graduate work in Bangalore, and a number go in for medicine. It is really terrible the discrimination against them in getting jobs and equal pay to men. Even our women's college only has one woman on the board.

More girls are taking such subjects as mathematics, physics and chemistry now because they feel that these subjects will help them to get better jobs. A number of girls take law, and make good lawyers. Men go to them as well as women, principally because they don't charge as much, and they work harder and take more care. Of course, their looks count too! Any girl with good looks can get on in the business world.

An acute problem in South India is that some families sacrifice a lot to finance their daughters' college education, and then find that the girls are unable to either get jobs or husbands. An informant said:

These girls will lead a miserable life. There are very few women's clubs so far, and so they have a very poor social life. Some may manage somehow to go on and get their M.A.'s, or even their Ph.D.'s. They may sell some property to do this. But their parents will be too poor to pay the large dowries, 10,000 to 15,000 rupees, which educated men demand. The solution is sometimes that the father will find a business man who is attracted by the girl's degree, but doesn't need the large dowry.

Even if they do get office jobs, they will find it difficult to adjust to working with men. It won't be possible, either, for men to treat them as friends; so they will lead very lonely lives. Women in this position can't talk freely to the young men around them, it would cause a scandal. I think that these girls gradually react to this situation by becoming bitter against men. They say they are against marriage, they talk of the miseries of married women, but in their heart of hearts they long to be married.

One case described by an informant stressed the difficulty which many women have in adjusting to the new role of working women. A young woman who obtained a degree in Commerce got a job as clerk in a bank. She was the first woman in that particular bank, and the first woman in her community to become a clerk. She, therefore, had no guidance as to how the new role should be carried out. Moreover, as it had not been the custom in her community for men and women to mix socially, she had had no experience in meeting strange men, and did not know how to react to her colleagues:

This girl doesn't work nearly as hard as the men. For example, whereas my husband stays at the bank until his work is finished, sometimes until 9, 10 or even 12 o'clock at night, the girl always stops working at five; so she often doesn't finish her work, and the men have to do it. The men are furious about it, but don't like to say anything to her. She says that as a woman she can't go home late at night alone, or in a taxi, or she will lose her reputation. She never mixes with the men at all at the office, or chats with them or enters into the office life. She just does her work and then leaves.

This case illustrates the difficulty of role adjustment in new situations. In this case the girl's male colleagues, accustomed to "male" clerks, did not know how to treat her as a clerk. The girl, too, did not know how to take over the impersonality of the working role. When a new situation arose for which she had no guidance, she tended to respond to it first of all according to her experience as a woman. The problem of getting home before dark was a real one to her, for her chastity is one of her most important attributes, and it will be questioned if she transgresses the patterns of behaviour expected of a woman. She thus responded to this new problem by playing a "female" role rather than a "clerk" role. This left her colleagues with extra work to do. They would not have hesitated to tell a male clerk that he must stay, but they too were confused by their own ambivalent attitudes to her. They too had been brought up to the custom that women must not be out alone after dark. And so a state of dissatisfaction arose: the men could not accept her wholly as a colleague because they were not used to women playing that particular role, nor could they accept her wholly as a woman, for after all she was there to do "male" work.

Thus each new occupational role taken over by women creates problems of adjustment of attitudes and behaviour. The opposition to the people playing new roles is caused by the uncertainty not only of the incumbent in the unfamiliar situation, but also of those who play related roles. Each one connected with the situation will have to make a minor or major adjustment.

Since people are probably more strongly conditioned to appropriate sex roles than to any others, the above type of conflict would be expected to arise whenever women enter a male-typed occupation and to last until both sides have gradually adjusted and women play their roles and are accepted as "workers" and not as women. Until that point is reached there will be conflict for the woman starting out on any career which has formerly been considered a "male" job. She will not face this problem when entering an occupation such as teaching, for women have long been accepted in this profession; so both they and the public have made the necessary accommodations.

The same kind of adjustment will have to be made by a man who enters a new caste occupation. If a Harijan, for example, instead of a woman obtains a degree in Commerce, and gets a position in a bank, he will be playing a new role for a Harijan. He will not be sure of the exact way to act, nor will his colleagues be sure of how they should treat him. He too is a newcomer and a "stranger." In the same way as a woman, he will find the adjustment difficult, for he too will have no guidance from his former life to direct him. His colleagues similarly will find many small problems in adjusting to a new conception of the type of person who should hold that particular job.[21]

Another important aspect of womens' work illustrated in the above case study is that women can be extremely lonely when working. In this case the young bank clerk lived at home, and therefore could get some social relaxation with her family, but for young girls who move away from their families to large cities the situation is much more difficult. According to an informant:

Girls working in Bombay can be very lonely, for they may not only be in offices with men with whom they find difficulty in mixing, but with people from different language groups. Moreover, they can't make contacts with other people the way men can; so, if anyone comes along that has her own background, they may become very close friends. This is one way in which men and women find people to marry in the cities, for when they work together, either in business or in research at the universities, they feel that they have a lot in common. And this is accentuated by the fact that there are few people with whom they can mix.

Men interviewees were more liberal in their attitudes to careers for women than were the women. About two-thirds of the sixty-two men expressing their views were in favour of women having careers, and a dozen more were willing with some qualifications. On the other hand, less than a third of the seventy-one women replying were favourable to the idea although about 50 per cent more thought women should have careers in certain circumstances. A breakdown of the women's answers showed that it is the single women with more education who believe most in women taking jobs.

Women interviewees gave the following reasons for favouring careers for their own sex: because they needed interests outside the home which would make them more alive and interesting and prevent their having to sit idly at home; because it would benefit society as there is a great need for trained people in India; because they would enjoy such professions as nursing and teaching; and because they would help with the family finances.

One of the few single women interviewees who had carried on her career rather than marrying had no intention of giving it up:

I am not married and I do not think I'll ever get married. I am too content with my present life as a doctor to contemplate it at this late hour. The reason I did not marry is that after my intermediate examinations I wanted to take up medicine. Father agreed to this in spite of Mother's plea that I

[21]Aileen D. Ross, "Symposium: Caste and Joint Family," *Sociological Bulletin*, vol. IV, no. 2, pp. 88–9. This discussion has been taken from the symposium on the joint family. Women of all countries have had to go through this same adjustment to "male" jobs.

should get married and then continue studying if I wanted. When I was in my third year of medicine, Father died suddenly and Mother was wild with grief. In the meanwhile Father had been making negotiations for my marriage with a certain young man of good background. Mother begged my suitor's people to give her a little time and then the marriage could be arranged. They refused to do so, and said that as they had plenty of girls in view if my mother could not get ready cash for them at once, she could say goodbye to all the arrangements. Mother did not know what to do. My maternal uncle urged her to get all her available cash and settle the marriage quickly. However, I knew that if she did this she and the rest of the family would suffer severe hardships after my expensive marriage was over. I decided on a bold step of action. I went to Mother and told her to cancel my marriage. I said that I would use half the amount which she needed for my marriage in finishing my medical course. I would qualify and become a doctor after which my practice would help to finance the family. Mother and the rest of the family were aghast and it was only after days of persuasion that I managed to win them around. I carried on with my studies, finished my course and started to practise. I educated my widowed sister's children and got the eldest married last year. Mother died three years ago and she said that she could never forget my unselfish act. Her words were enough praise for me, and I can only thank God that He showed me how I should act in that dark hour; so I have never married and I won't marry now. I enjoy my work, lead a happy family life surrounded by my sister and her children and do a bit of social work. I don't think marriage would have made me any happier. (Case 18)

The reasons given by the women interviewees who were against careers for women focused mainly on their traditional responsibilities to husband and children.[22] Qualifications to women having careers were also couched in terms of their home responsibilities. Some thought that if there were reliable women belonging to the same family to look after the children and help with the housework then careers might be successful.

I feel that women can work before marriage, but after marriage they should only work if they like it and the family needs financial help. If the money is not necessary, than I don't like their working. As a matter of fact there are many things women can do in the home to save money, such as making the children's clothes, teaching the children, and doing the cooking.

---

[22]Mrs. G. B. Desai, "Women in Modern Gujerati Life," Unpublished Master's Thesis, University of Bombay, Bombay, 1945, p. 130. In this study, 80 per cent of the women were against careers for married women. The reasons given were that as marriage is a full-time vocation, married women did not have time for careers; that it is not proper for women of high caste families to work; that many husbands do not like their wives working and neglecting the homes; and finally that it will also cause unemployment among men. Those who were in favour of careers gave the following reasons: to show men they have the capacity to earn; to show that women are not subordinate to men; to keep them occupied; to give them economic independence; and in case of financial necessity.

Women used to work and earn along with men in the villages. But they could do this while staying at home by keeping cows and selling the extra butter and milk. (Case 59)

The men who wanted women to have jobs or careers gave the following reasons: their extra income would help give the children a better education and more comforts and security; the wife would be happier if she were economically self-sufficient; it would make them as independent as men; it would prevent women gossiping and nagging; women should not live in a separate world from men but should have equal status and take equal responsibility. One said he preferred marrying a woman who was a doctor or a social worker as she would be serving her country.

Some, however, qualified their decision by saying that they were agreeable to careers for women as long as they restricted these to jobs which they were particularly suited for, such as teaching, nursing and social service. Another qualification was that they should not neglect their children. Still another that they should only take jobs after marriage if they were of benefit to society.

Objections were based on the important roles women play as wives and mothers. "Jobs are not for married women. A married woman should try to be an ideal housewife and a real mother and there will be a clash of duties if she takes a career after marriage." Another reason given was that they might lose their reputations through mixing with men. "I never trust the chastity of women who take up careers." Still other reasons were that they would lose their femininity, they would take jobs away from men, and people would laugh at the husband of a wife who worked.

Examples of these views are shown in the following typical interviews. In the first the traditional ideal of womanhood is stressed.

I feel woman's duty is to look after the house and children. Today taking up a career is more a fashion than a necessity. This results in women going astray. They get freedom which they haven't learned to handle as a boy has, and this sudden freedom will lead to misadventure, and all sorts of social and ethical problems.

Women are ideally suited to take care of the family and it is not right for them to take up jobs. If they do it will lead to promiscuity. The conception of Indian womanhood is strictly opposed to careers. First of all, all women should be ideal wives and mothers. To do this is an uphill task which requires full time and attention. (Case 148)

The second interview stresses the fear that the chastity of women, which is their most cherished possession, will be affected by careers.

I am dead against women having careers. Others may condemn me as an old-fashioned man, but I have seen with my own eyes the undesirable practices they indulge in and I am convinced that it is disastrous to send our girls either before or after marriage for a professional career. Sometimes their weaknesses will be exploited. I know several cases of this. Where is the stability and happiness of the home under such circumstances? We shouldn't allow girls to work in offices. At the most they could be allowed to do some voluntary social work during their leisure hours. And how will they spend the money? Usually on cosmetics or a few georgette saris. That money would be spent much more usefully if earned by a needy widow or an unemployed man. As long as we have unemployment, only people in need should take regular jobs. (Case 143)

The above interview shows that many men have accepted the idea that women can now move out of the homes to do voluntary social work. This new attitude is probably due to the influence of Gandhi and the Indian fight for Independence which had helped greatly in bringing the women out of their homes and giving them a conception of wider loyalties and responsibilities. The interviews also show that men have not yet accepted the idea of a change in the division of labour that would assign outside jobs equally to men and women.

As no man interviewed had a working wife, no light was thrown on the reaction of husbands who have experienced this new arrangement. A number of working wives, however, said that it was now impossible for them to wait on their husbands and children in the traditional manner.

We working wives have no time now to show our reverence for our husbands. My husband is headmaster, but I am also a head mistress, and I have a lot of work to get through before school. So in the mornings all I have time to do is to stand at the bottom of his bed and say: "Utha-Utha" (up you get!) and after that I am far too busy cooking for him to have any time to waste in worshipping him! (Case 56)

Besides the above-noted change in the attitude of the working wife to her husband, there will also be a shift in the division of labour between the two. The husband may find not only that his wife will not have enough time to care for all his needs, but that he may have to share in the work of the home himself. However, as urban wives are only beginning to share the social life of their husbands, this area will not be as difficult for them to cope with while working and running a house as it is for working wives in the Western World.

In spite of the more lenient attitude to wives working than is found in many Western countries, many Hindu wives and husbands still have to run the gauntlet of ridicule, particularly if the wife is working in a new field for women, for it takes the public a long time to adjust to this new situation. "A person who is first of his kind to attain a certain status is often not drawn into the informal brotherhood in which experiences are exchanged, competence built up, and the formal code elaborated and enforced. ... Many of these cause status dilemmas for the individual concerned and for people who have to deal with him."[23]

On the whole there was very little evidence from interviewees of either sex that Hindus are yet thinking in terms of the benefit that a career can give to the woman in terms of creative interest or fulfilment. The main points that are still stressed in considering its effect are the financial benefit to the family and its contribution to the good of the country.

## Summary

The essential shift in the relation of the family to the economic structure, when the economy of a society changes from that of simple agriculture, fishing or hunting to complex industrialization, is that the family is no longer a self-sufficient unit dependent only on local resources. Nor is it any longer a working unit with the labour of all members geared into one main occupation which fathers and sons follow and in which jobs are allotted on the personal basis of kinship rather than on rational factors of efficiency. Instead the family gradually becomes integrated into a work world in which the type of work varies for each member and each person's work may be at the mercy of worldwide economic conditions as well as local. This shift means that family members will no longer have a single unifying work interest, but typically each member will be working in a field of which other members know little. And the essential bond will not lie in the interest of the work and its common goal, but in the contribution each worker makes to the family purse and family prestige.

If the industrialization and urbanization of India continue, the former tightly structured caste system will gradually break down into a more or less open class one. Since a caste system does not permit mobility, it reinforces a rigid family system in emphasizing hereditary occupations and nepotism. The joint family also tends to discourage social mobility. On the other hand, industrialization brings about a movement of population both horizontally to the new urban areas, and vertically to the new social positions arising from new occupational opportunities. The new industrial society will also alter the former

[23]Everett C. Hughes, "Dilemmas and Contradictions of Status," *American Journal of Sociology*, vol. L (March, 1945), p. 353.

prestige hierarchy of the occupational structure, so that occupations which formerly held positions of great prestige may be superseded by new ones. As a result, ambitious middle-class young men will not necessarily want to follow in the occupational footsteps of their fathers and grandfathers. Thus a changing society opens up new vistas to achievement and success. It also presents young men and women with new occupational opportunities unknown to their parents.

As one of India's main economic problems has been that of the educated unemployed, the main ambition of parents of interviewees was to see their children well settled in life. In many cases this meant a desire for them to obtain a higher standard of living. These ambitions sometimes took the form of excessive pressure on sons to obtain degrees thought essential for important jobs. These jobs were often different from those of the father.

Change of occupation in a society in which it has been customary for a son to follow his father's occupation does not occur without strain and insecurity. Case studies highlighted many of the problems which both parents and sons face in attempting to fulfil these ambitions. These include the problem of financing adequate education for a good job, overcoming religious and caste barriers to jobs, knowing the right steps to take to find suitable occupations and acquire the right behaviour for them, and contending with an increased cost of living. Household expenses rise in the city. At the same time the son may still feel the obligation to carry out his traditional financial kinship responsibilities, such as helping to finance education for younger brothers and dowries for sisters.

The new media of mass communication, such as movies, magazines and newspapers, tend to inculcate some sons with the new industrial ambitions. Thus the "self-made" man arises, who carves out his own career, and in so doing tends to separate himself from his family and relatives. For as he has had little encouragement or assistance from his kin, he is not anxious to assume obligations on their behalf when he achieves success.

Middle-class married women are beginning to enter the work world and increasing contact with the outside world through college, movies, etc., has made some young girls career conscious. These women face such problems as having to adjust to "male" occupational roles in a society which still stresses the social separation of the two sexes, and the resistance of the public to their new role. Single women have difficulty in overcoming the social stigmas attached to the new freedom of behaviour which is necessary to carry on urban occupations.

The economic problems of older adults increase in the period of transition until their new position of insecurity is recognized and the government and other agencies step in to help them readjust to the new situation. The authority of the patriarch in the traditional joint family was so firmly established that it was probably not greatly affected by his economic contribution, but in an industrialized society a man's economic position has great bearing on his power; so his authority is likely to decline when he retires. Another problem of the retired father of a nuclear family is that the cost of raising his family is so great, particularly if he has had to financially assist relatives, that he has seldom saved enough to be self-supporting on his retirement. If his children still feel the traditional obligations to parents, this will not be a great problem. But if they have changed to more individualistic attitudes, then the retired father may feel himself a burden.

This chapter has shown the close interrelation of the economic and familial structures and that the way in which a family earns its living has great bearing on its structural form.

• *Chapter Seven* •

# EDUCATION AND THE FAMILY

TWO IMPORTANT STEPS must be taken by those who want to succeed in an industrialized society. First, they must achieve the appropriate education to fit them for a job, and secondly, they must find a job commensurate with their hopes and desires. These two steps are so interrelated that they could be said to co-exist in many parents' minds.

Training children for adult life is one of the family's primary functions. In a simple society it may be sufficient for parents to pass on the skills and knowledge with which they have solved their problems. But education for a highly industrialized society is far beyond their capabilities. And so formal systems of education develop with specially trained functionaries and elaborate equipment. Families will depend on these institutions to educate their children, and the education which they receive will in turn react back on family life. It will not only give the children new knowledge which will upset the old customary ways of living, but will also give them new ambitions and desires for new ways of living.

### Education in India

Before the British took over the control of India "the large number of indigenous schools were religious in character and regarded knowledge as the means of spiritual growth."[1] The British brought in their own educational system in 1814 with the purpose of educating some of the higher caste Indians, and through them passing on Western influences to the masses. By 1830, Macaulay had clearly stated the British policy: "We must at present do our best to form a class who may be interpreters between us and the millions whom we govern,

[1] Margaret E. Cousins, *Indian Womanhood Today* (Allahabad: Kitabistan, 1941), p. 90.

a class of persons Indian in blood and colour but English in tastes, opinions, morals and intellect."[2] Through this new education the British were gradually able to build up a large civil service in which educated Indians were able to find many new types of jobs which gave them security and tenure.[3]

From 1885 onwards the pressure to obtain English education increased rapidly.

This resulted in a very large increase in the school and college-going population. . . . Round about 1918–20 the proportion of scholars seeking to profit by College education . . . in Calcutta University to the total number of school students in Bengal was the highest in the whole world. . . . Young men from social groups which had no previous trade or traffic with education were now gambling with it. . . . Peasants were stinting themselves to send their young folk to schools and colleges.[4]

The introduction of the English language throughout the school system created a small group of English-speaking Indians who set the pattern of prestige, for they had acquired the language of the ruling class. "Thus English education created a new status group in the Indian social system and education became a means of acquiring higher social status. . . . For the castes and individuals who were already enjoying higher status English education was necessary to maintain that status."[5]

There are now thirty-one universities in India, and many technical and research institutes.[6] But the demands of a technical age, and the

[2]Dhurjati Prasad Mukerji, *Modern Indian Culture: A Sociological Study* Bombay: Hind Kitabs Ltd., (2nd ed., 1948), pp. 78–84.

[3]Mukerji, *Modern Indian Culture*, p. 104.

[4]I. P. Desai, *High School Students in Poona*, Deccan College Monograph Series, 12 (Poona: Deccan College Post-graduate and Research Institute, 1953), pp. 1–2.

[5]S. Mathai, "The Structure of University Education," in *The Teaching of the Social Sciences in India* (Paris: UNESCO, 1956), pp. 26–9. See Mathai for a list of these and the dates of their establishment. The way in which higher education has expanded can be seen in the increase in students. Before 1947, the total number of students in universities and comparable institutions was less than 250,000. Now they number about half a million. The number has almost trebled in technical and professional institutions, and in 1954 was nearly 125,000. The number of students in arts and science has doubled.

[6]*Ibid.*, p. 25. "The first Universities in India—those of Calcutta, Bombay and Madras—were established in 1857. By that time a number of other educational institutions had come into being, many of them set up by Christian missionaries, and others by the government. . . . The conflict that had arisen in the first decade of the nineteenth century between the advocates of Western learning and the champions of oriental education was more or less finally resolved in favour of the former by 1835, when it was laid down, under the influence of Macaulay, that government funds available for education were to be devoted mainly to support schools and colleges which imparted Western learning through the English language."

introduction of compulsory and free education by law, have crowded these institutions and made it difficult for many students to obtain seats, particularly for professional training in such fields as medicine and law.

As in most countries, women did not obtain formal education in India until much later than boys. The Christian missions played a large part in both initiating education for girls and popularizing it among the general public. Their first recruits for professional training were usually daughters of Christian Indian families and widows. Later Brahmo-Samajists and Parsees founded schools for girls, but the Indian government was slow in following suit. For the profound distrust of education for women all over India meant that, as there was no pressure on them to erect schools for girls, they spent their small resources on boys' schools and colleges.[7]

The type of formal education thought suitable for girls has changed markedly since the early schools. Whereas in 1823 girls were only taught to read, write and do simple accounts, by 1927 a large number had taken their B.A. degrees, and the whole outlook had changed to the point where the Rani Sahib of Sangli could say in her report at the Women's Conference on Educational Reform: "There was a time when the education of girls had not only no supporters but open enemies in India. Female education has by now gone through all the stages—total apathy and indifference, ridicule, criticism, and acceptance. It may now be safely stated that anywhere in India the need of education for girls as much as for boys is recognized as a cardinal need of progress—a *sine qua non* of national progress."[8]

In spite of this change of outlook, girls' education is still not taken as seriously as boys', and the amount of money expended on it is much less.[9]

[7]H. Gray, "Education," in *The Key of Progress: A Survey of the Status and Conditions of Women in India*, A. R. Caton, ed. (London: Oxford University Press, 1930), p. 27.

NUMBER OF GIRLS IN COLLEGE IN INDIA IN 1930

|  | Christian | Non-Christian | Total |
|---|---|---|---|
| Medical colleges | 219 | 95 | 314 |
| Training colleges | 98 | 17 | 115 |
| Arts colleges | 721 | 533 | 1,254 |
| TOTAL | 1,038 | 645 | 1,683 |

[8]*Ibid.*, p. 5.

[9]Desai, *High School Students*, pp. 45–6. "If a boy and girl from one family pass their Matriculation examination, and if the economic conditions do not permit to send both of them for further education, the girl will have to give up

My parents had great ambition for my brothers, but were not interested in their daughters' education. My two elder sisters had very little education, and were married quite early. Parents were more particular about getting good husbands for them. But they were very much interested in their sons' education and wanted all of them to get good incomes. The happiest day of Mother's life was when my eldest brother got a job and brought his first month's salary to her and prostrated before her. In regard to her daughters, the happiest day was when she first visited her daughter and son-in-law's house, and saw how happy they were. (Case 91)

The main problem in promoting their education has not been that women were thought incapable of learning as has been the case in many countries, but in the idea that education was futile for girls as it had no bearing on their future marital roles.[10] Moreover, in the days of child marriage, girls left school almost before they could read or write. Only in comparatively rare cases did a girl pursue her education after marriage.[11]

The Sarda Act which raised the age of marriage for girls to fourteen years had a vital effect on their education, for they then had more time to fill in before marriage and so could stay longer at school.[12] Public recognition of the need for a broader education for girls followed the report of the Hartog Committee in 1928-9: "We are definitely of the opinion that in the interest of the advance of Indian education as a whole, priority should now be given to the claims of girls' education in every scheme of expansion."[13] In the late 1940's women's education was given further impetus by the growing desire of men to marry educated brides,[14] and the gradual change in family structure, which deprived women of the former economic security of the large joint family, made parents increasingly aware of the importance of educating their daughters so that they would be able to look after themselves financially should the need arise. Finally, the teachings of

---

studies even if she is brighter than the boy. . . . The general attitude towards girls' education is similar to that towards the education of boys in backward classes. She is expected to do domestic work and if she gave priority to her studies she would be reminded that ultimately she has to mind the kitchen. Such an attitude may not prevail among very rich families."

[10]Cousins, *Indian Womanhood*, p. 95. "The whole current mentality. . . . to-day (is oriented towards the belief) that education for a girl is useless, a waste of time, and disturbing to their thoughts."

[11]*Ibid.*, p. 93. In 1947, Cousins says that it was becoming popular for young married girls after the birth of the "duty-child," that is, their first baby, to go back to school, sometimes they would even obtain academic degrees.

[12]Gray, "Education," p. 43.

[13]*Ibid.*, p. 4.

[14]Margaret Cormack, *The Hindu Woman*, (New York: Bureau of Publications, Teachers College, Columbia University, 1953), p. 52.

Gandhi and other Indian leaders of the need for equal rights for women have encouraged the spread of higher education to girls.

Not all the families included in this study showed a desire to educate their daughters beyond matriculation, but many did, and the daughters themselves were on the whole very keen to attend college.[15] One reason for their attitude lies in the fact that girls living in cities are becoming increasingly influenced by the attractions of the outside world, and attending college is one important way in which they can "safely" get in touch with them.

Higher education for girls in India is such a recent innovation that only a few of the mothers in the families interviewed had themselves gone to college. Table XII in Appendix I shows that only three of the mothers had received their B.A. degrees, and none had proceeded further. In comparison to this, thirty-three of the daughters and thirty-one of the female interviewees, a total of sixty-four daughters, had received their B.A. degrees, and seventeen their Master's and other degrees. At the other end of the educational scale, twenty-four mothers were illiterate, as compared to only two of the daughters. And thirty-nine mothers and twenty-three daughters were only able to read and write. These figures show that daughters of middle-class Hindus are now receiving a great deal more education than their mothers.

A similar trend was observed in the education of sons as compared with their fathers. Table XII shows that whereas half the fathers achieved an education only up to matriculation, the same proportion of their sons had obtained their B.A. degrees. And a large number of sons, fifty-nine, had obtained additional degrees.

Looking at the trend as a whole, it can be seen that children are now receiving more education than their parents, but that men are still ahead of women in the amount of education they obtain.[16]

In Bangalore there are two colleges for women, one a government college with 1,000 students, and the other, a privately owned institution, founded in 1948, with 600 students. The first college has had hostels (residences) for students for a number of years, the second built its first hostel in 1955. Women's hostels mean another step away

[15]Desai, *High School Students*, p. 45. In his study of Poona High School students, Desai found that 90 per cent of the girls wanted to go further than high school. He thinks that, as only a small percentage of these will in fact be able to do so, this may mean a new area of frustration for young girls and women. Of the boys, only 67 per cent wanted to study further than high school, 42 per cent wanted to go to college and 25 per cent wanted to take some other course of study such as technical training.

[16]The following table gives an idea of the general level of education of girls

from family influences for Indian girls, for it is one thing to take the step to acquire higher education and quite another to actually leave the jurisdiction of family, caste and relatives and live under the influence of outside authorities with girls from many different castes and religions. College staffs usually do all they can to see that girls of different communities and castes mix freely together.

Both colleges in Bangalore have many government scholarships and some students receive free tuition. This means that girls from families with relatively low incomes can now attend college. According to one college principal:

> Girls go to college in India at a much lower age than in most Western countries. Many begin college at fourteen years of age. About 25 per cent of the girls say they want to go on to postgraduate work, but only about 5 per cent in fact do. In all, there were about two hundred girls doing postgraduate work in Bangalore in 1955. Girls can enrol in any subject at Mysore University except engineering, but the majority of the girls who continue their studies after graduation go into teaching or medicine. The desire to become doctors influences their undergraduate work, and a large number of girls now take science rather than arts degrees. Parents are anxious that their daughters should broaden their horizons at college and are keen for them to perfect their English, for they believe that it is the door to the wider international world.

Women's colleges now have many extracurricular activities such as dramatic presentations, orchestras, classical dancing, debates and students' associations.

A recent innovation in many colleges is the pressure on students to do practical social work. Women students are taken to the poor districts of Bangalore, where they teach the people health practices and

---

in Indian cities. It shows a cross-section of married daughters from the Poona district classified by educational attainment and according to whether that education was considered adequate.

*Number of married daughters (City sample)*

|  | Considered adequate | Considered inadequate | Total |
|---|---|---|---|
| Illiterates | 43 | 60 | 103 |
| Up to Primary | 71 | 53 | 124 |
| Up to High School | 19 | 8 | 27 |
| Up to Matriculation | 10 | 2 | 12 |
| Higher or technical | 10 | 1 | 11 |
| TOTAL | 153 | 124 | 277 |

SOURCE: V. M. Dandekar and Kumudini Dandekar, *Survey of Fertility and Mortality in Poona District* (Gokhale Institute of Politics and Economics, Publication no. 27, 1953), p. 134.

how to care for their children. This is part of a movement which has spread all over India to teach children and young people a widening sense of responsibility.

Another innovation is the establishment of Departments of Home Science. These have roused some opposition, for parents not only do not understand their significance in training their daughters to be modern women but are also afraid that the girls will learn new ideas that will make them demand costly household equipment in their homes.

Not only do college graduates remain much longer in educational institutions than school children but while there, they are exposed to new ideas through a wider curriculum and broader friendships. Considering the deeply ingrained Hindu ideal of woman's place in the home, the rapidity with which college education has spread among women has been remarkable. This has been largely due to the conscious and unconscious acceptance by parents and daughters alike of the fact that they will now have to live in a wider world. One of my informants who said that hostels were good for girls because "they learned to get on with others" was in effect saying that girls from now on will increasingly have to meet people from all different sections of life. This is a great change for girls in comparison to their former secluded life.

In spite of this exposure to new trends, fewer women of this sample had been affected by their college and university experiences than men. A few of each sex said that they had not had any appreciable effect on their lives. The rest felt that their religious, political, and caste attitudes had been affected. Women, in particular, seemed to have got their first real interest in politics at college.

Thirty men and thirteen women had lived in hostels during their college days, and eighteen men and three women had lived with relatives while studying. An additional ten men had lived in boarding houses; one had lived with friends, and one, at the Y.M.C.A. These figures show that a number of respondents had lived away from home at an impressionable age. Change in attitude to other castes was a particularly noticeable result with those who had stayed in hostels which included people of several castes. One young girl said: "While at college I lived in a hostel where I met many girls and boys from different castes. I soon began to eat meat. This shocked my mother, and she scolded me about it. But Father pointed out that I could not possibly conform to all the old customs if I did not believe in them." (Case 7)

A number of respondents no longer carried out the religious rituals they had been taught as children. This did not mean that they had necessarily lost their faith, although several young men said they no longer believed in God, but only that they had given up such religious practices as saying prayers, reading religious books, visiting temples, or wearing the sacred thread.

Other customary ways which women had changed, or new ways of behaving that had been added, included: choosing their own husbands, marrying out of caste, having men friends, going to Christian schools, not sitting out for monthly periods, breaking caste rules such as eating meat and eating meals in the homes of people of other castes, attending mixed parties, marrying after puberty (for Brahmins), using an electric oven for cooking, eating in hotels, wearing the modern six-yard sari (for Brahmins), wearing lipstick, and divorcing their husbands.

Men had changed from the customary ways of their families by: breaking caste rules such as marrying into another caste, inter-dining with other castes and entertaining men from other castes in their homes. They had also eaten at hotels, eaten meat, cut their hair or grown moustaches contrary to caste custom, drank liquor, smoked, chosen their own wives, worn European clothes and eaten at tables rather than squatting on the ground.

The extent to which such changed behaviour led to conflict and tension within the family varied considerably. Quarrels over breaking family and caste customs, such as inter-dining, seldom led to family rifts unless they were so numerous that they finally totaled up to a crisis situation. But disagreements over marriage, education, careers and discipline often caused intense bitterness, and sometimes, as in the case of inter-caste marriage, meant the complete separation of the interviewee from his or her family.

Eating meat, too, seemed a serious break in caste behaviour, and would evoke much more antagonism than, for example, wearing lipstick or smoking. Staying out late at night and spending too much money were two other matters which caused a good deal of friction. Difference in political views from parents did not seem to occur very often, or cause much tension, and the wearing of shirts and ties is now so usual in cities that only parents and relatives who lived in isolated villages objected to it.

There was evidence that, in many instances, young men and women preferred conflict with their parents to the ridicule of comrades at "old-fashioned" behaviour. For example, one young man stood the anger of parents and relatives by cutting his hair rather than be made fun of by his friends. In this way peers are an important factor in change, and the gradual increase in the number of peer groups in India will probably be instrumental in accelerating the rate of change: both because they set patterns for new behaviour, and because they give the boy or girl, young man or woman, a supporting group in their adjustment to new conditions. Education could, therefore, not be said to be responsible for all change as such. It is rather the combination of the exposure to new ideas and patterns of behaviour along with peer group support and/or control that lead to changed behaviour.

Co-education has come slowly in most industrialized countries. In India the strict separation of the sexes in the large joint family has delayed its acceptance, for in such families the children were thoroughly trained in sex segregation at a very early age.[17] In a society in which this strict separation exists, neither sex achieves rewards for moving into the other world; so there is little incentive for boys and girls to mix, especially as the strong taboos against it mean punishment for a person who attempts to cross the sex line. The barriers to co-education, however, are gradually breaking down. Private experimental schools in large Indian cities now often teach boys and girls in the same class room.

The first girls to attend men's colleges in India were carefully supervised. But this supervision has been gradually lessened and now colleges present opportunities for young men and women to break through the barriers of sex segregation. One informant said:

Boys and girls don't mix at all in the pass courses at the university. Girls are allotted separate seats and automatically go to them. But the honours courses are smaller. There they mix, get to know each other, talk over courses, and even sometimes have coffee together. Men and women even stand chatting with each other in the corridors. But there is no "official" place for them to meet each other, there is no attempt on the part of university authorities or hostels to arrange meetings.

Psychology courses are looked on as "bad" because men and women mix so much in them. The X College for women also has a "bad" name because some of the girls go out with men. Occasionally, if a group of students are going on a mixed picnic, I will be asked to bring a girl along with one of her friends. She will go with me because I have a good reputation, and she knows she can trust me. But this is unusual. If I asked a girl to go and have coffee with me she would refuse—because she simply doesn't like doing it. Girls *don't* want to go out with boys. Now it is becoming the fashion for university students to go to mixed parties, but the majority of boys in Bangalore don't take girls out alone.

[17]The head mistress of a co-educational private school in Bangalore said that even three-year-old boys and girls will not take hands when playing games.

Indian girls who graduate from college, like their North American counterparts, are often given the somewhat derogatory title of "highbrow," for they form such a small percentage of the total number of Indian women that they have not been completely accepted either by the public in general or by young men in particular. They are said to work harder and be more conscientious than men about their studies, because they have fewer distractions; and to accept college discipline more readily because their training has made them more submissive.[18] They are freer to choose preferred subjects, for men must consider courses in terms of their future careers. But perhaps the main reason for the different attitude of men and women to their university work is that men students tend to be restless and frustrated at college partly as a result of the excessive pressure put on them by fathers and relatives and partly from their fear of the future. This restlessness has sometimes taken the form of student riots.[19] It has perhaps been enhanced by the banning of students' unions on many Indian campuses.

### Education and Ambitions

If the anxieties parents have in regard to their children are analysed, then their ambitions for their children are much better understood. In India, middle-class parents know full well the struggle that their sons will have to face in the work world, for to get a job at all, let alone a "good" job, sons must compete in an employment market in which the supply of jobs is far below the demand. Moreover, the cost of living in the city is higher than in the village and the family that moves to the city may feel compelled to continue to carry their share of the

---

[18]*Ibid.*, p. 52. "Generally girls want to go to school. . . . Boys, on the other hand, often try to avoid school. But girls like school, not so well as their homes, which are more secure, but they like school. They are usually better in their studies than the boys for that reason." In his study of the Poona high school students, Desai found that almost twice as many boys as girls said they were inattentive in school. A large proportion of these attributed the reason for their inattention to factors outside the class room such as economic conditions, ill health and "mental worries." See: Desai, *High School Students*, pp. 49–50.

[19]An informant gave these additional reasons for student restlessness: the strike pattern had been part of student behaviour even before they were encouraged to resist and strike for Independence in 1942; the distance between professor and student(modern students do not look up to their teachers as "gurus" as in the olden days); the professors have no hold over their students for they do not control their marks as in Western universities; (the central educational authority marks all examinations).

financial responsibilities of the large joint family in the native place. It is, therefore, possible that parents who appear to have very high ambitions for their children may in fact only be pushing their children's education because of their insecure economic situation.

Ambitions, too, are related to the background of the families concerned; so what might appear modest hopes for a son's future from one person's point of view may in reality be a very high goal from the relative position of his family. Moreover, a family living in a village may feel that their son has achieved great success when he obtains a job in the city where pay is high when in fact the same position may appear a very modest one from the point of view of a city dweller. This ambivalence means that in analysing people's ambitions it is safer to take the expression of their feelings on the matter of "getting ahead" rather than their actual achievements.

In a tightly knit family system one would expect consensus as to family goals. As far as "ambitions" are concerned, this would mean that all family members strive towards specific, clearly understood and agreed-on ends. A large number of the families studied did indeed seem to be united in their aspirations for family members. Most interviewees stressed their parents' ambitions, and did not mention father, mother or siblings having different ambitions. Since the sample was chosen from families in which one or more members had had higher education and a great many were Brahmins, it was not surprising to find that the great majority of parents were concerned over the education and future of their children, and that most of them were anxious to have them "get ahead" in the sense of achieving a higher standard of living than they themselves had enjoyed. "My parents wanted me to become an important, distinguished and powerful man," was not an unusual excerpt from interviews. Interviewees themselves also showed ambition to "get ahead" and a number were so ambitious that they were not at all satisfied with their parents' standard of living.

The sample of families represented different socio-economic backgrounds. Many of the interviewees had been brought up in homes where the parents had secure top positions in the business and social world. Their children had been surrounded by an atmosphere which promoted their ambitions as naturally as a farm family inculcates its children with love of the farm. No new unknown steps needed to be taken to achieve family ambitions. Sons merely had the responsibility of taking over positions which were held by fathers, or possibly to make slight advances over them. In any case, all the steps towards their goals were visible long in advance, and the whole family unconsciously helped to orient them to their adult positions. There was a minimum of strain for parents and children, for fathers were fairly sure that they could pass on their position to their children, and unless sons were rebels, they had utmost assistance in taking them over. The following example is typical of these young men or women:

My ambition in life is to be an IAS officer. None of us children are satisfied with our parents' standard of living. We are all equally ambitious and we have had very brilliant academic careers. One of my sisters is now in the United States on a scholarship, working for her Ph.D. One brother is studying engineering in the United Kingdom. I am quite confident that we will all be very successful in life. Our parents and relatives have had a good deal of influence in promoting our ambitions, for the atmosphere of our home was highly inspiring. My grandfather had many friends in high positions, and they used to often visit him at our house. (Case 144)

Another case shows the inter-stimulation in a family in which all the children are infused with the desire for higher education in order to get ahead.

I am not at all satisfied with the standard of living of my parents. My brothers and sisters are also very ambitious. One of my sisters was employed in the Public Health Laboratory as an Assistant after she matriculated. Later when she had accumulated leave, she finished her B.Sc. in chemistry and zoology. After that she was promoted and is now well off.

My eldest brother got his M.A. in literature, and now at the age of forty-five is studying law. Another sister did well in High School, and got scholarships through her college career. My next brother failed his Intermediate, which was a great shock to him, so he joined the services, earned some money, and then completed his B.Sc. and M.A.

From the very beginning of my college career I have had a strong desire to go abroad to study, for men returning with foreign degrees are held in high esteem, and can obtain responsible positions with fat salaries. (Case 48)

In many families, the parents' ambitions were expressed in such a helpful and unobtrusive way that the children were only aware of them indirectly.

My parents were keenly interested in our education. This was apparent to us in many small ways: for example, when exams came around, Mother would cook all sorts of extra nourishing foods to supplement our strength. She would come to the school and pick us up after our exams and find out how we had fared. Father also asked us often how we were getting on in school, and whether we wanted any extra tuition in any particular subject. Our parents wouldn't even give parties when we were studying for exams as they might be too noisy. Thus, it is to their unfailing enthusiasm that we owe our excellent progress in school. But they never forced us to do anything against our will: for example, my younger sister wasn't interested in music; so Mother stopped her lessons. (Case 7)

It was evident from interviews that in a few cases parents' ambitions for their children were largely shaped in order that the family might shine in comparison to those of relatives or caste members. One interviewee said: "My parents wanted us to be well educated because they wanted us to be cultured and intelligent and to be different from our community which has very few educated boys and even fewer educated girls." (Case 23) In other families fathers felt that they had achieved their ambitions for sons when the son's income was greater than their retiring income. "You have started where I have stopped."

Not all parents were highly ambitious for their children. In fact, a number seemed to be anxious to see that their children were properly educated only up to the point where they would be "well settled" in life. This meant for sons enough education to get a job which would give them an adequate standard of living, for daughters, enough for a "happy" marriage.

The above discussion has been concerned with families in which all family members were more or less united in their desire to get ahead as a family or to push some particular family member. Indian family members, may, of course, vary in the strength of their ambitions. Some may acquire incentives to move ahead, or push someone ahead, others may not. This situation may create strain, for even a husband and wife may not be equally ambitious or ambitious in the same way for their children.

Although, on the whole, a greater number of the fathers of interviewees were more highly ambitious for their children than mothers, on occasion the latter were the ones who were particularly determined to see that their children got education and good jobs.[20] In fact, several instances were cited in which mothers made great sacrifices, such as selling their jewels, to help finance their sons' education.

The two following cases are ones in which the father played the paramount part in encouraging children to do well in their studies, against oposition from relatives.

> My parents were very much interested in our education. Father in particular was very strict about it. He always felt very proud when any of us got distinction in class. The child's marks would be read out before all the family. The other children with low marks would feel humiliated. He was also very particular about music lessons for us girls. We were all taught the veena [a popular musical instrument]. I was so good at it that I was asked to play in public. Father encouraged me to do this in spite of opposition from our relatives. It was a proud day for the whole family when I gave my first radio programme. (Case 65)

[20]Studies have shown that mothers tend to be more ambitious for their children than fathers on the North American continent.

The second case is one in which a brilliant father who was a "mathematical genius" was very anxious for his daughter to go on to graduate education. Even after she was married and living with her in-laws, he urged her to take her B.Comm. so that she would be able to help in her in-laws' business.

Father wrote letter after letter stressing its importance and usefulness. But my mother-in-law wouldn't hear of it. She said it would bring a lot of complications and problems because my father-in-law's business was a joint business, and many of his sons were connected with it. After living twelve years with my in-laws I realize now that I would have landed in a lot of trouble if I had listened to my father. (Case 54)

Sometimes fathers are so keen for their sons to get on that they ride rough-shod over their wishes.

My parents are very anxious that their children should do better than they did. Father is prepared to spend any amount on my education. Even from early childhood Father was very particular that we should get a good education and big positions in life. He wanted me to be a barrister and hence much against my will I had to pass my law exams. He wanted my younger brother to be a doctor, but he did not yield and instead joined the Indian Army. My major interest is to study philosophy and literature, and go away for foreign study. Father will pay for this, but insists that I get married before I go, and take the girl with me. I don't like this idea at all, but as Father is adamant, I don't know what is going to happen. (Case 139)

Occasionally, the ambitions of a family will centre around one son. In one family the parents were helping a son to get a good job so that he could support the whole family.

I want to have a higher standard of living than my parents, and they want it too. They took intense interest in my studies. All my life they have inspired me, and given up many things to help finance my education. They have to finance the education of my younger brothers as well. But in spite of this they gave me everything they could in the expectation that I would get a good job and be able to support the whole family. (Case 136)

Reasons for mothers wanting their sons to get ahead vary considerably. Some mothers were financially insecure, and wanted their sons to get educated for jobs which would make them financially safe. One was afraid of her husband leaving her, and that she would be completely dependent on her sons. One interviewee said: "Because of the constant goading and advice of my mother I have always paid the maximum attention to my lessons, and have been successful in all my exams. My younger brothers have the same spirit. We all aspire to have a better standard of living and to be examples to the other relatives." (Case 47) Some mothers had been highly educated themselves, and were bound that their sons would have a college education. In fact, the ambitions of a number of mothers for their children were so high that when their husbands died they had carried the whole burden of financing the education themselves.

One exceptional case concerned a mother-in-law who was so keen to have her future daughter-in-law educated that she asked her mother to take her back until she had graduated, for usually mothers-in-law seemed to resent or be jealous of educated daughters-in-law. In another family it was the daughter herself who was ambitious to be educated and when her parents failed to help a brother came forward to assist her.

My parents had great ambitions for their sons, but weren't interested in their daughters' education. After Father's death I had finished my matriculation and wanted to go on to college. But Mother was against it. She thought it was time to marry me and that I should stop studying and stay at home. Finally, my youngest brother, who is an authority in our family, came on my side. He said that if the family wasn't willing to spend from the family income for my education he would do it from his own personal income; so he paid for my college education for two years, then I got a scholarship to finish it. Mother was afraid to send me to college for another reason. Our community is quite small and there are very few educated women in it, even highly educated men are rare; so if a girl becomes a college graduate it may be difficult to marry her and get an equally educated son-in-law. Even now Mother isn't very proud of my education. She feels that the higher education has given me new ideas such as taking a job, and she feels that I have had too much liberty. I am not very anxious to marry, but want to take up a career if I can get a suitable job. (Case 91)

Husbands vary in the amount of interest they take in their wives' education. The most usual pattern is for them to discourage higher education for their wives, but occasionally one will want to enhance his wife's education or accomplishments.

Father and Mother wanted to give me the best they could afford. They were interested in my education and wanted me to be well read. But the thing about which they were most anxious was my marriage. When they found a suitable match they stopped my education and I was married. After I went to live with my husband, he wanted me to finish at least up to Matriculation; so he coached me patiently for the exam. He was also very fond of music and encouraged me to sing and play the veena before his friends. (Case 70)

Many of the married interviewees showed great interest in their own children's education. A number said that they dreamt of their future happiness and prosperity. Several were struggling hard to finance their education and thought that their children's lives were of more importance than their own. Financing the education of their children was often a great burden and even meant sacrifice for the parents. "Our parents had trials and tribulations financing our education. Mother deprived herself of food and clothing to get my brother a diploma." "My parents starved for days in order to finance my college education."

Because of the earlier death of men, mothers were often left with the burden of financing their childrens' education. A number of cases showed that they often made great sacrifices to do this. "Mother kept up our expensive education after Father died with great financial difficulty." "Mother sold all her jewels to finance the family education."

In some families this responsibility is shared by the eldest son: "When I came to college Father died and Mother sold all her jewels to educate me and my younger brothers. Just at that time my eldest brother had been appointed to a good job, and he sacrificed everything for the sake of our education." (Case 154) On the other hand, the father normally bears the greatest burden of worry in financing his cihldren's education. Occasionally he uses this to goad his children to do well. "Father constantly reminded me of his sacrifice."

In well-knit, affectionate families, the children often appreciated this sacrifice to such an extent that it reinforced their feelings of responsibility to their parents. "All along my parents have sacrificed their comforts to educate me. I must prove worthy of this. I won't displease them in any way. It is my duty to look after their comforts and welfare when they grow old." Only a few interviewees said their parents had failed to assist them in any tangible way. "My parents only helped me with their prayers."

In view of the high ambitions of many parents and the personal sacrifice many underwent to educate their children, it was not surprising to find that interviews showed that a good deal of pressure was often put on sons to study. This might take a subtle form such as the expression of keen disappointment or sorrow when a son did not pass his examinations. In one case the home was said to be like a house at the time of death when a son failed, with all the women sitting in draggled clothes, weeping. In another house the mother shut herself in her room and wept for three days after her son's failure. This particular home was one in which the parents were extremely ambitious, and the eldest son had passed his examinations brilliantly. The son who had failed had had four tutors to try to help him get through his examinations.

Disappointment at the failure of a son might take the form of physical punishment such as caning. But the usual form was that of remonstration and constant nagging. This was often accompanied with disparaging comparisons between the son and his brothers, sisters and cousins. This seemed to be a most effective treatment for it was the kind most dreaded by sons. Several interviewees claimed that the constant reproaches of their parents had made them feel inadequate and unable to carry out the family expectations. When the four or five years of primary education and the six or seven years of middle and high school are added to the years many sons spend at college, it can be seen that pressure on them may last for many years. "My parents were never satisfied with my progress" shows the constant goading that one son must have endured. Another said:

My parents were very much interested in our education. But I think Father overdid it. He wanted me and my brothers to get high grades in our degrees; so he was never satisfied with us. He wanted us to read day and night and not spend time playing. He only allowed us two hours in the evening to play. He always cursed us if we didn't do our homework, and would even beat us at times.

I think my inferiority feeling is due to him, for he always told us that other children were far better than we were, and that we were all idiots. He would say this day in and day out, and it made a deep impression on me. His only thought in life was for his sons to get better jobs than he had and to lead decent, honest lives. (Case 154)

In the one Harijan family studied, the method used by the father was that of ridicule:

My parents were very strict about our study hours and regular attendance at school and college. I was always pitted against other boys at school and made fun of if I didn't get good marks. Father would always say that the caste Hindu boys were superior and I was good for nothing. He would sometimes say that I would never prosper in life. This always made me sick and I would openly swear and even abuse my father. I always wanted to show that I was as good as a caste Hindu. (Case 35)

In several families the father's nagging was so extreme that it appeared to have a boomerang effect, crippling the son's ability to study. One interviewee said:

Father always abused me when he heard that I was playing truant from school or didn't do my lessons. But I was often bored to death with school and would tell lots of lies to escape the torture of being confined in the class room. My father always compared me with other boys and told me I was good for nothing. I have always thought that I was quite above the average in ability, but I never did well in exams because I was always so afraid of failing that I could never concentrate. It wasn't really the exams themselves that I was afraid of, but of the way in which Father would treat me if I failed. Even now I am afraid of exams on this account. For although I am now an adult and married I am scared of what Father will think and say if I fail. I know he won't spank me, but still I can imagine how he will compare me with others. I know too how disappointed he will be if I fail—and this adds to my fear. It is this fear which has sapped my intellect. (Case 157)

In several instances, the boy's self-confidence was adequate for him to take nagging about school work as a matter of course; so it did not affect his competence. "My eldest cousin was much interested in my education. He constantly nagged me by pitting me against other boys. But I just didn't bother, his nagging was just routine and I got used to it." (Case 30)

Sometimes parents would insist on sons taking subjects which they disliked. This was effective with some sons but not with others. "My parents forced one of my brothers to be a doctor but my younger brother escaped their desire to make him an engineer and went into the navy instead." (Case 12)

A good deal of the anxiety for sons to do well at school and college is due to the belief that their success will reflect back on the family and eventually improve their standard of living. It may be that in a society in which children are expected to support their parents in their old age and help relatives in trouble that more pressure is unconsciously put on them. On informant told of a father who had saved every receipt for money spent on his son to show him later when he himself needed support. Extreme pressure can have tragic effects on the son who must bear the burden of family responsibility, and yet fails to equip himself with the university degrees which pave the way to a good job.

Interviews showed that not as much pressure is put on girls to study as boys. The great majority of women interviewees who said that their parents had been very interested in their education said that no excessive pressure was used. They had also had a wider choice in the subjects they had studied than the boys. "Mother and Father didn't force us to do anything against our wishes to get ahead" was a fairly typical remark. In fact, of the forty-three women reporting only seven said that their parents had put pressure on them to study or get jobs. One woman said:

My parents were so interested in our education that Mother actually moved to a city so that we could get a good education. But they weren't particular that we should be great scholars. They gave us the opportunities and conveniences and a proper atmosphere for studying well. There was no forcing. They taught me music and violin for three years as an accomplishment. When I didn't show much interest in it and gave it up, they didn't force me to continue. It was the same with my brothers. One was very interested in mechanics; so he took up engineering. The other was suited for office work; so he took up a pass course and got a job in a bank. There was no coercion on them of any sort to take particular subjects or take up any particular jobs. (Case 75)

As there are no comparable data, it is impossible to tell whether pressure on sons to study and do well in examinations is increasing or not. However, severals interviewees thought that it was, and their opinion, coupled with the increasing importance of education as India becames more industrialized, suggests that pressure is indeed greater now than before.

Of course, our parents wanted us to study. But they weren't mad or frantic about it. Even if we failed a class it did not shock them. My brothers were allowed to take up any subject they wanted to. When my fourth brother wanted to take up mathematics and go to Benares for his B.E., Father consented. When the other brothers wanted to just take the pass course, Father agreed. I think it was because there was no necessity to compete for government jobs. Our estate had plenty and could provide well for all the sons. One son wanted to take up business. Father said "yes" and gave him the necessary money to start out, but he and Mother weren't particularly proud of it. And when it failed a few years later and my brother lost all he had invested, they weren't very perturbed. (Case 66)

In a few cases parents showed little or no interest in the education of their sons after matriculation. It may be that they felt that they had sacrificed all they could to get their sons that far. Or, having several other sons to educate and daughters to marry, they could not afford to do more for one son. A few of these fathers lived on family estates and their sole ambition was to have a son inherit the family property and look after it. In such cases the father either did not consider that higher education would be of any practical use to his son, or else was so satisfied himself with village life that he did not see the necessity for his sons to be educated to leave.

All the sons interviewed were by no means highly ambitious, and as the sample under study was biased towards highly educated young men, it is quite possible that even a larger percentage of the general population has not yet acquired the ambitions of an industrialized society. One research assistant thought that a number of the young men he interviewed had no ambition at all although they had had a good deal of education. These young men had been pushed by ambitious parents, but after college had only been able to get minor clerical jobs. They grumbled continually about their pay, but made no attempt to improve their positions.

In summing up, it could be said that the majority of the parents of this study were anxious for their sons to obtain as much education as possible, and often pushed them in this regard. For some of these parents, no sacrifice was too great to make for their son's success. On the other hand, a small number of parents did not seem overambitious for their children, and there was no evidence that they had taken more than a mild interest in their education. A study of the ambitions of fathers for sons in Poona will be found in Appendix 4.

## EDUCATION versus MARRIAGE

Interest in the education of daughters was found in both the joint and the nuclear families of this study, but emphasis on it and pressure towards it were definitely higher in nuclear families and lower in large joint families.[21] On the other hand, although marriage was the chief goal of all parents for their daughters, it was in the large joint families that parents showed the greatest interest in their daughters' marriages, and the parents of nuclear families showed least interest. If this gradual change in emphasis is indicative of a general trend in attitude to marriage, it is easy to understand why the number of unmarried women typically increases as family structures change. Furthermore, none of the large joint families showed interest in the daughters working outside the home, whereas a number of the smaller joint and nuclear families showed a considerable amount of interest. Since education for the future role of wife and mother could be obtained within the family circle, daughters were not inculcated with ambitions for either formal education or a job outside the home in the joint family. Thus it is a relatively new thing for parents to think in terms of formal education for daughters, and still newer for them to harbour ambitions for their careers. Both these new atitudes are nurtured by city living and its concomitant economic insecurity. Case studies showed that most of the parents still stressed the type of education which would fit their daughters for marriage rather than for careers.

Yes, parents were interested in our education and educated us until we married. As soon as their daughters were fifteen or sixteen they began to look for husbands for them. When their marriages were settled, their education was stopped, for they considered settling a girl's life in marriage was

[21]Of the sixty-three families replying, forty-eight showed some or a lot of interest in their daughters' education, and the remaining fifteen families were not interested. Three of the large joint families were not interested as compared to two who were. Four of the eighteen small joint families were not interested, and fourteen were. Of the forty nuclear families replying, eight were not interested, and thirty-two were.

more important than her education. They wanted them to be well read, and that the minimum education for them should be Matriculation; so as soon as a girl matriculated they started looking for a boy. (Case 61)

Several informants said that the eagerness of young men to marry highly educated wives has somewhat diminished in recent years. Reasons for this are thought to be that, first of all, young men have found out that educated wives have a greater variety of needs, and so cost more to support; they expect more attention from their husbands and want to go out more with their friends; they do not expect to obey their husbands to the extent of uneducated girls; and finally they tend to make a relatively uneducated husband feel inferior. Parents too now seem loathe to select highly educated wives for their sons for they believe that they do not pay as much attention to the housework and do not fit as readily into the family pattern. They feel too that they are more likely to challenge their in-laws' authority, and are often restless and unhappy if they must live in a village without modern comforts.[22]

However, whether this trend to marry educated girls is changing or not, there is still plenty of evidence that many ambitious young men still want educated wives who can fit into the social life which will be part of their upward climb. One informant told of a young man who had been educated in Europe and whose family was trying to arrange his marriage to a girl whose family could give a large dowry. But the young man was not interested in the money for he wanted to marry an educated girl who would be a companion and share his views and interests.

Another important part of the education of daughters of middle-class families is that they must be well versed in literature and the arts. Many of the female interviewees had been brought up to play musical instruments, usually the veena. In fact, one interviewee said that her family considered music a "necessity of life." Often pressure

[22]An informant noted this difference in wifely expectations: wives that marry into a low servant caste are happy if they have plenty of grain in the house; a working man's daughter is happy when she marries, if her husband brings her home an occasional sari, and takes her out from time to time; but an educated daughter wants a great deal more attention and many more comforts.

Another informant spoke of the way in which the education of girls is affecting inter-religious marriages in northern India. He said that Christian girls are much better educated than their brothers, for the boys do not take their education seriously, and so do not get far. This means that there is a dearth of men of comparable education for the Christian girls to marry. However, a number of Hindu and Muslim men who attend universities want to marry educated girls instead of the more secluded women of their own religion. The higher education of girls is thus tending to cause some inter-religious marriages.

was put on unwilling daughters to practise, much in the same way as middle- and upper-class parents in the Western World try to train their daughters in "fashionable" musical instruments. Men often sought brides who could sing and play an instrument.

Another important accomplishment for the South Indian girl is classical dancing. This is a fairly recent innovation, as formerly it was not thought suitable for girls from "good" families. On the whole, this study shows that most young Hindu girls of the middle and upper classes are still educated with a view to marriage rather than to careers. However, a number of parents were anxious to have their daughters attend universities. Perhaps one of the main reasons for this new trend is that, with the change from child to adult marriage, the leisure time of girls must now be filled in up to nineteen or even twenty-five years. And college is one way of "keeping them busy" until marriage. Another reason mentioned by interviewees was that the difficulty of finding suitable mates for daughters sometimes forces parents to prolong their education further than they had first intended.

A few fathers seemed even more anxious to train their daughters for careers than were the daughters to be trained. "I have disappointed my father with regard to my education and career. He wanted me to take up law or study to be a doctor, but I wasn't interested in any of these things. I don't want to study at a university nor do I particularly want to tie myself down to a dreary job. I like to stay at home in peace." (Case 4) In another family the mother had done her best to give her daughters a liberal education and then was upset by the result.

> Mother was more interested in our education than father. She thought that by mixing with other children at school we would develop our characters more fully, and would help us to get jobs if we felt we wanted to work. She gave up a lot for our education, such as living far away from her family in Bangalore, where the education was better.
> But she was very disappointed when she realized that the rebellious attitude of my sister and myself—such as wanting to choose our own husbands, wanting equality for women, and having friends of all castes and religions—was all due to the education she had worked so hard for! None of my older sisters had dared go against her will, and so it was a shock for her when my younger sister wanted to marry a man of her own choice who belonged to another caste. And when another sister became a journalist and went out with a wider circle of friends and attended mixed parties.
> Mother felt it was a great irony that she, who had educated us in order that we might acquire more poise and be able to mix with people, should have to mourn the fact that her daughters were actually living up to those same ideas! (Case 11)

The brothers interviewed seemed even more anxious to have their sisters educated than were fathers. This might be due to the fact that brothers, who have always been financially responsible for sisters, are beginning to realize that their potential burden will be lighter if their sisters can look after themselves in financial crises. Education and training for a job will help them to do this. However, in spite of their desire to have well-educated sisters, they still preferred wives with just enough education to make them good housekeepers and mothers.

Interviews showed that the majority of young single women had a great desire for education and most of them wanted to take jobs after college. However, this might only be to while away the time until marriage, for even Western countries have not yet produced a large proportion of young women who want to continue working after marriage, particularly after having children.

Interviews also showed that a few married women wanted jobs outside the home. One of these had such a keen desire to be a doctor that she intended to go into training when her children were old enough to look after themselves.

Like some of the ambitious young male interviewees, a number of the young women were themselves bound that they would get higher education, even when parents and relatives opposed it. One woman could not stand the harsh treatment of her stepmother; so she lived in a college hostel for many years. which she preferred to home life. In another family, ego and her sister both insisted on going to college even though their father was not interested in educating them, and their mother was distinctly against it. In still another case the daughter finally won out against her mother and relatives and went to college. The following interview shows the struggle she went through to achieve her ambition.

My mother's only ambition was that her daughters should be well married. She didn't mind my being educated up to the end of high school, but she didn't want me to go on to college. I finally persuaded her to let me take my B.A., but later when I wanted to go on to my M.A. all my relatives flatly refused. And it was only after I had fasted for a whole week, and threatened to commit suicide that they finally gave in. At first they wouldn't give me money for my fees, but finally Mother relented and persuaded them to help me. One of the reasons that they did not want me to get my M.A. was that I would have been the first woman in my community to get such a degree, and they were afraid that it would affect my chances of marriage. (Case 85)

One young girl was finally able to get to the United States for graduate work after her parents had opposed her going to college.

The main reason for their opposition was that they were afraid that if their daughters were highly educated they might become too independent and eventually marry out of caste.

Only three single women said that they did not want to marry. One was an older woman who had already achieved a successful position as a lawyer, and another a woman who was extremely anxious to have a career.

It could be argued that Hindu girls have one great advantage over Western girls in college in that, as their marriages are still arranged by their parents, they do not have to worry about finding husbands themselves during their college years; whereas girls in Western colleges are often faced with two of the most difficult tasks of their lives at the same time—that of finding a husband and preparing themselves for future careers.

On the whole, this section could be summed up by saying that marriage, rather than a career, is still distinctly uppermost in the minds of both parents and daughters, and women's education, in the broad sense, is still largely oriented to this end. However, there is also a decided trend towards seeing that girls obtain higher education, for parents seem to be realizing that in the changing economic situation their daughters may have to look after themselves financially in some unforseen future situation.

#### Summary

All countries which become industrialized face the problem of reorganizing their educational systems to train their children for the new technological age. Schools and universities thus become increasingly important, both to give children a wider perspective and also to train them in the highly technical skills needed to run a complex society.

India has long recognized the necessity of educating its young people for their new urban responsibilities. Schools and universities have multiplied, and now all middle-class urban children are in touch with an educational system which can give them the necessary qualifications for urban life. However, the new economic order has not yet been able to supply enough jobs for the educated youth. Thus one of the major problems faced by Indians today is the fear of future unemployment. This results in extreme pressure on many boys to obtain high marks in school and college since degrees are thought of as gateways to jobs. Coupled with this pressure is that of the growing number of ambitious parents who want their children to improve their standard of living. Education too has always had high prestige in India, for the proportion of people with formal education has been small. In fact, so much pressure had sometimes been put on those interviewed that their self-esteem had been undermined and they had not been able to achieve the necessary self-confidence for sucess. Pressure to educate children may cause sibling rivalry and jealousy, for parents may not be able to give all their children equal educational opportunities, or they may pin their hopes on one, and the weight of their ambitions may be too much for him to bear. In any case, one of the greatest problems for sons, whether in joint or nuclear families, lies in their sense of failure if they do not achieve the high grades which their families deem necessary for their future careers. It is possible that much of the present-day restlessness of Indian students, shown in such forms as riots and strikes, can be accounted for by the intense pressure on middle-class boys by fearful, insecure or ambitious parents.

The encouragement of higher education for girls has been one of the greatest innovations in India in recent years. Part of this is due to the belief that educated girls will be able to get better husbands, and part to the growing realization that women in the nuclear form of family are no longer financially secure, for they may have to earn their own living in later life and perhaps help to support other family members. It is also due to the growing opportunities for married women to work outside the home and so add to the family income. The main problem for highly educated girls lies in the fact that whereas their former training consisted of informal education received in the home for their future roles of housekeeper, wife and mother, today those attending colleges often acquire ambitions for a wider world than the household. College and university life will also give them more self-assurance and independence, which will react on their former subordinate position in marriage to both husband and in-laws. This may cause problems of adjustment in marriage, for an educated girl may find it difficult to live with an uneducated and "old-fashioned" husband or mother-in-law, or both. Her more up-to-date knowledge gleaned from such courses as Home Economics and Child Psychology will almost assuredly affect her own attitudes to the customary ways of dealing with these home problems, and her contacts with girls from other castes and religions will weaken the force of many former caste taboos. Thus the women of the household will gradually cease to be the strong backbone of family tradition and caste customs.

Another problem for educated girls, which shows the interrelation of education with the economic structure, is that, as there is no co-education in India (except in a few private schools) even at the college level, only girls who go on to postgraduate work come into contact with men in the educational field. This tends to prevent their competing successfully occupationally with men, for they will not have had the informal training which will help them to adjust to the "male" work world.

Since the conception of middle-class women working outside the home is not as well established as that of men working, young women are not as subject to family pressure as boys, and are able to still choose the courses which they want to take more than boys.

The main problems in their obtaining higher education lie in the difficulty of financing their education; the greater need for their services at home; their failure, in competition with men, to obtain the limited number of university seats; and in the attitudes that education for women is unsuitable and a waste of time, as it is not necessary for married life.

In a technological age the educational system is the main channel through which business or professional success is possible. In opening up new vitas of knowledge and new occupational opportunities, education has had the effect of both promoting new ambitions and spreading these ambitions to a larger proportion of the population. This is in contrast to the traditional Hindu philosophy of life, which, by stressing the spirit of resignation as a supreme virtue, tended to minimize the importance of personal ambition and to lessen expectations of purely personal advantage. The sample of families interviewed had higher ambitions for their children than would normally be expected in a cross-section of the total Hindu population. The majority of the families showed unanimity over family goals, but sometimes the father was the prime enthusiast and pusher, and sometimes the mother. Occasionally motivations to get ahead came to children throughs teachers or the media of mass communication. These "self-made" men often have such a difficult struggle to obtain the education which will help them achieve their goals that they have to concentrate all their efforts, time and money, on their own careers. This tends to cut them off from former family ties.

In this study, family type seemed the most important variable in determining the degree to which the family was affected by the educational structure, for the nuclear families showed more interest in the education of their children, particularly of daughters. Age too had some bearing on attitudes to education, the younger generation showing more enthusiasm for it than the older. Difference in caste background, however, did not seem to be important in determining desire for education, for the ambitious young men from non-Brahmin castes were as eager as Brahmins to obtain it.

One thing which showed the confusion of attitudes that comes with changing educational standards was that many of the young men were anxious that their sisters should be well educated, but were less desirous of marrying educated wives, for as personal needs and desires increase with education educated wives are likely to make more demands on husbands. This attitude contrasted with the desire of some young men to marry educated wives who would be more companionable.

This short analysis shows the interrelation of the educational and family structures, and that in an expanding industrial society one cannot be fully understood without the other. This particular study has done no more than scratch the surface of all the facets of this interaction, and merely opens up the subject for further study.

• *Chapter Eight* •

# CHANGING FRIENDSHIP AND MARRIAGE PATTERNS

STRUCTURAL CHANGES do not occur in a vacuum but cause related changes in attitudes and behaviour. The traditional joint family provided its members with a wide enough group of people to make it a satisfactory recreational unit. But the small nuclear family impels its members to seek friendships outside the family circle. These will normally include members of the opposite sex, for boys and girls, as well as men and women, cannot avoid social contacts in the city. These contacts are functional in that they prepare them for the new division of labour and for more freedom of choice in marriage.

The Hindu attitude to marriage has come down from the ancient Vedic times when it was regarded as a social and religious duty. Even today it is looked on as a sacrament, "and no normal man or woman must die without receiving it."[1] For this reason, Hindu parents have always considered the marriage of their children one of their most sacred duties. But it is difficult for them to accept the new marriage patterns which are more appropriate for an industrial than an agricultural society, such as: the right of men and women to choose their

---

[1] Irwati Karve, *Kinship Organization in India*, Deccan College Monograph Series No. 11 (Poona: Deccan College, 1953), p. 130. Karve says that in many communities if a woman dies a spinster, the marriage ceremony is performed with her corpse, and then she is burned with the honours due a married woman. See also K. M. Kapadia, *Marriage and Family in India* (London: Oxford University Press, 1955), p. 160. "Marriage is said to be essential for a woman because that is the only sacrament that can be performed for her." This is probably why marriage comes to be regarded as the actual commencement of life for women. See also Mrs. Sinclair Stevenson, *The Rites of the Twice Born* (London: Oxford University Press, 1920), p. 46. "It is impossible for any English person to realize what marriage means to an Indian. No early Victorian old maid ever gave it the supreme place in her thoughts that it naturally seems to assume amongst Hindus."

own mates, the new emphasis on romantic love, and, perhaps most difficult of all, the breaking-down of caste endogamy.

## The Social Life of Men and Women

In the traditional joint family social life and recreation were largely confined to family members and relatives. The taboo on the social mixing of the sexes meant that the women of the household formed their own social group. But there were enough of them in each house to share mutual interests and supply affectional support. River banks, where women went to bathe, clean vessels or wash clothes, were important mileus for entertaining gossip.

The men had brothers, uncles and cousins close at hand to share their interests and with whom they could relax. Children too would normally have many cousins, as well as siblings, to play with, and their similar family background made for congenial companionship. In this way the joint family provided a ready-made social life for all ages and both sexes. Visits from distant relatives for weddings and other family festivals kept the wider kinship group in touch. Outside this circle, villagers and fellow caste members supplied neighbourly contacts.

The smaller family of the city, however, is no longer large enough to supply a satisfactory social life. Moreover, city life develops many kinds of groups whose interests claim the attention of the different family members. These divide families in their leisure-time activities, and each one gradually finds friends of his own outside the family circle.

This trend was shown in interviews, for the young men were definitely tending to rely more on their peers than their families for recreation. Their friends were often new ones and came from a number of castes and religions. Thirteen of the men said they had been completely cut off from their childhood friends since moving away from home. Most of the sixty-six male interviewees said that although they had had many friends when growing up,[2] they were mainly from their

[2]The main types of recreation the men indulged in when growing up were walking, unorganized games, and chatting. Some of the boys went in for organized sports. Other forms of amusement were going to the movies, getting into mischief, swimming, wrestling, playing, and reading. A few said they were too busy working on the farm or studying to have time to play.

Of the sixty-three who mentioned participation in formal groups, twenty-eight had belonged to youth organizations and thirty-five had not. The only organizations mentioned were the Boy Scouts, Cubs, and Rovers. There are as yet few youth organizations or summer camps of the western type for boys in India, and so they do not help to train young men to mix with different kinds of people, or learn administrative and leadership skills, as they do in the West.

own neighbourhoods and after the age of six were of their own sex. As Hindus tend to live as near relatives or people of the same caste as possible, many of these children were probably of similar caste background.[3] It is only at school, in youth organizations, or later at college that boys of different castes and religions meet.[4] Some college hostels have mixed membership. College life also provides the opportunity of making casual acquaintances in classrooms, through extracurricular activities, and at restaurants with a wider variety of people. It is in these restaurants that a young man may become accustomed to eating with people of other castes for the first time. The army and business are other media through which caste contacts may be widened.[5] It is evident that, as young men tend to go to college, enter business or the army in larger numbers than young women, they have more channels through which they can build up new friendships and primary groups.

[3]Fifty-three boys had played with children of different castes, and sixteen of these had also played with children of different religions. But on the whole their playmates came chiefly from their own caste and religion. Several families had made an effort to see that their children mixed with children from other castes.

[4]Several young men ate with men of other castes in restaurants, but would not go to their houses to eat. One of the reasons for this is that they would probably have to break their caste dietary rules if they did and might even pollute the food or drinking water of the house they visited. Another reason is that the women of the house are usually more caste bound than men, and might resent a man from another caste entering their homes.

The problem of a Harijan interviewee in trying to make friends with boys of other castes is seen in the following interview: "I had very few friends when I was young. The few I had were my relatives. When I was in primary and middle schools, I craved for the company of my classmates, but I could not make friends. In school I had to sit with one or two of my community on the last bench. Other boys would not come anywhere near us. If by chance some boys came to play with me, it would usually end up badly for both of us. The boys' parents would spank them for having played with an untouchable, and later those boys would always bear a grudge against me and treat me with contempt. Sometimes I would play with neighbours (caste Hindus), and if their parents found out that their children were playing with me, they would say—so loudly that all could hear—that they had an awful time on account of Harijans because their children had to bathe every time they played with us. They would even say that we were polluting the house and street. In order to avoid these bitter experiences, my parents strictly forbade me to play with any castes other than our own. This gave me a deep feeling of inferiority. When I went to high school, I joined an organization which preached equality and fraternity amongst Hindus. This gave me the opportunity to mix with boys of all castes without being victimized. From then on I lost a lot of my feeling of inferiority and began to assert myself."

[5]John Seeley, R. Alexander Sim, and Elizabeth Loosley, *Crestwood Heights* (New York: Basic Books Inc., 1956), pp. 292–3. Studies such as Crestwood Heights show that development of primary group relationships is one of the important by-products of men's clubs and associations:

"[A] businessmen's association, devoted primarily to furthering the financial interests of its members, may produce intimacy as a by-product. Such a group

Middle-class incomes are so low in India, and pressure to study so great, that on the whole the social life of the young men of this sample seemed rather meagre. Clubs, organized sport, or games such as golf or tennis are often too expensive, and only the wealthiest can afford radios or cars. The movies afforded the best cheap means of amusement, but most of the leisure time and holidays of the young college men were spent in walking and chatting with their friends. Few could obtain part-time jobs to augment their incomes.

Many of the young men said that their friends now meant more to them than their relatives or family and that they spent more of their leisure time with them than with their brothers. Friends were said to be helpful and affectionate, and to act as advisers. Several said that they confided in them and trusted them to a greater extent than they did brothers or sisters. They also spoke of the great influence they had had in changing their ideas, interests and attitudes and in giving them support in standing out against parental authority. Those who had moved away from home to large cities stressed the importance of their new friends so strongly that it is possible that the adjustment to a new environment depends largely on the ability of a person to find friends who will replace the warm, intimate relations of family and neighbourhood. These new friends will be facing many similar problems and so will be even more effective than the family in giving advice and providing psychological support, particularly if parents have never lived in cities and are unfamiliar with the problems which their children encounter in them.

Interviews showed that the social life of women is still largely confined to their families and relatives in South India, and that festivals and family ceremonies are still their main means of recreation. However, girls are beginning to make friends outside the kinship circle

---

might not be too different from a service club, which has intimacy as its aim but is also useful in promoting business or professional contacts. . . .

"Though mixed with other attractions, the element of intimacy in clubs and associations is none the less significant. Together with occupation, they have become important auxiliaries in creating a solidarity which cannot now be achieved solely within the primary group. It is perhaps inevitable that there should be many such external ties for each individual in a society which stresses independent activity dissociated almost entirely from the kinship system or other habitual primary ties. A man's business or professional affiliations in Crestwood Heights may hold out to him more emotional security than his family circle, and they are most certainly essential to his earning power. Indeed, the club or association is in itself a form of psychological shelter, almost equivalent in potency to the protection afforded by the office or the home. As one male informant, . . . said of his club, 'That's where you can *really* feel at home.'"

at school as the number of educated girls increases. Some of the interviewees had attended Christian schools or convents, where they had met girls from a wide range of religions and castes for the first time.[6]

Young middle-class girls are still carefully chaperoned. Usually their parents or an older brother will escort them to exhibitions, festivals, or dramas. They are sometimes allowed to go out alone for walks in the afternoon or to the pictures with their girl friends. But their mothers must know where they are going, and in Bangalore they are expected to be home by six o'clock.

Most of the women interviewees said that they no longer went with the friends they had grown up with, for either they had little in common with them or their friends had moved away on marriage. Most of them had made new friends as adults, but this seemed to be more difficult for women than men, as they had fewer ways of meeting other women. This means that middle-aged women are often very lonely when they first move to the city although married men are beginning to spend more of their leisure time with their wives and children in the cities. Colleges and universities are as important meeting places for women as they are for men. Some join women's clubs, but they are such recent innovations for women that their husbands often object, or they may be too expensive. However, clubs are one of the first steps many Hindu women take in moving out into a wider social life. Once they have become accustomed to mixing with different types of women and have learned some of the rituals and skills of carrying on associational life, they may then go on to work in the more formally organized welfare and philanthropic associations. Ghandi had a great deal of influence in encouraging Hindu women to take an active interest in social work, but they still have a long way to go before the traditional views of responsibility change to an acceptance of a wider range of obligations than to their families, relatives, religion and caste. Shopping is beginning to become a pastime for women, and some are also joining study groups.

[6] Young girls do not often have much leisure time in India, for they must assist their mothers with the housework. The women of this sample had spent what leisure time they had in reading, sewing, chatting, entertaining friends of the same sex, or playing musical instruments. Few had played organized games or taken part in sports, nor had they belonged to a wide variety of youth organizations. The only three mentioned were the Girl Guides, the Blue Birds, and the Red Cross. Of these, fifteen had belonged to the Blue Birds; twenty-six, to the Girl Guides; and ten, to the Red Cross. They served the same function for the girls as for boys, namely, to give them the opportunity of meeting a wider circle of people, to help them use their leisure time constructively, and to teach them leadership skills.

Single women who are working have a much more restricted social life than young men, but the majority in this sample seemed content with it. Their leisure-time activities were much the same as when they were young girls and consisted of reading, visiting other women friends, chatting and doing embroidery. One or two entertained men in their homes, and two of the interviewees said they went out with men. Otherwise their friendships were only with women.

In most parts of India, boys and girls are still trained for a separate adult social life. They usually play together freely as children, but after the age of six there is a gradual separation of the two sexes until, after the age of ten or twelve, segregation is almost complete. This training makes it difficult for many young people to change their attitudes and behaviour to the opposite sex when they grow up. Fifty-five of the men interviewed said that they had never gone with girls as adolescents, in contrast to thirteen who had, and very few of the girls had gone with boys at that age. Even at college age it is still considered very bold for a girl to talk to one of her brother's friends when he visits her home, to speak to the brother of a girl friend if he is at home when she calls, or even to answer the door should she know that a man has knocked.

The degree to which this strict separation of the two sexes is maintained varies, of course, in different parts of India and among different caste and religious groups. Informants said that, on the whole, girls mix with boys much more freely in northern India than in the south. Anglo-Indians, Christian Indians, and the Hindus who have become urbanized and taken over the Western pattern of boy-girl relationships, all tend to allow more social contacts between boys and girls than the traditional Hindu families. Boys and girls belonging to the former groups often attend co-educational schools, where they become accustomed to being together.[7] This association tends to continue as they grow older, and somewhat the same pattern of dating arises among them as is found in the Western world. However, they do not escape the criticism of the general public in the smaller cities and towns, and the girls in particular are sometimes regarded as having rather questionable reputations.

Training to maintain the distance between the sexes is done both

[7]Co-educational schools in India do not necessarily mean that boys and girls are friends, for teachers, as well as parents, or perhaps because of parents, are anxious to keep them apart. Sometimes in these schools girls must leave the classroom before the boys, and they usually sit on opposite sides of the room and at separate tables at meals. A number of male interviewees said that they had had no opportunity, at school, college, or even in the army to meet girls.

formally and informally. Formal means include keeping boys and girls apart in play and at school. Informal training is accomplished through the early indoctrination of sex mores of distance. On the one hand, the boy is taught from an early age that friendly relationships with girls are bad and immoral. On the other, he is taught through the epics and myths of his society to regard women with great respect. For example, he must not talk to them, and, when looking at them, must look at their feet rather than their faces. Even strange women must be treated in this respectful way. One result of this training is that boys are often afraid to talk to girls when they have the opportunity to do so in case they might offend or insult them, or they are not able to talk to them naturally as they would to friends of their own sex.

In spite of this early training, twenty-two of the forty-two male interviewees who mentioned their relationship with the opposite sex said that they had had girls for friends. Some of these appeared to be mere "acquaintances" whom they had not actually taken out alone. A few had "dated" them in the Western sense of that word, and one or two of these claimed that they had had "affairs" with them.[8] Nine others said that although they would have liked to take girls out, they had had no opportunity of meeting them. The remaining twenty had not made friends with girls for the following reasons: fear of criticism from family and friends, feelings of guilt, lack of common interests, not enough pocket money, and the belief that it would be inappropriate or even immoral to do so. Some went so far as to say that such friendships would lead to "vice" or "corruption." On the other hand, interviewees who had taken girls out socially were often equally vehement in their attitudes to sex segregation, saying that it was "tragic" and would lead to an over-idealization of women by men and men by women which would cause disillusionment on marriage. Several young men had dodged the problem of parental and public criticism by taking girls out secretly.

The clash between old attitudes and new desires is seen in the following interview: "I had opportunities at college to make friends with girls who were my classmates, but I was not able to do so, for although I found it thrilling, I felt the modern girls lacked modesty.

[8]Those who had taken girls out socially had entertained them by taking them to the movies, restaurants, or dancing, or to picnics with a group of other boys and girls. An occasional brave young man had visited a girl in her home. That these friendships sometimes blossomed into love affairs was seen in five cases in which this had occurred. A few others said that their relations with girls were "very intimate," but this did not seem to infer a sexual relationship as it might have in the West.

There is something vulgar about a girl who goes with boys and haunts coffee houses. I have never been able to reconcile my wish to have girl friends and still respect women of that type." (Case 120)

"Society girl" is the term which has been coined by some men students to describe a girl who is beginning to defy some of the social conventions. By this term they mean that the girl is independent, goes out without an escort, has boy friends, and wears the latest fashions in dress. Usually she is an educated girl. The attitude of the boy to her, in general, is said to be that of contempt, and the majority of young men say that they do not like this type of girl although they take her out.

The attitudes of the female interviewees to going with men showed much the same variation. Only a few girls who had been exposed to Western influences accepted it, and even they found it very difficult to carry out, for opposition from the public, relatives and parents, and their own inner feelings of guilt were difficult to overcome. The opposition of the public is shown in the unwelcome attention many young girls receive when out alone. Boys on bicycles will follow them, calling out to them, or boys will line up on the street and make comments as the girls pass. Unmarried couples receive much the same attention.[9] The main problem in going out with boys, however, lies in the fact that young girls who transgress the deeply laid mores surrounding the appropriate behaviour of the two sexes are in great danger of losing their reputations, for even a slight deviation from the norm, such as walking with a young man in the street, or even bowing to him in passing will imply sexual involvement. And the girl, in the opinion of the public, will have lost her most cherished attribute—chastity. Given this traditional attitude to the separation of the sexes, it was not surprising to find that very few young women went out socially with men alone.[10] Moreover, as not many young men have taken over

[9]Prawer R. Jhabvala, *Amrita* (New York: W. W. Norton & Company, Inc., 1955), pp. 52–3. See this novel for a description of Amrita's dislike of going to a café alone with two young men, and her embarrassment, when there, at the interest of the men in the restaurant in her: "She did not dare look up, for she knew she was being scrutinized from all sides; as was every woman tolerably young and pretty." One informant said that he thought the attention young girls received from young men is due to the fact that the segregation of the two was beginning to break down, and yet there were so few ways in which they could meet naturally. He said that at one of the universities in North India men students used to throw darts at the girls in class and tease them in other ways until normal ways of meeting them were introduced.

[10]One young interviewee said that about 50 per cent of the girls in her class at college went out with boys, although a number of them had to do so secretly. Another said that this figure was far too high and that this new behaviour was so

the new dating pattern, not many girls get invitations to go out, or meet boys who might invite them.

Another factor which keeps many young people from dating is that they find it difficult to know how to entertain each other. A few families allow their daughters to have their men friends at home, where they can talk in peace. But as most parents will not allow this, girls who are determined to have boy friends will meet them secretly, either at cafés or at the movies.

One Christian girl who had defied the conventions and gone out with men spoke of the great difficulty of meeting them without the scrutiny of parents or public. Once her escort had to motor for miles out of the city before they could talk alone. The only sanctioned places to meet, for those allowed to go out, is in the home under the watchful eye of parents or relatives, at the movies, or—for a very few—at dances. There are thus very few opportunities for young people who are breaking through the age-old patterns to test out their relationship in a natural environment. Informants said that boys, too, find it difficult to adjust to the new pattern of behaviour of calling on girls at their homes.

Nine out of the sixteen single women who said that they had men friends went out with them, but this was usually in the company of others, or if they were known to be close friends of the family. Ten single women said they had no men friends, and only four of the young married women of this sample had had men friends before marriage.

On the whole, the interviews showed that young men seem much further ahead in their desire to have friends of the opposite sex than do young women. This is probably due to the fact that they are more in touch with the outside world, and are more influenced by romantic Western films and novels than are the girls.[11] The main problem here is that, when the attitudes of parents and young women lag behind those of the young men, it is extremely difficult for the young men to meet girls in a natural way. This often causes intense emotional strain, and may well be one of the most difficult areas of adjustment when changing family patterns develop the need for closer relations between the two sexes as a basis for a wider choice in marriage.

---

shocking that the numbers engaging in it were largely exaggerated. An older woman interviewee, who had attended a Catholic college some years ago, said that in her class of 150 boys and 40 girls, only one Hindu girl went out with men.

[11] Western films can have the opposite effect, for the life they picture is so far from the traditional mores that it often shocks Hindus. To older Hindus, in particular, it looks as though friendships between men and women lead to much immorality and family disorganization.

In summing up this picture it can be said that a decided shift is taking place towards freer social contacts between boys and girls, and men and women. However, since companionship between the two sexes could lead to marriages outside the traditional endogamous boundaries, there is still much resistance to this new pattern. This resistance occurs not only on the part of parents and relatives but also on the part of many young men and women themselves, who either find it too difficult to face the problems involved in making the new adjustment or have been so thoroughly trained in traditional attitudes that they feel guilt or anxiety when trying out the new behaviour. Only the few who are able to stand out against public opinion, who have the support of parents and relatives, or who have equally strong support from peer groups are able to pioneer.

The effect of the social separation of the two sexes in adolescence and as young adults is seen in the problem of a growing number of married couples when they move from their original communities to far-away cities. Not having learned the social skills of mixed social intercourse, wives often cannot face breaking the sex barriers to join their husbands in mixed recreation. This was shown in that, on the whole, the married women of this sample did not share their husbands' social life. Several men said that their wives were entirely cut off from the company of men other than male relatives, and only a few single men wanted their future wives to share their social life or meet their men friends.

Very few clubs as yet have mixed memberships in India. This is not only due to traditional attitudes of segregation but also to the fact that wives might interfere with their husbands' freedom to break caste rules, such as drinking, smoking or eating meat.

The lack of training and the unwillingness of some wives to take over the new patterns of mixed social life mean that it is often difficult for an ambitious husband to get the support for his career that a wife can give. One informant illustrated this in talking about one of his friends who had moved to Bombay from a small town with his wife and two children.

In Bombay he got a good job with a salary of 1,500 rupees per month. This meant that he must mix more socially, but his wife was unwilling to do this. She did not like going to the parties that he had to attend. She won't allow any smoking or drinking in her house, which makes it difficult for him to entertain his business friends.

Her husband talks from time to time about her ability to cook and look after their house, but in reality people can sense that he is very disappointed in her. He would like her to go out more and make friends with his acquaintances.

Some husbands have their wives trained to play the necessary new social role. This may give them greater confidence and make them more at ease in the new situation.

Hindu parents are often so busy providing the family income and looking after the household and children that they have little leisure time. If they do go on a trip, it is usually to visit relatives. But relatively low incomes and heavy family expenses, especially when children must be educated and married, prevent much travelling for pleasure; so Hindu middle-class families do not typically go away on holidays as Western families tend to do.

Older men who can afford clubs are able to get the major part of their recreation in them. Other ways in which they pass the time are reading and taking long walks. The main leisure-time activity of most grandparents, however, seems to be observing religious practices, as this example shows: "After his retirement my father did a little of the shopping for the house. The rest of the time he spent in poojas in the morning, resting in the afternoon, and in the evening he went to the temple or read religious books." (Case 51) Elderly women may help with some of the housework, but their main interest in later years will also be religion. They may spend some of their time reading or going for walks with women friends.

By and large, Hindu grandparents still feel themselves to be an integral part of the family life, and few have to face the anxiety and sorrow of finding themselves, in their old age, without a warm, intimate family group for both affectional and economic support; so even though their friends may gradually die, the household will provide many and varied interests. Moreover, as the attitude of respect to elders is by and large still maintained by the younger generation, the grandparents retain a feeling of worth and self-esteem which is often lost in societies in which older people are no longer thought of as a necessary part of the family circle.

## Changing Marriage Patterns

### Age of Marriage

The age of marriage of both men and women in India has varied from time to time and region to region as well as with religion, caste, and language differences. Even when the age is supposedly set by custom, it varies according to the convenience of the families concerned. Other factors which have affected it down through the ages are famine, pestilence, harvests or a rise in prices. Even astronomers' predictions of auspicious times for marriage can alter it. But the main consideration which determined the girl's age of marriage until recently was that she was supposed to marry before she attained puberty. This custom was due to the high regard for the chastity of women, which was assured by her marriage before she could lose her virginity, or be suspected of having lost it.

Another reason for early marriages, according to Kapadia, was that marriage meant that the bride shifted from the domination of her father to that of her husband. And it was easier if this transfer occurred before the girl arrived at the age at which she could question his authority. Pre-puberty marriage for girls began in the higher castes and was gradually taken over by the whole society. In this way the custom began with high prestige and continued until the latter half of the nineteenth century when changing circumstances altered attitudes to it.[12]

After various attempts to abolish child marriages, the Child Marriage Restraint Act was passed in 1929. This legally raised the age of marriage for boys to eighteen and for girls to fourteen. As the Act had not the necessary force to make it effective it was strengthened by an amendment in 1939, which made the imposition of stricter penalties possible.[13] In spite of these laws, hundreds of child marriages still take place all over India. On the other hand, well-educated girls tend to marry at a later age. But 25 years is now considered the limit, and girls have difficulty in finding husbands after that age.

Child marriage meant that the bride learned to fit into the ways of the new household and carry on its traditions to a much greater extent than girls who marry at a later age, for the child bride changed her environment before she had become too strongly attached to her parents and family, and before she was too deeply immersed in family customs to be able to change to those of the new home. As she was in a subordinate position to her husband and in-laws she had to fit into the new pattern with no chance of asserting her own individuality. She had little protection or support if she found a domineering mother-in-law and jealous sisters-in-law ready to harass her. Moreover society

---

[12]Karve, *Kinship Organisation*, p. 138. It was also a matter of prestige to have one's children sought in marriage before puberty. Some parents even contacted marriage for their children before they were born.

[13]K. M. Kapadia, *Marriage and Family in India*, (Madras: Oxford University Press, 1956), p. 155. "Whoever disobeys such injunction shall be punished with imprisonment of either description for a term which may extend to three months, or with a fine which may extend to one thousand rupees, or with both." In spite of these laws hundreds of child marriages still take place all over India.

did not sympathize with her because "these are social conventions."[14] Karve, Kapadia and Cormack all refer to the possible psychological shock that early marriage may have been to many young girls.

Mrs. Das gives a graphic picture of the experiences of a child bride when she arrived at her husband's home:

> There she is the central object of curiosity; her garments, ornaments, behaviour are minutely examined, compared, criticized. She must be absolutely obedient to all, instantly willing to render any service demanded by any older person. She may not speak unless spoken to, may not wear what she pleases, may not buy, choose, or order anything on her own initiative. Her sisters-in-law spy upon her every action and she is sharply reproved for any shortcoming.... In an affluent family, some single uninteresting task is assigned to her, such as picking over rice, drudgery with no educative quality whatever. The strict discipline of obedience is suddenly substituted for the lax indifference or indulgence of the parental home, and is her only training and education....
> Detailed accounts of their experiences I have heard from the lips of Indian women themselves. Generally the first weeks and months had been passed by these brides in the husband's home in passionate homesickness, and intense feeling of forlornness, bewildered shyness, and agonizing self-consciousness....
> Not until she had herself borne a son did life grow bearable. The coming of her first son was like a great warm glow; it won her immediate consideration and automatically gave her the right to hold up her head somewhat and find a voice. Pride in her son became the main consolation of her life; the rearing of this son and attendance upon the slightest wish or need of her husband her supreme duty."[15]

Kapadia suggests that the problems faced by the girl when married as a child are much lessened for girls who marry at a later age. For well-educated girls of eighteen years of age or over are more able to assert and protect themselves. They are more independent at the time of their marriage and probably have more education than their mothers-in-law. Many of them now have a weapon in that they can threaten to leave their in-laws' home and set up separate households with their husbands.

When these differences in independence and age are taken into consideration, it can be seen that a later age of marriage for girls

[14]*Ibid.*, p. 155. "She passes through tensions all alone and attempts to adjust herself to the situation, relying, as every Hindu woman does, on the mercy of God and seeking her consolation in the philosophy of *karma*."

[15]Freida M. Das, *Purdah: The Status of Indian Women* (New York: Vanguard Press, 1932) pp. 104–12. This description by Mrs. Das described conditions which prevailed with child marriage. They would be different for cross-cousin marriages where the young bride went into a familiar home where she would live with relatives whom she already knew.

may be one of the most disruptive factors in the continuity of family rituals, particularly if the bride has been influenced by modern ideas of nutrition, child training and other family matters.

In one of the most recent studies of age of marriage Kapadia found that some 25 per cent of the girls married before seventeen years of age, a third when seventeen or eighteen, about 22 per cent at the ages of nineteen and twenty, 17 per cent between twenty-one and twenty-four, and 4 per cent from twenty-five to twenty-seven years of age.[16] Thus, three-quarters of the marriages occurred after the girl was seventeen years of age. As his sample included 256 graduate teachers it may be biased towards educated women, but if this is so it shows the important bearing that education has on the age of marriage.

The difficulty of securing jobs by persons of low educational qualifications has driven more and more persons to seek higher education and higher education has invariably meant comparatively late marriages. Since young men nowadays prefer educated girls . . . education of girls has ceased to be a fashion and is becoming more and more a necessity. Inevitably this has resulted in postponement of marriage. Increasing resistance on the part of young men to get entangled in matrimony till they are settled in life, has also operated in the same direction. The difficulty of securing suitable young men for girls and the difficulty of meeting the marriage expenses are other factors that have contributed to a rise in the marriageable age.[17]

The general upward trend in the age of marriage in India was supported in this study both by the age at which married interviewees had married and the age at which single interviewees wished to marry. Since no comparable studies seem to have been done for men it is difficult to know whether their age of marriage has changed as radically in recent years as that of women. But many references to bridegrooms would suggest that it has. Education has also affected it. However, there is some indication that the same phenomenon may be developing in India as on the North American continent, in that sons are likely to marry before their education is finished, and live with their family until well enough established to set up separate homes of their own. This enables them to marry at an earlier age. These marriages tend to be encouraged by Hindu parents.

Sixteen of the eighteen single men giving an opinion on this point said that they did not want to marry until they were economically secure. "By the time I am twenty-nine years old I should have my Ph.D. and a lucrative position. Then I will think of marriage." The

[16]Kapada, *Marriage and Family*, pp. 64, 150, 151.
[17]*Census of India*, 1950, vol. XIV, Part I, pp. 107–8 Bangalore: Director of Printing, Stationery and Publications at the Government Press, 1954).

above figure combined with the figures of marriage shown in Table VI for married interviewees shows a definite trend to an older age of marriage for men although it is not as marked as the difference shown in the same table for the age at which the older women interviewees were married and the age at which single women wish to marry. Fourteen women interviewees had been married by the time they were thirteen years of age and twenty-eight by the time they were eighteen

TABLE VI

AGE OF MARRIAGE OF MARRIED INTERVIEWEES COMPARED TO AGE AT WHICH SINGLE INTERVIEWEES WISH TO MARRY

| Age (yrs.) | Age of marriage | | | | Desire to marry | | | |
|---|---|---|---|---|---|---|---|---|
| | Old marrieds | | Young marrieds | | Single men | | Single women | |
| | Husbands | Wives | Husbands | Wives | Husbands | Wives | Husbands | Wives |
| 10–13 | — | 12 | — | 2 | — | — | — | — |
| 14–15 | — | 4 | — | 5 | — | — | — | — |
| 16–18 | 6 | 7 | — | 12 | — | 4 | — | — |
| 19–24 | 13 | 4 | 19 | 14 | — | 14 | 4 | 7 |
| 25 and over | 9 | — | 15 | — | 25 | 4 | 5 | 1 |
| Total | 28 | 27 | 34 | 33 | 25 | 22 | 9 | 8 |

years old. A larger number of the younger married women had been married between nineteen and twenty-four than the older married women. In contrast, the single men seemed to prefer wives in this age bracket, and none of the single women wanted to be married before nineteen years of age.

Not only the age at which men and women marry, but also *the difference in age* between husband and wife is important in determining their relationship. The traditional attitude that the wife is completely subordinate to the husband and must look up to him as a god is more likely to fit in with a large difference in age than equal age. If the age difference changes, and at the same time women become more equally educated to men, then the traditional attitude between husband and wife is likely to break down into one of more equal authority and more companionship.

For both men and women interviewees, those of single status were more anxious to have less difference in age between partners than the married people had actually achieved. Since many of the young marrieds of both sexes were equal in age to the single men and women—the figures seem to indicate that, although single men and women are anxious to lower the age between them and their prospective spouses, when they actually marry they do not succeed in getting mates of the age they desire. In other words, the traditional age difference in marriage still prevails although many now do not want it.

This may be due to the fact that even young men and women who want to make their own marriage choice find they must still rely on their parents' help. And it may be either difficult to persuade parents to change their ideas about age or difficult for parents to find mates of the "non-traditional" age difference. There was a greater average age difference between the young married women of this sample and their husbands (8.9 years) than the older ones (7.9 years). The young and older married males showed approximately the same average difference, that is 7.5 as compared to 7.4 years. These figures suggest that the age difference between married couples is not changing as rapidly as might be expected, for the older marrieds have a slightly lower age difference than the younger married people.

Some age difference was noticeable for the different types of families. In joint families the older married females were, on the average, 8.2 years younger than their husbands as compared with 7.6 for those in nuclear families. For young married females, the difference was much greater, 10.8 years for joint families and 6.8 for those coming from nuclear families. There was also a marked difference for single woman interviewees—those from joint families desiring to marry husbands about six years older than themselves, and those from nuclear families wanting only about three years' difference.

Single men interviewees, coming from joint families, wanted an average of six years' difference whereas those from nuclear wanted 5.7 years between themselves and their wives. The difference between the two sexes in this regard suggests that women are much more anxious than men to cut down the traditional age difference, and to be more on an age level with their husbands. It was also evident that respondents from nuclear families were more eager to have a lower age gap between husband and wife than those coming from joint families.[18]

One informant stressed the antipathy felt by Hindus to men who marry women older than themselves: "It is almost a sin for a man to marry a woman older than himself. The wife is expected to touch the feet of her husband, how can she if she is older than he is?"

---

[18]Srinivas, *Marriage and Family*, p. 63. Srinivas says that the difference in age between husband and wife varied from six months to twenty years in the Mysore Census of 1901. The average for all classes was ten years. Special statistics showed the mean age of males to be nine years more than females.

## Arranged Marriages

In the traditional joint family parents were morally obliged to find mates for their children and the children to accept their choice. As the marriage contract was looked on as an agreement between two families rather than between two young people, love was not necessary as a basis for marriage selection, nor was courtship a necessary prelude for testing the relationship. The Hindu ideal had no regard for individual taste, and in fact, rather feared it, as it might upset the adjustment of the bride to her new household. Thus marital choice was subordinate to group ends. Manu did recognize mate selection by mutual choice, but he placed it far down on his list of preferences, and looked on it as highly undesirable. Love between husband and wife was the result of marriage in the Hindu view, not the prelude to it.[19]

Instead, therefore, of judging their future partners on their own merit, each partner in the traditional Hindu system had an ideal mate in mind and emotions felt toward this ideal mate were expressed as a matter of natural duty toward the actual mate, at least at the beginning of the marriage.

Freedom of choice in marriage is now accepted by a few of the Hindu families that have been influenced by Western patterns, and whose family structure has changed so that this method of mate selection is appropriate. But that it is not yet a widely accepted pattern was shown in that all varieties of marriage selection were found in the families of the sample under study. In a few families ego or his siblings had had their mates chosen in the traditional manner.

My marriage was settled by my parents and my husband's relatives after matching our horoscopes. I never had any choice as I was hardly ten years old. My husband was eighteen. We never saw each other before the regular ceremony. First my mother-in-law and sister-in-law came to see and approve me. Then the whole family came to see me. Then the wedding was settled, after the preliminary discussion about dowry. I married my daughter when she was eleven years old and she too did not have any choice. (Case 84)

In the above case, the future bride and groom did not see each other before the ceremony. Sometimes, however, they were allowed to see each other before marriage. The formality of these visits is described in the following interview. "My brother's marriage was arranged by my father. My brother did not have much say in it, but he was given the opportunity of seeing the girl before marriage. Their meeting was supervised and they could not exchange any ideas or even talk together." (Case 149)

[19]Rabindranath Tagore, "The Indian Ideal of Marriage," in *The Book of Marriage*, ed. Herman Keyserling (New York: Blue Ribbon Books, 1920).

The gradual change to more participation in the choice of a mate is shown in the following excerpt:

I was ten years old and my husband was nineteen when we were married. My parents saw him before our marriage, and his parents saw me, but we didn't see each other until the actual marriage ceremony. In the last few years a new practice has sprung up called "seeing the girl." That was the practice when my daughter was married. She and her future husband saw each other, but weren't allowed to speak to each other. But when my granddaughter was married, the boy and girl talked together and were given the liberty of going out together before their wedding, although it was arranged by the parents. (Case 82)

However, even when sons are given more freedom of choice the parents still do most of the arranging or at least must approve his choice. The following case is one in which the son had gained economic independence by moving to Bombay for more education and a job and yet wanted his parents to choose his wife.

Even though I want to marry immediately after getting my Ph.D. I have not given much thought to the girl I will marry. I am relying on my father to find a girl for me so that I won't have to bother about it. However, my parents have allowed me to have final choice in the matter. Maybe they've done so because they know full well that I won't go against their wishes. (Case 141)

This view is quite different from that of a North American young man of the same age, for normally he would have been dreaming about the kind of girl he wanted to marry for many years.

TABLE VII

Desire of Single Interviewees to Choose Marriage Mates as Contrasted with Amount of Choice of Married Interviewees

|  | Complete choice | Some choice | No choice | Totals |
|---|---|---|---|---|
| *Women* | | | | |
| Single | 7 | 7 | 5 | 19 |
| Young married | 3 | 13 | 5 | 21 |
| Older married | 2 | 10 | 10 | 22 |
| Total no. of women | 12 | 30 | 20 | 62 |
| *Men* | | | | |
| Single | 18 | 21 | 3 | 42 |
| Young married | 2 | 8 | 10 | 20 |
| Older married | — | 7 | 4 | 11 |
| Total no. of men | 20 | 36 | 17 | 73 |
| Total | 32 | 66 | 37 | 135 |

Table VII shows that there is a decided desire on the part of a number of the single young people interviewed to have more choice in the selection of their marriage partners than the older married interviewees had actually had. Of the forty-two single men replying to this question, eighteen wanted complete choice, twenty-one some choice and only three were willing to rely completely on their parents' choice. On the other hand only two of the young married men had had complete choice, as compared to eight who had had some choice and ten who had not had any. None of the older married men had had complete say in choosing his wife.

Of the single women, fourteen wanted complete or some choice as contrasted to five who were still willing to have their parents choose their husbands. Three of the young married women had had complete choice, and thirteen had had some, in contrast to two of the older married women who had had complete choice and ten who had had some choice. But ten of the latter women had had no say whatever in choosing their husbands. Two of the single women did not want to marry, and a few did not want to marry until they were around twenty-five years of age.

One caution in interpreting the above figures is that, even though single men and women say they want complete choice in their marriage partners, they may not be able to achieve it. Therefore, Table VII should be seen as an indication of a desire for more choice rather than being interpreted as a trend to more actual freedom of choice. The Table does show that there are still a substantial number of young men and women who depend to some extent on their parents' choice. In consideration of the feelings expressed in interviews it would seem that the change that has so far taken place is that instead of the former practice of parents and relatives making the complete decision or giving their children the opportunity of selecting from a group of picked candidates, now the young people themselves tend to select the person they want to marry, and ask their parents' approval of their choice.

It is important to note that with the system of arranged marriages the boy receives "proposals" as well as the girl. In this sense the girl may have more freedom to select her husband than in the system of free marriages in which women supposedly have to wait to be chosen.

Some young married interviewees were so much in favour of individual choice in marriage that they had decided to allow their own children complete freedom.

Some of the reasons given by men for not wanting to break the custom of arranged marriages were that these marriages had been going on for centuries and had been happy, freedom of choice was "romantic nonsense," and that it was such an important decision that the parents' help was necessary.

Of the few interviewees who stated opinions on the use of horoscopes to determine suitable mates only one single man and one woman said they disbelieved in them. Most of the married women believed in their use. The desire to "match horoscopes" is often mentioned in marriage advertisements in Indian newspapers.[20]

Personal choice in marriage is such a relatively new idea in India and is so disrupting to the established mores that it is seldom won without a struggle in which even distant relatives may play a part. In the following interview with an informant a young girl was determined to make her own choice.

> I have told my parents that I will absolutely not have an arranged marriage. They told our relatives and they came to me, not in anger, but to reason with me. They told me to think of the family name, and how my decision would affect my brothers and sisters. I'm still more of a family member than an individual to them. Finally, they decided that they would let me marry into any caste, but not into any religion.

In the above case, the girl had also had to fight to get higher education. When her family and relatives found they could not persuade her to submit to their control of her marriage they decided that it was better to let her have her own way rather than remain unmarried.

Young men as well as young women have difficulty in acquiring the right to marry the person they want to as the following interview shows:

> In my community marriages are arranged by parents, and the parties concerned, especially the girls, have little voice or choice in the matter. But as far as I am concerned I don't want my parents to interfere in my marriage. I must have full freedom to select my own partner in life. I hope my father won't stand in my way. But I have heard that he is trying to force me to get married by negotiating for the daughter of a very rich man in our locality. (Case 139)

A few felt very determined to marry girls of their choice. One said: "I will never tolerate the old-fashioned way of arranging marriages. Boys and girls should have sufficient opportunity to know each other

---

[20]Bachmann, *On the Soul of the Indian Woman*, p. 186. The horoscope came into general use from A.D. 400 on. This date coincides with the beginning of child marriage. Parents wanted a super-natural sign to show that their arrangements for their children's futures were approved. Parents today often insist on it in order to free their own consciences from the heavy responsibility of choosing bridegrooms. Bachmann suggests that, on the one hand, belief in the horoscope shows faith in the irrevocability of destiny, on the other, an attempt to bring about this destiny and determine it beforehand.

well before they enter into the sacred union of marriage. They should know each other's weak as well as strong points." (Case 48)

Even attempting to break down some of the minor customs associated with marriage cannot be achieved without criticism from family and relatives.

I was eighteen and my husband was twenty-five years old when we married. He was not satisfied with seeing me formally but insisted on talking to me alone. This was quite a new idea for the family, and our relatives were very critical. But my husband insisted, and so our family had to agree. After our engagement he went even further. He took me out alone for walks, to the movies and to visit his friends—which caused a great deal more criticism. My parents too were very perturbed by this behaviour. (Case 95)

In the above case, one of the main reasons for criticism would lie in the fact that this unusual behaviour would cause gossip. Should anything then prevent the wedding the girl's reputation might be so ruined that she would not be able to get another husband. Thus, every precaution must be taken to guard a girl's reputation until the marriage ceremony is over. That the attitude of interviewees to freer choice in marriage is supported by newspaper articles seems to infer that choice in marriage has made an impression on Hindu public opinion.

May I ask whether we are going to refuse to board an omnibus because our grandfather travelled by bullock carts? Culture and social custom are never stagnant; . . . Educated girls with fully developed personalities . . . are still revolting against the absurd custom of marrying a man on the basis of a meeting in a drawing room zealously supervised by the two families . . . in full formation like two rival hosts waiting for the battle to commence. For, strange as it may seem "arranged" marriages are still the order of the day at most levels of society though the theory that marriage should be the outcome of romantic love is accepted by most. . . . It may be unwise to build marriages on mere physical attraction, which is, after all, ephemeral, but hasn't a loveless marriage less chance of succeeding than a marriage based on attraction to start with? Besides, if we concede the emancipation of women, the necessity for educating them and granting them equal rights, it logically follows that they should be granted the right to choose their own partners. . . . A marriage of choice may have its own disadvantages, but with the present trend towards a general equalisation and the modern emphasis on the personality and its development, this seems to be the best way of building up a happy marriage."[21]

If the views of the young people of this sample are at all representative of the younger generation, it would seem that the present generation of educated middle-class urban young men and women seem to

[21]Leela Bhaskraiya, "Addressed to the Bride-to-be," *Deccan Herald*, Nov. 28, 1954.

be moving towards the desire to have more or complete freedom in marriage choice, and are against undue interference by parents or relatives in their choice. And parents now often acquiesce to their demands. As one interviewee said: "My youngest sister is working in Delhi. Mother and I are trying to get her married, but whenever we find a boy she doesn't like him. She has her M.A. and wants him to have one, too, or even a higher degree; so at last we have given her her liberty to choose her own partner." (Case 52)

College and postgraduate work at universities gives both boys and girls the opportunity of coming into contact with the opposite sex. Another way is through business, but as careers for young girls are still frowned on, only the most modern girls yet take up office work. An informant said:

Young men feel they may find their future wives by themselves at work or when doing research. For example, they may work in an office where there is a girl from their own locality. The similarity of background will draw them together. If they come from the same language group, it will be a strong tie. They will grow together, and this may result in marriage. They wouldn't have been drawn together in this way at home, because they would have had no opportunity to get to know each other. They will be able to defy their guardians, too, because they will be economically independent.

Another development which is similar to the North American pattern is that friends and colleagues now often consciously or unconsciously try to push young people into marriage.

I have once and for all decided not to marry. Many of my friends have tried in vain to get me to develop an interest in some girl so that we would ultimately be married. Once they tried to do this at the university. While I was working for my Ph.D., there was a girl in the same department working for the same degree. Even though we were from different regional backgrounds, we had certain traits in common. We had the same idealistic approach to life and we developed a close and intimate relationship by working together.

All this made the others feel that we were in love with each other. I don't know to this day what her feelings were for me, but I only had affection and regard for her—not love. But people began to associate our names together.

One day at a post-graduate picnic our professor suggested that each one of us give details in turn regarding our would-be partners. Everyone began to give long and detailed descriptions. When my turn came, I felt very nervous and awkward. However, I mustered up enough courage to say that I had decided not to marry. But if any girl was prepared to break my decision, I would marry her. Immediately my professor pointed out my friend, and said that she was the girl to break my decision. Later I heard that it was all a calculated attempt on the part of my professor and other friends to bring us together. (Case 145)

Several cases in which sons or daughters had been forced to marry men or women whom they did not want to showed the conflicts which may arise when fixed marriage patterns are challenged by changing conditions. One young man felt that his whole career had been ruined because his parents had insisted he marry before he had obtained his university degree, and the expenses of married life had prevented him from ever finishing it. In one extreme case the parents had even locked their son up, when he was seventeen years of age, until he consented to marry a girl of their choice. After the wedding he refused to consummate the marriage, and there had been friction and conflict ever since because of his underlying resentment towards his parents and his dislike of his wife.

In two other cases there had been much family conflict because the sons insisted on marrying girls with whom they were in love. In one of these, the boy's marriage to his cousin had been arranged since their childhood, but when he went away to college, he was influenced by modern ideas and finally married an "up-to-date" girl.

However, the complete acceptance of most women of their parents' choice of husband came out clearly when they discussed the qualities which they desired in them. The married women interviewees often were at a loss to answer this enquiry. Some laughed, as though it was a very strange question. Most answered in these terms: "I was too young to think of his personality," "I wasn't old enough to want special qualities." "After marriage I just accepted my husband as best." And the older married men answered much in the same way: "I was married at seventeen, my wife was eleven. I hadn't any idea of what qualities she should have."

This disinterest in the personalities of husbands or wives was also seen in the lack of desire of many single men and women to know the boy or girl before marriage. However, a few of the young married women suggested that although husbands must be accepted as they are, they sometimes dreamt about them. "In practice we accept our husbands as they are. Our picture of the ideal husband was a college daydream."

The qualities in husbands and wives desired by the interviewees who felt they could answer this question are shown in Table VIII, and fell into seven main categories.

Table VIII suggests that when Hindu men and women do, in fact, think of the qualities which they most desire in mates, those pertaining to "character" are considered most important. This means that the picture of a desirable mate is still in terms of reliability rather than

## TABLE VIII
### Qualities Desired in Mates*

|  | Men | | Women | |
| --- | --- | --- | --- | --- |
| Qualities† | Single | Young marrieds | Single | Young marrieds |
| Character | 41 | 3 | 17 | 11 |
| Equality | 34 | 7 | 12 | 3 |
| Well educated | 28 | 1 | 9 | 2 |
| Home role | 21 | 7 | — | — |
| Personal appearance | 16 | 2 | 1 | — |
| Sociability | 13 | — | 4 | — |
| Personal relationship | 10 | — | 12 | 5 |
| Total‡ | 163 | 20 | 55 | 21 |

*Not enough of the older married men and women expressed views to make it worth while recording.

†The qualities included in the following categories were: *Character*: for wives—highly moral, modest, chaste, virtuous, noble, pure; for husbands—generosity, integrity, courage, courtesy, trustworthiness, truthfulness. *Equality*: companion, friend, partner, co-worker, guide. *Personal relationship*: loving, understanding, sympathetic, helpful. The Home role desired by men in their wives included her being a good mother and housekeeper, and accomplished.

‡Several interviewees mentioned more than one quality.

a question of the qualities which affect the personal relationship between husband and wife. A similar expression on the part of North American young men and women would very probably stress personal qualities above all others. In this study, whereas "personal relationship" was second in importance for women, it was of least importance to men. Although both mentioned sympathy and understanding among the personal qualities desired, only one woman and two men mentioned "love." And the two men responding couched this in terms of "loving" wives, which seems to imply the love on their side. Affection was only mentioned by one young married woman.

Equality was important to both men and women. This suggests a new trend in the relationship of husband and wife. Four of the women mentioned "companionship" in this category, and thirteen men. Seven other men mentioned "friendship." Seven of the single men said that they did not want to dominate their wives, and four single women did not want their husband to "boss." An informant said:

Girls used to be told of Sita, and her attitude to her husband, from childhood on. They were told that she had all the virtues of a model wife. Their fathers, mothers, and grandparents told them that they must submit to their husbands as they would be the head of the house; so girls got married with the idea that they would give in to their husbands. The first three months after marriage were said to be very exciting because they were finding out what their husbands were like. If it didn't turn out well, a girl would say it was just "karma"—that they had to go through this period of unhappiness and they might as well get it over in this world or they would have it in the next.

But nowadays girls tend to say that Sita was "goffey" to take what she did. They are beginning to think that they are not the only ones who should adjust in marriage. Before they made the whole adjustment.

Twenty-eight men wanted well-educated wives. A good education for husbands is so important that a fairly common pattern is for parents to finance the education of a prospective son-in-law. They may send him abroad for a foreign education which will help him get a better job when he returns. This is looked on as insurance for the family's future.

There is now a tendency among moneyed people to find intelligent and promising boys and send them on for higher education on condition that during their studies, or on their completion, they will marry the daughters of the people who sponsor them. In this way boys who aren't in a position to pursue studies are dragged into an alliance which they may not really like. For, in the course of their studies they are likely to befriend some other girls, this may develop into love, and so the marriages of convenience often prove irritating to both parties. (Case 48)

The women interviewees did not seem to be concerned about the personal appearance of their husbands, but eighteen men wanted beautiful wives. However, ten of these qualified this to "moderately" beautiful for "too much beauty is dangerous." That only one man stressed "fair" is interesting in view of the fact that a fair-skinned bride has been considered of great importance in India down through the ages. The women's lack of interest in the appearance of their future husbands fits in with the relative unimportance of men's looks in India.

Wealth was only considered to be important by one young married woman and one single man. Seven men said that money was of no importance to them in considering a wife. In fact, a few young men seemed afraid that a wealthy wife would not fit into their family's way of life, and would feel superior to her husband.

To sum up, although the young men and women of this sample showed some modern trends in their attitude to marriage and the relationship between husbands and wives, the majority thought of their spouses in terms of characteristics which were more related to a large family unit than a small one. That the once clear-cut picture of the ideal husband and wife are no longer true, however, is shown in the somewhat confused ideas that were held by single men interviewees of the type of girls they wanted for wives.

One thing I am quite certain of is that I shall never marry a girl from a village. The girl should not be very young, at the most three years younger than me. She should be neither rich nor poor. She must be physically fit to do any strenuous work, and quite smart and intelligent. I'm not very particular about her having higher education, but she should at least have passed the Intermediate exam.

I don't want to marry a girl from another caste, and her social status should be similar to mine. Above all the girl should be ready to undergo any type of hardship, to nurse my parents in their old age, and make them happy. My parents have had a happy married life full of mutual understanding and appreciation. I, too, should like to have something like that. To be brief, my wife should be an ideal woman like my mother or aunt. I don't mind giving her full freedom, but on no account will I allow her to work outside the home or pursue a career, for I want my wife definitely to be in charge of the home and family. (Case 141)

The extent to which the views of a few of the young men have changed from the traditional picture of a wife is seen in the following interview:

I want to marry a talented girl, well educated and beautiful. I don't mind about her caste, but I would try to avoid inter-communal marriage in the interest of my parents, brothers and sisters. I am now twenty-eight years old, and I want to marry a girl of about the same age. It is easy for me to get a rich girl from my native place, but I am not after money. Anyway, I don't want to marry an old-fashioned girl. I should like to know the girl I am to marry beforehand, and should also like her to know me well. This is very essential, for if you know the girl before marriage much of the subsequent problems the arranged marriages are having could be avoided.

I want to marry a girl of the same age because I want her to be a true companion in life. She also must be used to city life.

I believe in giving my wife full freedom of opinion and discussion, for married life should be a partnership, with the wife as equal partner. I want to live in a separate house of my own after marriage. (Case 138)

*Dowry*

Finding a husband for a daughter is made more difficult for some by the need to pay a dowry to the bridegroom. The dowry system was unknown in Vedic times and seems to have been a comparatively recent development. It is supposed to have arisen with the custom of child marriage which gave men a wider choice of brides; so fathers had to induce men to marry their daughters by offering large presents and dowries.[22] Nowadays dowries include jewellery, silver, and brass

[22] Hedwig Bachmann, *On the Soul of the Indian Woman: As Reflected in the Folklore of the Konkan* (Bastora, India Portuguesa: Tipografia Rangel, 1942), pp. 67–71. The author says that the Mahabharata speaks of the "Danar Dakshena," that is, the idea of handing over women to their future husbands with the "dakshena" which was to ensure her support. She suggests further that the dowry had the object of making the wife completely dependent on the husband in

vessels for the home as well as a sum of money. The actual cost of the dowry to a parent depends on the social and economic position of the family and the education of the bridegroom. Minor considerations are the girl's beauty and education.

Srinivas says that in certain parts of South India the bridegroom price is standardized and varies with the academic qualifications of the boy. An England-returned bridegroom can demand as much as 5,000 rupees.[23] One interviewee said that parents in her caste must spend at least 50,000 rupees in dowry and other expenditures for the marriage of a daughter. In order to raise the money the father will often have to even mortgage the ornaments of his wife, and perhaps those of his daughters-in-law as well. His relatives may have to do the same to help him out. This means that the father will spend the rest of his life trying to liquidate this debt, unless his sons get the equivalent of the dowry back through the dowries of their brides when they marry. It can, therefore, be seen that an ambitious father who is seeking an alliance for his daughter which will heighten the prestige of the family may have to pay a considerable amount for this privilege.[24] This bargaining element in marriage often places a family in a very difficult position, for parents may be forced to marry their daughters to boys whom they would otherwise have not considered suitable.

The financial burden of the dowry is one of the main reasons that daughters are less welcome than sons on birth. Ideally, the cost of the dowry is really an exchange of money between two families, for the dowry paid out for the daughter is balanced by the dowry paid into the family for the son. However, an unequal number of daughters, or a poor bargaining position at the time of the daughter's marriage, tends to affect many families adversely. Many Hindu proverbs show the problems which this system engenders. An informant voiced the current feeling of many parents this way:

---

money matters. In reality the dowry is equivalent to the daughter's rightful share of the family wealth which is transferred to her husband through the marriage. It would possibly be more correct to say to her father-in-law for in most cases the husband does not get control of the dowry.

[23] Srinivas, *Marriage and Family*, p. 57. Srinivas quotes the list of dowry items demanded by a lower middle-class bridegroom. In a recent debate in the United Provinces Legislative Council some dowries mentioned were: for an I.A.S. official, Rs 30,000 to 40,000; for men in the provincial services, Rs 20,000 to 25,000; for engineer and medical graduates, Rs 10,000 to 14,000; and for lecturers in colleges and universities, Rs. 4,000 to 5,000.

[24] Kapadia, *Marriage and Family*, pp. 128–9. Even paying a large dowry, without getting an especially important man, will add to the prestige of the family.

For the past few decades "dowry" has become a word which signifies worry and even terror to most parents who have daughters. It has come down to the level of hectic bargaining in a market place where price is ruled by supply and demand. When there are only a few eligible bridegrooms and a large number of parents with brides, prices for grooms sky-rocket and in the scramble the winner finds he is economically exhausted.

One problem encountered by a number of the families interviewed was the element of blackmail which can enter into dowry negotiations. Original agreements about the amount of dowry are sometimes changed and the prospective in-laws make a series of claims on the girl's family which they cannot refuse since the girl is the one who suffers the onus of public opinion if the marriage is not carried through.

My daughter has had a lot of trouble with her in-laws. Although I was a widow and wasn't earning any money, I tried my best to satisfy their demands for a dowry and other articles. When the marriage was settled, they all came to our place and we had a discussion about the list of articles, such as silver vessels to be included in the dowry. But during the marriage ceremonies they added many things to the list which I was not prepared for. By then it was too late for me to back down. We tried our best to satisfy them. Even after my daughter's marriage they used to send urgent demands at every festival for something, such as a diamond ring or a wrist watch. I wept for five or six years I was so miserable for my daughter. (Case 57)

Another recent writer stresses the intensity of feeling about the problems involved in the dowry system.

An abominable evil is the system of bridegroom-buying politely called the dowry system. This insidious disease is now wide-spread. . . . Economic pressure which has made young men put off marriage till they can stand on their own feet has made most of them more unscrupulous in exacting a dowry. . . . We boast we are a people with a spiritual outlook; and we profess that the initiation into knowledge and marriage are the two major sacraments "in a boy's life. . . ." The bride is the sahadharmini, the spiritual partner of the bridegroom. Nowadays marriage is no more a spiritual covenant, not a partnership of wedded souls, but a commercial transaction. Some of the bridegroom's elders, who drive a hard and squalid bargain are seemingly very "pious" persons.

The young bridegroom, who is supposed to have been initiated into the transcendent wisdom of the Upanishads on the day of his Upanayanam, is now taught not to look for beauty of person and charm in his spiritual partner, but to think of the money she will bring him. A sacrament has been turned into sacrilege.[25]

[25]Kar, "A Solution to the Dowry Problem," *Aryan Path*, Nov., 1954, p. 523. These attitudes are also stressed by Srinivas, *Marriage and Family*, p. 59, "[the institution of bridegroom-price] has reduced many people to bankruptcy, cast them into the clutches of the money-lender, equated marriage to a bargain and, worst of all, has subjected innocent girls to daily insults in their parents' home."

Further remarks from an informant show other effects of the dowry system.

As a result of the dowry, young girls are sometimes given in marriage to very elderly men, at times as old as their fathers. These men accept a small dowry or none at all—if they are very old they themselves offer the girl a dowry. In such an unequal marriage the dreams of a young girl are shattered, her ambitions are stifled. . . . If there are children by a previous wife, the position of the young wife is miserable. There is every chance of her becoming a widow at an early age. Her intolerable condition finds release sometimes in suicide.

Sometimes the young girl isn't able to satisfy the lust of the elderly husband.

Daughters-in-law who come with a small dowry are treated with contempt by in-laws. The richer ones are more favoured and treated better. Poorer ones are made to drudge. The husband of such a girl looks small in the eyes of the brothers. All these things lead to ill-feelings among daughters-in-law and brothers-in-law.

There are instances when the wedding ceremonies are being gone through that the bridegroom's party demand more cash and presents. As the bride's father has no more to offer the marriage stops. The poor girl's life is then doomed, and the chance of her marrying has dwindled.

Another point that the above writer brings up against the dowry system is that the education of the girl is sometimes neglected as parents have to save up for her dowry.

Considering the strength of the feeling against the dowry system, it is pertinent to enquire into its persistence, and the functions, other than the obvious ones, it may serve. Some people believe that the dowry system is intimately connected with caste, for as long as the choice of the girl is restricted to the few suitable men in her own caste, competition for them will entail dowries. Srinivas believes that it still plays an important function as it has been the means of providing many poor students with enough money to complete their education. It has also been indirectly the means of helping to raise the age of marriage, for middle-class and poor men have to wait until they find a bridegroom for their daughters who will fit their purse or until they can save enough money to "set forth confidently in search of that rare game, the bridegroom." Another function it has played is to force parents to go beyond their caste barriers to find bridegrooms for their daughters from other sub-castes.[26]

Still another function it serves is to help young people to set up house with the money and gifts received. This, of course, if the

[26]Srinivas, *Marriage and Family*, pp. 59, 60. Srinivas speaks of the "desperate demand for bridegrooms among the Brahmans."

husband does get possession of the money. "Sometimes he doesn't get a pie though it is taken in his name. His father has absolute right over it, and disposes of it as he likes. In most cases he spends it on his own daughters' marriages."

Not all communities have the dowry system. Their attitude is seen in the following excerpt from an interview.

We do not follow the dowry system in my family, although other communities in my native place think it is a necessary evil. We think it is below our dignity to give money along with a girl. When this is done, it becomes a business proposition, and as marriage is one of our most sacred institutions it should not be reduced to such a commercial level. (Case 145)

A number of the men and women interviewed who objected strongly to dowries did so on the grounds that it was "a costly and stupid custom," "a shameful practice," "an insult to manhood," "an evil custom." Several thought that the government should make it illegal. Only a few of the men and women interviewees who replied to the question were in favour of them. One of these stressed the asset they were to ugly girls.

The banning of dowries will make the parents' lot still worse. What will happen to girls who are a bit dark and ugly? At least because of the dowry system parents are able to give them some sort of decent lives. No doubt forced marriages do lead to a little unhappiness, but can you say that anybody in this world is completely happy? At the present time poor parents are suffering with the dowry system; when it is banned, parents of ugly girls will suffer. (Case 72)

Indications of a revolt from the traditional system is shown in the opinion of interviewees and in Srinivas' remarks: "a few idealist youths are refusing to accept Varadakshine, and a few families are braving public opinion by sending their girls to schools and not bothering about their marriage at all.[27] Individual boys are refusing to accept dowries on marriage and at a recent session of the All India Marwari Conference in Calcutta girls of that community set a bold example by taking a vow not to marry if a dowry was demanded.

The problem in attempting to uproot such a deeply laid custom lies in its intricate relation with the whole marriage system.

### Engagement

In traditional practice the engagement period was short in India and seemed to serve the function of giving the parents time to prepare for the marriage ceremony and collect the equivalent of the Western

[27]*Ibid.*, p. 60.

"trousseau." It was possibly a time in which the future couple got instruction in details of married life, if not sex education. But it was not thought of as a time in which to test the relationship so that the couple would be able to judge whether they were suited to each other in personality and interest.[28] In fact, they did not usually see each other until the wedding. This practice still holds in orthodox Hindu families. Couples coming from less orthodox families are now sometimes allowed to meet under the strict supervision of relatives. Modern parents may allow them to go out alone together. Some idea of the extent to which young Hindus now want to test out their relationships with their future marriage partners is shown in their idea of how well they want to know them before marriage.

TABLE IX

DEGREE TO WHICH MARRIED INTERVIEWEES KNEW THEIR MATES BEFORE MARRIAGE COMPARED WITH DESIRE OF SINGLE INTERVIEWEES TO KNOW THEIRS

| Marital status | Never knew or do not want to know | Saw once | Knew slightly or want to know a little | Knew or want to know very well | Total |
|---|---|---|---|---|---|
| Older married | 10 | 11 | 3 | 5 | 29 |
| Younger married | 12 | 16 | 3 | 8 | 39 |
| Single men | 7 | — | 5 | 19 | 31 |
| Single women | 2 | — | 9 | 6 | 17 |
| TOTAL | 31 | 27 | 20 | 38 | 116 |

Table IX shows that only a few of the married interviewees had known their mates at all well before marriage. The majority had either never seen them, or only seen them once, whereas about three-quarters of the single men and a large number of the single women wanted to know them well. But not many wished to lengthen the engagement period. Only a few thought it should last over a year, and a large number wanted it to last from two to three months, which is the traditional length of time. Engagements are rarely broken, particularly by the girl's family, for it suggests scandal, and the girl may suffer to the extent that she will find it difficult to get another husband.

[28]Willard Waller and Reuben Hill, *The Family* (New York: Dryden Press, 1951). In chap. 12, "The Engagement: A Bridge to Marriage," Waller and Hill give a very good description of the function of the engagement in North America. One of their hypotheses is that it gives the couple the opportunity of avoiding faulty mate selection which often ends in divorce.

Very little sex information is yet given Hindu girls, for the traditional view is still held that she learns about the sexual side of marriage from her husband. This has often meant that the girl is deeply shocked by her first sexual experiences.[29] Some of the more modern girls manage to get books which tell them some of the physical factors of sexual intercourse, but informants said that many girls dread marriage because they are afraid of this aspect of their relation with their husbands.

## Wedding

For hundreds of years weddings have been the most important social events for high-caste Hindu women. "They are her dinner parties, her 'at homes,' and her concerts. In fact, a wedding is to a Brahmin what her London season is to the wife of the ordinary country squire in England."[30] In former days they were also the occasion for visiting relatives and, as they normally lasted many days, were an important device in keeping the larger kin group in touch. The time schedule of urban living, as well as the increased cost of city weddings, has cut down the number of days the celebrations last, but weddings are

---

[29]See Margaret Cormack, *The Hindu Woman* (New York: Bureau of Publications, Teachers College, Columbia University), pp. 117–19.

The experience of one modern young woman interviewee and the attitude of her mother are shown in the following interviews:

*Daughter.* "I don't know why mother was so reticent about talking to us about sex. She avoided the subject, and expected us to likewise treat it with loathing and disgust. She looked on the facts of sex as something which all women had to endure, but the least said about it the better. Her attitude was that even though one knows that a gutter exists it does not mean one should go and look at it.

"Her attitude had the effect of making us blush with guilty shame whenever we consciously or unconsciously came across anything which pertained to sex. Needless to say we never discussed these things amongst ourselves, the subject was taboo in our house.

"It was only after I became engaged that my fiancé, learning of my amazing ignorance, insisted on my reading certain good books on the subject. Even at that time mother evidently expected us to behave as if we were still ignorant of the facts of life, and we never had the courage to disillusion her."

*Mother.* "In the old days girls were married at a much earlier age than now, and consequently they grew up both physically and mentally much more swiftly than the girls of today. It was unnecessary for parents to give them an elaborate explanation of the facts of life, for it was assumed, and rightly, that the girls would learn of them themselves. For in the joint families they had an opportunity of studying the facts of marriage and birth at close quarters. But nowadays we haven't this close family group, and girls are not as close to their parents as before because of their education and wider choice of friends. But there are other ways of finding out about the facts of sex, and I believe that they will know them when they reach the right age and it isn't necessary for parents to tell them themselves."

[30]Stevenson, *Rites of the Twice Born*, p. 58.

still important symbols of prestige, and are still carried out punctiliously and traditionally.[31]

Many Hindus spoke of the enormous cost of weddings and said that it was almost inevitable for parents to go into debt for the rest of their lives when they married a daughter.

The expense involved is enormous, ranging from a thousand rupees to five thousand. The chief obstacles to cutting down the expenses are vanity, a tendency not to depart from tradition, and among the Brahmans, the rapacity of the bridegroom's party. Persons stinting expense everyday on the barest necessities of life, will let themselves go financially at marriages and funerals. The most frequent excuse for asking loans of co-operative societies is "son's or daughter's marriage!" . . . In order to escape the excessive cost, more and more people are resorting to one-day marriages. . . . Non-religious or Civil Marriages are not yet introduced in the State, though the few who want it get married in the Civil and Military Station, Bangalore. This form of marriage is the least costly, though it is the other pole of public opinion.[32]

These expenses can be further visualized when they are totalled up for all of India:

Weddings in India account for the conversion of Rs. 150 worth of bullion into ornaments or refined bullion every year.

Ornaments worth Rs. 20 crores are annually required for 20 lakhs of weddings at an average of Rs. 100 per bride.

In all a sum of Rs. 125 crores is needed yearly to adorn 5 crores of Indian girls before their marriage. In this wedding-gold economy with an annual turnover aggregating to Rs. 680 crores, two Lakhs of goldsmiths families scattered throughout the country make a living.

Getting these facts at the All-Indian Bullion Traders' Convention here yesterday, the President of the Bombay Bullion Association, Mr. Jawala Prasad Tiwari said: Compare this with the annual cotton crop worth Rs. 100 crores, oilseeds worth Rs. 100 crores, or even cereals worth Rs. 380 crores.[33]

The actual wedding ceremonies and feast are not the parents' only anxieties at this time. Almost as worrying is the problem of entertaining literally hundreds of relatives of both the bride and the groom and keeping them all relatively content.

Many servants are hired for weddings. But in spite of them everyone in the house will have lots to do. Weddings keep us busy for months ahead and weeks afterwards, for hundreds of people and even far distant relatives come and must be looked after. It is the bride's people's responsibility, too, to look after the groom's family and relatives. They are usually very critical, and even a small mistake won't be excused. (Case 54)

[31]*Census of India*, 1951, vol. XIV, Mysore, p. 107. "One day marriages which were exceptional thirty or forty years ago have now become general. . . ."
[32]Srinivas, *Marriage and Family*, pp. 60–1.
[33]*Deccan Herald*, Feb. 13, 1955.

In former days the approaching wedding was an exciting but also a fearful prospect for the young girl. But as marriage was looked on as her inevitable fate, it was accepted as part of her life experience. It was also looked on as the beginning of life for women: "the bride enters through the gate into life on her wedding day.[34] This attitude makes marriage a greater event in India than in many other societies. It is symbolized by the jewel or piece of gold that is fastened around the neck of the newly married bride which symbolizes the possession and mastery of the husband, and thus has greater significance than the western engagement ring.

On the other hand, the young girl is leaving the security of her own family and moving into a strange environment. Karve describes the attitudes to the bride leaving home in olden days and the apprehension of her family about the new home she was going to. If the young bride was unfortunate enough to enter a house in which her in-laws were hostile, she might have a very hard time which might last until she herself became head of the domestic side of the household.[35] Now the bride is older and has had more experience when she is married. This does not always mean that her problems will be lessened, but it does mean that she will be more able to stand up for herself, and the growing opportunity for middle-class women to work outside the home gives her some feeling of security and more bargaining power.

The traditional marriage patterns which have been described above gradually give way as new circumstances arise to alter the family structure. Several changes which are causing a marked revision in the expectations of the behaviour of husbands and wives will be discussed in the following sections of this chapter.

### New Marriage Trends

The discussion of the age of marriage, weddings, and the dowry system has shown some of the changes which are going on in the traditional marriage pattern. However, the dynamic forces of urbanization and industrialization have introduced new elements into the marriage picture. Some of these are the view that romantic love is a

[34]Bachmann, *On the Soul of the Indian Woman*, p. 27.
[35]Karve, *Kinship Organisation*, pp. 103–4. "Only when she becomes a mother can she be a little freer, but only when the mother-in-law is old or dead does a woman have freedom of speech and behaviour. If the husband dies when the bride is but young, she is branded as an inauspicious woman and her lot is hard. This is an ancient sentiment. . . . In modern times, whatever misfortunes fall to a house within a year of bringing in a new bride are ascribed to the inauspicious qualities of the bride."

necessary prelude to marriage, the possibility of divorce, and the gradual acceptance of the idea of inter-caste marriage.

*Romantic Love*

Romantic love as a basis for marriage is not unknown in India, in fact, it is often mentioned in the Epic literature,[36] but is so exceptional that it is not in the customary expectations, for the partners seldom have a chance of meeting in a way in which they can form romantic attachments. However, many girls seemed to feel that they had "fallen in love" with the men chosen for them to marry.

The three older women interviewees who had had what approximated to "love marriages" did not appear willing to talk of this aspect of their married life. This seems to imply that they were not proud of the fact, and this, in turn, implies that romantic love is not yet accepted as a prime basis for marriage.

Other cases showed that parents are not pleased when sons or daughters want to marry the people they fall in love with. One boy who had fallen in love with a girl from a lower caste found himself in a very difficult dilemma:

My love affair has caused me great trouble, for my intense love of the girl and my devotion to my parents cannot be reconciled. My parents don't like our engagement, and I cannot displease them, but on the other hand I cannot give up my girl who has done so much for me. She is responsible for my progress and the bright future which everyone says is ahead of me. This problem is my greatest headache at the present time. (Case 45)

In several other families, parents tried their best to break the proposed love marriages of their sons or daughters which they referred to as "madness." One girl was so upset by the continuous harping of her parents and relatives and the tension at home that she married the boy to get away from it.

In another case the daughter was cut off by her family after marrying a boy with whom she fell in love.

Mother wouldn't agree to our marriage because my husband didn't have much education, or a good position. She also thought that he was too old for me. His father objected to me on the grounds that we didn't belong to the same caste. I tried to explain to my parents about his real qualities, but they weren't impressed. We sent an invitation to both our parents for the marriage, but none of them came. After it they cut off all connection with us. I have seen my mother and father in public places and at meetings since, but they never even speak to us. We aren't anxious to recognize them either, or for any close contact with them. (Case 80)

[36] Johann Jakob Meyer, *Sexual Life in Ancient India*, (London: George Routledge & Sons, Ltd., 1930) chap. 10.

One problem in regard to romantic love is that several informants said that many young men and women are now being influenced by the portrayals of romantic love which they see in Indian as well as Western movies. These give them such high expectations that they become disillusioned with the men or women they marry.

Taking into consideration the few "love marriages" in this sample, along with the still strong desire of many interviewees to have arranged marriages, and the type of "qualities" expressed by the sample as desirable in their mates, it is evident that the theme of "romantic love" as a basis for marriage is still not very deep or widely spread in the family mores of India today.[37]

In the stage of transition from one family form to another, the romantic type of love can be a disturbing thing, for it will tend not only to cause deviation from firmly established family patterns, but also to upset such formerly close relationships as those of mother and son, brother and sister.

*Inter-Caste Marriage*

The fact that men are more exposed to new ideas may account for the more lenient attitude to inter-caste, inter-racial and inter-religious marriage of men interviewees as compared to women. Table X shows that roughly two-thirds of the men thought inter-caste and inter-religious marriages should be permitted, but only about half wanted inter-racial marriages. The two main reasons they gave for wanting inter-caste marriages were that they helped to break down the caste system, and that caste barriers should not prevent love marriages. Ten young men stressed the importance of these marriages in helping to make the "good society." "This alone can wipe away untouchability and caste distinctions."

TABLE X

OPINION OF INTERVIEWEES ON INTER-CASTE, INTER-RELIGIOUS AND INTER-RACIAL MARRIAGES

|  | Inter-caste | | | Inter-religious | | | Inter-racial | | |
|---|---|---|---|---|---|---|---|---|---|
|  | Yes | No | Number replying | Yes | No | Number replying | Yes | No | Number replying |
| Men | 44 | 16 | 60 | 20 | 12 | 32 | 30 | 24 | 54 |
| Women | 26 | 35 | 61 | 9 | 33 | 42 | 9 | 34 | 43 |
| TOTAL | 70 | 51 | 121 | 29 | 45 | 74 | 39 | 58 | 97 |

[37] Srinivas, *Marriage and Family*, p. 60. Srinivas remarks that it is uncommon even amongst the educated middle classes.

A number of those who favoured inter-caste, inter-religious and inter-racial marriages, however, qualified their remarks by saying that the couple must be financially self-sufficient as no support would be given them by their families. Several others spoke of the problems and unhappiness such marriages would bring to the children and parents of the couple.

Women interviewees seemed less interested in the possibility of intermarriage widening community barriers than men. Several who did not believe in intermarriage between castes thought marriages should be allowed between sub-castes. Only about a quarter of those stating opinions were in favour of inter-religious or inter-racial marriages. About half wanted inter-caste marriages. Their main reason against these types of marriage was that the couple would have difficulty in adjusting to other caste customs. As one interviewee said: "I do not believe that inter-caste marriages will be successful because religious and caste rules are so deeply rooted in us that we will not be able to blend ourselves with people brought up with different ideals and customs. And parents will not be able to take the girl back if the marriage is unsuccessful." (Case 88) Other reasons given were that in marrying a man from another caste a girl cannot return to the security of her own family; that the consequences will fall more heavily on the children; and that those holding strong religious beliefs will feel guilty about breaking so many rules of caste segregation.

Those in favour of inter-caste marriages stressed much the same reasons as the men, namely that marriage was a matter of personal adjustment and that the couple should be able to choose their own mates. One woman showed a very tolerant attitude: "I am going to give my two sons and daughter free choice in their marriage partners. Inter-caste or love marriages will be successful if parents have broad ideas and children are brought up in a broad-minded atmosphere." (Case 71)

In spite of the liberal attitudes of male interviewees to inter-caste marriages, not many had actually married out of caste, nor had members of their families.[38] Several said that although they did not believe such marriages to be bad or evil, society still did, and they would be adding to their problems by going against public opinion.

[38]*Census of India*, 1951, vol. XIV, Mysore p. 107. "Though exceptions are found here and there, endogamy of caste and exogamy of gotra or totem are still the rule." See also Noel P. Gist, "Caste Differentials in South India," American *Sociological Review*, vol. 19, no. 2 (April, 1954), pp. 127–8. Gist reaffirms the impression received by this writer that marriages are tending to take place more readily between sub-castes of the same main castes, particularly among the more sophisticated Hindus.

Several women interviewees, however, had married men from other castes and had not found the expected opposition. In fact, a number of informants said that even though the couple might be at first outcaste, reconciliation usually eventually occurred, especially after the birth of a child.

My brother married a girl from another caste, and you can imagine how this shocked our whole community. I remember someone coming and questioning Grandmother about it. They pretended to be very sad about the whole affair. I can still hear Grandmother say to them—although she had been crying and miserable just before they arrived—"Well, there's no use going on about it now. My grandson has done something which he felt he should do. Let us leave him in peace. My only prayer is that he and his wife will always be happy. If they wish to come and stay with us, they are welcome."

On the other hand, a number of cases were mentioned in which the families had done all they could to prevent such a marriage.

When I was taking my M.A., I met a boy who filled me with hope and courage to fight the problems of life. He made me stand on my own. At that time my mother and uncle—my father was dead, and my uncle lived with us—had received several proposals of marriage for me. But I refused to marry any of them, for in all the men I found an important lack—that culture and humanness that I found in my friend. I could have married a man with money and high status, but I could not imagine marrying for comforts alone.

Mother was hysterical with rage and uncle was so annoyed when they found that I was in love with my friend that they imposed very strict restrictions on me. I was not able to go to the college library or work on research for my degree. I had no peace of mind. I felt as though I was in prison. I had nothing but cruelty at home. They made me swear that I would never see him again. Then one day my uncle brought in some men who showed me a photograph and tried to make me say it was my friend, for they wanted to molest him. All this made me sick and desperate. I hated my uncle.

Then they arranged a marriage for me and only told me at the last moment. I was horribly shocked and didn't know what to do. Finally, I decided to put an end to my life, and I attempted to jump down a well. My mother found out and stopped me at the last minute. She told me I had no right to commit suicide, for it would interfere with my sister's marriage, for people would think I had had an affair with someone. I felt as though I had not even liberty over my own life, and it was true, I could not die because of the effect it would have on my family. Finally, I managed to stop my marriage through stubbornness. (Case 85)

Men can often get away with breaking such caste rules as eating meat, for they can conceal their actions from other caste and family members. But inter-caste marriages cannot be hidden. And as marriage perpetuates caste customs, it is the real stronghold of the caste system.

Like religious and racial endogamous rules, caste endogamy is so complexly integrated with the rest of the Hindu society that it cannot give way without many unforeseen repercussions. The attitudes of the sample of men and women interviewed for this study could be summed up by saying that many of the modern minded believe that inter-caste marriages should be permitted. But as they know the problems entailed in this basic change, they are not always willing to pioneer provided suitable partners can be found within their own caste or sub-caste. A very strong emotional bond, a determination to go to the extreme of revolt against family practices, or some practical gain in the form of wealth or social position seem necessary to overcome the difficulties. A final conclusion from all the evidence that could be found seems to show that the crisis of inter-caste marriage can be met in the joint family by bringing back the children of such a marriage into the family fold.

*Divorce*

As marriage has always been a sacrament in India, it could not be dissolved at the mere will of the participants. Rather the couple remained married until separated by death, and indeed, women were supposed to remain bound to their husbands even after death. This meant that widowhood was regarded as a state of celibacy and second marriages were theoretically taboo. Thus divorce was not sanctioned, nor was it upheld by the sacred Hindu writings.

However, men were allowed more leniency in marital matters than women, for in earlier times they were permitted to have several wives although the general tendency was towards monogamy.[39] In recent times, a few castes have permitted divorce, but many of the higher castes have not sanctioned it. And only in a few cases has the wife been allowed to give up her husband.[40]

Baroda was the first state to bring in legislature permitting the dissolution of marriage in 1942. This act favoured the wife in that she was given permission to divorce her husband when he did not carry out his marriage obligations, was excessively cruel or a drunkard. This meant that the man had now to be as faithful to his wife as she to him.[41] And in effect gave women an equality with men before the law

[39] Kingsley Davis, *Human Society*, p. 420. "Both polygamy and concubinage were permitted but did not occur frequently. Also religious and secular prostitution occurred. These institutions allowed the male but not the ordinary female to escape the rigorous limitation of indissoluble wedlock."

[40] For discussions on divorce, see Alan Gledhill, *The Republic of India* (London: Stevens & Sons, Ltd., 1951), pp. 204-6, 217-19.

[41] Kapadia, *Marriage and Family*, see pp. 169-71 for full details of this act.

which was never formerly accorded. Other recent changes in the divorce laws have evoked much discussion and bitterness. But the fact that such legislature has been introduced, and is at least accepted by some Indians, shows that the general attitude to divorce must have changed considerably in recent years. The opinion of the interviewees on the matter probably mirror those of the general public for they showed a marked difference in attitude.

Of the sixty-five women giving an opinion, eleven thought divorce should be completely free, twenty-seven believed that it should be given for certain grounds, sixteen in exceptional circumstances, and eleven that it should never be permitted. The women who favoured completely free divorce did so partly in terms of their desire for equality: "Why should one partner have the right to desert the other?" "Why should the weaker sex be silent sufferers?" They thought, too, that legal divorce would not necessarily mean the break-up of many families. "People will not rush to the courts if it is legalized." The suffering of women was mentioned by many as a reason for divorce. "It will be a boon to women suffering untold misery because they have no legal right to separate. Divorce is better than a living death. It may help girls deserted by their husbands on flippant excuses." (Case 69) Some saw it as a safety-valve to arranged marriages. "In a country where forced marriages are in vogue, divorce is the only solution."

The women who were completely against divorce gave the following reasons: divorce cheapened the sanctity of marriage, it was not necessary as girls are now old enough at marriage to give their consent, it threatened the chastity of women, it would affect the country's morality, and it would make marriage unstable. "A real Hindu wife would prefer death than to live with a second husband."

On the whole, men interviewees were less inclined to accept divorce than women. Of the sixty-six replying, only four thought divorce should be completely free. Ten men believed that it should be granted on certain grounds and forty-one only for exceptional circumstances. Eleven thought that it should never be granted. The grounds they stipulated for divorce also differed from those suggested by women. Whereas women thought serious diseases, such as leprosy, venereal diseases, tuberculosis, and incurable diseases, were the most important grounds for divorce, they ranked only second on the men's lists. First with them came incompatibility, and third came insanity. Impotency, not mentioned by women, ranked fourth with men.

The stress on incompatibility seems to suggest a new attitude to the marriage relationship. Those mentioning it put it in such terms as: "Divorce should be given for differences in temperament, personality traits and marital adjustment." "When married life becomes unhappy owing to differences in personality and interest, divorce is the only solution." One young man advocated special agencies to deal with marital adjustment.

Those against divorce gave similar reasons to the women, such as: "Divorce and sacramental marriage are contradictions and so why think of divorce?" "Divorce shouldn't be a farce as it is in America. If it is, sex will become the major consideration and this will affect family life." "Divorce will destroy the whole conception of chastity and sanctity of the Hindu woman."

If the views expressed by this sample of interviewees are indicative of the feelings of Indians in general, then it would appear that divorce has not yet gained general acceptance, and that many conflicts will centre around this crucial aspect of the marriage pattern in the years to come.

## New Marriage Problems

In every society, ideal mates are defined in such a way that people who do not approximate these definitions often have difficulty in getting married, and may be forced to take mates whom they would not ordinarily have chosen. People with physical handicaps or defects typically have poor bargaining power. In India, the daughter of a family which has transgressed the mores may have difficulty in finding a husband. In one of the families of this study it even took about eight years to arrange the marriage of a daughter whose sister had left her husband. Finally, her parents found a man, who was the son of a very rich high-class family, but who was completely blind in one eye and partly in the other. The girl accepted him, and both he and his parents were so thankful to her that they treated her well.

In most societies the beauty of woman has a very important bearing on her successful marriage. The Hindu society has been no exception to this rule, and even an "ugly" sister may interfere with a girl's chance of marriage. This is due to the custom, which is usually rigidly adhered to, that the eldest daughter must be married before the younger ones. In one case the eldest daughter was tall, thin and ugly, and as she was not likely to attract a husband, the younger sister was learning a trade for she was afraid that she would never have the opportunity of marrying. As Hindus are particularly careful of family "blood," an unmarried elder daughter casts suspicion on younger daughters.

The difficulty that someone with a physical defect or poor appearance has in finding a mate is not a new problem in India, but if the choosing of a mate is gradually left more and more in the hands of the individual concerned, and the well-organized family and kin assistance which was available in the past is withdrawn, then it is likely that fewer of these people will be able to find mates.

Another attitude that may be becoming more prevalent is the reluctance of some young men and women to marry. Five of the single men interviewed did not want to marry. Reasons given by them were the desire to devote themselves to their country or to a religious life; no interest in marriage; and the conviction that marriage brings unhappiness and that the economic responsibilities of a father were too great to assume.[42] One young woman was so absorbed in her work that she had not thought of marrying.

As women become more self-sufficient financially and psychologically, it is possible that more will reject marriage if they cannot find satisfactory mates, in other words, that they will find alternatives to marriage. As one interviewee put it: "Mother wanted me to marry after getting my degree. But three years have passed since I graduated and in spite of several proposals I've decided not to marry unless I meet a man who suits me perfectly. I'm not willing to have a second best as a husband. I feel, too, that my present life is full and interesting; I have my books and my music." (Case 4) However, the fate of an unmarried woman is particularly difficult in a country such as India where marriage is still thought of as the only possible role for a woman.[43]

Some of the recent problems of marriage have been caused by the higher education of women, which tends to make them want to marry men with an education equal to or better than their own. As the number of educated women increases, and as Hindu men seem still inclined to prefer women with less education than themselves, more women will probably remain unmarried. Several of the single women

---

[42]Mrs. C. A. Hate, *Hindu Woman and Her Future* (Bombay: New Book Company, 1948), p. 185. Hate's study shows that out of a sample of 263 unmarried girls, 13 per cent have decided not to marry.

[43]Srinivas, *Marriage and Family*, p. 126. See also Hate, *Hindu Woman*, p. 48. "An unmarried woman is cursed by the gods, and has no hope in this life or the next. If a married woman faithfully discharges her duties to her husband, and is obedient to her mother-in-law, etc., she may hope to be born again in the form of a man, and later perhaps merge into the great God."

interviewed were afraid that they would not be able to find satisfactorily educated mates. This desire to marry men of equal education may outweigh caste and religious factors.

These, then, are a few of the problems which arise when there is a change in the attitudes which centre around one of the most crucial family relationships—that of husband and wife.

## Summary

The nuclear family is too small to provide, in itself, a satisfactory social life. Moreover, other factors in the city, such as the rise of many interest groups, gradually draw parents and children outside it for recreation and entertainment. When this takes place, the social life of women, on the whole, undergoes an even greater change than that of men, for they must learn to find new social contacts outside the home as well as mix with strange men and women. The loss of the large group of women typical of the joint family household means that many women have no one to advise them or help them in times of family crisis. This forces them to seek more impersonal, and probably more up-to-date, channels of information on family matters, such as women's magazines. It may be that, as women are the main carriers of family tradition, the separation of married women in nuclear families from the adult bearers of the traditional family lore may cause family change to occur more rapidly.

Husbands and wives are beginning to share a common social life, but there is not as yet any clear trend in this direction, nor have many new ways arisen to facilitate greater companionship between them. Some of the young men and women of this sample were still so bound by the traditional attitude to the separation of the sexes that they did not have any inclination to mix socially with the opposite sex. Other more modern-minded young men and women, especially those who had moved from South India to Bombay, had taken over the Western pattern of dating. But their efforts are still hampered by public opinion and by the fact that they have few chances of meeting members of the opposite sex. This means that the necessary prelude to personal choice in marriage has not yet been established.

As marriage is the ritual through which the continuity of the family is regulated and assured, utmost care is taken in all societies to see that the appropriate people marry. In traditional societies the new marriage partner must fit into the total family pattern; so family elders control the choice, as they are in a better position to assess the new members' qualifactions. Personal compatibility of husband

and wife is not as essential as it is in the nuclear family where the husband-wife relationship is the pivot of the structure.

Up to the present Hindus have usually insisted on caste, language and religious endogamy although crises might necessitate marriage beyond these boundaries. It is possible that socio-economic and educational factors may now become even more influential in determining marriage choice, and ambitious young men and women may begin to prefer to marry out of caste as long as their prospective mates have the desired economic and educational characteristics. However, as the traditional boundaries for marriage are still firmly set, and as going beyond them upsets other aspects of married life, it is not likely that they will lose their total significance in the near future.

Opinions of those interviewed as to inter-caste, inter-religious and inter-racial marriages showed that on the whole the attitudes of young men and women were likely to be more liberal about these matters than their actual practice. However, marriages between members of sub-castes are increasing. If inter-caste marriage does occur, most families seem to find means of reincorporating the couple into the family circle after an initial period of rejection.

Interview data showed that some of the former traditional marriage patterns are tending to change. The dowry system, for example, although still practised, is being questioned, and there are even a few young people who refuse to accept it. Where it is still accepted— and its claims become more insistent when there is great competition for mates—it is usually a heavy financial burden for parents, particularly when there are many daughters to marry and few sons to bring in compensating dowries through their own marriages. Weddings, too, have changed greatly in the past few decades. Not only have some of the elaborate rituals been eliminated, but the length of the ceremonies has been shortened to a few days. New types of recreation and relaxation for both men and women now take the place of the social functions which weddings formerly served. One possible outcome of this change is that weddings will no longer serve the function of reuniting the large kinship group, and so one more important means of keeping the larger family unit together is disappearing.

Other changing marriage patterns which are having an even more profound effect on family relations are the changing age of marriage and the trend to greater personal choice in the selection of mates. Girls now marry at a much later age. This has had repercussions on the whole roster of family relationships. Besides altering the relation between mother and daughter and brother and sister, it has had great effect on the husband-wife relationship, and on the wife's relationship with her in-laws. Girls may now marry as late as twenty-five years of age without too much criticism from family and friends. At this age they are able to handle their own households and children. Moreover, as they will be more mature on marriage, their in-laws will not be able to mould them as fully to their traditional family customs. This is likely to cause greater varieties of family behaviour than before. Wives, too, will have a quite different relationship with their husbands, and, if the difference in age between the two decreases—as seems likely—the wife will no longer be in such a subordinate position. On the other hand, she will be more of a companion to her husband than before.

One trend which seemed fairly clear was the growing desire of young men and women to have more say in the choice of their husbands and wives, and coupled with this, a greater desire to see more of their prospective mates during the engagement period. However, the deeply laid patterns surrounding arranged marriages are still so persistent that few means have yet arisen by which either of these can be accomplished. Colleges, universities and business provide the best means of bringing the two together, but the mores surrounding the chastity of women are so strong that many young women risk losing their reputations unless they are very careful to follow the old patterns. One change which has appeared, and may be indicative of future change, is that the college peer groups are tending to put pressure on others to date, and exerting some control over choice of dates—and mates. If this is so, they are following the pattern of other highly industrialized societies.

Other trends related to the marriage pattern were observed in slight changes in the picture of the ideal mate, and the desire for the romantic type of love as a basis for marriage. This latter wish seemed, as yet, to exist more in the dreams of interviewees' than in their actual demand when they came to marry.

Marriage is a complicated process involving many aspects of behaviour. It is not to be expected that all its facets will be affected in the same way or at the same rate. By no means all interviewees had changed their attitudes to, or expectations of, marriage, but enough spoke of deviations from the traditional picture to suggest the beginnings of some fundamental changes. Since the mores and folkways surrounding marriage are usually very deeply set, any grave disruption of these customary ways of behaving will cause much emotional resistance. This can be seen in India in the recent controversy which has occurred over the introduction of new legislation in regard to divorce.

• *Chapter Nine* •

# SUMMARY AND CONCLUSIONS

THE MAIN PURPOSE of this study was first of all to try to add to the knowledge of the way in which changing conditions alter family structures, and secondly to illustrate these remarks by using examples from a society whose traditional family system is being radically altered by the new technological era. Substantial enough evidence from the sample of families studied was found to permit certain generalizations. However, the study opened up so many new areas of family behaviour and relationships that could not be substantiated in the short period of the research that the main conclusions will appear more in the form of hypotheses for future study than verified statements.

If the intricate and complex relationships of a small family unit make it impossible to study every aspect of its behaviour at one time, it is still more difficult to analyse all the infinite detailed behaviour of a large extended kinship group. Thus the particular aspects of family life chosen for this study were some of those which were known to be especially affected by changing outside conditions.

The main interest in the study did not lie in trying to assess whether the traditional Hindu family, is moving towards the small family unit, found in its extreme form among the middle classes of modern Western urban cities, but rather in attempting to analyse the factors which are tending to break up the large joint family, and to seek out the main ways in which these changes are affecting family roles. As some type of joint family seems to be still the main form in India, it is one of the countries in which the problems of change to a nuclear unit can be most vividly and dramatically seen.

The sample of families interviewed for this study had certain variables in common in that they were all Hindu, and roughly from the same socio-economic class. The interviewees lived in cities, and some members of their families had had higher education. But as their caste and language backgrounds varied it was possible to see whether these variables did, in fact, have much influence in causing or preventing family change. One factor which tended to confuse some of the findings was that, as the sample was drawn from South India, some of the families still maintained matrilineal elements although their main structure was patrilineal in character. However, the difficulties which arose from this were more superficial than real, for the same basic problems of change were found to occur in all the families interviewed.

On the whole, caste and language, income and social class seemed to have little bearing on the reactions of the families to changing conditions, for the same ambitions, conflicts, and tensions were found in all caste and language groups and in the different social classes. The type of family structure, however, had a decided relation to the rate of change. The majority of the 141 interviewees, for example, who said that they no longer followed the family customs they had learned as children came from nuclear familes, whereas about one-third of those coming from joint families said that they still followed the traditional family customs wholly or in part. Interviewees who had been brought up in orthodox homes, or in closely knit joint families, also felt that they had changed less from the customs learned as children than did those who had grown up in "progressive" homes. This is due to the fact that a closely knit family holds the allegiance of its children, and they tend to feel happy and secure in the old ways and the support of their parents and relatives. On the other hand, so-called "progressive" parents help to pave the way for change in their children. They not only present models for this change, but also allow their children to develop their own initiative and individuality, and train them to handle their new independence. Well-educated, broad-minded and tolerant parents were also mentioned as being able to move with the changing times, and their children had tended to change with a minimum of conflict. Age, marital status and number of generations in the city were other important variables which seemed to effect family change.

It was expected, and found, that few of those interviewed had completely changed their way of life with change in family structure. Most of the interviewees had accepted some new patterns of behaviour relatively easily, others with difficulty; and still others had been resisted. This shows that individuals, like institutions, do not change rationally or consistently; rather they may accept changes in areas to which they are open, and stubbornly reject others. Changing behaviour, too, was often accepted by interviewees in principle although the particular individuals concerned said that they themselves could or would not indulge in it. Several of the young men, for example, who said they were completely in favour of inter-caste marriages, said that they themselves intended to marry girls from their own castes.

The subtle factors which bind people together in groups are extremely hard to break down into measurable units. So far the best clues have been obtained by verbal statements. But, as people often speak in terms of group attitudes rather than their own, sometimes acts rather than words may show the intensity of a feeling. This was why the actual acts of assistance given to other members were recorded, as well as their verbalizations, when the changing feelings of obligation to different family members were being studied.

The analysis of the different substructures of rights and duties, authority and affection, showed the great complexity of family relationships. The main problem in such an analysis lies in the fact that these substructures, although interrelated, do not necessarily change at the same rate, for adjustments may be made in, say, the lines of authority, and these may not coincide with changes taking place in the structure of responsibility.

The spatial position of the households of different family units was considered an indication of the extent to which they saw, and consequently influenced each other. Moreover, as women are the main media through which the traditional lore of the family and society is passed on to the next generation, the geographical separation of families into nuclear units has had great effect in accelerating the rate of change. Formerly the early marriage of women, and their incorporation into their husband's household at a very impressionable age, meant that even the minutest detail of family behaviour could be transmitted through them to the next generation. Now that Hindu women marry at a much later age, and are tending to establish separate homes of their own, they escape the former rigorous training in their husband's home. This will give them more opportunity to use their own initiative, and will have a profound bearing on the rate of change.

No matter whether the structure of a family is joint or nuclear, every member must carry out a certain portion of the division of labour, and bear some of the family responsibilities, but the type of work expected of each position, and who does it, as well as the people who are assisted, who helps and what type of assistance is given, will be determined by the historical background of the society. Normally a clear division of labour, based on age and sex, is found in simple societies. And usually the responsibilities of family members extend only to the border of their immediate intimate groups, such as their kin, caste or neighbourhood. However, a complicated industrial society mixes people up, and women as well as men move out into the work world, so that sex and often age roles become confused. Responsibilities, too, tend to widen in scope and becomes more impersonal, and governmental and other agencies gradually grow up to replace the former personal assistance. Many expressions of inner conflict and guilt felt by interviewees, when they did not live up to the traditional expectation of obligation, showed the dilemma of people when circumstances force them to alter their patterns of assistance.

One of the most crucial aspects of family structure resides in the hierarchy of power and control. This structure may or may not have supporting emotional elements, such as sentiments of affection or respect. In the traditional large joint family the eldest male member is the pinnacle of the hierarchy, and has considerable power over all other members. On his death, authority passes to the next eldest male and so on down the line. The wife of the eldest male has the controlling position over the household. Theoretically, in such a system, sons will be given little practice in exerting authority, particularly those who are not heads of households. But the father of a nuclear family must bear the heavy burden of responsibility alone. He must also have enough initiative to make important decisions without consultation with other male kinsmen. Thus a son who establishes a separate household, far away from the jurisdiction of the large kinship group, enters a world in which he must be able to handle decisions and initiate ideas. Much of the present-day conflict between parents and children, in most societies, highlights the problems which emerge when family form changes and whereas sons try to exert more independence parents do not understand that they must train them for their new emancipation. Daughters, too, owing largely to their growing economic insecurity in the nuclear family, must learn to play more independent roles. This necessitates changes in the structure of male-female authority, and also introduces the problem of training sons and daughters for their new roles. The new independence of the young people will be supported by peers, and reinforced by the media of mass communication, as well as by the confidence which the children may glean from their ability to obtain more up-to-date education than their parents.

The affectional relationships of family members will also change with changing family form. For, first of all, whereas in the traditional joint family the affections of each individual family member were diffused over a large group, in the nuclear unit they are concentrated on a very few people. This makes the emotional load of a small family intense. And secondly, changes in the affectional strength of the different family relationships will occur and may cause just as much inner and outer conflict as changes in the feelings of obligation and authority. One of the major adjustments in this realm in the Hindu family will lie in the change of the son's devotion from his mother to his wife, which is the expected pattern in small nuclear families. Another important change will occur in the brother-sister tie, for although it is close in the nuclear family, it is by no means as important as that between hsuband and wife and parents and children. Other major changes in affectional relations will be expected to occur in the development of a closer affectional bond between father and children, mother and daughter. It is possible, in fact, that the latter change, along with the closer husband-wife relationship, may compensate the mother for the loss of the close emotional tie with her son.

Feelings of affection and obligation towards the large circle of relatives will diminish as the family changes form. Although the large family circle will still be important on ritual occasions, such as weddings, little sentimental feeling may remain for distant relatives. Even uncles, aunts and grandparents may be so separate in interests and outlook, as well as geographical distance, that there will remain little common ground to serve as a basis for affection. On the whole, in this study, there seemed to be indications that a sense of family obligation lasted longer than feelings of love and affection, for a number of cases were cited in which distant relatives had been helped although those who gave the help actually disliked them. This may mean that feelings of guilt for not bearing the expected share of family responsibility, inculcated in childhood, continue more persistently than any other training, and are, therefore, the most enduring ties of kinship. Such inner feelings play an important part in group security, for they can be depended on to be effective in holding the group together, even when there is little affection between the different members and no active public opinion to shame them into familial duties.

In a study of the family it is necessary to keep in mind that all the structure of a society are functionally linked.[1] And that in times of rapid change, these structures do not necessarily change concurrently. It is also important to note that the structures are integrated through the personalities of the members of which they are composed. And that it is "through the direct person-to-person interaction of individuals occupying differentiated statuses" that the relations between groups are mediated.[2]

[1] Robin M. Williams, Jr., *American Society* (New York: Alfred A. Knopf, 1951), p. 487.
[2] *Ibid.*, p. 488.

Williams's illustration of the way in which the economic structure affects the family shows that the economy of a highly industrialized society is in many ways incompatible with a stable family structure.

Since an emphasis upon occupation as a primary determinant of social station necessarily implies a lessened role for kinship, a reduction in the size and scope of the basic family unit becomes a meaningful consequence of our elaborately differentiated occupational structure . . . much evidence supports the conclusion that the small-family system results in part from competitive occupational placement in a dynamic economy, as when economic changes force families to disperse. Competitive occupational placement seems to strain family solidarity, creating pressures both toward reduction in size and toward insulating certain family roles from the competitive matrix. The absence of the worker from home and family during his occupational activity has, as one consequence for family structure, the mother-centered pattern of training, and the lack of an occupational apprenticeship of sons to the father. Whatever degree of father-son discontinuity is thus introduced is reinforced by rapid changes in occupational opportunity (as well as by the pattern of upward social mobility). Still more generally, the removal of economic production from the home radically affects the total pattern of family relations. It would seem that the most important fact is not the loss of economic functions as such but the reduction in intrafamily . . . interaction centered upon purposeful common goals, and affective patterns.[3]

Another profound way in which industrialization affects the family is in the greater opportunity it gives sons and daughters to move away from the family stem. This is due to improvements in transportation and an increase in work opportunities as caste occupational barriers break down. This separation removes them from the jurisdiction of the family and thus lessens its authority over them. As the son is no longer working under his father, he is obliged to exert his own initiative. This new freedom will be reinforced by the introduction of new material incentives, which will develop a new standard of aspirations. In this way ambitions to "get ahead" are promoted, and these in turn involve more time spent on education and preparation for work. All this has bearing on the age of marriage, the son's wish to choose his own wife, his desire to live separately from his family, and many other factors which greatly diminish the solidarity of the large family group.

One of the major problems of the first member of a joint family to move to the city is that, as he is ordinarily earning more money than his kinsmen in the village, they feel he should share his extra good fortune with them as of old. Nor do they tend to understand the higher

[3] *Ibid.*, pp. 494, 495.

expenses of the city where material symbols such as dress, good residences and clubs, must be acquired to support and enhance occupational positions. He is thus working "in accordance with the patterns of an economy based on individual initiative, but his consumption patterns are dictated by the traditions of a collective system. The conflicts that arise from this, as regards both the earner and the group out of which he has come, can be serious."[4]

As the educational system of a society evolves to assist children to take over adult roles, it can only be judged in terms of the type of society the children will meet as adults. In the highly industrialized and individualistic countries of the West, the qualities which educators try to develop are initiative, independence and creativeness, for these are the qualities which they believe will best enable a child to survive in a highly competitive world. But, these are precisely the characteristics which will make a child unfit for life in a simple, tightly structured society, such as the isolated Indian village, where he must fit into a niche in a system of closely integrated primary groups—his family, caste and community. No matter how rapidly India changes, it will probably be many decades before urban influences will have so spread to isolated villages that a school system geared to an industrial society will be functioning in all parts of India. On the other hand, as there is much migration from rural to urban areas in India, parents who do not train their children to become independent, or see that they get the formal education which will equip them for city life, will find that their children will have difficulty in adjusting.[5]

The newcomers will also face the problem of finding suitable models for their new work and social behaviour. In the village they will have

---

[4]Melville J. Herskovits, "The Problem of Adapting Societies to New Tasks," in *The Progress of Underdeveloped Areas*, Bert F. Hoselitz, ed. (Chicago: University of Chicago Press, 1952), pp. 101, 102. See also, Talcott Parsons, "The Social Structure of the Family" in *The Family: Its Function and Destiny*, Ruth N. Anshen, ed. (New York: Harper & Brothers, 1949), p. 192. "The isolation of the conjugal family ... as characteristic of the American system is the mechanism for freeing the occupation-bearing and competing member of the family from hampering ties which would both inhibit his chances and interfere with the functioning of the [economic] system. This applies, of course, both to his emancipation on maturity from his family of orientation and to the segregation of his own family of procreation from those of his brothers."

[5]Supplying different types of education for different sections of a society is a dilemma which all countries have faced as they have changed from rural societies to urbanized ones. In its essence, it is a question of timing. That Indians are fully aware of this problem is shown in the many conferences on education, and references to the subject in newspapers and journals.

been largely brought up on the idealized conceptions of adult roles found in the Mahabharata and Ramayana, which are not appropriate for urban adjustment.

Once the educational system is recognized as the main channel to jobs which offer more money and greater prestige, pressure will be put on children to get grades at school which will enable them to get a university education, particularly in families where the parents have been influenced by urban ambitions. On the other hand, some sons will themselves be influenced by the incentives of an industrialized, urbanized society and so want to get the degrees which will enable them to "get ahead." Once the mechanisms which promote these incentives, such as movies and radio, penetrate the rural areas, a rapid movement of people to the cities in the hope of a higher standard of living will take place. It should be noted, however, that not all the highly ambitious people in India automatically move away from the villages, for many can still maintain positions of power and prestige in their native places.

In a country such as India in which the new urban occupational opportunities have not caught up with the expansion of the educational system, the pressure on children to get high grades at school and university will often be excessive, and sons, in particular, will find it difficult to fulfil the expectations of their elders. Even those who do acquire higher degrees may find it impossible to get jobs commensurate with their ability when they graduate. Much anxiety and frustration will, therefore, be generated until the occupational openings are more in line with the number of people trained for these positions.

From the point of view of changing family solidarity, modern schools and universities can be seen as media through which children are separated from their parents in education and outlook. Not only do they acquire new knowledge in them of which parents are ignorant, but their horizons are also widened through mingling with children of different religious, economic, caste and language backgrounds.

A major result of this is that the new roles they learn to play no longer fit in with those of their parents, or of siblings who have not shared their experience. Faris and others agree that family disorganization is often the result of poorly articulated roles, a condition which is much more typical of complex societies than of simpler ones. "Since role structuring is designed for reciprocal or matched behaviour, a lack of it results in a breakdown of socially integrated behaviour processes with the release of intense anxiety or other signals of emotional distress."[6] This means that the two main problems of family unity are, first of all, individual adjustment to new expectations of roles and, secondly, the adjustment of family members to changes which occur in the roles other members play. Two important criteria in this context are the clearness with which roles are defined, and the rate at which new role expectations arise. For, even if a person has been prepared adequately for his adult roles, conditions may have changed when he comes to play them, so that the role he is ready to play has a "backward reference" to behaviour no longer appropriate. Moreover, his behaviour will tend to contain residues of responses which he has acquired from previous experiences, and these may have lost their adjustment value.

One factor which complicates an analysis of the effect of changing roles on family conflict is that every family member not only plays a succession of roles during his lifetime, such as son, brother, father, uncle and grandfather, but must also enact a number of these roles concurrently. Moreover, the family drama involves such intimate relations that it is a very intricate operation to dissect and examine the interaction of all members. Waller and Hill have suggested three dimensions of adjustment in family relations. First, the individual member must adjust individually to the crisis situation; secondly, he must adjust as a pair in terms of his "opposite" position, for example, a husband to his wife; thirdly, there must be an adjustment in terms of the whole family. The complexity of this total adjustment increases with the number of family members involved.[7]

As marriage is of crucial importance for the continuation of the family, particularly in relation to its caste, class or religious position, all societies see that it is closely supervised and guarded. The traditional Hindu pattern of mating was similar to all extended kinship systems, in that the new mates had to fit into the large family kinship group, and take over a particular portion of the division of labour. Thus the personal adjustment of the husband and wife was not of such paramount importance as it is in the small nuclear family in which the marriage relationship is pivotal, and where it is often impossible for them to carry out their difficult family roles unless their relationship is personally satisfying.

[6]John F. Spiegel, "New Perspectives in the Study of the Family," Address at Annual Meeting, National Council on Family Relations, September 2, 1953. See also Robert Faris, *Social Disorganization* (New York: Ronald Press, 1948), pp. 21, 27, 29.

[7]Willard Waller and Reuben Hill, *The Family* (New York: Dryden Press, 1951), chap. 12.

... in a peculiar sense which is not equally applicable to other systems the marriage bond [in the American society] is the main structural keystone of the kinship system. This results from the structural isolation of the conjugal family and the fact that the married couple is not supported by comparably strong kinship ties to other adults. Closely related to this situation is that of the choice of a marriage partner. It is not only an open system in that there is no preferential mating on a kinship basis, but, since the new marriage is not typically incorporated into an already existing kinship unit, the primary structural reasons for an important influence on marriage choice being exerted by the kin of the prospective partners are missing or at least minimized.[8]

Marriage in societies with small family systems thus becomes a matter of more individual choice. As many aspects of family behaviour revolve around the marriage relationship, many other changes, often of a subtle nature, take place when more individual choice is introduced. For example, more sanctioned opportunities for young people to meet to test out their reactions to each other evolve and women acquire more freedom to move with the opposite sex, and also learn how to look after themselves when they are no longer under parental protection.

Highly industrialize countries tend to produce a number of men and women, particularly in the upper classes, who fail to marry. They thus forfeit the high prestige of the married status, but compensations arise in the form of new definitions of their roles, such as the change from the "spinster" to the "career woman."

One change than can be seen in the Hindu marriage pattern is the increasing desire of young brides to live separately from their in-laws. Modern mothers tend to encourage this move, and may even try to find for their daughters husbands who live separately. On the other hand, their affection for, and dependence on their sons make them still want to have them live on in the parental household after marriage. This arrangement will provide the mother-in-law with the assistance of a daughter-in-law in the household work, and will keep her son close to her. Sons are often anxious to fit in with this arrangement because of their own warm relation with their mothers, and because many fear shouldering the responsibilities of a family by themselves. Some are also anxious to keep an eye on their share of the family property.

Changes in marriage patterns involve such deep emotional adjustments that many sociologists think that the extensive marriage conflict in North America can be attributed to these changes. It is also due to

---

[8]Talcott Parsons, "The Structure of the Family," pp. 182, 183.

the confusion of the husband and wife in trying to adjust to their new roles, changing sex mores, the shifting position of women and the uncertainty of how to bring up children.

As the total elements of the various family roles have been somewhat segmentalized throughout this study, for purpose of analysis, it is now appropriate to draw the picture together by briefly describing the major changes which will take place in each family position as family structures change. In doing this, it must be remembered that, as the structure of roles is designed for reciprocal or matched behaviour, changes in one role cannot occur without changes in the complimentary role. Thus, the position of the women of the family cannot equalize with that of the men unless the position of the latter becomes more subordinate than before. And the husband's emotional feelings for his wife cannot strengthen without a relative weakening of those for his mother. Nor can children become more independent unless parents lose some of their authority over them, nor older people maintain their former positions of prestige when children are receiving more recognition.

In traditional family systems elder members are not thought of as problems, for they have important positions in the household. But in industrialized societies the knowledge, experience, and skills of the older people no longer relate to the present, for it is impossible for them to keep pace with a dynamically changing society. The importance of their functional position thus declines, and with it their authority, and much of the respect and prestige that formerly went with it. These changes will bring older people many frustrations and anxieties. They will experience a loss of self-esteem, and may even feel intense social isolation. They may find it difficult to understand the revolts of their children and grandchildren against them.

The attitude to older people in India has not yet changed enough to have made their problem as striking as it is on the North American continent, but the problem of redefining their authority and responsibility was apparent in many case studies.[9] The new science of geron-

[9] Waller and Hill, *The Family*, pp. 442, 443. The authors quote a study by Dinkel of aged grandparents in Minnesota who had somewhat similar conflicts to those of older people in the Hindu family. The Minnesota grandparents were born around 1855 on farms; so their attitudes represented the rural ways of life of a pioneer society, which clashed with the urban values and behaviour of their children. The grandparents did not receive the respect which they had expected, and were hurt when their children referred to them as being old-fashioned and out-of-date. Nor would the children play submissive roles when the old people tried to exert their authority. All this led to much conflict between the two generations.

tology shows that the change in their position has been critical enough in the Western World to have crystallized public opinion into action.[10]

The main change in the role of the father will lie in his having to shoulder the major family responsibilities unaided by other male relatives. These will be particularly heavy in the financial area, for higher standards of living in the city, as well as growing demands for higher education for daughters, as well as for sons, and, perhaps more competition in finding husbands for his daughters, will all make his financial burdens heavier. He will be the chief earner, and may have to support his sons, and their families, until they are well settled in life, particularly if the son is taking graduate degrees at the university, and cannot financially assist until a relatively late age. The father, too, instead of having a large group of male relatives to consult on important matters, will now have to rely on the advice of his wife and children. This will tend to undermine his authority, and bring about more equalitarian relations between them. However, the necessity of making decisions for a common family goal may promote more companionship between husband and wife, father and children. The father's social life will change from intimate contacts with relatives, and close neighbours, to impersonal relations with a wide variety of people. He will gradually have to learn to accept his wife as a companion, and share a mixed social life with her.

On the whole, the father in this changing scene could be called the "forgotten man," for in the literature and propaganda of the times it is the changing position of woman that is emphasized rather than that of the man. It is true that women must also make new role adjustments, such as working outside the home, but no matter how difficult

---

[10] Pius Okigbo, "Social Consequences of Economic Development in West Africa" (*Annals of the American Academy of Politics and Social Science*, vol. 305, May, 1956), pp. 129, 130. Okigbo shows how the position of older people changes with economic development and expansion: "So long as the socio-economic goals were designed to meet the requirements of mere subsistence, the demands of the aged, the poor, and the infirm were rudimentary. The social unit could, without greatly depressing the consumption level, meet this requirement. But the level of living has been rising steadily. The needs of the unemployed, the disabled, and the old have risen with the needs of the wealthy, and the obligation to meet the needs of the indigent and nonproductive members of the household has become increasingly onerous. Even the expense of feeding the unemployed has become burdensome. Evasions of responsibility are, therefore, more frequent now than they were two decades ago. It would appear that indigenous institutions for the maintenance of social cohesion are breaking down and that something ought to be done to replace them if the social disorganization that is thus exposed is to be remedied. . . . If the indigenous institutions are not suitable for the transition from the old to the new order, then the responsibility must be taken over by the state or some other agency."

this is, they are often stepping into positions of recognized prestige; whereas the position of the father is definitely declining from one of great authority and power to a relatively equalitarian position. Much of the conflict between father and child, husband and wife, could be profitably studied in the light of the problems entailed in this profound shift.

There are four major changes in the position of the mother of the household. The first is that she will gradually become the chief pivot around which the family life revolves. Formerly, the male head of the household not only made the main family decisions, but had such authority over all members that he was literally the pivot of the large kin group. It was his responsibility to see that all these people fitted into the total picture as smoothly as possible. Hence he was the chief mediator through which peace was maintained between different generations, the two sexes, and new people coming into the system, such as daughters-in-law. Urban life has introduced so many complex factors that a small family living in the city must now have a rigorous time schedule if it is to function at all efficiently. In modern urban families it is the wife who takes over the function of seeing that the complicated time schedules of different members are co-ordinated and carried out.

Secondly, the mother must learn to shoulder more responsibility alone, without the support and advice of a large group of women. Thirdly, she may have to work outside the home to augment the family income. If so, she adds another role to her repertoire, one which, at the present stage of women's position in India, is so uncharted that it entails all the uncertainties of a pioneer job. Finally, she may have to learn the intricacies of behaviour necessary for a mixed social life, and she must also acquire a new circle of women friends. On the other hand, the increasing companionship of her daughters—who will now marry at a later age—and her husband will tend to compensate for the loss of the intimacy of the large group of kinswomen and her close affectionate relationship with her son. These problems of the father and mother entail basic personality changes, for the submissive, self-sacrificing attitude of the former "ideal" mother and wife, and the strict authoritarian, distant, "ideal" of the father are no longer functional in the modern urban family.

The major task for the son will be to fit himself for, and finally obtain, a job which will be both financially adequate and psychologically rewarding. The present unemployment among educated Indians, and the breaking down of caste occupational barriers, leaves him to face an impersonal work world, where success depends on his ability to compete effectively, rather than on family or caste sponsorship. The severity of this problem for many young Hindus was shown in the fact that their main conflicts centred around the fields of education and careers. Pressure on them begins at school, and even when suitable jobs are obtained, continues in the form of the financial pressures entailed in raising a family, for the standards of aspiration in India tend to outrun rises in income. Conflicts in this area enumerated by interviewees supported the hypothesis that the major anxieties of young men in India centre around economic rather than sexual factors.

Another of their problems is to become independent of parental control. It may be significant in this regard that the men interviewed had had more conflict with their parents in nuclear than joint families. Another of their problems will be that of finding a wife who fits in more with their own personalities rather than with the total family structure. Still another problem lies in learning the social skills which will help them to develop a group of supporting friends, for a strong in-group can cushion the change from the intimate large family unit to the impersonal city in an effective way. Friends of their own age can also instruct them, directly and indirectly, in the new urban folkways and mores.

The main problems of young women do not seem as difficult, on the surface, as those of young men, for they can still remain in the security of the family while trying out new patterns of behaviour. Their most difficult problems will probably centre around marriage and in-laws for some time to come. About one-third of the young married, and half the older married women, spoke of quarrels and friction with their in-laws, and several married women ascribed the peacefulness of their lives to the fact that they lived in separate homes of their own. Fewer conflicts were mentioned with husbands, but were often very upsetting when they occurred.

The young woman who blazes a new trail, however, will have many anxious moments. Some of her main tasks will be to enlarge her circle of both men and women friends, to find some means of obtaining greater freedom of choice in marriage, and to establish a new relationship with her husband in which love and companionship will be predominant features. As the economic insecurity of the small family unit increases, she too will have to seek the education which will fit her for jobs in the work world, and later will have to adjust to these new positions.

Practically all the interviewees said that their families had been closer, and that they had clearer conceptions of their roles as children than as adults. This was particularly true of those brought up in orthodox homes or villages. For there parents still trained their children in the security of the old patterns of behaviour, and many brought them up so "automatically" that they did not pass on their own anxieties or uncertainties, as do many modern parents. The phenomenon of the "problem child" will probably appear as Hindu parents become more unsure of their positions in relation to their children, and less able to train them for their new, and perhaps unknown, adult roles.

One of the difficulties in understanding the different family relationships in this study was that, although a good deal of information in regard to the main traditional family roles was available in literature and studies, many of the minor relationships were not adequately enough described to act as standards by which change could be measured. The expected strong mother-son tie, for example, was found to prevail in most families, but it was not certain whether this relationship pertained to *all* sons, or only one. For in the families studied, the mother was often found to love her eldest or youngest son best, and then perhaps prefer a daughter to her second son. In other words, although we can say that certain family relationships have stronger affectional bonds than others, we know little about the order of preferences when there are several sons and daughters in one family. Another example of this problem lies in the brother-sister bond, for the study showed that a brother might love one sister intensely, and be indifferent to or actually dislike another.

Still other relationships on which only general observations could be found were those of the sons' wives living within their in-laws' household. A good deal has been written about the eldest daughter-in-law, who becomes head of the household after her mother-in-law, but the others have been paid little attention. Again, the power and position of the eldest brother is clear, but very little seems to have been written on the extent to which the subordinate position of younger brothers throughout their lives eventually leads to frustrations and friction.

These, then, are some of the many questions which have arisen in the course of the study. Indeed, this study was typical of all research, in that it opened up far more questions than it answered.

The disorganizing effects of rapid social change have been so marked in many countries in recent times that interest has often focused on them rather than on the new patterns of behaviour which are emerging. Only the greatest catastrophe seems to be able to so cripple a society that it is not eventually able to readjust to new conditions. Disorganization can thus be seen as the prelude to reorganization.[11]

As the leading industrialized countries did not have the experience of other countries to guide them through their transition from agriculture to industry, they had to work their way by means of painful trial and error to new adjustments. Societies now on the threshold of similar industrialization need not, and probably cannot, follow their solutions in detail, but by observing their experiences they have the opportunity of foreseeing some of the problems which lie ahead, and thus are able to somewhat temper the impact of change. In India, the Indian government has already organized schemes, or is planning them, which will cushion many aspects of change which Western countries were not prepared for at similar stages of industrialization. Pension and hospitalization schemes, for example, are well advanced if not yet actually in practice.[12] India is thus able to plan some of the consequences of change, so that its disrupting effects will be met before they can distress too many people. Other areas in which India is reorganizing in response to change is perhaps more apparent to students than to many Indians. In relation to children it is most evident in the field of education. Industrialization was not far advanced when India was able to take over an educational system which had been slowly worked out in the more advanced industrialized countries. This enabled it to provide its people immediately with the type of education which could teach them the attitudes and skills appropriate for an industrialized society. Schools have multiplied rapidly in recent years, as well as nursery schools, sport facilities, youth clubs and associations. All of these tend to take young boys and girls further away from the influences of the family, not only making them more independent, but also helping them acquire friends outside the kinship group.

Knowledge of how to handle practical and emotional family problems, formerly passed down by elders, is now being disseminated by newspapers, women's magazines and books on child psychology. And child study associations and parent and teacher organizations are be-

---

[11]Herskovits, "The Problem of Adapting Societies to New Tasks," p. 104. Herskovits speaks of the continuous process of relearning that results from the constant readjustment which people must make to changing environmental and group conditions.

[12]Milton Singer, "Cultural Values in India's Economic Development" (*Annals of the American Academy of Politics and Social Science*, vol. 305, May, 1956), pp. 81–91.

ginning to replace the traditional family councils on child problems. In this way the trained expert is tending to replace family lore. The impersonal nature of these new media of education permits a more rapid presentation of new ideas, thus tending to help keep the adjustments more in line with change.

Other new types of organization which are arising, such as men and women's clubs, professional associations, study groups, and welfare agencies, are all new ways in which adaptations are being made to changing times. Another major reorganization is occurring in the area of primary relations. Widening circles of friends for people of all ages, and an increasing dependence on peer groups for intimate social contacts, show the trend away from the companionship of relatives. These new groups not only supply much of the affection formerly obtained in the large kinship group, but also provide a milieu, particularly at adolescence, in which new patterns of behaviour can be learned. Finally, perhaps the greatest change is taking place in the relationships of men and women. It is possibly in this area that most resistance to change is found, and new means of assisting adjustment are slowest to arise.

The strength of the traditional Hindu society in the past, and its ability to resist many disrupting forces, such as the invasion of foreign conquerors, seems to have lain mainly in the close integration of its religion, caste system and joint family. It was not until the British invaders introduced the new technological forces of the modern age that the powerful solidarity of the society was undermined, and significant changes in caste and family occurred. The traditional Hindu culture can still be found, almost untouched, in remote villages and regions of India.[13] But in other areas nearer the large urban centres, many Hindus must now adapt to a way of life, in a single lifetime,

[13]Humayun Kabir, "Higher Education in India and the Study of the Social Sciences," Introduction to *The Teaching of the Social Sciences in India* (UNESCO, 1956), pp. 16–18. "In India . . . the old social forms have continued and still have considerable vitality. . . it is only with the outbreak of the second world war that the full impact of modern industrialization was felt by India. The processes which were initiated then have continued with increasing force and with a more conscious purpose in independent India. There are no doubt some sections of the people who are opposed to change and seek to cling to the old pattern of life. They are however fighting a losing battle and it may truly be said that after the attainment of independence, the process of modernizing the country has been accepted as a deliberate policy of the nation. India is today passing through a transformation of a primarily agricultural rural community into a new society where industry and modern modes of life will take an increasing share. Old social institutions have decayed or are in a process of fast change."

## SUMMARY AND CONCLUSIONS

which has gradually evolved over a period of many centuries in other countries: that is, the changes which many Hindus must now adjust to are much more drastic than those faced by people living in more hghly industrialized countries. However, enough Hindus have already adapted to the new urban way of life to act as guides and interpreters to those that follow.

Many studies have shown that the new forces are beyond the family's control. Some individual families may play a rearguard defence for a time, and some sort of joint family system may continue for many decades, as it has in parts of Europe which have been relatively isolated from the total complex of industrial and urban forces. But this will not necessarily disprove the hypothesis that, if a full complement of technological forces impinge on family structure, it will alter. What remains to be done is to isloate, and then test, the many different facets of industrialization and urbanization, in order to better understand the ones which tend to modify family structure, and those which help to maintain, or reinforce the traditional system.

# Appendixes

## APPENDIX I

### Method and Sample

As the purpose of this research was to open up areas of conflict attendant on family change rather than to attempt to get strict statistical indices of change, no questionnaires were used. Instead, an interviewing schedule was gradually developed, based, at first, on much preliminary reading and interviewing of a general nature. The main interviewing was done by a research team of six Hindus. Of these, two men had their Master's degrees in psychology and one in sociology; one woman had her Master's degree in psychology, and one had majored in sociology for her Bachelor's degree. The last member of the team was an older housewife who had had experience in interviewing. When the research assistants began to interview, weekly seminars were held at which their interview data were thoroughly discussed. As insight into the Hindu family increased, the breadth of interviewing was constantly widened and deepened. Particular insight was obtained by discussing the case studies thoroughly with each interviewer.

The main task of interviewing was left to the research team as it was felt that a Western person would not be able to put interviewees at their ease as rapidly as Hindus, nor be able to master the intricacies of language. All members of the team could interview competently in several languages. It was also considered preferable for interviewers to work by themselves rather than act as interpreters.

In all, the team spent a total of thirty-one months interviewing. A large number of the interviewees were interviewed several times. On the average the interviews lasted from two to five hours.

The interviewers were given complete freedom in choosing their interviewees as long as they kept to the main background characteristics of the sample. This meant that they could interview friends or acquaintances, and so be in a more favourable position to both get information and interpret findings. They could also interview in more relaxed situations, such as the interviewee's own home. All interviewees seemed able to discuss many intimate aspects of family affairs with the interviewees without entailing much resentment or resistance.

The problem of translating interviews from one language to another was always present. However, as many of the same trends were found in interviews made by different research assistants interviewing in various languages with a variety of different people, confidence was felt in the validity of the translations.

The main disadvantage of the indirected method of interviewing is that the student may not get accurate enough data to tabulate precisely. But as this method permits shadings of feelings, and many subtle aspects of family life to be ascertained, the advantages far outweigh the disadvantages, especially in an exploratory study. It also gives new insight as the study progresses.

In order to differentiate the various people who gave information for the study, those interviewed by the team are called "interviewees," "respondents," or "ego," whereas the additional people who were interviewed in view of their general knowledge of India are called "informants."

The intention of the study was both to interview a homogeneous enough group of people to be able to generalize for their behaviour, and to explore some of the main areas of strain attendant on family change. Thus, while the study concentrates on Brahmin middle- and upper middle-class young men and women, a number of people from other castes and older age groups were included in order to test the variables which were thought to be most important in promoting or restricting family change. For the same reason, interviewees were chosen who lived in a variety of family types.

The sample, therefore, is not homogeneous, and the tables of statistics throughout the study should be looked on more as summations of the interview material rather than as valid statistical generalizations. Another warning is that the detailed findings of this research only apply to the actual sample of people studied. All generalizations for India as a whole have been made with great caution and only if supported by other studies.

A more detailed analysis of the background characteristics of the 157 interviewees follows.

*Caste and Mother Tongue*

Of the 157 interviewees, 53 women and 57 men came from the Brahmin caste. The remaining 47 interviewees came from a number of castes including Vokkaligia, Naidu, Kshatria. Coorg, Reddy, Sindhi, Mudaliar and Lingayat. The Brahmin interviewees included people from a number of sub-castes such as the Madhva, Smartha, Vaishnavite and Deshastha. One Harijan (untouchable) young man was interviewed to throw some light on the problems of a highly educated man of that caste.

The mother tongue of 62 interviewees, 20 women and 42 men, was Kannada; of 28 women and 17 men (45) Tamil; and of 9 women and the same number of men (18) Telegu; 6 women spoke Marathi; and the remaining 10 women and 16 men had a variety of mother tongues.

*Income and Social Class*

The income and social class position of the fathers of interviewees varied considerably. The term "social class" was not defined for interviewees, for so little is known of its characteristics in India that it was thought better to take the respondent's feelings on the matter rather than to tie him down to a set formula worked out by the researcher. Of the sample, 111 considered themselves to be middle class, while 25 claimed to be upper class. Some of the middle-class interviewees were able to place themselves fairly exactly, for 10 of the 111 said they belonged to lower middle-class families, whereas 13 said they were from the upper middle classes; 25 interviewees did not place themselves, and 18 did not report income.

AVERAGE MONTHLY INCOME OF FATHERS IN TERMS OF SOCIAL CLASS

| Social class | Average monthly income of father |
|---|---|
| Lower middle | 189.5 |
| Middle | 273.0 |
| Upper middle | 845.8 |
| Upper | 1,053.5 |
| TOTAL: Sample of 136 | 472.5 rupees per month |

The above figures show that the estimations of class position fitted in roughly with the family income. These data suggest that there is a definite relation between income and social class position amongst Hindus. However there were variations in income in that 1 middle-class father was receiving 1,000 rupees per month, 4 upper middle had salaries from 1,000 to 2,000 rupees and 13 upper-class fathers were receiving from 1,000 to 2,500 rupees. One had a high income of 4,160 rupees.

*Home and Number of Generations in City*

Of the interviewees, 25 came from villages and 27 from towns; 33 were born in other cities than the ones in which they were living at the time of this study. Thus 85 of the interviewees were not living in their original homes when interviewed. On the other hand, 69 had grown up in Bangalore, the city in which the research centred. Three did not report.

A number of the interviewees were living in hostels (college residences) when interviewed. Others were living with relatives while attending college. It is probable that most of these interviewees came from towns and villages, and might not return to them later. Information from interviewees on the number of generations their families had lived in the city is far from complete, but 48 said they were the first generation to live in the city, 20 the second and 6 the third generation; 4 said they had lived 4 generations or more in cities.

*Marital Status and Age*

The sample purposely sought interviewees of all adult ages, for it was thought that this would be one of the most significant variables in explaining differences of attitudes and behaviour. However, the study concentrated mainly on young single and married men and women, and the few older men and women were interviewed mainly to get some idea of the impact of change on older people, and to use their attitudes as a comparison for those of the younger respondents.

As the Census for Mysore defines young men and women as being between 15 and 30 years of age, the married respondents were divided into two categories. They were called "young marrieds" if they were 30 years of age or younger, "old marrieds" from 31 years of age on. The number in each category and their average age is given in Table XI.

## TABLE XI
### Marital Status and Average Age of Interviewees

| Marital status | Men | | Women | | Total no. of interviewees |
| --- | --- | --- | --- | --- | --- |
| | No. of interviewees | Average age | No. of interviewees | Average age | |
| Single | 51 | 26.6 | 25 | 24.92 | 76 |
| Young married | 22 | 27.25 | 26 | 27.35 | 48 |
| Old married | 11 | 39.25 | 22 | 35.97 | 33 |
| Average age of sample | 84 | 28.57 | 73 | 29.11 | 157 |

*Education*

The education of the families interviewed is shown in Table XII.

## TABLE XII
### Education of Fathers, Mothers, Siblings and Interviewees

| Amount of education | Fathers | Mothers | Brothers over 18 years of age | Sisters over 18 years of age | Male interviewees | Female interviewees |
| --- | --- | --- | --- | --- | --- | --- |
| Illiterate* | — | 24 | 1 | 2 | — | — |
| Literate | 18 | 39 | 13 | 22 | — | 1 |
| Middle School | 7 | 23 | 3 | 49 | — | 6 |
| Matriculation and S.S.L.C. | 33 | 19 | 36 | 67 | — | 18 |
| Intermediate (college) | 13 | 2 | 30 | 9 | 3 | 8 |
| Bachelor's degree | 30 | 3 | 99 | 33 | 34 | 31 |
| Master's degree | 7 | — | 14 | 9 | 21 | 3 |
| Ph.D. | 1 | — | 1 | — | 8 | — |
| Other degrees† | — | — | 35 | 1 | 15 | 4 |
| No information | 48 | 47 | 19 | 21 | 3 | 2 |
| Total‡ | 157 | 157 | 251 | 213 | 84 | 73 |

*Literate means the ability to read and write only.
†Other degrees included: LL.B., B.E., B.T., L.M.E., etc.
‡27 interviewees had no brothers over 18 years of age, and 41 had no sisters over that age.

This table shows that the families were fairly highly educated, and that the children on the whole had achieved much higher education than their parents. This suggests either that the families illustrate the rapid increase in education which has occurred in India in the past 25 years, or that they are families which have had high ambitions for their children and have stressed education as a means of achieving their goals.

The figures show the new emphasis on education for women, for more than half the mothers whose education was ascertained were no more than literate, whereas only one daughter had not progressed beyond mere literacy, and none was illiterate. Moreover, the women interviewees whose

APPENDIXES

education was below matriculation were the older married women. Sons too show a decided increase in education over their fathers.

*Family Type*

When the family composition of the interviewees was analysed, it was found that they came from four main types, namely, large joint families, small joint families, nuclear families and nuclear families with dependents. These types have been described in chapter II.

However, it was found that caution must be used in interpreting the influence of family type on the interviewee, for, although the family in which interviewees grew up had had great influence on them, the type of family they were living in at the moment of the interview might only be a temporary phase in their lives, and so might not influence them to any great extent.

Table XIII shows the classification of the case studies in terms in their family type and marital status, and Table XIV gives the number of times each term paper was quoted in the script.

TABLE XIII

CASES CLASSIFIED ACCORDING TO MARITAL STATUS AND FAMILY TYPE

| Type* of Family | Men | | | Women | | | |
|---|---|---|---|---|---|---|---|
| | Married | | Single | Married | | Single | Total |
| | Old | Young | | Old | Young | | |
| Type A | 92 | 112, 133 | 31, 32, 48, 50, 114, 141, 153, 154 | 59, 81, 84, 88 | 74 | 19, 27, 85 | 19 |
| Type B | 43, 45, 111, 123, 151 | 40, 41, 103, 115, 124, 125, 130, 157 | 30, 33, 35, 36, 37, 38, 47, 120, 121, 143, 144, 155, 156 | 57, 60, 62, 65, 76, 83, 87 | 61, 73, 78, 89 | 3, 4, 8, 12, 15, 21, 22 | 44 |
| Type C | 46, 105, 113, 146 | 44, 99, 102, 116, 126, 128, 129, 131, 132, 134, 152 | 29, 96, 97, 98, 100, 101, 104, 107, 109, 117, 118, 122, 135, 136, 137, 138, 139, 140, 142, 145, 147, 148, 149, 150 | 17, 53, 58, 70, 71, 82, 86, 90, 94 | 2, 10, 13, 18, 23, 51, 52, 54, 55, 56, 64, 67, 69, 72, 80 | 5, 7, 9, 11, 14, 20, 24, 25, 26, 28, 49, 79, 91, 93 | 77 |
| Type D | 42 | 108 | 34, 39, 106, 110, 119, 127 | 6, 63, | 1, 66, 68, 75, 77, 95 | 16 | 17 |
| TOTAL | 11 | 22 | 51 | 22 | 26 | 25 | 157 |

*See pp. 34–7.

## TABLE XIV
### Number of Quotations from Each Interview Used in the Manuscript

| Number of times each term paper was used | Number of term papers |
|---|---|
| 1 | 38 |
| 2 | 25 |
| 3 | 14 |
| 4 | 2 |
| 5 | 3 |
| 6 | — |
| 7 | 3 |
| Total number of papers quoted | 85 |
| Total number of papers in sample 157 | |

## APPENDIX II

NUMBER OF HOUSEHOLDS PER 1,000 HOUSES AND DISTRIBUTION BY SIZE OF 1,000 SAMPLE HOUSEHOLDS OF RURAL AND URBAN POPULATION

| State, city and district | Households per 1,000 houses | Total population in 1,000 households | | | Small (3 members or less) | | Medium (6 members) | | Large (7-9 members) | | Very large (10 members or more) | |
|---|---|---|---|---|---|---|---|---|---|---|---|---|
| | | Persons | Males | Females | Number | Persons | Number | Persons | Number | Persons | Number | Persons |
| Mysore State | 1,202 | 5,412 | 2,830 | 2,582 | 217 | 486 | 520 | 2,630 | 209 | 1,624 | 54 | 672 |
| Bangalore Corporation | 1,454 | 5,556 | 3,016 | 2,540 | 210 | 467 | 540 | 2,742 | 177 | 1,371 | 73 | 976 |

SOURCE: *Census of India*, 1951, vol. XIV, *Mysore*. Part I, *Report*, Table 6.2, p. 263.

## APPENDIX III

FAMILY COMPOSITION OF 1,000 HOUSEHOLDS OF THE GENERAL POPULATION

| State, city and district | Sample household population | | | Heads of household and their wives | | Sons of heads of households | Daughters of heads of households | Other male representatives of heads of households | Other female representatives of heads of households | Unrelated persons | |
|---|---|---|---|---|---|---|---|---|---|---|---|
| | Persons | Males | Females | Males | Females | | | | | Males | Females |
| Mysore State | 5,288 | 2,723 | 2,565 | 878 | 850 | 1,141 | 906 | 628 | 792 | 76 | 17 |
| Bangalore Corporation | 5,556 | 3,016 | 2,540 | 968 | 871 | 1,201 | 823 | 806 | 822 | 40 | 25 |

SOURCE: *Census of India*, 1951, vol. XIV, *Mysore*. Part I, *Report*, Table 6.3, p. 264.

## APPENDIX IV

SONS WITH COMPLETED EDUCATION CLASSIFIED ACCORDING TO THE LEVEL OF EDUCATION ATTAINED AND LEVEL OF EDUCATION DESIRED BY FATHER

|  | City sample Number of sons with educational level | |
| --- | --- | --- |
|  | Attained | Aimed at |
| Illiterates | 56 | 8 |
| Up to primary school | 172 | 53 |
| High school | 62 | 31 |
| Up to matriculation | 50 | 107 |
| Higher | 38 | 120 |
| Not stated | 4 | 43 |
| TOTAL | 382 | 382 |

SOURCE: V. M. Dandekar and Kumudini Dandekar, *Survey of Fertility and Mortality in Poona District* (Gokhale Institute of Politics and Economics, Publication no. 27, 1953), p. 123.

## APPENDIX V

### Age Distribution of 1,000 Married Persons of Each Sex

| State, city and district | Males | | | | | | | | Females | | | | | | | |
|---|---|---|---|---|---|---|---|---|---|---|---|---|---|---|---|---|
| | 0–14 years | | 15–34 years | | 35–54 years | | 55 years and over | | 0–14 years | | 15–34 years | | 35–54 years | | 55 years and over | |
| | 1951 | 1941 | 1951 | 1941 | 1951 | 1941 | 1951 | 1941 | 1951 | 1941 | 1951 | 1941 | 1951 | 1941 | 1951 | 1941 |
| Mysore State | 1 | 1 | 375 | 429 | 481 | 452 | 143 | 118 | 32 | 41 | 669 | 702 | 266 | 232 | 33 | 25 |
| Bangalore Corporation | 1 | – | 428 | – | 443 | – | 128 | – | 13 | – | 687 | – | 260 | – | 40 | – |

SOURCE: *Census of India*, 1951, vol. XIV, *Mysore*. Part I, *Report*, Table 6.8, p. 269.

## APPENDIX VI

Married Daughters Classified by Age and Marriage and According to Whether the Age was Considered Appropriate

| Age at marriage | Number of married daughters | |
|---|---|---|
| | City sample | Non-city sample |
| Not later than 14 | 126 | 431 |
|   Considered appropriate | 100 | 266 |
|   Considered too early | 26 | 165 |
| 15–21 | 140 | 69 |
|   Considered appropriate | 134 | 64 |
|   Considered too late | 6 | 5 |
| Above 21 | 11 | — |
|   Considered appropriate | 7 | |
|   Considered too late | 4 | |
| Total | 277 | 500 |

Source: V. M. Dandekar and Kumudini Dandekar, *Survey of Fertility and Mortality in Poona District* (Gokhale Institute of Politics and Economics, Publication no. 27, 1953), Table 7.12, p. 133.

## APPENDIX VII

Indian Legislature Pertaining to Family Life

| | |
|---|---|
| 1829 | Abolition of Sati Act |
| 1856 | Hindu Widow Remarriage Act |
| 1870 | Infanticide Act |
| 1872 | Special Marriage Act |
| 1892 | Legislature against Child Marriage |
| 1925 | Indian Succession Act |
| 1928 | Hindu Inheritance (Removal Disabilities) Act |
| 1929 | Child Marriage Restraint Act |
| 1929 | Hindu Law of Inheritance (Amendment) |
| 1930 | Hindu Gains of Learning Act |
| 1931 | Sarda Act (Age of Marriage) |
| 1933 | Legislature on Property Rights of Women |
| 1937 | Aryan Marriage Validating Act |
| 1937 | Hindu Women's Right of Property Act |
| 1946 | Hindu Marriage Disabilities Act |
| 1946 | Hindu Women's Right to Separate Residence and Maintenance Act |
| 1949 | Intercaste Marriage Validating Act |

# Bibliography

This bibliography only includes books and articles used in this study.

### A. The Traditional View of Hindu Family Life

AIYAR, C. S. RAMAKRISHNA. "The Hindu Joint Family," *Hindu Law Journal*, vols. III, IV (Madras: Commercial Press, 1921–2).

BACHMANN, HEDWIG. "*On the Soul of the Indian Woman: As Reflected in the Folklore of the Konkan*, 2 vols. (Bastora, India Portuguesa: Tipografia Rangel, 1942).

DAS GUPTA, T. C. *Aspects of Bengali Society from Old Bengali Literature* (Calcutta: University of Calcutta, 1935).

GHURYE, G. S. *Caste and Class in India* (Bombay: Popular Book Depot, 1950).

KAPADIA, K. M. *Hindu Kinship* (Bombay: Popular Book Depot, 1947).

MEYER, JOHANN JAKOB. *Sexual Life in Ancient India*, vols. 1 and 2 (London: George Rutledge and Sons Limited, 1930).

SHASTRI, SHAKUNTALA, Rao. *Women in the Sacred Laws* (Bombay: Bharatiya Vidya Bhavan, Champatty, 1953).

——— *Women in the Vedic Age* (Bombay: Bharatiya Vidya Bhavan, Champatty, 1952).

SRINIVAS, M. N. *Marriage and Family in Mysore* (Bombay: New Book Co., 1942).

STEVENSON, Mrs. SINCLAIR *The Rites of the Twice Born* (London: Oxford University Press, 1920).

TAGORE, RABINDRANATH. "The Indian Ideal of Marriage," in *The Book of Marriage*, Herman Keyserling, ed. (New York: Blue Ribbon Books, 1920).

THOMPSON, E. *Suttee: A Historical and Philosophical Account into the Hindu Rite of Widow-Burning* (London: George Allen and Unwin, Ltd., 1928).

### B. Contemporary Studies and Novels of Indian Life

ACHARYA, HEMALATA. "In an Immigrant Artisan Community," in "Symposium: Caste and Joint Family," *Sociological Bulletin*, vol. IV, no. 2 (Sept. 1955).

AGARWALA, B. R. "In a Mobile Commercial Community," *ibid.*

AIYAPPAN, A. "In Tamilnad,"*ibid.*

*All-India Rural Credit Survey*, vol. II, *Report of the Committee of Direction, Department of Research and Statistics, Reserve Bank of India*, (Bombay, India, 1954).
BEALES, ALAN R. "Interplay among Factors of Change in a Mysore Village," in *Village India*, McKim Marriott, ed. (Chicago: University of Chicago Press, 1955).
BILLINGTON, MARY F. *Women in India* (London, 1895).
BLUNT, E. A. H. *Social Service in India* (London: His Majesty's Stationery Office, 1946).
CATON, A. R. ed. *The Key of Progress: A Survey of the Status and Conditions of Women in India* (London: Oxford University Press, 1930).
*Census of India*, 1950, vol. XIV, Part I (Bangalore: Director of Printing, Stationery and Publications at the Government Press, 1954).
——— 1951, vol. XIV, Mysore.
CORMACK, M. *The Hindu Woman* (New York: Bureau of Publications, Teachers College, Columbia University, 1953).
COUSINS, M. E. *Awakening of Asian Womanhood* (Madras: Ganes and Company, 1922).
——— *Indian Womanhood Today* (Allahabad: Kitabistan, 1947, revised edition).
CRANE, ROBERT I. "Urbanism in India," *American Journal of Sociology*, vol. LX, no. 5 (March, 1955).
DAS, FRIEDA M. *Purdah: The Status of Indian Women* (New York: Vanguard Press, 1932).
DAVIS, KINGSLEY. *The Population of India and Pakistan* (Binghamton, N.Y.: Vail-Ballou Press, Inc., 1951).
DESAI, Mrs. G. B. "Women in Modern Gujerati Life," Unpublished Master's thesis, University of Bombay (Bombay, 1945).
DESAI, ISHWARLAL PRAGJI. *High School Students in Poona*. Deccan College Monograph Series no. 12 (Poona: Deccan College, 1953).
——— "The Joint Family in India—An Analysis," *Sociological Bulletin*, vol. V, no. 2 (Sept., 1956).
——— "An Analysis" in "Symposium: Caste and Joint Family," *Sociological Bulletin*, vol. IV, no. 2 (Sept., 1955).
DESAI, N. A., "Impact of British Rule on the Position of Indian Women." Unpublished Master's thesis, School of Economics and Sociology, University of Bombay (Bombay, 1951).
DUTT, G. S. *A Woman in India* (Life of Saroj Nalini) (London: Hogarth Press, 1929).
FORSTER, E. M. *The Hill of Devi* (London: Edward Arnold and Company, 1953).
GANDHI, MOHANDAS KARAMCHAND. *Women and Social Injustice* (Ahmedabad: Navijivan Publishing House, 1942).
GIST, Noel P. "Mate Selection and Mass Communication in India," *Public Opinion Quarterly*, vol. XVII, no. 4, (Winter, 1953), pp. 481–95.
——— "The Ecology of Bangalore, India: An East-West Comparison," *Social Forces*, vol. 35, no. 4 (May, 1957), pp. 356–365.
GLEDHILL, ALAN. *The Republic of India* (London: Stevens and Sons Ltd., 1951).

GHURYE, G. S. "Age at Marriage," *Marriage Hygiene*, vol. 1 (Feb., 1935).
GOUGH, E. KATHLEEN. "The Social Structure of a Tanjore Village," in *Village India*, McKim Marriott, ed. (Chicago: University of Chicago Press, 1955).
GRAY, HESTHER. *Indian Women and the West* (London: Zenith Press, 1943).
GUPTA, G. C. "Role of Husband and Wife among Working Class Families," Unpublished dissertation for Diploma in Social Service Administration, Sir Dorabji Tata Graduate School of Social Work (Bombay, 1951).
HATE, Mrs. C. A. *Hindu Woman and Her Future* (Bombay: New Book Co., 1948).
KABIR, HUMAYUN. "Higher Education in India and the Study of the Social Sciences," Introduction to *The Teaching of the Social Sciences in India* (UNESCO, 1956).
KAPADIA, K. M. *The Hindu Marriage and Divorce Bill: A Critical Study* (Bombay: Popular Book Depot, 1953).
——— "Views and Attitudes of University Graduates in the Hindu Community on Marriage and Family Relationships," *Sociological Bulletin*, vol. III, no. 1 (March, 1954).
——— "Changing Patterns of Hindu Marriage and Family," *Sociological Bulletin*, vol. IV, no. 2 (Sept., 1955).
——— "Changing Patterns of Hindu Marriage," *Sociological Bulletin*, vol. III, no. 2, (Sept., 1954).
——— "Rural Family Patterns," *Sociological Bulletin*, vol. V, no. 2, (Sept., 1956), pp. 111–26.
——— *Marriage and Family in India* (Madras: Oxford University Press, 1956).
KAR, "A Solution to the Dowry Problem," *Aryan Path* (Nov., 1954),
KARVE, IRAWATI. *Kinship Organisation in India*, Deccan College Monograph Series no. 11 (Poona: Deccan College, 1953).
KENNEDY, BETH C. "Rural Urban Contrasts in Parent-Child Relations in India," *Indian Journal of Social Work*, vol. XV, no. 3 (Dec., 1954).
MANDELBAUM, DAVID G. "The Family in India," in *The Family: Its Function and Destiny*, Ruth Anshen, ed. (New York: Harper and Brothers, 1949).
MANSHARDT, C., ed. *The Child in India* (Bombay: D. B. Taraporevala Sons and Co. Ltd., 1937).
MARRIOTT, McKIM, ed. *Village India* (Chicago: University of Chicago Press, 1955).
MERCHANT, K. T. *Changing Views on Marriage and the Family* (Madras: B. G. Paul and Co., 1935).
MUKERJI, DHURJATI PRASAD. *Modern Indian Culture: A Sociological Study* (2nd ed., Bombay: Hind Kitabs Ltd., 1948).
MURPHY, GARDNER. *In the Minds of Men* (New York: Basic Books Inc., 1952).
NAIDU, SAROJINI. *Women in Modern India* (Bombay: D. B. Taraporevala Sons and Co., 1929).
O'MALLEY, L. S. S. *Modern India and the West* (London: Oxford University Press, 1941).

PAUL, CHERAYATH L. "A Research in Marital Adjustment within a Selected Group of Hindus," Dissertation for Diploma in Social Service Administration, Sir Dorabji Tata Graduate School of Social Work (Bombay, 1940).
——— "Problems of Family Maladjustment with Reference to Hindu Society in Bombay Presidency," Dissertation, Sir Dorabji Tata Graduate School of Social Work (Bombay, 1940).
PRABHU, PANDHARINATH. "Social Effects of Urbanization on Industrial Workers in Bombay," *Sociological Bulletin*, vol. V, no. 2 (Sept., 1956), pp. 127-43.
ROSS, AILEEN D. "An Approach," in "Symposium: Caste and Joint Family," *Sociological Bulletin*, vol. IV, no. 2 (Sept., 1955).
SAHGAL, NAYANTARA. *Prison and Chocolate Cake* (London: Victor Gollancz Ltd., 1954).
SARMA, N. A. *Woman and Society* (Baroda: Padmaja Publications, 1947).
SINGER, MILTON. "Cultural Values in India's Economic Development," *Annals of the American Academy of Political and Social Science*, vol. 305 (May, 1956).
SRINIVAS, M. N. "The Industrialization and Urbanization of Rural Areas," *Sociological Bulletin*, vol. V, no. 2 (Sept., 1956).
URQUHART, MARGAET M. *Women of Bengal* (2nd ed., Mysore: Wesleyan Mission Press, 1926).

## C. SOCIOLOGICAL THEORY AND STUDIES PERTAINING TO THE FAMILY IN OTHER CULTURES

AI-LI, S. CHIN. "Some Problems of Chinese Youth in Transition," *American Journal of Sociology*, vol. LIV (July, 1948).
BOSSARD, JAMES H. S. *The Sociology of Child Development* (Rev. ed., New York: Harper and Brothers, 1954).
BURGESS, E. W., and H. J. LOCKE. *The Family* (New York: American Book Company, 1945; 2nd ed., 1953).
COMHAIRE, JEAN L. "Economic Change and the Extended Family," *Annals of the American Academy of Political and Social Science*, vol. 305 (May, 1956).
DAVIS, ALLISON, BURLEIGH B. GARDNER, MARY R. GARDNER. *Deep South* (Chicago: University of Chicago Press, 1941).
DAVIS, KINGSLEY. *Human Society* (New York: Macmillan Company, 1949).
——— "The Origin and Growth of Urbanization in the World," *American Journal of Sociology*, vol. LX, no. 5 (March, 1955), pp 429-37.
FARIS, ROBERT. *Social Disorganization* (New York: Ronald Press, 1948).
GREEN, ARNOLD W. *Sociology: An Analysis of Life in Modern Society*, (New York: McGraw Hill Book Company, Inc., 1952).
HERSKOVITS, MELVILLE J. "The Problem of Adapting Societies to New Tasks," in *The Progress of Underdeveloped Areas*, BERT F. HOSELITZ, ed. (Chicago: University of Chicago Press, 1952).
HUGHES, EVERETT C. "Dilemmas and Contradictions of Status," *American Journal of Sociology*, vol. L (March, 1945).

KIRKPATRICK, CLIFFORD. *The Family as Process and Institution* (New York: Ronald Press Company, 1955).

Koos, EARL L. *The Middle Class Family and Its Problems* (New York: Columbia University Press, 1950).

LANG, OLGA. *Chinese Family and Society* (New Haven: Yale University Press, 1946).

LEVY, Jr., MARION J. *The Family Revolution in Modern China* (Cambridge, Mass.: Harvard University Press, 1949).

——— "Some Sources of the Vulnerability of the Structures of Relatively Nonindustrialized Societies to Those of Highly Industrialized Societies," in *The Progress of Underdeveloped Areas*, BERT F. HOSELITZ, ed. (Chicago: University of Chicago Press, 1952).

LINTON, RALPH. "Cultural and Personality Factors Affecting Economic Growth," in *The Progress of Underdeveloped Areas*, BERT F. HOSELITZ, ed. (Chicago: University of Chicago Press, 1952).

MINER, HORACE. *St. Denis: A French Canadian Parish* (Chicago: University of Chicago Press, 1939).

MURDOCK, GEORGE P. *Social Structure* (New York: Macmillan Company, 1949).

OKIGBO, PUIS. "Social Consequences of Economic Development in West Africa,"*Annals of the American Academy of Political and Social Science*, vol. 305 (May, 1956).

PARSONS, TALCOTT. "The Social Structure of the Family," in *The Family: Its Function and Destiny*, Ruth Anshen, ed. (New York: Harper and Brothers, 1949).

PARSONS, TALCOTT, and A. M. HENDERSON. *Max Weber: The Theory of Social and Economic Organization* (New York: Oxford University Press, 1947).

RIESMAN, DAVID. *The Lonely Crowd* (New Haven: Yale University Press, 1950).

RYAN, BRUCE. "The Sinhalese Family System," *Eastern Anthropologist*, vol. 6.

SPIEGEL, JOHN F. "New Perspectives in the Study of the Family," Address at Annual Meeting, National Council on Family Relations, Sept. 2, 1953.

WALLER, W., and R. HILL. *The Family* (New York: Dryden Press, 1951).

WILLIAMS, ROBIN. *American Society* (New York: Alfred A. Knopf, 1951).

# Index of Authors

Agarwala, B. R., 9, 10, 12, 22, 26, 44
Aiyappan, A., 21, 22

Bachmann, H., 6, 61, 98, 102, 105, 110, 115, 140, 141, 142, 143, 145, 146, 154, 155, 158, 160, 254, 260, 268
Beales, A. R., 23, 93
Bhaskraiya, L., 255
Blunt, E. A. H., 4, 29
Bossard, J. H. S., 40
Burgess, E. W., 27, 28, 29, 92, 96, 154

Chin Ai-Li, 134
Comhaire, J. L., 21
Cormack, M., 106, 123, 125, 163, 164, 211, 247, 266
Cousins, M. E., 208, 211
Crane, R. I., 18, 19

Dandikar, K., 213
Dandekar, V. M., 213
Das, F. M., 247
Das Gupta, T. C., 18
Davis, A., 22
Davis, K., 5, 11, 14, 19, 20, 26, 273
Desai, A. R., 183, 190
Desai, G. B., 47, 107, 108, 143, 202
Desai, I. P., 9, 10, 11, 23, 30, 33, 34, 41, 74, 77, 78, 209, 210, 211, 212, 217
Dube, S. C., 37

Forster, E. M., 141

Gandhi, M., 156, 193, 212
Ghurye, G. S., 181, 182, 193
Gist, N. P., 27, 271

Gledhill, A., 273
Gore, M. S., 69
Gough, E. K., 92
Gray, H., 210, 211
Green, A. W., 30, 136, 137

Hate, C. A., 276
Henderson, A. M., 91
Herskovits, M. J., 286, 295
Hill, R., 265, 288, 290
Hughes, E. C., 205

Jhabvala, P. R., 242

Kabir, H., 296
Kahl, J. A., 184
Kapadia, K. M., 37, 235, 246, 247, 248, 261, 273
Kar, 262
Karve, I., 3, 4, 5, 6, 7, 8, 9, 10, 12, 13, 15, 18, 22, 29, 34, 68, 116, 162, 235, 246, 247, 268

Lang, O., 92, 170
Levy, Jr., M. J., 29, 30, 31, 52, 61, 99, 115, 118, 121, 144, 147, 169, 173
Linton, R., 16, 25, 28
Locke, H. J., 27, 28, 92, 96, 154
Loosley, E., 237

Mandelbaum, D., 6, 10, 11, 29, 93, 101, 116, 146, 154
Markandaya, K., 198
Mathai, S., 209
Meyer, J. J., 141, 158, 269
Miner, H., 64
Mukerji, D. P., 68, 182, 209
Murphy, G., 139, 175, 194

Nehru, J., 182

Okigbo, P., 291

Parsons, T., 30, 91, 180, 286, 289

Rauf, M. A., 26
Reisman, D., 92
Ross, A. D., 201
Ryan, B., 83

Sahgal, N., 24
Sarma, N. A., 147
Seeley, J., 237
Sim, A. R., 237
Singer, M., 68, 295

Spiegel, J. F., 288
Srinivas, M. N., 5, 6, 17, 20, 54, 61, 84, 116, 117, 120, 141, 143, 150, 151, 155, 158, 169, 170, 171, 173, 250, 261, 263, 264, 267, 270, 276
Stevenson, S., 61, 235, 266

Tagore, R., 251

Urquhart, M. M., 12, 68, 107, 115, 146, 148, 150, 155

Waller, W., 265, 288, 290
Weber, M., 91
Williams, Jr., R. M., 284, 285

# Index of Subjects

AFFECTION: changes in, 282–4; demonstrations of, 161; in the family, 100, 136–8; in joint family, 15, 31, 50, 137, 175–9, 283; in nuclear family, 175–9, 288, 289; of relatives, 175–9. *See also* Love; Sentiments

Ambitions: of brothers, 187; of children, 25, 42, 48; of daughters, 219–22; and education, 217–26; effect of new, 285; of fathers, 186–7, 220–2, 229–31; of husbands, 222; in joint family, 218; of mothers, 220–2, 229–31; of parents, 188, 211, 217–22, 226, 227, 232, 233; of self-made men, 71; of sons, 185–90, 218–21, 226, 228; urban, 287; of women, 197–204, 230

Anglo-Indians, 198, 240

Anxiety: over education of children, 225; of parents, 185, 186; in relation to employment, 185, 187, 287

Aryans, 12

Assistance: burden of, 77–9; estimation of, 81; financial, 76, 80; givers and recipients of, 77–84; and nepotism, 77; to relatives, 84; type of, 77, 79, 89

Associations: function of, 237–9, 296

Aunt: and assistance given, 77; authority of, 112, 113; conflict with, 17; and relation with nieces and nephews, 167, 168; and her subordinate position as widow, 113

Authority: of aunts, 112, 113; of bride, 101, 102; between brothers, 108–11; between brother and sister, 110, 111; of brother-in-law, 119; changes in, 132–5; "direct," 92; family, 91–135; of father, 98–101, 103; of father-in-law, 113, 114; of grandfather, 92–8, 103; of grandmother, 94–8; of head of household, 92–8; of husband, 105–8, 117, 121; "indirect," 91; in joint family, 9, 15, 29, 31, 283; of mothers, 101–4; of mother-in-law, 114–18; of relatives, 103, 104; between sisters, 110, 111; of sister-in-law, 119, 120; of son, 132; and strain, 96, 97, 135; substructure of, 91–135, 282, 283; "traditional," 91, 93; of uncle, 111, 112; of women, 101. *See also* Power

BABIES: desire for, 139, 145; punishment of, 124, 125

Bangalore, 27, 43, 189, 212, 213, 216, 239

Barrenness of women, 141, 143, 155

Bombay, 43, 44, 85, 100, 109, 164, 187–9, 201, 244

Brahmins, 4, 45, 68, 105, 186, 193, 234; and problem of getting jobs, 194; *versus* non-Brahmin, 193, 194

Bride, 105, 113, 119; attitude of, 268; authority of, 101, 102; and child marriage, 48, 49, 246, 247; conduct of, 114–16; and desire to live separate from in-laws, 289; in patrilineal-patriarchal system, 14, 49. *See also* Daughter-in-law

British, 6–18; education under rule of, 208–11; rule of, 182, 183; unification of India under, 18

Brother: ambition of, 187; and assistance given, 77, 80; authority of, 108–11; duties of, 69, 70, 108; eldest, 108, 109; jealousy of, 17, 109, 162; and relation with brother, 42, 162, 163; and relation with sister, 110, 163–5; sacrifice for education, 223. See also Men

Brother-in-law: authority of, 117; relation to brother's wife, 174, 175

Brother's wife: relation with brother-in-law, 115, 174, 175; relation to co-wives, 173, 174

CAREERS
of sons, 186
of women, 197–204, 206; attitude to, 256; attitude of men to, 200–4; attitude of women to, 200–4; marriage and, 198, 202–4; and problem of getting jobs, 199–201, 203–5; type of, 198

Caste, 92, 97; ambitions in, 182, 183; and attitude to divorce, 273; "backward," 193, 194; as basic structure, 7; boundaries of, 3, 5; Brahmin, 4, 45, 68, 105, 186, 193, 194, 234; and the breaking of its rules, 215, 272; change in attitude to, 214; and change to social classes, 181–5; changes in, 5, 22, 26, 182, 296; effect of education on, 232; effect of industrialization on, 181–5; and endogamy, 236, 278; and function for family, 4, 14, 281; Gandhi and, 24; and importance in family changes, 281; Kshatriya, 193; and outside friendships, 237, 239; and outside marriages, 49, 270–3, 278; penalties, 5; size of, 4; Sudra, 193; Vaisya, 4, 193. See also Sub-caste

Caste council, Panchayat, 5, 6

Census: definition of, 9; of India, 4, 33, 198, 267, 271; of Mysore, 198

Ceremonies, 79, 84, 85

Change: in affection, 283, 284; in authority, 132–5; and conflict, 215; in customs, 182, 214, 215; disorganizing effects of, 294, 295; in divorce, 273, 274; in education, 286, 287; in family structure, 28, 99, 178, 179, 281, 284; in friendships, 235–45, 277, 296; to independence, 134, 135; in India, 23, 25; in joint family, 3–32, 53, 172, 205–7, 296; in laws, 26; in marriage, 235, 245–79, 289, 290; in models, 195, 286, 287; in population 23; in roles, 287, 288, 290–3; in theories of family, 27–32

Chastity: of women, 98, 242; of women who work, 203, 204

Child marriage, 48, 246, 247

Children: affection for parents of, 139–43; ambitions of, 25, 42, 48; change in independence of, 134; desire for, 139, 145; in joint family, 17; obedience of, 128; "problem child," 294; punishment of, 122–7; and relation with father, 100, 101; training of, 57, 58; and veneration for mother, 142; work of, 54, 56, 58. See also Daughter; Son

China, classical family in, 8, 52, 121, 147, 170

Christians, 198, 228, 239, 240, 243

City, 53, 80, 85, 86; division of labour in, 20; education in, 25; families in, 57; growth of, 19, 20; influence of, 25; joint family in, 21, 22; size of household in, 39, 44

Clubs: function of, 238, 239, 296; for men, 237, 238, 245, 296; with mixed membership, 244; for women, 239, 296

Co-education, 216, 240

College: in Bangalore, 212, 213; Department of Home Science in, 214; effect on women of, 214; friends at, 237, 239, 240, 256; hostels, 48, 212, 214, 237; social work in, 213, 214. See also Education; Universities

Conflict: between brothers, 42, 162; and changing behaviour, 215; in the family, 16, 17, 40, 43, 47, 257; father-children, 101; father-son, 99, 100, 146, 293; husband-wife, 127, 156, 157; mother-in-law–daughter-in-law, 17, 43, 146, 169–72; mother-son, 146; with relatives, 176; between wives, 43

Communities: Marwadi, 22; Sindhis, 22

Cousins: in joint family, 168; in nuclear family, 168

Co-wives, relation with wife, 173, 174

Crises, 288; of death, 38, 39, 46, 66, 101, 223; in India, 22, 23, 48

DATING: attitude to, 242, 243; of interviewees, 241–3
Daughter: ambitions of, 219–22; and assistance given, 77, 79; dependence of, 104, 105, 118; desire for a, 145; education of, 151, 227–31; and inheritance of property, 11; marriage of, 227, 228; obligations of, 45, 62, 63, 68, 70–5; relation with father of, 145, 146; relation with mother of, 104, 105, 149–52; work of, 58–64. *See also* Women
Daughter-in-law: changing position of, 172; and conflict with mother-in-law, 17, 116–18, 146, 168, 169, 171, 172, 176; her desire to live in separate house, 170, 171; as a mother of sons, 114; and relation with brothers-in-law, 115; and relation with father-in-law, 113, 114, 168, 169; and relation with mother-in-law, 169–72, 222; subordinate position of, 114–18, 169; suicide of, 117; training of, 61–4. *See also* Bride
Death, 46, 101; of grandfather, 38, 39; of mother, 66; of men, 223; and transfer of duties, 64, 65
Dependent: definition of, 36; members, 45
Discipline: of eldest brother, 109; in family, 94, 103, 132; by father, 100, 103; by grandfather, 103; by mother, 103; strictness of, 122–4
Dislike, in family, 136–79. *See also* Conflict
Division of labour, 87. *See also* Work
Divorce: attitude of men and women to, 274–6; changes in laws of, 273, 274
Dowry: changing attitudes to, 262–4, 278; system of, 260–4; financial burden of, 25, 261; function of, 263
Dravidians, 12, 13
Duties, 8, 10, 15, 30, 31, 42, 58, 283; allocation of, 52, 53; religious, 68, 69; substructure of, 52–90, 282, 283; transfer of, 64–7. *See also* Obligations; Responsibility

ECOLOGICAL SUBSTRUCTURE, 29, 33–51
Educated unemployed, 190–3, 206, 231
Education, 18; and ambitions, 217–26; anxieties over, 225; attitudes of boys to, 217; attitudes of parents to, 227–31; attitude to women's education, 211, 214, 230; under the British, 208–11; co-education, 216, 240; of daughters, 151, 227–32; desire of girls for, 212, 213; and desire of men to marry educated wives, 234; family separation caused by, 47; and higher education of women, 25, 43, 45, 46, 48, 50, 212, 213, 232; in India, 208–17; of interviewees and their families, 301; and jobs, 248; and joint family, 22; and marriage, 211, 213, 227–31, 234, 247, 248; of men, 209, 210, 221, 223–6, 231; and pressure on children, 25, 209, 221, 223–6, 231; prestige of, 209; and reform, 210; and sacrifice of parents for children's, 25, 199, 223; trend in, 212; Western, 22; of women, 25, 61, 63, 64, 210–14, 221, 226–32. *See also* Co-education
Educational system. *See* College; Universities
Employment: anxieties in regard to, 185–7; in Madhya Pradesh, 198; of women in Mysore state, 197, 198
Endogamy: caste, 236, 278; racial, 278; religious, 278; rules of, 5
Engagement. and desire of men and women to know mates before marriage, 265; and dowry, 260–5; duration of, 264, 265; function of, 265
Exogamy, 23

FAILURE: attitude to, 223; to get jobs, 193; punishment for, 223
Family: affection in, 136–79; authority in, 91–135; changes in, 28, 38, 53, 74, 99, 178, 179, 205–7, 284, 285, 296, 297; in China, 8, 52, 121, 147, 170; companionship in, 27–9; conflict in, 16, 17, 40, 43; cycle of, 35, 36, 41, 50, 64, 65; definition of, 27–31; demonstrations of affection in, 161; discipline in, 94, 103, 132; disorganization of, 287; division of labour in, 53, 58–64, 87, 282, 283; duties in 9, 14, 42, 67–76; feuds in, 24, 47; hatred and dislike in, 136–79; and income, 41,

42, 44; and the Institutional theory, 27–9; in modern America, 138, 179, 180; nuclear type of, 21–8, 38; as a producing and consuming unit, 41; return to village, 22, 23; solidarity of, 33, 38, 41, 177–9, 287, 293, 294; strain in, 44; theories of, 27–33; and types A, B, C, D, 28–38; village, 8, 10; in the West, 21, 172; work in, 180–207

Joint: affection in, 283; ambitions in, 218; aunt in, 167; authority in, 9, 15, 29, 31, 283; boundaries of, 3; and brother-sister relation, 163–5; changes in, 3–32, 296; in city, 21, 22; closeness and affection of, 175–9; conflict in, 16–18; cousins in, 168; definitions of, 9, 21; desire to remain in, 47; discipline in, 94, 103; dowry system in, 260, 261; duties of, 8–11, 14, 15, 282; father-daughter relation in, 145, 146; father-in-law in, 168, 169; financial arrangements of, 42, 283; functions of, 10, 14–16; husband-wife relation in, 153–62; interior of household, 40; legal basis of, 10; marriage in, 227, 251, 277, 288, 289; mother-daughter relation in, 150–2; mother-son relation in, 146–9; older people in, 290, 291; relation of brothers in, 162, 163; relation of mother-in-law to daughter-in-law in, 169, 172; relation of uncle and aunt with nieces and nephews in, 166–8; and size of household, 33–5, 38; stability of, 14, 22, 26, 177; strain in, 16–18, 115; structure of, 6–18, 28, 29; worship in, 11, 12

Nuclear, 21–8, 38; affection in, 175–9, 288, 289; authority in, 283; brother-sister tie in, 165; closeness of, 175–9; duties of, 283; education of daughters in, 227, 228, 233, 234; and function in modern society, 180, 181; marriage in, 288, 289; older people in, 197, 290, 291; relation of brother-in-law with sister-in-law in, 175; relation of cousins in, 168; relation of father-in-law and daughter-in-law in, 169; relation of sisters-in-law in, 174; relation of uncle and aunt with nieces and nephews in, 167; stability of, 177

Problems, solutions to, 295, 296

Types, 34–8; A, 28, 29, 34–6; B, 29, 35, 36; C, 29, 35–7; D, 29, 36–8; and change, 281; and education, 233

Father: ambitions of, 186, 187, 220–2, 229–31; and assistance given, 77, 80; change in authority of, 132–4; change in role of, 291, 292; and conflict with son, 99, 101, 146; domination of, 99; punishment of children, 100, 122–7; and relation with children, 58, 100, 103, 139–43; and relation with daughter, 145, 146; and relation with son, 143–5, 168, 169. *See also* Grandfather; Household, Head of; Men; Parents

Father-in-law: authority of, 98, 101, 103, 113, 114; and relation with daughter-in-law, 113, 114, 168, 169; and relation with son-in-law, 113, 114

Festivals, 11, Dasara, 144, Divali, 84; religious, 25

Feuds. *See* Family

Financial arrangements: of family, 11, 41, 42, 44, 93, 94; and mental health, 191

Friendships: in the army, 237, 240; between men and women, 159, 241–4; of boys, 235–7; in business, 237; between castes, 237, 239; changing patterns of, 235–45, 277, 296; at college, 237, 239, 240, 256; and control over behaviour, 215; of girls 235, 238, 239; importance of, 176, 216, 236, 238; inter-religious, 237, 239; of men, 235, 237; of women, 235, 238–40

GANDHI, 24
Gods, 10–12, 15
Guilt, feelings of, 67, 131
Grandchildren: affection for grandparents, 138, 139; punished by grandmother, 124; and relations with grandparents, 92–8, 103. *See also* Children
Grandfather: and affection, 138, 139; authority of, 92–8, 103; and discipline, 103; effect of death of, 38,

39. *See also* Household, Head of; Grandmother; Grandparents; Men

Grandmother: and affection for grandchildren, 138, 139; authority of, 94-8; personality of, 97; position of, 38, 39; and punishment of grandchildren, 124. *See also* Grandfather; Grandparents; Women

Grandparents: and affection, 138, 139; and assistance given, 77; and influence in home, 57. *See also* Grandfather; Grandmother; Old Age

HARIJAN, 193; education of, 224; problems of, 200, 237
Hatred, in Hindu family. *See* Conflict; Dislike
Hearth, 9, 10, 29, 30
Horoscope, 251, 254
Hostel, 48, 212, 214, 237
Household, 29, 31; composition of, 34, 36, 37; effect of son moving to own, 39, 41; interior arrangement of, 40; of large joint family, 38; reasons for remaining in one, 41-6; reasons for separate dwelling for, 46-51; size of in relation to type of family, 33-5, 38; spatial arrangement of, 38-40
  Head of: authority of, 92-8; and financial position, 11, 93, 94. *See also* Father; Grandfather
Husband: age of marriage of, 249, 250; and assistance given, 77-9; and change in husband-wife relation, 149, 161, 162, 204, 259, 260, 277; authority over wife of, 105-8, 117, 121; and conflict with wife, 156, 157; and demonstration of affection for wife, 161; and desire to choose wife, 252-4, 279; and "oneness" with wife, 155, 156; qualities desired in wife by, 257-60; and relation with father-in-law, 113; and relation to in-laws, 172, 173; and relation with wife, 13, 103, 105-8, 152-62, 244, 245. *See also* Men

ILLNESS, 34, 39, 75, 76
Income, 9; and expenditure, 10, 11, 181; of family, 41, 42; responsibility for, 64, 202
Independence: changes in, 134, 135; of children, 286; and completely independent men and women, 130, 131; and completely dependent men and women, 128; desire for, 49; and higher education for girls, 25; and obedience, 129-31; and partially dependent men and women, 129, 130.
India: economy of, 8; education in, 208-17; fight for independence: 24, 25, 71, 198, 217; and nationalism, 182; and solutions to problems, 295
Individuality: effect of city on, 21, 21, 26; trend to, 49
Industrialization, 18-24, 26, 27, 29, 107; and ambitions, 226, 287; effects of, 18, 181-90, 205, 206; effect on family of, 22, 28, 285, 296, 297; and effect on the self-made man, 187-90; and effect on standard of aspirations, 185-7; and new oportunities, 182
Inheritance, 11, 26, 42
Insecurity: economic, 50, 185; financial, 89; of old people, 196, 197; and pressure on children's education, 221
Jealousy: of brothers, 17, 109, 162; of cousins, 168; of husband and brother-in-law, 119; mother-daughter, 165; sibling, 142, 143; of sisters, 17, 166; of sisters-in-law, 164, 173, 175
Junior levirate, 174

KANNADA, 6
Kinship group, 12-14; bonds of, 29, 50; closure of, 22; limits of, 12. *See also* Relatives
Kitchen, 9, 10, 40, 54

LANGUAGE, 18, 209
Laws, 26, 211, 246; of inheritance, 10, 11, 23, 26, 44
Linguistic group, boundaries of, 3-5, 7
Literatures: on brother-sister relation, 165; epic, 7, 8, 241, 269; Hindu, 116, 137, 142; on husband-wife relation, 153, 157, 160; on mother-in-law–daughter-in-law relation, 150, 170; proverbial, 117, 141, 142; on relation of sisters-in-law, 173; Sanskritic, 8; Vedic, 142

Love: in the family 136–8; and marriage, 155, 159, 257, 269, 270. *See also* Affection; Romantic Love; Sentiments

MAHABHARATA, 7, 8, 141, 153

Manu, 15, 155

Marriage, 42, 63, 96, 103–5, 119; age of, 48, 49, 245–50, 278, 279; attitude of parents to, 14, 105, 113, 227–31; and bride, 48, 49, 119; and careers for women, 198, 202–4; changing patterns of, 235, 245–79, 289, 290; child, 48, 246, 247; and choice of mates, 252–7, 279, 288; of cross cousins, 13, 14, 38; of daughters, 227, 228; and difference in age of husband and wife, 249, 250; and duty to marry children, 235; and education, 211, 213, 227–31, 234, 247, 248; effect of friends on, 256; family conflict because of, 257; Hindu ideal of, 251; importance for women of, 235, 276; importance of, 277; and increase in single men and women, 230, 276, 289; in joint family, 227, 251, 277, 288, 289; and later marriage, 247; new problems of, 275–7; and pressure to marry, 257; romantic love in, 155, 159, 259, 270; and Sarda Act, 211

Arranged, 12, 250–60; attitude to, 251, 279; changing pattern of, 251–7; and desire of husbands to choose wives, 252–4, 279; and desire of women to choose husbands, 252–7, 279

Inter-caste, 49; attitudes of men to, 270–3, 278; attitude of parents to, 272, 273; attitudes of women to, 270–3, 278; in sub-castes, 271

Inter-racial, attitude of men to, 270, 271, 273, 278; attitude of women to, 270, 271, 278

Inter-religious, 228; attitude of men to, 270, 271, 273, 278; attitude of women to, 270, 271, 278

*See also* Romantic love

Matriarchal system, 12, 13

Matrilineal system, 12, 13, 38, 111, 119

Meals, 9, 10, 40, 55

Men: attitude to divorce of, 274–6; attitude to marriage of, 270, 271, 273, 278; attitude to women's careers of, 200–4; changing customs of, 214, 215; clubs of, 237, 238, 244, 245, 296; education of, 209, 210, 221, 223–6, 231; friendships with women of, 241–4; social life of, 236–45. *See also* Brother; Father; Grandfather; Husband; Son

Method of this study, 298–303; quotations from each interview in, 303; sample, 280, 281, 298–303

Mitakshara, 10, 11, 93

Mobility, 14, 23; occupational and social, 20, 39, 41, 51

Models: in a changing society, 158, 286, 287; in modern society, 195, 196; Sakhu, 115; Savitri, 158; Sita, 158, 258

Mother: ambitions of, 220–2, 229–31; affection for children, 139–43; authority of, 101–4; change in role of, 292; as a consultant, 102; death of, 66; and punishment of children, 103, 122–7; and relation with daughter, 104, 105, 150–2; and relation with son, 97, 102, 105, 118, 146–9, 152, 172; sacrifice of, 61; taking father's role, 64–7; and training of children, 57, 58; work of, 55–7. *See also* Grandmother; Parents; Women

Mother-in-law: authority of, 114–18; and conflict with daughter-in-law, 17, 43, 116–18, 146, 169–72; and conflict with son over daughter-in-law, 168, 169, 171, 172; cruelness of, 117, 118; jealousy of daughter-in-law for, 170; and relation with daughter-in-law, 117, 169–72, 222

Movies: 191, 238, 239, 243

NEPHEW: relation with aunt of, 167, 168; relation with uncle of, 36, 47, 166, 167

Nepotism, 14, 77

Niece: and relation with aunt, 167, 168; and relation with uncle, 36, 47, 166, 167

OBEDIENCE: of children, 128; of daughters, 61; family, 106, 133;

in later life, 128–31; in moral matters, 128; in practical matters, 128; of sister, 111; of wife, 107

Obligations, 11, 42, 46, 50–2; of bride, 48; changing, 90; in cities, 45; of daughters, 45, 62, 63, 68, 70–5; evasion of, 43, 44, 82; family, 9, 14, 42, 67–76; to older members, 45; philosophy of, 67; reciprocal, 81–3; to relatives, 39, 67–76; of sons, 4, 11, 44–6, 60, 66, 68, 70–5, 83, 85; in villages, 45; of women, 81–4. *See also* Duties; Responsibility

Occupation: changing prestige of, 181, 184, 185; and education, 248; family, 180–207; pressure on children to get jobs, 190–2; search for jobs, 185–7; of university graduates, 185. *See also* the Educated unemployed; Work

Occupational problems: 206; Brahmin, 193, 194; and the educated unemployed, 190–3; models, 195, 196; of old age, 196, 197; of women, 197–205

Old age, 3, 75; attitude to, 45, 46, 245; and economic security, 196, 197, 207; in joint family, 290, 291; in nuclear family, 197, 290, 291; prestige of, 196, 197; problems of, 290, 291; of widow, 43

PANCHAYAT, 5, 6, 93

Parents: affection for children of, 139–43; their ambitions for children, 188, 211, 217–22, 226, 227, 232, 233; anxiety of, 185, 186; and assistance given, 77; attitude to education of, 227–31, 233, 234; attitude to marriage of, 227–31; and changing relation with children, 152; and desire for children, 139; and sacrifice for children, 45, 199, 223, 226, 227. *See also* Father; Grandparents; Mother

Patriarchal system, 12, 13

Patrilineal system, 12–14

Patrilocal system, 12, 14

Power, 30, 31; definition of, 52; institutionalization of, 121, 122; substructure of, 91–135. *See also* Authority; Household, Head of

Pooja room, 40, 54, 56, 63

Pregnancy, 34, 121

Pressure: to get jobs, 190–2; to study, 190–2

Property, 9, 29, 42, 43; division of, 10, 11, 24, 38, 48, 49; and laws of inheritance, 10, 11, 23, 26

Punishment, 121–8; avoiding of, 126, 127; of babies, 124, 125; as beating, 100; as caning, 223; of children, 122–7; and disparaging comparisons, 224; by father, 100, 122–7; by grandmother, 124; by mother, 122–7; as nagging, 223–5; as teasing, 122, 123; as ridicule, 224; as scolding, 122, 123; as spanking, 122, 123; other types of, 124

RAMA, 158

Ramayana, 7, 8, 153

Relatives, 33–6; and assistance given, 77, 78, 83, 84; authority of, 103, 104; closeness and affection of, 175–7; conflict with, 176; definition of, 31; responsibility for, 39, 67–76. *See also* Kinship group

Religion, 92; and friendships with other religions, 237, 239; and outside marriage, 228, 278; rituals and ceremonies of, 11, 12, 83–6

Research for this study: findings of, 280–97; problems of, 294

Responsibility: acts of, 76–81; of brother, 69, 70, 108; family, 9, 14, 42, 67–76; to relatives, 39, 67–76; sense of, 59, 69, 90; of sons, 4, 11, 44–6, 60, 66, 68, 70–5, 83, 85. *See also* Duties; Obligations

Rights, 30, 31; of joint family, 8–10, 15; substructure of, 52–90, 91, 282, 283

Rivalry: sexual between father and son, mother-in-law and daughter-in-law, 168, 169; of sisters-in-law, 174

Romantic love, 13, 29; and love marriages, 257, 269, 270; in marriage, 155, 159, 269; new emphasis on, 236; problems caused by, 270

SACRIFICE: of brother, 223; of parents, 45, 61, 223, 226, 227; of sons, 45

Sample: caste and mother tongue of interviewees, 299; education of fathers, mothers, siblings, and interviewees, 301; family type of interviewees, 302; home of interviewees and number of generations in city, 300; income and social class of interviewees, 299, 300; marital status and age of interviewees, 300–2; of this study, 23, 27, 280, 281

Self-made man, 233; ambitions of, 71; industrialization and, 187–90; problems of, 188, 189

Sentiments, 29; in the American family, 138; changes in, 138, 282–4; substructure of, 136–79. *See also* Affection; Love

Separation of the sexes: attitude to, 236, 242; attitude of girls to going out with boys, 216; effect of in city, 244, 245; training for, 240, 241

Servants, 56, 63, 65

Sex, problems of, 191, 266

Sister: and assistance given, 77; jealousy of, 17; power of, 110, 111; and relation with brother, 110, 111, 163–5; and relation with sister, 111, 165, 166; responsibility of, 111. *See also* Women

Sister-in-law: authority of, 119, 120; jealousy of, 173, 175; and relation to husband's brothers, 174, 175; and relation of wife to husband's sisters, 120, 172–174

Social class: caste system to, 181–5; characteristics of interviewees, 299, 300

Social life: of boys, 236; of children, 236; of husband and wife, 244, 245; of men, 236–45; of older people, 245; of women, 236, 238–45, 277

Social work: in colleges, 213, 214; interest of women in, 239

Son: ambitions of, 185–90, 218–21, 226, 268; and assistance given, 77, 79, 80; attitude to, 142; authority of, 132; birth of a, 101; career of, 186; change in role, 292, 293; conflict of, 293; and conflict with father, 99, 101, 146, 168, 169; and conflict with mother, 146, 149, 152; and desire for a son, 145; education of, 221, 223–6, 231; effect of moving to own household on, 39, 41–3, 51; emancipation of, 99, 100; and inheritance of property, 11; legal rights of, 10; obligations of, 11, 44–6, 60, 66, 68, 70–5, 83, 85; occupational mobility of, 39, 41, 51; and relation with father, 99, 101, 143–6, 168, 169; and relation with mother, 97, 102, 105, 118, 141, 146–52, 172; work of, 58–60. *See also* Men

Son-in-law: relation with father-in-law of, 113, 114

Standard of living, 42; in cities, 25, 26, 198; and desire for a higher one, 185–7, 206

Strain, 65; between aunt and nieces and nephews, 167; and authority, 96, 97, 135; between brother and sister, 110; in family, 16–18, 44, 73, 115, 179; between mother and son, 146, 149, 152; in new dating pattern, 243; between sisters, 166; between sisters-in-law, 120

Student riots and strikes, 217

Sub-caste, 4, 7

Substructure: abstraction of, 31; of authority, 91–135, 282, 283; ecological, 39, 33–51; of rights and duties, 52–91, 282, 283; of sentiments, 137–79, 282–4

Suicide, of daughter-in-law, 117


UNCLE: and assistance given, 77, 80–3; authority of, 111, 112; and boarding of nephew, 166; conflict with, 17; and education of nephew, 166; and relation with nieces and nephews, 166, 167

Unemployment, 75; detrimental effect of, 191–3; and the educated unemployed, 190–3, 206; in Mysore State, 190; and transfer of duties, 65

Universities: and B.A. degrees, 210; and degrees obtained by men and women of this sample, 212; and effect on women, 214; and matriculation, 210, 212, 213; modern, 287; in India, 209; and number of students, 209, 210, 212; opportunity of boys and girls to mix at, 216. *See also* College; Education

Urbanization: and change in village life, 23; and dissolution of joint family, 21; effect of, 19, 20, 28, 49, 205; and growth of cities, 19, 20

VILLAGE, 6, 7, 14, 18–21, 44, 47, 53, 59, 68, 69, 74, 92; boundaries of, 3; and family life, 8, 10; return to city from, 22, 23

WEDDINGS, 83–5; changing pattern of, 268, 278; cost of, 25, 266, 267; importance of, 266, 268; problems of, 267; as symbols of prestige, 266, 267

Widow: dependence on son, 148; in old age, 43; and Sati, 105; subordinate position of, 34, 114; work of, 69

Wife: age of marriage of, 249, 250; and change in relation with husband, 149, 161, 162, 204, 259, 260, 277; and companionship with husband, 159; and conflict with husband, 156, 157; as consultant of husband, 102, 159, 160; and desire to choose husband, 252–7, 279; personality of, 103, 153, 161; and power in domestic sphere, 107; and qualities desired in husband, 257–9; and relation with husband, 13, 103, 105–8, 152–62, 244, 245; and relation to sister-in-law, 43, 120, 172–4; role of, 153, 154, 156–60; subordinate position of, 102, 103, 105–8, 117, 154. *See also* Women

Women: ambitions of, 230; and attitude to barrenness, 141, 143, 151; and attitude to divorce, 274–6; and attitude to marriage, 235, 251, 270, 271, 276, 278; and attitude to studying, 217; authority of, 101; careers of, 197–204; change in role of, 215, 293; chastity of, 98, 203, 204; at college, 214; education of, 25, 61, 63, 64, 210–14, 226–33; and friendships with men, 241–4; higher education of, 212, 213; and illiteracy, 213, 301; obligations of, 81–4; and problems of changing role, 293; social life of, 116, 155, 236–45, 277, 296; and strain, 17; work of, 54–8

Single: ambitions of, 230; and desire to marry, 230; responsibility for family income of, 64, 202; social life of, 240; "Society girl," 242. *See also* Careers of Women;

*See also* Daughter; Grandmother; Mother; Sister; Widow; Wife

Work: of boys and girls, 58–64; of bride, 63; of children, 54, 56, 64; and division of labour in the family, 54, 282, 283; of family, 180–207; of grandparents, 57; of men, 54–8; and search for jobs, 185–7; of women, 54–8. *See also* Occupation

Worship, 9, 11, 12, 29. *See also* Pooja room

www.ingramcontent.com/pod-product-compliance
Lightning Source LLC
Chambersburg PA
CBHW020245030426
42336CB00010B/621